46-37.

Mi 1 April 2010

ft®

0

er

AD PRESS™

WILEY COMPUTER PUBLISHING

John Wiley & Sons, Inc.
NEW YORK • CHICHESTER • WEINHEIM • BRISBANE • SINGAPORE • TORONTO

Publisher: Robert Ipsen
Editor: Theresa Hudson
Developmental Editor: Mike Mulcare
Managing Editor: Angela Smith
Technical Editor: Joel Semeniuk
Copy Editor: Faithe Wempen
Text Design: Carol Leyba
Composition: Ed Kotzen
Indexer: Joan Green
Consulting Editors: Donis Marshall, Trudy Neuhaus

Designations used by companies to distinguish their products are often claimed as trademarks. In all instances where John Wiley & Sons, Inc., is aware of a claim, the product names appear in initial capital or ALL CAPITAL LETTERS. Readers, however, should contact the appropriate companies for more complete information regarding trademarks and registration.

The Gearhead Press trademark is the exclusive property of Gearhead Group Corporation.

This book is printed on acid-free paper.

Published by John Wiley & Sons, Inc., New York

Published simultaneously in Canada.

This publication is designed to provide accurate and authoritative information in regard to the subject matter covered. It is sold with the understanding that the Publisher is not engaged in professional services. If professional advice or other expert assistance is required, the services of a competent professional person should be sought.

ISBN: 0-471-06116-6

Printed in the United States of America.

10 9 8 7 6 5 4 3 2 1

A Note from Gearhead Press

Gearhead Press is dedicated to publishing technical books for experienced Information Technology professionals — network engineers, developers, system administrators, and others — who need to update their skills, learn how to use technology more effectively, or simply want a quality reference to the latest technology.

Gearhead Press emerged from my experience with professional trainers of engineers and developers: people who truly understand first-hand the needs of working professionals. Gearhead Press authors are the crème de la crème of industry trainers, working at the companies that define the technology revolution. For this reason, Gearhead Press authors are regularly in the trenches with the developers and engineers that have changed the world through innovative products. Drawing from this experience in IT training, our books deliver superior technical content with a unique perspective that is based on real-world experience.

Now, as an imprint of John Wiley & Sons, Inc., Gearhead Press will continue to bring you, the reader, the level of quality that Wiley has delivered consistently for nearly 200 years.

Thank you.

Donis Marshall
Founder, Gearhead Press
Consulting Editor, Wiley Computer Publishing

Gearhead Press Books in Print

(For complete information about current and upcoming titles, go to www.wiley.com/compbooks/)

Books in the Gearhead Press Point to Point Series

Migrating to Microsoft Exchange 2000
by Stan Reimer
ISBN: 0-471-06116-6

Installing and Configuring Web Servers Using Apache
by Melanie Hoag
ISBN: 0-471-07155-2

Books in the Gearhead Press In the Trenches Series

Windows 2000 Automated Deployment
by Ted Malone, Rolly Perreaux, and Mike Young
ISBN: 0-471-06114-X

Robust Linux: Assuring High Availability
by Iain Campbell
ISBN: 0-471-07040-8

Dedication

This one is dedicated to Rhonda, Angie, and Mandy. You make it all worthwhile.

Acknowledgments

Writing a book is a team project and I was backed by a great team in putting this one together. Thanks to Donis Marshall, Publisher of Gearhead Press, for giving me the opportunity to write this book and put into words what I do for a living. Thanks to Trudy Neuhaus, publishing consultant, for keeping all the pieces of the project connected. And thanks to all the other people at Gearhead who worked on the book — you did a great job of making my writing coherent.

Special thanks to Mike Mulcare, the developmental editor. We have worked together on a couple projects and working with Mike is always a pleasure. Mike has a knack for figuring out what I am trying to say, and then pushing me to make it clear for the rest of you. Thanks to the technical editor, Joel Semeniuk, for editing the book, and who together with Bill Toews and Rod Giesbrecht provide a challenging and interesting place to work at Imaginet Resources Corporation.

But most of all, thanks to my wife, Rhonda, and my daughters, Angela and Amanda. Everyone warned me when I started this project that it would consume my life and my family would have to live without me. Everyone was right. Thanks to the three most important people in my life for hanging in there. I felt your support every step of the way. I promise I will get the fall yard work done in the spring.

Contents

Introduction

MICROSOFT EXCHANGE SERVER IS ONE of the most successful Microsoft products, with approximately 35 million users relying on Exchange Server for their e-mail. Exchange Server 4.0 was introduced in 1993 as a replacement for Microsoft Mail Server (MS Mail). Most organizations were slow to adopt Exchange Server 4.0 because it was seen as difficult to implement and maintain. The introduction of Exchange Server 5.0 in the spring of 1997 marked the beginning of a widespread acceptance of Exchange as a messaging server. Version 5.0 introduced many new capabilities as well as fixed many of the problems with Exchange Server 4.0. The release of Exchange Server 5.5 later in 1997 marked another step forward in the Exchange evolution with its dramatically improved database engine and its Internet protocol support.

Exchange Server 5.*x* is now implemented in almost every possible networking environment, from small businesses with single servers to large corporations with multiple sites. By including Exchange with the integrated Small Business Server, Microsoft has made Exchange available to small offices with only a few users. At the other extreme, Fortune 1000 companies are implementing Exchange in large worldwide networks with hundreds of thousands of users. According to a survey done by the Radicati Group, nearly half of the Fortune 1000 companies and over half of the Fortune 50 companies have either already implemented Exchange Server as their standardized e-mail system or are planning to do so.

NOTE: You can order the complete report from the Radicati Group online at http://www.webcom.com/radicati.

There are many reasons for Exchange Server's success. The Radicati Group has determined that the Total Cost of Ownership (TCO) of using an Exchange messaging platform is significantly lower than the TCO for Lotus Notes and Domino Server, Exchange's largest competitor. Exchange Server 5.5 provides a new database engine that enables the information store to grow up to 16 terabytes (TB), which means that a single server can support a much larger number of users. Exchange 5.5 also provides powerful support for the Internet mail protocols, a crucial feature now that Internet mail has become almost as ubiquitous as the telephone as a communication medium. In addition, Exchange 5.5's option of configuring a network into multiple sites provides flexibility and scalability for large organizations trying to integrate thousands of users in multiple locations into single messaging system. As Exchange has proven successful, it has also become the first platform that software companies consider as they develop new messaging-enabled applications.

Exchange 2000 Server is set to continue this success story. Exchange 2000 Server offers some great enhancements that make it even more reliable and scalable than previous versions. These enhancements include the following:

▲ Integration with Microsoft Windows 2000 Active Directory as a single directory service for storing users, mailboxes, and configuration information.

▲ Enhancements to the information store, including increased overall capacity and the ability to partition the database into smaller units for backup and restoration.

▲ Integration with Internet Information Services (IIS) 5.0, in which Internet protocols for a variety of e-mail clients are now implemented.

▲ Enhanced Web Store access methods, providing developers with powerful new options when designing applications for Exchange 2000 Server.

Due to these enhancements, many organizations that are currently using Exchange Server 4.0 or 5.*x* are now contemplating a migration to Exchange 2000 Server. Exchange Server 2000 requires Windows 2000 Server and Active Directory, so as organizations evaluate an implementation of Windows 2000, they can at the same time think about whether they also want to move to Exchange 2000 Server.

The migration from Exchange Server 4.0/5.*x* to Exchange 2000 Server is probably the most complex migration that most companies' IT departments have ever undertaken, because there are so many planning issues and required related activities. For example, an organization cannot implement Exchange 2000 Server without first implementing Windows 2000 Active Directory. This means that as a company plans to migrate, key IT decision makers must consider a number of issues prior to actually implementing Exchange 2000 Server. These issues include the following:

▲ Designing the Active Directory forest configuration and planning the upgrade path to Windows 2000 Server.

▲ Completing the actual upgrade process from a Windows NT domain structure to Windows 2000 Active Directory for at least some part of the organization.

▲ Integrating the existing Exchange Server 4.0/5.*x* organization with Active Directory.

Only after these preliminary steps are completed is the company ready to migrate to Exchange 2000 Server.

A company must plan the Exchange 2000 Server implementation as it implements Windows 2000 and Active Directory. The fact that the company is migrating to Exchange 2000 Server has important implications for the design of the Active Directory forest. In addition, some of the migration tools provided with Exchange 2000 Server can help simplify the upgrade from a Windows NT domain-based network to Active Directory. How a company decides to integrate the Exchange Server 4.0/5.*x* organization into Active Directory has a direct influence on what the Exchange 2000 Server organization looks like.

In addition to organizations that are currently using Exchange Server 4.0/5.*x*, many companies currently using other e-mail systems, such as Lotus Notes and Domino, Novell GroupWise, or MS Mail will also look seriously at migrating to Exchange 2000 Server. The issues for these organizations are similar to the issues confronting companies migrating from Exchange Server 4.0/5.*x*. For example, before migrating, an Active Directory forest must be in place. During the migration process, the organization may also need to support some form of coexistence, either for a short time or for the foreseeable future.

All these factors make the migration to Exchange 2000 Server a complex task. This book is designed to be a guide on that path. It walks you through the complexities of performing a successful migration regardless of your starting point.

What Is in This Book?

This book follows a fictitious airline, North American Air, as it migrates to Exchange 2000 Server. This company has locations throughout the United States and Canada and has many thousands of users supported by a variety of servers. This book begins by examining the company as it exists today — an organization running Microsoft Windows NT 4.0 as the network operating system and Exchange 5.5, Lotus Notes, and MS Mail as the e-mail systems. Chapter by chapter, this book follows the company through the migration planning process, and then through the implementation of Windows 2000 Active Directory.

After demonstrating Active Directory implementation, the book addresses the important issue of coexistence between Active Directory and Exchange Server 4.0/5.x. Following this, this book deals with the first installation of Exchange 2000 Server and the coexistence issues with Exchange Server 4.0/5.x raised by the presence of Exchange 2000 Servers in the organization. And finally, the book examines options and processes for completing the migration and provides some important tips for managing an Exchange 2000 organization.

While this book addresses many non-Exchange 2000 Server topics along the way (for example, the migration to Windows 2000 Active Directory), the focus is always on Exchange and how the installation of Exchange 2000 Server affects each part of the process. At each step along the way, the North American Air scenario provides a context for the discussion, but the ultimate goal of the scenario — and of the entire book — is to help readers with the network environments in which they are working.

The book consists of five parts, explained in the following sections.

Part 1: Introducing the Exchange 2000 Migration

This part begins by discussing the reasons why a company might migrate to Exchange 2000 Server. The first chapter enumerates the enhancements and improvements offered in Exchange 2000 Server. Chapter 2 compares Exchange 5.*x* and Exchange 2000 Server to provide experienced Exchange 5.*x* administrators a quick look at what has changed both conceptually and practically.

Chapter 3 introduces the business scenario upon which this book is based. This scenario provides a realistic focus for the book by following a fictitious company, comparable to many of the large corporations that run Exchange Server 4.0/5.*x* today, through the planning and implementation of an Exchange 2000 Server migration. The company used in the scenario includes multiple Windows NT 4.0 domains and corporate locations and multiple Exchange Servers 5.*x* that are spread across several sites. The scenario is complex, but the book divides its migration process into separate steps as much as possible, so that you can focus on the part of the scenario that applies to the company with which you are working.

Part 2: Planning

Chapters 4 and 5 focus on the planning that a corporation needs to do before beginning the migration. The migration is an expensive and time-consuming process, so one of the first tasks in the planning process is to determine the reason(s) why the corporation should migrate. In any company, the IS infrastructure is a tool for achieving corporate goals, so one of the first steps in a migration is to define how this migration assists the company in achieving those goals. These chapters describe a sample planning process and discusses the creation of the migration team and the types of information the team needs to gather to plan the migration. They also explain how a team can map out the entire migration process, including the Exchange 2000 Server organizational structure design and the steps and processes needed to implement that structure.

Part 3: Migrating to Windows 2000 Active Directory

Exchange 2000 Server requires Windows 2000 Active Directory, so the first step after the planning is complete is to implement Active Directory in at least some part of the organization. Chapter 6 provides an overview of the process of migrating to Windows 2000 Server (and Active Directory), with a focus on how the Exchange 2000 Server migration affects, and is affected by, the domain migration. This book does not provide a detailed description of all the options for domain migration, but rather an overview. Chapter 7 contains vital information about implementing and configuring the Active Directory Connector, which synchronizes the directory service between the existing Exchange 5.*x* organization and Active Directory.

Part 4: Migrating to Exchange 2000 Server

This part comprises the largest portion of the book and covers three important information areas.

Chapter 8 discusses migrating a single location or Exchange 5.*x* site in a single NT domain to Exchange 2000 Server. There are two reasons why this book begins by focusing on a small migration.

▲ Most companies begin by migrating a single location rather than trying to migrate the entire network at once. Even in a large organization with multiple sites, this is the best way to minimize the disruption of mail services for the corporate e-mail users and to limit the potential for disaster if the migration runs into serious problems.

▲ For a small company with a single location, this chapter includes almost all the information needed to migrate to Exchange 2000 Server.

Chapter 9 discusses the coexistence of Exchange 2000 servers with existing Exchange 5.*x* servers. This is an important topic, because in all but the smallest organizations, the corporation does not migrate to Exchange 2000 Server in a single step, but requires at least some period in which both Exchange Server versions are in use and must be supported. The topics covered include interoperability between sites using Exchange 5.*x* and routing groups using Exchange 2000 Server as well as mixing the two Exchange servers in the same site. When interoperability issues are handled well, there should be only minimal disruption of e-mail services during the migration process.

Chapter 10 covers completing the migration to Exchange 2000 Server. It discusses a variety of approaches to finishing the migration, along with tips for optimizing the process. This part of the book ends with an overview of migration issues for other e-mail systems, such as Lotus Notes and MS Mail, along with more details about enhancements that Exchange 2000 Server brings to a corporation.

Part 5: Managing and Maintaining the Exchange 2000 Server Organization

The last part of the book discusses the migration results and reviews the procedures for managing and maintaining an Exchange 2000 Server organization. This part focuses on maintenance and monitoring and includes information on managing and troubleshooting message routing in the organization (Chapter 11), implementing some of the new features in Exchange 2000 (Chapter 12), and monitoring and backing up Exchange servers (Chapter 13). This part also addresses disaster recovery preparation and techniques. When you have completed the migration and implemented the monitoring and backup procedures covered in this part, your organization is well prepared to enjoy the benefits of Exchange 2000 Server.

What Is *Not* in This Book?

No book can cover every topic related to Exchange 2000 Server, and this book does not attempt to do so. Topics that are *not* covered in detail in this book include the following:

▲ **The day-to-day administration of the Exchange 2000 Server organization.** Chapter 2 discusses Exchange 2000 administrative tasks in contrast to how they were performed in Exchange 4.0/ 5.*x,* and the last three chapters cover some of the administration procedures you use to manage and maintain your Exchange

2000 organization, but this book does not look at all configuration options in detail.

▲ **Active Directory planning and migration.** Complete coverage of Active Directory migration could fill a whole book. This book provides an overview of the process and explains some of the options for the migration, but focuses on how the Active Directory configuration affects the Exchange 2000 Server migration.

▲ **Client software issues.** This book focuses almost entirely on working with the server end of an e-mail system. For experienced e-mail administrators, Exchange 2000 Server introduces very few new e-mail client issues.

▲ **Developer topics.** This book briefly mentions some of the enhancements that Exchange 2000 Server provides for developers who are writing server-based applications. The focus of this book is platform migration, not Exchange 2000 Server application development.

Who Should Buy This Book?

This book is for anyone involved in a migration to Exchange 2000 Server. Its audience can range from network architects who provide the high-level planning for the migration to the network administrators who do most of the actual implementation. This book also provides useful information for organizations that are only beginning to think about the reasons for, and the process of, migration. The book focuses primarily on migration from an Exchange 4.0/5.*x* e-mail system, but if you are migrating to Exchange 2000 Server from any other e-mail system, much of the information presented in this book might prove valuable to you.

This book assumes that you have experience in administering an Exchange 4.0/5.*x* organization and are familiar with Windows NT 4.0 domain management. It also assumes that you are familiar with implementing Windows 2000 Server and have some understanding of the concepts and process of implementing Active Directory.

Part 1

Introducing the Exchange 2000 Migration

Chapter 1

Why Migrate? Exchange 2000 Enhancements

EXCHANGE 2000 SERVER OFFERS significant enhancements over previous versions of Exchange. It replaces the Exchange directory service of previous Exchange versions with Windows 2000 Active Directory and offers tight integration with Windows 2000. Exchange 2000 also is integrated with Internet Information Services in Windows 2000, resulting in more configuration options and greater scalability when supporting the Internet messaging protocols.

Exchange 2000 has changed in other ways as well. For example, the information store has been redesigned so that more mailboxes can be stored on one server without sacrificing performance and disaster recovery flexibility. In addition, Exchange 2000 can operate as an instant messaging or conferencing server, opening up new possibilities for collaboration within organizations. Exchange 2000 also has been improved as an application server, with its Web Store providing more flexibility for storing and accessing information on the Exchange server.

But is Exchange 2000 the right solution for your organization? Migrating to Exchange 2000 from earlier versions of Exchange can be a complex task. Before you decide whether to migrate your organization to Exchange 2000, you should consider some of the benefits you'll reap in return for going through the work of migrating. This

chapter provides a summary of the product enhancements in
Exchange Server 2000.

> **NOTE:** *For ease of reading, I use Exchange in this book to refer to
> Exchange 2000 Server. To draw a comparison between Exchange
> 4.0/5.x and Exchange 2000, I include 2000 to be specific. To refer to
> previous versions of Exchange, including Exchange 4.0, 5.0, and
> 5.5, I use Exchange 4.0/5.x. For most of the concepts discussed in this
> book, there is little difference between the three earlier versions of
> Exchange. To refer to a particular version of Exchange (for example,
> Exchange 5.5, Service Pack 3), I use the specific version information.*

Active Directory Integration

One of the biggest changes in Exchange 2000 is that it no longer has
a directory service of its own. Exchange 4.0/5.x has two directory services: the Windows NT directory service and the Exchange directory
service. You work with mailboxes in Exchange 4.0/5.x independently
of user accounts in Windows NT. This can result in confusion and
duplication of effort in some cases. For example, groups in NT and
distribution lists in Exchange 4.0/5.x are separate, even though the
same users appear in both. This situation has changed in Exchange
2000. There is now only one directory service with which you will be
working — Windows 2000 Active Directory.

Windows 2000 Active Directory is a major change for Windows
NT administrators. For the first time, Microsoft has produced a
directory service and network operating system that is scalable to any
size organization. Active Directory provides services for administering users and groups and managing domains, as does Windows NT.
By employing a hierarchical forest and domain structure, however,
and by using Kerberos as the authentication protocol, Windows 2000
networks provide enhanced management flexibility and are much
more scalable. Organizational Units (OUs) enable you to split a
domain into multiple components, providing the opportunity to delegate administrative tasks to users and assign them a limited set of
administrative rights. OUs also enable the use of Group Policies, a
powerful tool to manage the users' working environments. Through

Group Policies you can automatically install software, configure user desktops, and limit user access to system components.

Exchange benefits from its integration with Active Directory in many ways. I describe some of them in the following sections.

User and Group Management

One of the first benefits that you'll notice in Exchange 2000 is that you now administer users, groups, and mailboxes using a single interface: the Windows 2000 Active Directory Users and Computers management console. Using this one tool, you can create users and create the mailboxes for the users. You can also create groups and then mail-enable the groups so that they can be used as e-mail distribution lists. When Exchange 2000 is installed in a Windows 2000 domain, every user object and group object in Active Directory Users and Computers has several additional tabs that can be used to configure the Exchange properties for the user or group.

This change is much more than a simple administrative interface change, however. The concept underlying user account administration also has changed. When you create a mailbox on an Exchange 4.0/5.*x* server, you create a mailbox object and then specify a Windows NT account as the owner as one of the attributes on the mailbox. In Exchange 2000, when you create a user account and a mailbox, one of the user account's attributes identifies the account as the owner of an Exchange mailbox. Exchange 2000 does not have a directory service of its own; all the directory information must come from Active Directory.

A second benefit to the integration with Active Directory is that you can now create three types of user objects, depending on the security and mail requirements of a user:

▲ **Mailbox-enabled user.** A *mailbox-enabled user* is both a security principal and the owner of a mailbox. This means that the user can have both a mailbox on an Exchange server and access to network resources.

▲ **Mail-enabled user.** A *mail-enabled user* is a security principal with a custom e-mail address rather than a mailbox on the Exchange server. This type of account is useful for users who require access to the network but receive their e-mail on a different system.

▲ **Contact.** A *contact* is a pointer to an external e-mail address. The user has neither network access nor a mailbox on an Exchange server. In Exchange 4.0/5.*x*, a contact was called a custom recipient.

Notice that there is no option to create a user who has a mailbox but is not a security principal. As in Exchange 4.0/5.*x*, every mailbox in Exchange 2000 must have a domain account associated with it. To access an Exchange mailbox, Active Directory must first authenticate the user.

Group management has also changed in Exchange 2000. When creating a new security group in Active Directory, the administrator can create a *mail-enabled group*. (This was called a *distribution list* in Exchange 4.0/5.*x*.) A mail-enabled group shows up in the global address list (GAL) and on the Security tab when assigning permissions to network resources. If the group is a universal security group, the group and its membership list can be viewed as a distribution list anywhere in the Active Directory forest. This is similar to viewing the membership of a distribution list in Exchange 4.0/5.*x*. All the members of a distribution list are visible in the GAL regardless of which NT domain actually contains the account. A global group or a domain local group can also be mail-enabled and used as a distribution list, but viewing the membership of the group across the forest becomes more complicated. You must decide what types of mail-enabled groups to use in Active Directory when planning the Windows 2000 Active Directory structure with Exchange 2000 in mind.

Integrated Security

Security in Exchange 2000 is integrated with Active Directory security. Every visible object in the Exchange 2000 System Manager is an Active Directory object, and as such, is part of the Active Directory security model. Every Active Directory object has an Access Control List (ACL) that determines what level of permissions a user or group has to that object. This applies to Exchange objects as well. For example, in Exchange 2000 you can create a routing group connector, which is used to connect routing groups (similar to a site connector in Exchange 4.0/5.*x*). This object appears in both the Exchange System Manager and the configuration partition in Active Directory. When an administrator tries to change a setting on the routing group connector, Exchange 2000 checks the administrator's permission level in Active Directory. It applies the change only if the administrator has permission to change the Active Directory object. Another example of Exchange security's integration with Windows 2000 is that the user must be authenticated in Active Directory before accessing an Exchange mailbox.

This security integration can be useful. For example, in Exchange 4.0/5.*x*, you use a distribution list to assign permissions to a public folder, but use a Windows NT domain group to assign permissions to resources such as folder shares or printers. In Windows 2000, because the same group is used for both security and as a distribution list, the same group object can be used to assign permissions in both places.

Another example of integrated security's usefulness is evident when delegating administration, which is covered next.

More Administration Options

Another benefit of Active Directory integration is that you now have more options in how you administer your Exchange 2000 organization. In an Exchange 4.0/5.*x* organization, you could assign permissions to the whole organization, to a site (which gave you the rights to manage recipients in that site), or to the configuration container in a site. In Exchange 2000, you can be much more precise in how you assign permissions, including what types of permissions you assign and where in the organization you assign them. Additionally, you can create multiple administrative groups to match your organization's requirements. For example, you may want to create an administrative structure in which one group of Exchange administrators has full control over all of the Exchange servers in their office, another group of administrators has the right to manage user accounts and mailboxes in all locations, and a third group has the right to manage only the connections between the locations.

This administrative control is possible because of the way Exchange 2000 is integrated with Active Directory. As mentioned earlier, you can manipulate the ACL on an Active Directory object, which allows you to precisely manage the level of permission any user or group has to Exchange 2000 objects. You do not need to manage the permissions by directly changing the permissions on an ACL; in most cases, Exchange 2000 provides wizards that guide you through the process of setting the permissions exactly as you want them.

The improved administration options enable you to delegate both Exchange and Active Directory administrative tasks in your organization. In Active Directory, one of the main purposes of an OU is to make it easy to delegate administrative duties. For example, you may want to give the Human Resources (HR) department in a particular city the right to create and modify user objects for new hires in that city, but not to perform any other administrative tasks anywhere in the organization. You can accomplish this by creating an Active Directory group that includes all the users from the HR department. Then create an OU that contains the user accounts for that city, and run the Delegation of Control wizard to assign precisely those permissions to the HR group. If you also want the HR department to be able to create mailboxes for new employees, you can create an administrative group for that city within the Exchange System Manager and then run the Exchange Administration Delegation wizard to give the group permission to create the mailboxes. To create mailboxes, the group needs at least Exchange View Only Administrator permissions.

Figure 1-1 illustrates the relationship between the OU and the administrative group for assigning permissions as just described.

Custom Management Tools

Closely linked to the enhanced administration options are the new administration tools that can be used to manage Windows 2000 and

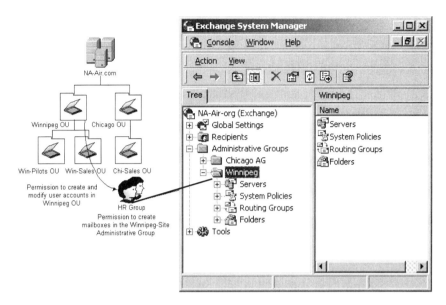

*Figure 1-1: Delegating Permissions to OUs
and Administrative Groups.*

Exchange 2000. All the administrative tools for Windows 2000 are available as snap-ins in a Microsoft Management Console (MMC), as are the Exchange 2000 administrative tools. Since all of the administrative tools use the same interface, you don't have to remember the specifics of many different interfaces.

The MMC enables you to customize the tools that you see when you open the console. For example, if you are responsible for administering the entire Exchange organization, including all servers, public folders, and connections between routing groups, as well as user administration, you can create a custom MMC that includes all of the tools you need for those activities in a single console.

To manage everything in Exchange 2000, you need the following MMC consoles:

▲ **Exchange System Manager,** to manage most of the Exchange settings

▲ **Active Directory Users and Computers,** to manage user accounts and mailboxes

▲ **Internet Services Manager,** to manage Internet Information Services (IIS)

You also may want to add the Event Viewer, Performance Logs and Alerts, and Services snap-ins to provide you with tools for monitoring your Exchange servers. You can add all of these consoles as snap-ins to a single MMC so that you can manage everything from one interface.

When you add a snap-in, such as Event Viewer or Services, you can specify which server you want to monitor using this tool. That way you can create a console to monitor all the Exchange servers in your location.

You can also limit what is visible in the console. Rather than add a number of tools to one console, you can add one snap-in to the console and then create a custom interface so that only certain parts of the interface are visible to the intended administrator. For example, I described earlier how you could delegate administrative tasks, such as creating users, to the HR department. To make this administration as simple as possible, you could create a management tool that enables the members of that department to see only the OU in which they are creating the users. You can also create a Taskpad, such as the one in Figure 1-2, that enables the HR staff to create additional users by opening a shortcut on the desktop and typing the required information rather than accessing the full MMC. Exchange 2000 also provides extension snap-ins that you can use to manage parts of the whole Exchange organization, such as the SMTP virtual servers or the public folders. For example, you can create a custom MMC to which you add just the SMTP snap-in, enabling only the management of the SMTP virtual servers from that MMC.

NOTE: A Taskpad is a customized MMC that provides a custom management tool for users with specific administrative tasks. To create a Taskpad, open a blank MMC and add one of the administration snap-ins (for example, the Active Directory Users and Computers). Then right-click the OU that will be the focus of the Taskpad and select New Taskpad View. The New Taskpad View wizard leads you through the process of creating the Taskpad. After you have created the Taskpad, you can make it available to the user who will perform the administrative tasks.

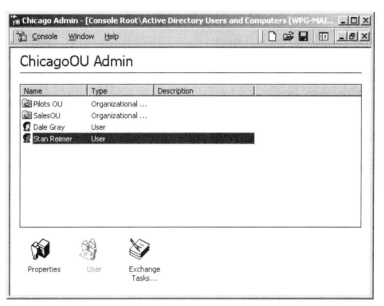

Figure 1-2: Creating and Managing User Accounts and Mailboxes Using a Custom Taskpad.

Better Client Support

Exchange 2000's integration with Active Directory provides at least two improvements in how you support clients.

The first improvement is in the area of e-mail client installation and configuration using Group Policies within Active Directory. Group Policy is a powerful tool for installing and configuring software on client computers, as well as setting restrictions on what changes the users can make to their desktops. For example, if you support Outlook Express or Outlook Web Access clients, you can use the Internet Explorer options available under the Group Policy administrative templates to limit and configure the clients. If you support a MAPI client such as Outlook 2000, you can install a copy of the program on every desktop in the organization by using Group Policy. Using the Custom Installation wizard from the Office 2000 Resource Kit, you can create a transform file that will install a completely preconfigured installation of Outlook 2000. Once the software is installed using Group Policy, it can repair itself in the event of damage and is easy to upgrade. Group Policy has many other features, but from an Exchange administrator's perspective, this option to configure clients automatically is the most useful.

The second improvement to client support as a result of Exchange and Active Directory integration directly benefits the users in an organization. Windows 2000 Active Directory is a Lightweight Directory Access Protocol (LDAP) compliant directory, which means that it is searchable using many different LDAP clients with powerful options when configuring the searches. Users can locate other mail recipients by searching Active Directory using any attribute. For example, suppose a user wants to send a message to all the users who report to a certain manager. If the organization information has been filled in for all the users in Active Directory, she can search for users that have that manager's name in the Manager field and then select all of the names as mail recipients.

You can also use LDAP queries to build an address list (called an Address Book View in Exchange 4.0/5.x). For example, you could create an address list of all contacts in a particular city that are working with a certain department. You can build the address list using an LDAP search in the Exchange System Manager. After the address list has been created, e-mail users can access the list by selecting it as the Address Book through their MAPI e-mail clients.

> **NOTE:** *Clients use LDAP primarily to search LDAP-compliant directories. In addition, developers use LDAP when writing applications to modify the information in the directories.*

Configuration Information

In addition to user and group information, Exchange 2000 also stores virtually all configuration information in Active Directory. When you open the Exchange System Manager, the Exchange server contacts the closest domain controller and requests the Exchange configuration information from the configuration partition in Active Directory. The configuration partition provides information about the entire Exchange organization. This includes enterprise-wide information, such as the administrative and routing groups and the connections between different routing groups. Active Directory also stores server-specific information, such as the number of storage groups and mailbox stores, the number of virtual servers, and how the virtual servers are configured. Whenever the Exchange server needs information about the entire Exchange organization, it checks Active Directory. Figure 1-3 shows some of the Exchange configuration information stored in Active Directory.

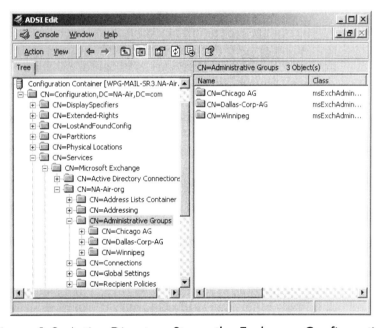

Figure 1-3: Active Directory Stores the Exchange Configuration Information.

Storing all data centrally in Active Directory has two implications for you as an Exchange administrator. First, because Active Directory holds the information that Exchange needs to start, you must make sure that the Exchange server always has a fast and reliable connection to a domain controller (for configuration and some user and group information) and to a global catalog server (for universal group information). If the server cannot contact a domain controller when it starts, it cannot start the Exchange services.

Exchange 2000 and Active Directory Schema Changes

For Active Directory to become the storage location for all this Exchange information, Microsoft had to extend the schema for Active Directory considerably. In fact, Exchange 2000 makes over 1000 changes to the schema. The changes are made when you install the first Exchange server into a forest, or when you run the Exchange setup program with the /forestprep switch.

Second, this dependency on Active Directory affects disaster recovery. Because all the configuration information for Exchange is now stored in Active Directory, you can use this information when you need to rebuild a server. If a server has crashed completely, you can reinstall Windows 2000 using the same computer name, and then install Exchange using the /DisasterRecovery switch. As long as Exchange has access to a domain controller during the recovery, it can read the configuration information from Active Directory and use it to return the server to its predisaster state. (Chapter 13 includes a much more detailed discussion of the process of disaster recovery.)

Information Store Enhancements

The second important enhancement to Exchange 2000 is the redesigned information store architecture. The basic technology for the database engine that underlies the information store has not changed. Exchange still uses transaction logs and rollback recoverability for reliability and redundancy. However, the ways you can organize the database have changed dramatically. You can now support a much larger database and take advantage of more options and higher performance for backup and restore operations.

Storage Groups and Stores

Exchange 2000 introduces a new way of organizing your Exchange databases on the server. In Exchange 4.0/5.x you can have only one private store and one public store on each server, with each store reaching a maximum size of 16 terabytes in Exchange 5.5. As the database size increases, managing the database becomes more complex. In particular, a very large database will take a long time to restore if the hard disk storing the database fails. While the database is being restored, none of the users on the server can access their mailboxes until the entire database is restored. The only way to decrease the size of the database in Exchange 4.0/5.x is to install an additional server and then move user mailboxes to the second server.

With Exchange 2000, however, you can partition your database on a single server into more manageable units. To make this possible, Exchange supports separate stores and storage groups. A *store* is a database that can be used to store user mailboxes (called a *mailbox store* in Exchange 2000) or public folders (called a *public folder store* in Exchange 2000). A *storage group* is a collection of stores that are grouped together for administrative purposes, and that share a single transaction log. In Exchange 2000, you can create up to four storage groups per server and up to five stores per storage group. This means that you can take one large database and partition it into up to 20 separate databases.

!   **EDITION ALERT:** *Exchange 2000 ships in three different editions: Exchange 2000 Server, Enterprise Server, and Conferencing Server. To support multiple databases and unlimited database size, you need to implement Exchange 2000 Enterprise Server. I include notes throughout this book indicating other differences between the editions.*

Database partitioning makes restoring data from backups more convenient. You can restore each store in a storage group individually. If the hard disk on which you are storing your Exchange databases fails, you can begin your restore with the most important store first. You can then mount just this store, and any users with mailboxes on the store can begin using their e-mail. You then can continue to restore the stores one at a time, bringing them online as soon as each store is available.

A storage group is a collection of stores that share one transaction log. When a message is sent to any mailbox or public folder store in a storage group, the message is logged in a single transaction log, regardless of the store for which the message is intended. This means that, in most cases, you back up the storage group as a single unit. While it is possible to back up the stores individually, it is quite inefficient to do so because you need to back up all the transaction logs with each individual store backup. Because all the stores in the storage group are linked to the same transaction log, configuring the transaction log location and circular logging is done at a storage-group level. Almost all other database-related settings, such as mailbox limits, are configured on each individual store.

In most cases, you do not want to turn on circular logging, but in Exchange 2000 you have the option of doing so for a specific storage group. For example, if you are using Exchange as a newsgroup server and you are making the newsgroups available as public folders, you are probably not concerned about providing redundancy for those folders. You can put all stores for the newsgroups in one storage group and then enable circular logging for that one storage group.

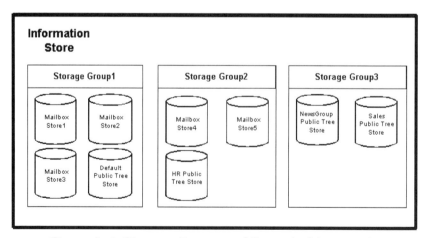

Figure 1-4: Storage Group and Store Architecture in Exchange 2000.

Figure 1-4 illustrates how you can now configure storage groups and stores on a single Exchange server.

Each store in Exchange 2000 can be of unlimited size, but because you can now use multiple stores on a server, stores no longer needs to be as big as they were in Exchange 4.0/5.*x*.

Other Information Store Enhancements

Exchange 2000 includes a number of other improvements to the information store. Here are some examples.

Native Content Store

In Exchange 4.0/5.*x*, there is a single database file (Priv.edb or Pub.edb for the private store or the public store respectively). In Exchange 2000, however, there are two files associated with each store (for example, priv1.edb and priv1.stm for the first mailbox store). The .edb file is similar to the file in Exchange 4.0/5.*x*; it stores the mail messages in the native Exchange Rich Text Format. The .stm file is used to store messages that are sent in Multipurpose Internet Mail Extension (MIME) format.

Having two files decreases the time it takes to read from and write to the database because MIME messages no longer have to go through conversion. When a message arrives in MIME format in Exchange 2000, it is saved without conversion in the .stm file, and the header is written to the .edb file. In Exchange 4.0/5.*x*, in contrast, every message is converted to the Exchange format when it arrives.

If a user reads a message from an .stm file using an Internet mail client, such as Outlook Express or Netscape Communicator, the message does not need to be converted because it is already in the correct format for the client. If a client opens a message in the .stm file using a MAPI client, such as Outlook, the message is converted by the server and presented to the client in its native format. If the MAPI client does not change and save the message, the message remains in the .stm store after the client closes the message. Using the native content store improves server performance because it has to convert only the messages that need to be converted.

Multiple Public Folder Trees

In Exchange 4.0/5.*x*, you are limited to a single public folder tree on a server. All public folders on the server have to be created under the default tree, and the hierarchy of public folders is replicated to all servers with a public store. In contrast, in Exchange 2000, you can create multiple public folder trees, and then create the public folders in a more logical location. To create a new public folder tree, you must associate a public folder store with the tree, creating a one-to-one relationship between a public folder tree and a public folder store.

One of the advantages of using multiple trees is that the information about the new tree is replicated only to locations that also have a store dedicated to that tree. For example, if you have one location in your company at which there are a number of public folders that do not apply to any other company location, you can create a new public folder tree in that location and put all the location-specific folders into that tree. Information about that tree will not be replicated anywhere else in the organization. The primary limitation with using multiple public folder trees in Exchange 2000 is that the additional public folder trees can be viewed only from Web clients and NNTP clients. Microsoft has stated that the next version of their MAPI client will be able to view multiple public folder trees.

Full-Text Indexing

Exchange 2000 can be configured to create a full-text index of the content of any store. This greatly speeds up the search process when clients search the messages in a store for a particular message. In Exchange 4.0/5.*x*, the entire database must be searched to find a message containing a certain word. In Exchange 2000, however, the server creates an index of the store, and a client can search the index rather than the entire store. To optimize this feature's performance, you can configure Exchange to update the index during off-peak hours.

Full-text indexing has some limitations in Exchange 2000, in that it is based only on full word searches (for example, a search for "data" will not return a message with the word "database" in it) and it can search only message headers, message bodies, and attachments.

This means that you cannot use the full-text index search to search for all messages sent by a certain recipient. However, Exchange still supports the old searching method that enables you to search for message properties, such as sender. Exchange automatically combines the results of the two search methods so that when you search for messages from a specific recipient with certain words in the subject, Exchange searches for the subject word using the full-text index and then searches just this result set for the message sender.

Internet Information Services Integration

The third significant change to Exchange 2000 is its integration into Microsoft Internet Information Services (IIS). In Exchange 4.0/5.*x*, the Exchange server handles all protocol support, regardless of the protocol being used (MAPI, X.400, IMAP4, SMTP or any other protocol). Unless you want to install Outlook Web Access, you do not install IIS on an Exchange 4.0/5.*x* server because of the additional resources that it would consume. In Exchange 2000, however, all the Internet protocols have been moved out of the Exchange process and are now supported by IIS. This means that every Exchange server must now be running IIS. IIS is installed by default when you install Windows 2000 Server; when you install Exchange on the same server, it adds to and enhances the protocols supported on the IIS server.

NOTE: One of the implications of Exchange 2000's dependence on IIS is that you also have to learn how to administer IIS. While you do very little actual administration of the Exchange properties in IIS, understanding how IIS functions is essential in troubleshooting Exchange messaging issues.

Exchange Protocol Architecture

Integration with IIS results in a different protocol architecture in Exchange 2000. In previous versions of Exchange, all the protocols are integrated in the information store process. In Exchange 2000, the only protocols that are still integrated into the information store process are MAPI and X.400. While MAPI continues to be important in an Exchange organization to support the most full-featured clients, X.400 is supported primarily for connectivity with older X.400 e-mail systems. All the Internet protocols have been moved into the IIS process (inetinfo.exe) in Exchange 2000.

Internet Protocol Support

Exchange 2000 supports the same set of Internet protocols that are supported in Exchange 4.0/5.*x*, with many of the same configuration options at the protocol level. There are, however, some significant changes. One of the most important of these is the enhanced importance of the SMTP protocol in Exchange 2000. In Exchange 4.0/5.*x*, when two servers in the same site need to exchange messages, they use remote procedure calls (RPCs) to pull the messages from each other. When you set up multiple sites with Exchange 4.0/5.*x*, the preferred method of connecting the two sites is with a site connector that uses RPCs to communicate between the servers. You can configure an Internet Mail Service connector to connect sites, but the preference is to use the site connector because it is faster and easier to configure. One of the most problematic issues with RPCs used by the Exchange 4.0/5.*x* servers is bandwidth. In most cases, you need at least 128 Kbps of available bandwidth to use the RPC-based site connector. If you have much less bandwidth than that, the RPCs time out too frequently, resulting in unreliable communication.

In contrast, Exchange 2000 uses SMTP as the protocol for most inter-server communication. SMTP has become the standard for all Internet e-mail. It uses a single TCP/IP port, making it easier to configure routers and firewalls. When two Exchange 2000 servers are in the same routing group, they send messages to each other using SMTP.

The preferred connector between routing groups in Exchange 2000 is the routing group connector (RGC), which also uses SMTP. An Exchange 2000 server uses an RPC to communicate with another Exchange server only when the other server is an Exchange 4.0/5.*x* server that is in the same site or routing group, or when the Exchange 4.0/5.*x* server is the bridgehead server in a remote site and the two servers are using a site connector to communicate.

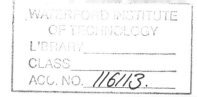
One of the advantages of SMTP is that it can be used on a network link with less bandwidth than was required when using RPCs. As long as the network link is reliable, it can be used for SMTP regardless of its bandwidth. You might want to revisit the site boundaries you have established in Exchange 4.0/5.*x* in light of the reduced bandwidth requirements of Exchange 2000; previously unsuitable connections may now be usable.

Multiple Virtual Servers

The Exchange 2000 relocation of Internet protocol support to IIS provides you with a couple of other interesting possibilities when configuring Exchange 2000 servers. One of these is the option of supporting multiple virtual servers for a particular protocol. For example, you could use the same computer to provide your connection to the Internet e-mail and to operate as an SMTP bridgehead server between two routing groups. For the Internet connection, you may want to set restrictions on who can use the connection, specify the maximum message size that can be sent on the connection, and configure the server to prevent the relaying of e-mail messages. For the bridgehead server connection, you may not want to configure any restrictions, but you may want to schedule the delivery of messages to occur only during off-peak times to preserve bandwidth on the WAN connection. This scenario is easy to configure using Exchange virtual servers.

The virtual server in Exchange 2000 is based on virtual servers in IIS. To create additional virtual servers in IIS, you need to have multiple IP addresses (and preferably multiple network cards) for the server, or use multiple port assignments. You follow the same procedure when creating multiple SMTP servers. First, install two network cards in the Exchange server and configure one with an IP address and virtual server to provide the Internet connection. Then use the second network card, IP address, and virtual server to provide the bridgehead server connection. You can implement virtual servers for any other Internet protocol using this same methodology.

Distributed Internet Protocol Services

Integrating Exchange and IIS in Exchange 2000 enables you to distribute tasks related to the Internet protocols between multiple servers. Normally, when clients access an Exchange 2000 server using the POP3 protocol, they connect to the POP3 virtual server on the server where their mailboxes are located. Allowing this connection to their Exchange server raises a security concern if the clients are connecting to their mailboxes across an Internet connection. Exchange 2000 enables you to set up a front-end/back-end server configuration. In this configuration, all the clients connect to one or more front-end servers across the Internet, and the front-end server forwards the request to the back-end server. When a client logs on to the front-end server, the server checks in Active Directory for the mailbox location for the client and then forwards the request to the correct back-end server. Figure 1-5 shows you what this configuration looks like.

! **EDITION ALERT:** *To support the front-end/back-end configuration, you need to install Exchange 2000 Enterprise Server.*

This front-end/back-end server configuration also provides options for distributing the workload onto multiple servers. For example, suppose you want to require your Internet clients to encrypt all the e-mail sent across the Internet using S/MIME. Encrypting and decrypting messages is a CPU-intensive activity that you may want to offload onto another server. Such offloading is easy to configure using front-end/back-end servers. You can configure the front-end server with a high-end RAM and CPU configuration that has limited hard disk space, and the back-end server with a large hard disk system that is optimized for access speed. Then you configure all the clients to use S/MIME and to connect to the front-end server. The front-end server can take care of all the encryption and decryption, while the back-end server functions primarily as a database server and as the server for internal MAPI clients. You can easily balance the load across the front-end servers by using Network Load Balancing provided with Windows 2000 Advanced Server, by using DNS round robin, or by implementing a hardware load balancing device. The load on the back-end servers is balanced by distributing user mailboxes across multiple servers.

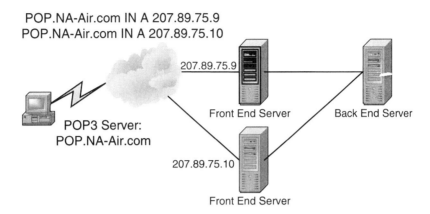

POP.NA-Air.com IN A 207.89.75.9
POP.NA-Air.com IN A 207.89.75.10

207.89.75.9

Front End Server   Back End Server

POP3 Server:
POP.NA-Air.com

207.89.75.10

Front End Server

Figure 1-5: Distributed Services for POP Servers in Exchange 2000.

Outlook Web Access

Integrating the Internet protocols with IIS also changes Outlook Web Access (OWA) in Exchange 2000. OWA is a favorite user feature in Exchange 5.*x* because it enables users to access their mailboxes from anywhere on the Internet using only a Web browser.

OWA is the only option in Exchange 5.*x* that provides a front-end/back-end configuration similar to that described in the preceding section. You install OWA on a front-end server running IIS. When a user connects to the front-end server, the server uses Active Server Pages and RPC connections to the back-end server to access the content of the user's mailbox.

In Exchange 2000, the basic concept is similar, but the way you implement it is very different. Instead of using Active Server Pages and RPCs, Exchange 2000 uses Distributed Authoring and Versioning (WebDAV) and HTTP to communicate between the two servers. WebDAV provides enhanced options for reading and writing to the information store using HTTP. When you set up OWA in Exchange 5.*x*, you have to configure the OWA server with the back-end server to which it would connect. In Exchange 2000, however, the front-end server contacts an Active Directory domain controller to determine

23

the mailbox location for the client, and it can connect to any back-end server.

OWA in Exchange 2000 also offers some enhancements for clients. For example, in Exchange 5.*x*, you can access your mailbox by typing the Uniform Resource Locator (URL) of the Exchange server followed by the Exchange Virtual directory. The URL looks something like this:

```
http://mail.NA-Air.com/exchange
```

After connecting to the OWA server, a logon page appears on which you type your mailbox alias; then you log in and access your mailbox. You can still use the same URL in Exchange 2000 OWA, but it checks the name you are currently logged in with to see whether your credentials match the credentials for a mailbox in the organization.

As a shortcut, you can type:

```
http://mail.NA-Air.com/exchange/youralias
```

to open your mailbox, where *youralias* is the account under which you are logged in. The server prompts you for your credentials only if your current credentials do not match those required to access the mailbox.

You can also type:

```
http://mail.NA-Air.com/exchange/youralias/inbox
```

to go directly to your inbox. If you know the subject for a message, you can even open the message directly from the URL. For example, you can type:

```
http://mail.NA-Air.com/exchange/youralias/inbox/
    holidays.eml
```

to open the specific message.

You can even include commands as part of the URL. For example, you can type:

```
http://mail.NA-Air.com/exchange/youralias/inbox/
    ?cmd=new
```

to open the new message template to create a new e-mail message.

Using Internet Explorer (IE) 5.*x* also increases client functionality. IE 5.*x* supports drag-and-drop, enhanced rich-text formatting, and more options than earlier IE versions for creating and moving folders. All the OWA clients provide additional features as well, such as support for embedded objects and multimedia messages and access to public folders that contain contact or calendar items.

Administration and Routing

Exchange 2000 also changes the way the Exchange organization is configured, both for administrative and message-routing purposes. The single Exchange 4.0/5.*x* concept of a site is replaced in Exchange 2000 by administrative groups that can be used to configure administrative rights and routing groups that can be used to configure message routing.

Delegating Administration with Administrative Groups

Perhaps the closest analogy for an administrative group in Exchange 2000 is the Organizational Unit (OU) in Windows 2000 Active Directory. The OU is designed primarily to group users, computers, or other Active Directory objects into logical groupings so that they can be administered the same way and by the same group of administrators. This is exactly the same function that the administrative group serves in Exchange 2000. The administrative group is designed to split your Exchange organization into smaller blocks for the sake of administration.

An administrative group can contain almost any type of Exchange object. For example, the default *First Administrative Group* contains a Routing group, a Servers container, a Chat Communities container, and a Public Folder container. You also can add other objects such as System Policy containers and Conferencing Service containers to the administrative group. If you create additional administrative groups, you can move the contents of any of these containers to any other administrative group, with the exception of the servers in the Server container. This provides a great deal of flexibility in how you design the administration of your Exchange organization.

> **NOTE:** *One big difference between OUs in Active Directory and administrative groups in an Exchange organization is that you will almost certainly have more OUs than you will have administrative groups. The default installation of Exchange 2000 has only one administrative group, and that is adequate for most small to medium-sized companies.*

As discussed earlier, one way to configure administrative rights is to delegate permissions based on the administrative groups. There are many other ways that administrative groups can be used to partition your Exchange organization into multiple administrative units as well. For example, if you have multiple locations with Exchange administrators at each location that should have full control of the Exchange servers at that location, you can create separate administrative groups for each location. You might, for example, have a group of administrators responsible for the message routing between routing groups. You can create an administrative group that has all the routing groups and the connectors between routing groups in it and then assign one group of administrators full control of only that administrative group. Alternatively, you might have a Public Folders Administrators group that manages all of the public folders for the entire organization. You can create an administrative group, move the Public Folder container into it, and assign the Public Folders Administrators group full control.

Controlling Message Flow with Routing Groups

In Exchange 4.0/5.*x* you use sites to control message routing through the organization. In Exchange 2000, this functionality is supported using routing groups. Like in Exchange 4.0/5.*x*, all the servers in the same routing group should be connected with a reasonably fast, reliable network connection. All the message routing within a routing group are routed using a single hop, as each server can directly communicate with each other server in the routing group. The only significant difference between message routing in an Exchange 4.0/5.*x* site and message routing in an Exchange 2000 routing group is the protocol used to send the messages. In Exchange 4.0/5.*x*, the servers use RPCs to communicate within the same site; in Exchange 2000 this intra-routing group message transfer is handled through SMTP.

When you create multiple routing groups, you have to create the connectors between the routing groups manually. Again, the concepts are very much the same as routing between sites in Exchange 4.0/5.*x*. You can use a variety of routing group connectors to provide the connections between the groups, which include using the configurable options of scheduling message delivery, configuring bridgehead servers, and tracking messages. However, there are two important changes in Exchange 2000. Once again, the protocol of choice when servers are communicating between sites is SMTP rather than RPC. The only other available protocol is X.400, which is included in Exchange 2000 primarily for backward compatibility, but can be used to connect routing groups as well. One of the important advantages of SMTP is that it supports significantly slower network connections than RPC.

The second change is much more significant, especially for large corporations with multiple locations. The process of building and maintaining the message routing table has been completely revamped in Exchange 2000.

In Exchange 4.0/5.*x*, the routing information is kept in a Gateway Address Routing Table (GWART), which is a compilation of all the routes and address spaces that each server knows about. The server uses the GWART to make routing decisions when transferring messages between sites. The GWART has two major drawbacks. First, it has no way of dynamically detecting whether intra-site links are up or down, and as a result, no way of rebuilding the routing table. Second, it is unsophisticated about rerouting messages if a connection along a chosen route through the site topology is down.

Exchange 2000 replaces the GWART with the link state table, which addresses these two limitations well. Every server has a copy of the link state table, which is an up-to-date copy of the routing topology of the entire Exchange organization. The link state table is dynamically updated; when a route goes down, all of the Exchange servers in the entire organization are informed of the failed connection and the servers then reroute messages around the failed link until it is available again. If a link fails while a message is being routed, the Exchange server that detects the failed route can reroute the message, or hold the message in a queue if no other route to the routing group is available.

When you migrate an Exchange 4.0/5.x organization to Exchange 2000, by default each administrative group is mapped to an existing Exchange 4.0/5.x site. Each administrative group also contains a single routing group containing all the servers in that site. After migrating all the Exchange 4.0/5.x servers to Exchange 2000, you can switch the Exchange organization to native mode instead. This enables you to reconfigure the routing group topology of your organization by moving servers into appropriate routing groups.

Exchange System Policies

System policies are another useful component when administrating the Exchange 2000 organization. System policies are similar to group policies in Active Directory, in that you can create one policy and link it to multiple locations in the organization. The policy is then applied to all the objects that fall under its scope. The types of policies available in the Exchange system policies are different from the types of policies available under group policies, but the basic application is similar.

There are four types of system policies that can be configured in Exchange System Manager:

▲ **Recipient policies.** Recipient policies are used to add additional e-mail addresses to all of the recipients affected by the policy. You can create various filters to specify who will be affected by the policy.

▲ **Server policies.** Server policies are used to configure message tracking on servers.

▲ **Mailbox store policies.** Mailbox store policies are used to define the default public store, the offline address list, the database settings such as when the online maintenance will take place, mailbox size limits and deleted item retention settings, and configuring full-text indexing.

▲ **Public store policies.** Public store policies are used to configure the online maintenance schedule, default replication scheduling for public folder replication and limits, such as size and age limits, for public folders.

All of these policies can be created within Exchange System Manager and then applied throughout the entire organization. System policies simplify administration by grouping a set of objects and configuring one policy for all of them. This makes it easy to change a setting in multiple locations at one time. For example, you could use a single system policy to configure the mailbox limits on all mailbox stores at a maximum of 10 MB. If you wanted to change the limit to 12 MB, you could change the setting on the system policy and the change would be applied to all of the mailbox stores.

Exchange 2000 is much more than just an e-mail server. In these last two sections of the chapter I discuss two of the enhancements to Exchange 2000 that make the server the center of other communication activity as well as the back-end server for applications.

Real-Time Collaboration Tools

Instant messaging, the chat server, and conferencing services provide real-time collaboration alternatives to the traditional communication choices of e-mail and telephones.

Instant Messaging

Microsoft Exchange Instant Messaging provides an instant communication platform to members of an Exchange organization. The client used in instant messaging is similar to the client used for MSN Messenger and provides many of the same features. Users can specify other users to appear on their messaging contact lists, and then the client software and server work together to provide continuous information about the online status of those contacts (called *presence information*).

The Exchange server performs a number of tasks as the instant-messaging server. First, the user account on the server must be instant messaging-enabled because whenever any user tries to log on to Instant Messenger, the user permissions are checked. Once a user is logged on, the server begins to store the presence information about the user and informs all the users who have listed the client as a contact of the user's online status. The instant messaging servers can also be configured in a front-end/back-end configuration, where the front-end server is configured as a messaging router and the back-end server is the client's home server.

Chat Server

Exchange 2000 also provides a full-featured chat server that can be used to set up chat rooms on the server and then service chat clients. The chat server is also available in Exchange 5.*x*, but not many clients have implemented it. The chat server in Exchange 2000 is based on the Internet Relay Chat (IRC) protocol and enables people within the corporation to "meet" in chat rooms to discuss issues of common concern. The Exchange 2000 version of the chat server has increased scalability, integration with Active Directory, and an auditorium mode option that can be configured for one-way communication, such as a broadcast chat with an important guest or executive.

!

EDITION ALERT: *To support a chat server, you need to install Exchange 2000 Enterprise Server.*

Most corporations see instant messaging and chatting as Internet applications and have not implemented them as business applications. Instant messaging will not replace the telephone for a long time. Traditional business practices, such as meetings and conference calls, are certainly still much more accepted than chat rooms in most companies. However, some organizations, including Microsoft, have implemented these tools and are using them to replace many of the traditional practices. Having these options available allows organizations to begin exploring other options for enhancing communication between users.

Conferencing Services

A totally new enhancement in Exchange 2000 is the conferencing service, which you enable by installing the Conferencing Server. Conferencing services are similar to using T.120 applications, such as Microsoft NetMeeting. Exchange 2000's conferencing services improve on NetMeeting's stand-alone capability, however, in several ways.

NetMeeting can be used independent of any server to create a "meeting room" for sharing information. You can create a meeting using NetMeeting and then have other people join your meeting. In that meeting you can share information using a chat program, share a common white board for diagrams, transfer files between computers, listen to audio, and view video images from each other, as well as share applications for remote control. Any users with NetMeeting installed on their computers can create meetings and invite other people to join them. Running NetMeeting in this configuration, however, has several serious limitations. First, it can take a great deal of network bandwidth because the computer hosting the meeting has to set up a TCP/IP unicast session with each other computer that is part of the meeting. This creates serious problems if any users joining the meeting are across a WAN link because of the limited bandwidth. In addition, when the meeting host goes offline, the meeting ends. There is also no way of scheduling meetings with NetMeeting and no option for automatically joining meetings to which you have been invited.

The conferencing services in Exchange 2000 address these limitations. When Exchange is used as a conferencing server, the server uses multicast to communicate with all the clients in the meeting rather than a unicast session for each one separately. The Exchange server is the meeting host rather than a workstation. This means that the conference uses much less network bandwidth. You can also configure Quality of Service (QoS) settings in Active Directory to improve the quality of the meetings for users across slower WAN connections.

Using a client, such as Outlook 2000, you can also schedule meetings just as you would schedule any other meeting. When you schedule a meeting, you invite a resource that serves as the meeting room. You can invite other people to the meeting and when they accept the meeting it shows up in their calendar as a regular meeting. By right-clicking the meeting in the Calendar and selecting Join Meeting, they can join the online meeting. They can even join the meeting using just a Web browser. (Although a client, such as Net-Meeting needs to be installed on the computer to get full functionality.) Figure 1-6 shows what an online conference looks like using Internet Explorer version 5.0.

!

EDITION ALERT: *The conferencing service is available only if you have Exchange 2000 Conferencing Server installed.*

Conferencing services include data conferencing, as well as audio and video conferencing if the client computers are equipped with appropriate hardware.

Using Exchange 2000 conferencing services opens possibilities for replacing some standard meetings with a much cheaper option (compared to traveling to meetings) but it remains to be seen to what extent corporations will accept it as an alternative.

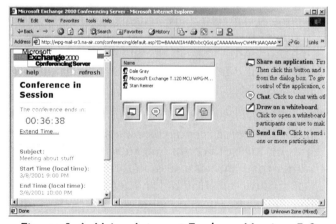

*Figure 1-6: Using Internet Explorer Version 5.0
for Online Conferencing.*

Developer Tools Enhancements

Microsoft would like to extend the functionality of Exchange 2000 by having developers write applications using Exchange as an application server. To make this possible, Exchange 2000 provides several new options for accessing and manipulating data in the information store on the server. Microsoft frequently refers to this technology as the *Web Store*, which is essentially the information store and the Web-based options that can be used to work with the information in the store.

Accessing the Information Store

Exchange has always provided access to the information store using standard e-mail clients. For example, a POP client or an IMAP client can read e-mail messages from the information store, and an SMTP client can send mail to the information store. A MAPI client has always provided the most full-featured access to the information store. For developers, the Exchange Information Store in Exchange 4.0/5.*x* can be accessed using Collaborative Data Objects (CDO), which uses MAPI calls to access data on the server. Using this tool the developer can write applications in Visual Basic (VB), C++, or a scripting language, such as VBScript or JavaScript, to create the application to use Exchange as an application server.

Exchange 2000 still supports most of the previous options for accessing the information store, but also adds a number of new ones. One option that is no longer supported is making client calls using CDO. With Exchange 2000, CDO can be used only on the server where the data is stored. Some of the new options are:

▲ **Installable File System (IFS).** When you install Exchange 2000 on the server, the installation process maps drive M: to the information store and loads the IFS to provide simple file access to the information store. Drive M: appears as a normal drive in Windows Explorer, as well as from a command prompt, and you can use it the same as any other drive.

▲ **Access using Web folders.** Web folders are installed as part of Office 2000, Windows 2000, and Internet Explorer 5.*x*. To use Web folders you can create a new network place in My Network

Places in Windows 2000 or a new Web folder through My Computer in Windows 9x or Windows NT and point the folder to a URL, such as:

```
http://Exchange servername/Exchange/youralias/Inbox
```

This network place is then available as a destination when you are saving any kind of file from a Web-enabled application such as Office 2000. When you select the Web folder as the destination for the save, the file will be saved into your inbox. You can also create the URL to point to a public folder that allows you to use the public folder as a storage location for any kind of file.

▲ **URL addressing.** URL addressing is used from within an application to access information in the information store. For example, a developer could use the following URL to access a particular document in a user's mailbox:

```
file://./backofficestorage/domainname/MBX/useralias/
   inbox/document.doc
```

Table 1-1 explains the components of this URL. Using this URL, the developer can access the document and then manipulate it, including options such as changing the content of the document or changing properties of the document.

▲ **Modifications to ADO and CDO.** A developer can use ADO and CDO to access and manipulate information in the information store. The main difference between ADO and CDO in Exchange 2000, compared to previous versions of Exchange, is that rather than use MAPI to access the information store, these tools now use the Exchange OLEDB provider (EXOLEDB). Using EXOLEDB allows the developer to access the information store in familiar ways, including accessing records and record sets and even using SQL-like queries.

Table 1-1: Components of a Web Store URL

URL Component	Explanation
File://	Used to connect to the information store rather than using an Internet protocol
./	Refers to the current server

Table 1-1: Components of a Web Store URL (Continued)

URL Component	Explanation
Backofficestorage	Refers to the information store (M: drive)
Domainname	Specifies the domain where the information store is located
MBX	Specifies the mailbox store. If this URL refers to a public folder, this part would be *Public Folders*
Useralias/inbox	Specifies the user mailbox and the folder in the mailbox
Document.doc	Specifies the document this URL is pointing to

Exchange Server Events

In Exchange 2000, you can use events and event sinks on the server. This enhancement helps developers create applications for Exchange 2000.

An *event* is simply an action that occurs on the server. For example, an event occurs when a user saves a message into a public folder or a message is sent to a particular user. An *event sink* is a piece of code called whenever an event happens. In Exchange 2000, an event can be a transport event, a protocol event, or an information store event. A *transport event* is triggered when a message moves through a server, allowing you to modify the process of dealing with the message, or even change the message itself. A *protocol event* is called whenever a message is transferred using SMTP, providing options for screening or rerouting messages.

An *information store event* can be almost any action that occurs in the information store. For example, saving a message to a public folder is an information store event. As a developer, you can write an event sink that is triggered by an event, such as saving a message to a particular public folder. You can also use timer events that trigger an event sink if someone does not respond to a particular e-mail for a certain period.

The Exchange events allow developers to create business applications that depend on a workflow process. For example, suppose your company implements a policy for approval of travel requests that involves several steps and several different people. You can create a public folder containing a custom form that the employees fill out to make a travel request. Then you can create the workflow process and connect it to the public folder. For example, the first step in the approval process might be to forward the request to the employee's manager for approval. You could write an event sink that is triggered when a message is saved to the folder that extracts the sender's name from the message, checks in Active Directory for the employee's manager, and then forwards the request to the manager. The manager can then approve or reject the request and you can define different actions in the workflow depending on what the manager does. You can continue to design the workflow process, forwarding the message to the appropriate people until the entire policy has been implemented.

NOTE: This is very much an introduction to the developer options available in Exchange 2000 but this is as far as this book goes. If you need more information, the MSDN site (http://msdn.microsoft.com) has thorough information about developing for Exchange 2000. Microsoft is strongly pushing companies and individuals to write applications using Exchange 2000 and is providing a great deal of information to make this possible.

Conclusion

Migration to Exchange 2000 is an attractive option for many corporations. Microsoft's goal in designing Exchange 2000 was, first, to integrate Exchange into Windows 2000's Active Directory. The second goal was to make Exchange more scalable and reliable. They certainly seem to have achieved these goals. With the changes that have been made to the information store, allowing multiple storage groups and stores, a single powerful server is able to support many more mailboxes, while still providing much quicker recovery from database disasters. This, combined with improved support for clustering servers, means that you can consolidate smaller servers into fewer, more powerful servers. In many companies, this can help decrease the total administrative effort needed to maintain the corporation's servers. In addition, moving the Internet protocols into IIS means that you can set up front-end/back-end server configurations, allowing you to scale your support for these protocols to almost any size. Microsoft's third goal was to provide enhanced administration options, which they have achieved using administrative groups and system policies.

This chapter has described many of the new features that are part of Exchange 2000. In the next chapter, I give you a closer look at some of these features, specifically comparing them to Exchange 4.0/5.*x*. The goal of the next chapter is to introduce many of the concepts and procedures that are part of Exchange 2000 by comparing them to something you know well—Exchange 4.0/5.*x*.

Chapter 2

Comparing Exchange 4.0/5.x and Exchange 2000

ONE OF THE BEST WAYS TO LEARN something new is to compare it to something you know well. You already know Exchange 4.0/5.x well, and that gives you a good start on learning Exchange 2000. Both Exchange 2000 and Exchange 4.0/5.x are messaging servers, so many of the concepts and administrative processes are similar between the two versions. One of this chapter's goals is to build on what you already know in Exchange 4.0/5.x and apply it to Exchange 2000.

At the same time, many concepts and procedures in Exchange 2000 have changed significantly from Exchange 4.0/5.x. Exchange 2000 is a significant upgrade, and mastering it requires learning many new administrative skills. This chapter addresses the changes that have been made and contrasts what you already know about Exchange 4.0/5.x with the way things are done in Exchange 2000.

In this chapter, I briefly review how a particular feature is implemented in Exchange 4.0/5.x, and then compare it to the Exchange 2000 implementation. This will help you learn how Exchange 2000 works and how to perform some basic administration before I begin discussing the migration to Exchange 2000 in later chapters. Many of the concepts introduced in this chapter are useful to understand when you are planning and optimizing the migration process.

Administration Interface Changes

The administrative tools for managing the Exchange organization have changed in Exchange 2000. The Exchange System Manager is now a Microsoft Management Console (MMC) snap-in, as are all the other administrative tools for Windows 2000. In addition, many of the components have been moved to different locations in the management tool. Figure 2-1 shows the Exchange System Manager interface. Table 2-1 provides an overview of some of the changes that have been made to the administrative tools.

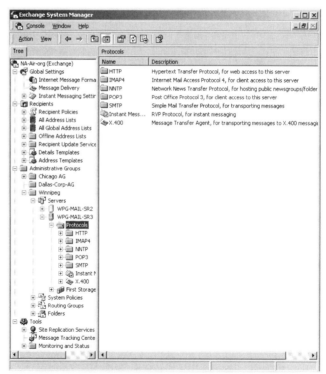

Figure 2-1: The Exchange System Manager.

Table 2-1: Modifications to the Exchange Administration Tools

Exchange 4.0/5.x Administrator	Exchange 2000 System Manager
Address book views	Renamed *address lists* and moved into the Recipients container, which also includes Recipient Policies, Global and Offline Address book views, and the Exchange templates.
Folders	Now appears inside a specific administrative group container, but is still used to administer public folders.
Global address list (GAL) and Recipients containers	Do not appear the same way in Exchange 2000 because the list of recipients is now based on the users in Active Directory. You can view the GAL by opening the Default Global Address List properties and clicking Preview.
Site container	Administrative groups and routing groups have replaced sites. Each administrative group is listed in the Administrative Groups container, with the routing groups listed inside the specific administrative group.
Configuration container	The closest comparable container is an administrative group.
Connections container	Now located in the Connectors container, in *administrativegroup/routinggroup*.
Addressing	Now located in the Recipients container.
Directory replication	Not applicable anymore because of the Active Directory integration.
Monitors	Now configured on each individual server and in the Tools container. Improved routing management between routing groups has replaced the Link Monitor function.
Protocols, site and server level	Now located on the virtual servers for each protocol. The virtual servers are listed *administrativegroup/ Servers/servername/Protocols*.
Servers	Now reside in two different places: *administrativegroup/Servers*, and *administrativegroup/routinggroup/Members*. Almost all the server administration is done on the object in the administrative group.

Table 2-1: Modifications to the Exchange Administration Tools (Continued)

Exchange 4.0/5.x Administrator	Exchange 2000 System Manager
DS site configuration	Has been relocated to the Recipients container. The custom attribute configuration requires an Active Directory schema change.
Information store site configuration	Configured on the mailbox and public folder stores. Configuration of multiple stores is done using system policies. The stores are located in *administrativegroup* /Servers/servername/storagegroup.
MTA site configuration	Configured on the protocol virtual servers under each server.
Site addressing	Configured using recipient policies. The routing functionality is implemented by a link state table.
Private information store	Located in *administrativegroup*/Servers/servername/ *storagegroup*. Now called a *mailbox store*.
Public information store	Located in *administrativegroup*/Servers/servername/ *storagegroup*. Now called a *public store*.
Directory service, message transfer agent, and system attendant	These objects do not have equivalent objects in Exchange 2000. Most of the functions from these objects are configured on the server object and the virtual protocol servers.

NOTE: When you first open the Exchange System Manager, it does not show the administrative group and routing group containers. This provides a simplified user interface for small organizations that have only a single routing group and administrative group. To make these containers visible, right-click the organization name in the System Manager and select Properties. On the General tab you can change the view to include these containers.

Both the Exchange 4.0/5.*x* Administrator program and the Exchange 2000 System Manager can be used to administer the entire Exchange organization. However, with the System Manager you can modify the MMC to include only the part of the organization that you are administering.

Recipient Management

The difference between the Exchange versions becomes obvious when you begin working with the mail recipients in your Exchange organization. Not only has the interface changed, but many of the concepts have changed significantly because of the integration with Active Directory.

Creating Mailboxes and Distribution Lists

In Exchange 4.0/5.*x*, there are two ways to create Exchange recipients. When you install the Exchange Administrator program and User Manager for Domains on the same computer, the installation process installs the mailumx.dll, which creates a link between the two administration tools. Then, when you create a new user in User Manager for Domains, you have the option of creating a new mailbox on the Exchange server at the same time. Alternatively, you can create a user account that is the owner of a mailbox when you create the mailbox itself using the Exchange Administrator. Whichever process you use, you create two separate directory objects — one in the Windows NT domain and one in the Exchange directory — as well as creating the actual mailbox in the information store. One of the attributes for the Exchange directory object is the Security Identifier (SID) of the Windows NT account that owns the mailbox. The Windows NT object contains no Exchange-specific information.

Exchange 2000 creates and administers only one directory object in Active Directory for each recipient. The actual process of creating a new user in Exchange 2000 is not that different than it was in Exchange 4.0/5.*x*. If you have an Exchange server installed in your Active Directory forest and you create a user using Active Directory Users and Computers, the last screen of the wizard asks whether you want to create a new mailbox for the user. However, when you create the mailbox, you merely assign an attribute to the user object that identifies it as the owner of a mailbox; you do not create a second directory object. Figure 2-2 shows the interface for creating the mailbox. When you create the mailbox, you can choose which server, as well as which mailbox store on the server, will host the mailbox.

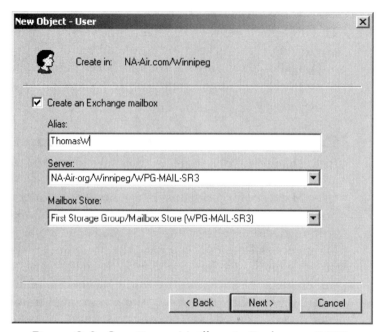

Figure 2-2: Creating a Mailbox in Exchange 2000.

You use the same interface to modify the Exchange attributes for the user. To create a mailbox for a user who does not have a mailbox or to move or delete a mailbox, you locate the user in Active Directory Users and Computers, right-click the object, and choose Exchange Tasks. To modify any other Exchange attributes, you right-click the user and select Properties. As shown in Figure 2-3, four Exchange-specific tabs are now available for each user object.

NOTE: *The Exchange Advanced tab is visible only if you select Advanced Features from the View menu.*

The configuration options for each user are similar to the options that were available for directory objects in Exchange 4.0/5.*x*. In Exchange 2000, however, you perform the administration using Active Directory Users and Computers. Individual user objects do not show up in the Exchange System Manager at all. The only visible reference to individual users is when you check the mailbox size for a user for each mailbox store.

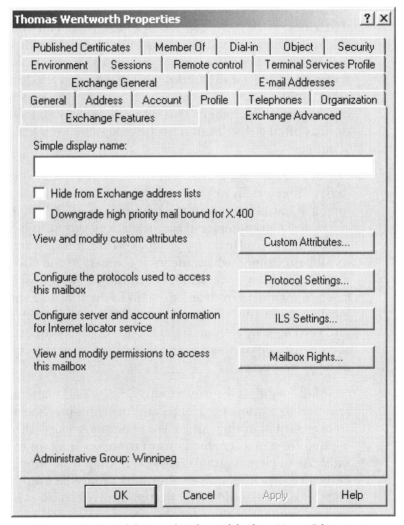

Figure 2-3: Additional Tabs Added to User Objects in Exchange 2000.

While the procedures for administering users have not changed a great deal, administering distribution lists has changed much more significantly in Exchange 2000. In Exchange 4.0/5.*x*, a distribution list is a group of recipients that provides an easy way to send e-mail messages to many users at once. The distribution list in Exchange 4.0/5.*x* is not a security principal, so you cannot assign permissions to that group (with the exception of assigning permissions to public folders). Distribution lists can include users from any domain in the organization, as well as custom recipients. However, because Exchange 4.0/5.*x* and Windows NT have separate directory services, you cannot create a link between groups in Windows NT and distribution lists in Exchange. This often means a great deal of duplication, as often a distribution list has the same members as a group in Windows NT.

One of the results of integrating the Exchange directory into Active Directory in Exchange 2000 is that such duplication is no longer required. You can now take any group in Active Directory Users and Computers and *mail-enable* the group. When you mail-enable an Active Directory group, you are configuring the group as a message recipient, which means it appears in the GAL as a distribution list. You can work with this group just like a distribution list: you can add members from any domain in the forest (if you use a domain local group or universal group), you can add contacts to the group, and you can send e-mail to the group. In addition, because it is also a security principal, you can use the group to assign permissions to network resources.

Mail-enabling security groups decreases the amount of effort required to administer groups and distribution lists, but it also raises some group planning issues. For example, to view the entire membership for a mail-enabled group from any domain in the forest, you must use universal groups. However, when designing the Active Directory structure, universal groups should be used only minimally, or at least you should avoid putting individual users into universal groups, because of the Global Catalog replication implications. This raises an important planning issue that you need to address as you plan to implement Active Directory and Exchange 2000.

NOTE: *I discuss the planning involved when implementing security groups as distribution lists in Chapter 5.*

Managing Address Lists

In Exchange 4.0/5.*x*, you can create additional address book views to partition a large GAL into smaller units. This limits the list of recipients that users are able to see in their address list and is often done for security reasons to prevent users from seeing a certain group of addresses. Address book views are also used to provide a smaller, more navigable address list. To create the address book view, you have to decide what properties to use to sort the GAL and then create the address book view using the Exchange Administrator. For example, you might sort the GAL using the City attribute. However, Exchange 4.0/5.*x* creates a separate address book view for each unique property value. If you sort the list based on the City attribute, an address container is created for each city, while you might have wanted to create an address book view for one particular city.

In Exchange 2000, address book views are replaced by address lists, which provide considerably more flexibility when partitioning the GAL. When creating an address list, you can sort the GAL based on any Active Directory property or combination of properties. You can even create an address list that includes recipients from only selected servers or mailbox stores. In addition, you can specify a single list rather than creating multiple lists. For example, if you want to create an address list for only one city, you can do so without creating an address list for all the cities.

To create an address list, use the following procedure:

1. Open the Exchange System Manager and expand the Recipients container and then the All Address Lists container.

   The All Address Lists container contains all the default address lists created when Exchange was installed.

2. Right-click All Address Lists and select New/Address List.

3. Type a descriptive name for the address list and click Filter Rules.

4. Use the filter rules to sort the GAL so that only selected recipients are included in the address list. Figure 2-4 shows the interfaces you use to create the address list.

a. On the General tab, select the type of recipient to include: for example, Contact, Users with Exchange mailboxes, and so on.

b. On the Storage tab, select which Exchange servers and stores to include in the filter.

c. On the Advanced tab, select the attribute(s) by which you want to filter. To do so, click the Field button and select the attribute for which you want to search. Then select the Condition (Is(exactly), Starts with, and so on.) and select the Value you want to match. For example, you can create a query where you filter by the User/City property, using a condition of Is(exactly) and a value of Dallas.

5. After selecting the criteria, click Add.

6. If you want to make the search more specific, add additional criteria.

7. To see the list that the current criteria returns, click Find Now; Exchange performs the query and returns the current results.

To view the actual LDAP query that was used to create the address list, right-click the address list and select Properties. You can also modify the address list criteria from this location.

The address lists in Exchange 2000 appear in the client interface exactly the same way as address book views did in Exchange 4.0/5.*x*. You can set an address list as the default address book for your users. If you want to limit the visibility of an address list so that certain users cannot see a particular list, remove read permission to the address list object in the Exchange System Manager.

You can also use the LDAP filtering procedure to create custom global address lists and custom offline address lists. This can be useful if you are hosting more than one company's mailboxes on a single Exchange server and you want to limit the visibility of the mailboxes. You can create a custom GAL and a custom offline address list for each company based on the company name. Then you assign the correct permissions to control which global address list is visible to the users in each company. To configure the default offline address book for recipients on different stores, you can edit the properties of the store.

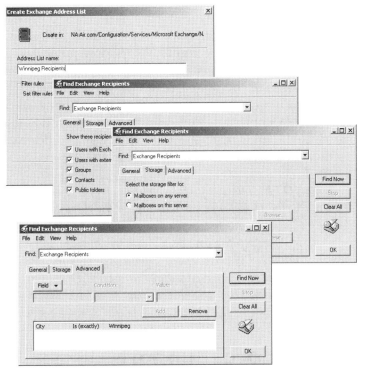

Figure 2-4: Creating an Address List.

Managing Recipient Policies

In many organizations, users have more than one e-mail address. Sometimes this is necessary because one company has taken over another and wants to continue to use the e-mail addresses for both companies during a transition period. In other cases, companies use alternate e-mail addresses to identify some employees' departmental affiliation. For example, the members of the sales department might have two e-mail addresses: *alias*@NA-Air.com and *alias*@sales.NA-Air.com.

In Exchange 4.0/5.*x*, you have two options for configuring this. One way is to configure the additional address for each recipient's mailbox. At the site level, you can configure an additional e-mail address for all the recipients in that site by adding the address in the Site Addressing Properties dialog box.

Exchange 2000 uses recipient policies to provide a much finer level of management for multiple e-mail addresses. To create a new recipient policy, you right-click the Recipient Policies container in the Exchange System Manager and select New/Recipient Policy. You can then use the same LDAP query interface that you used to create the address lists to select a group of recipients. In the Sales department example, you would select all users with Sales listed as their department. Then you would click E-mail Addresses and add the additional e-mail address to the selected users.

> **NOTE:** *The Recipient Update Service is responsible for updating the Active Directory information for the domain when you make changes to the address lists or to the e-mail addresses using recipient policies. To speed up the processing of any changes you have made, you can right-click the Recipient Update Service for your domain in the Exchange System Manager and click Update Now. By default, the Recipient Update Service runs every 15 minutes. You can modify the frequency in the Recipient Update Service properties.*

Internet Protocol Support

One of the biggest changes in Exchange 2000 is the way it implements Internet protocols. In Exchange 4.0/5.*x*, the default configuration for every server supports all Internet mail-related protocols so that users can connect to the server using POP3, IMAP4, NNTP, SMTP or LDAP clients. The protocol options can be configured at the site level, individual server level, or user level. By default, the lower levels inherit any settings configured at a higher level. All the Internet protocols, with the exception of LDAP, are implemented within the information store process in Exchange 4.0/5.*x*. (LDAP is integrated within the directory service process.) The only way to stop and restart the individual protocol components is to stop and restart the information store.

Internet Protocol Architecture

In Exchange 4.0/5.x, the protocols are integrated into the information store and directory service processes; in Exchange 2000 this support has been integrated into Internet Information Services (IIS).

Support for all the protocols except MAPI and XAPI (which is used for X.400) has been moved into IIS. All that remains of the other protocols are the protocol stubs that provide access to the Exchange InterProcess Communication (EXIPC) layer. The EXIPC is essentially a queuing layer between the information store and IIS designed to provide fast communication between the two components.

Because the protocols are integrated into the information store and all run in the same process in Exchange 4.0/5.x, communication between the components is fast. The EXIPC provides advanced queuing functionality using shared memory between the two processes, also resulting in fast access. Within the EXIPC, there is a queue for each protocol. Within IIS, the protocols are implemented as virtual servers with single or multiple virtual servers for each protocol. Figure 2-5 shows the architecture in Exchange 2000.

The other important change with the way protocols are implemented in Exchange 2000 is an increased reliance on SMTP. The preferred protocol for all mail exchange is now SMTP, both within and between routing groups. RPCs are still supported, but only when the Exchange 2000 server communicates with an Exchange 4.0/5.x server in the same site or when the Exchange 4.0/5.x server is a bridgehead server in a remote site. The X.400 protocol also is supported, and you can configure it to provide connectivity between routing groups, but you should use it only for slow network connections or to use an existing X.400 link.

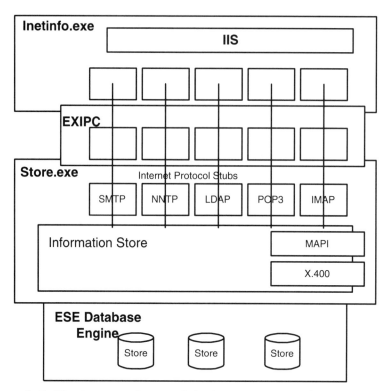

Figure 2-5: The Internet Protocol Architecture in Exchange 2000.

There are several advantages to using SMTP. First, SMTP is faster and more reliable than RPCs. In addition, because all Internet e-mail servers use SMTP, the Exchange 2000 server is fully compatible with Internet e-mail standards. You can also use SMTP across a much slower link than RPCs, which require about 128 Kbps of bandwidth. The primary consideration for network connectivity between servers in the same routing group becomes reliability rather than bandwidth with Exchange 2000. Because of the decreased bandwidth requirements, you may want to review the site boundaries used in Exchange 4.0/5.*x* to determine whether you want to use the same boundaries in Exchange 2000.

There is another important change in the way SMTP is implemented in Exchange 2000, one that has broad implications. As part of the architectural changes, the duties of the message transfer agent (MTA) in message routing have also been moved into SMTP. In Exchange 4.0/5.*x*, when a message is routed between servers, the MTA receives the message from the information store, determines the best route to transfer the message, and then performs the transfer. In Exchange 2000 this whole functionality is located in SMTP.

> **NOTE:** *The importance of the MTA has diminished considerably in Exchange 2000. The only time the MTA is used is when routing mail through an X.400 connector to a remote routing group or other e-mail system, or when using an MTA-based connector such as the MSMail connector.*

To provide this functionality, the SMTP component includes several subcomponents that are involved in every message transfer on the Exchange server:

▲ **Advanced queuing engine.** Exchange 2000 uses the queuing engine several times during the process of delivering a message. When a message first arrives at the server, it waits in a queue for the message categorizer to determine its destination. After the message has been categorized, the queuing engine moves it into the correct queue based on whether the message is going to a mail client with a mailbox on the server or to a remote location.

▲ **Message categorizer.** The message categorizer accepts a message from the queuing engine and determines its destination. That destination could be the local server, another server in the same routing group, another server in a different routing group, or a server on the Internet or across some other connector. The message categorizer also performs a number of other functions, such as expanding distribution lists, checking for any limits (such as message size), and determining how many copies of the message need to be sent. To perform most of these functions, the message categorizer must be able to connect to a domain controller or a global catalog server to look up the directory information.

NOTE: The message categorizer in Exchange 2000 is implemented in a .dll called PHATCAT.DLL. And you thought that the developers at Microsoft didn't have a sense of humor.

▲ **Routing engine.** The routing engine determines the optimal path for a message as it leaves the queuing engine. The routing engine provides information on how to route messages between routing groups or to a connector outside the organization.

Server Message Flow

Like Exchange 4.0/5.*x*, Exchange 2000 is made up of separate components that perform different functions as a message moves through a server. To understand how the messaging process works, let's take a look at how a message flows through a server. Figure 2-6 shows the process of moving mail through a single server.

The following steps detail this process.

1. The message arrives at the server.

   The message could arrive at the server through several different interfaces, such as the following:

   ▲ SMTP transport from another server

   ▲ Information store from a MAPI client

   ▲ Information store from an MTA connector (X.400 or other MTA-based connector)

2. The message waits in a pre-categorizer queue in the advanced queuing engine. Regardless of where the message originated, the process on the server is the same.

3. The message categorizer collects the message from the queue and determines the destination(s) for the message.

   The message destination could be one or more of the following:

   ▲ **The local information store.** The message moves to the post-categorizer queue for the local information store.

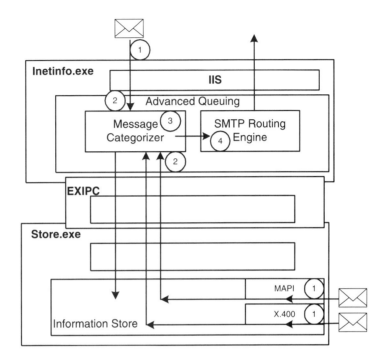

*Figure 2-6: The Message Flow Process through an
Exchange 2000 Server.*

▲ **A MTA connector.** The message moves to the post-categorizer queue for the local information store, and then to the MTA for delivery.

▲ **A remote SMTP server in the same organization.** The message moves to the post-categorizer queue, and then to the local domain queue after the routing engine determines the best route for delivering the message.

▲ **A remote SMTP server in a different Internet domain.** The message moves to the post-categorizer queue and then to a queue for delivery to the remote domain.

NOTE: You can monitor the status of each of these queues by expanding the SMTP virtual server container in the Exchange System Manager.

4. If the message is intended for a remote SMTP server, the message is passed to the SMTP protocol engine, which then attempts to deliver the message.

One important difference between this process and the one used in Exchange 4.0/5.x is that all messages follow this process, including messages between users with mailboxes on the same server. In Exchange 4.0/5.x, if a message is sent from one user to another on the same server, the MTA is not involved in sending the message, as the information store handles the entire delivery. In Exchange 2000, the message is always transferred through the advanced queuing engine and the message categorizer. This enables event sinks to be linked to the message categorizer to customize the message or the delivery. For example, you might create an event sink that adds a corporate logo to all messages as they pass through the message categorizer. If the message were not sent to the message categorizer, it would be more difficult to create a customized process for dealing with the messages.

Configuring Protocol Virtual Servers

By moving the Internet protocols into IIS, Exchange 2000 offers more flexibility in administering Internet protocol servers. In Exchange 4.0/5.x, each server provides protocol support through the information store, and all mailboxes on the server inherit the settings configured on the server by default. To change any individual settings, you have to change the properties on each mailbox. In Exchange 2000, however, you can implement multiple virtual servers for each protocol and then configure each of the servers with different settings.

Having multiple virtual servers for a protocol can be advantageous. For example, suppose that you use a single Exchange server to send and receive mail both to the Internet and to internal recipients on other servers. With multiple virtual servers, you can set different security levels for Internet e-mail than for internal corporate mail. If Internet bandwidth is an issue, you might also limit the size of messages sent to the Internet but allow internal messages of any size. You might also set up two virtual servers providing Internet mail connectivity, with one server used for all secure e-mail using S/MIME and the other server used for all other Internet mail. All of these options are easy to configure by creating additional virtual SMTP servers.

NOTE: You can create additional virtual servers for any of the Internet protocols. The process of creating and configuring the servers is much the same for all the protocols, so I focus on just the SMTP server as an example of this procedure.

To create an additional virtual server in Exchange, you must have some way of uniquely identifying each virtual server on the physical server. To do this, the virtual servers must have unique IP addresses, port numbers, or — if the virtual server is an HTTP server — host headers for each virtual server. Therefore, before you set up additional virtual SMTP servers, you need to configure multiple IP addresses for the server (and preferably multiple network cards) or configure both the virtual server and the SMTP clients to use a different port number for each virtual server.

NOTE: You configure multiple virtual servers the same way that you configure virtual servers in IIS. In fact, because of the integration between IIS and Exchange, you are configuring virtual IIS servers.

To create and configure virtual servers, use the following procedure:

1. Expand the Administrative Groups container and expand the administrative group that contains the server you are configuring.

2. Expand Servers/*Servername*/Protocols/SMTP. The default SMTP virtual server is listed in the details pane.

3. Right-click SMTP and select New/SMTP Virtual Server. Type a descriptive name for the virtual server.

4. If you have multiple IP addresses on the server, select the IP address that this virtual server should use. If you are using the same IP address with a different port number, accept the default to complete the wizard.

5. If you selected a unique IP address, the virtual server automatically starts. If you are using a single IP address, the server cannot start until you assign a different port number for the server. To do this, right-click the server and select Properties. Click Advanced and edit the port number for this virtual server. When you close the Properties dialog box, the virtual server starts.

You can use the Properties sheet to configure the settings for the virtual server. I cover the process of configuring virtual servers in more detail in Chapter 10.

Figure 2-7 shows the interface that is used to configure SMTP virtual servers.

After you configure the virtual servers, you need to configure the client connections to the servers. If you are working with internal clients, you can configure your DNS server with host records pointing to the two IP addresses, or you can configure the clients to use a different port, depending on which virtual server they are using. In most cases, configuring the Exchange server with two IP addresses is preferable because it is much easier to configure one DNS server than to configure multiple clients to use a different port number. If you use both virtual servers to receive mail from the Internet, and you want to use one for secure e-mail, you need to configure the MX records on the external DNS server with two different mail server names and IP addresses.

Configuring virtual servers for the Internet e-mail protocols provides a great deal of flexibility in your server configurations using a limited number of actual servers.

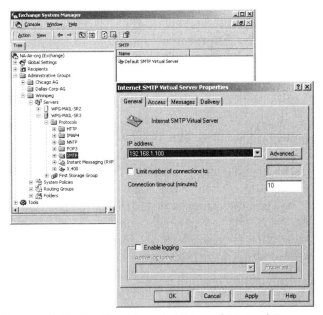

Figure 2-7: Configuring Additional Virtual Servers.

Outlook Web Access

Exchange 5.*x* implements Outlook Web Access (OWA) using a completely different architecture than any other component. OWA is part of IIS, which can be running on the same computer or a different computer than Exchange Server. When a client connects to the IIS server using a Web browser, the server uses Active Server Pages (ASP) to create MAPI connections using RPCs to connect to the Exchange server. OWA in Exchange 5.*x* is a separate component in the installation process, and requires that IIS 4.0 (or IIS 3.0 with ASP support) be installed on the computer before installing OWA. To place OWA on a computer other than the Exchange server, you install just the OWA component on that computer.

Exchange 2000 implements OWA using the HTTP virtual server and you configure it much like any other Internet protocol. By default all servers in Exchange 2000 are enabled for OWA support because of the HTTP support included in IIS. In an environment that does not use distributed servers, a client can connect to any

Exchange server using a Web browser. When the client first connects to the server, the server checks Active Directory to authenticate the user and to determine which server is the user's home server. The client Web browser is then redirected to the client's home server. The communication between IIS and Exchange uses HTTP and Web-DAV through the EXIPC.

With a distributed server configuration, the client connects to the front-end server. The front-end server looks up the user name in Active Directory to authenticate the user and also to determine the user's home server. However, the front-end server does not redirect the client browser to the back-end server, but rather uses HTTP and Web-DAV to connect to the IIS component on the back-end server. IIS on the back-end server then communicates with the information store through the EXIPC. Figure 2-8 compares the two options for connecting to Exchange 2000 using OWA.

> **NOTE:** *The security configuration options for OWA have not changed significantly in Exchange 2000. If you are using OWA using distributed servers, you are still limited to basic authentication. If you put OWA on the same server as the information store, you can use NTLM or Kerberos authentication.*

Configuring Distributed Servers

Implementing distributed servers in Exchange 2000 is easy but requires careful planning. To set up front-end and back-end servers, you have to install Windows 2000 and Exchange 2000 on both computers. In most cases, you should configure the front-end server without any mailboxes. That's because after you have configured a server as a front-end server, any mailboxes on it are no longer accessible using an Internet protocol. (They are, however, still accessible when using MAPI clients.) The best way to configure the front-end server is to move all the mailboxes off the server before making it a front-end server, or to configure it as a front-end server immediately after installing Exchange.

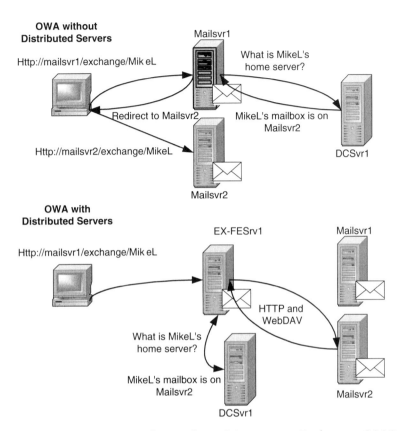

Figure 2-8: OWA and Distributed Servers in Exchange 2000.

To configure a server as a front-end server, you access the server properties in the Exchange System Manager and select the This is a front-end server check box. You can then disable the information store service on the server. You can configure distributed servers in any combination of front-end or back-end servers, using as many servers as you require. For example, if most of your users are using MAPI clients, you might have several back-end servers and a single front-end server. On the other hand, if most clients are using an Internet protocol, you might have several front-end servers and only a single back-end server. This is especially true if you are using any security options that include encryption to handle client access.

Configuring Administration

In Exchange 4.0/5.*x*, large organizations with multiple locations are usually split into multiple sites. You can create additional sites for a variety of reasons, the most important of which is usually message routing. However, creating multiple sites also creates an administrative and security boundary. This means that you can assign permissions at the site level and those permissions apply to the entire site. In Exchange 2000, the functions of administration and routing are split into two separate configuration groups — administrative groups and routing groups. You configure message routing through routing groups and security and administration through administrative groups.

Sites Versus Administrative Groups

Permission configuration is pretty simplistic in Exchange 4.0/5.*x* and does not provide the flexibility that many organizations require. There are three primary places to assign permissions in Exchange 4.0/5.*x*: at the organization level, at the site level, and at the site configuration level. If you have administrative rights at these three levels, you have administrative rights to the organization and the site because of the way the permissions are inherited by lower-level containers in the hierarchy.

Sites in Exchange 4.0/5.*x* provide an administrative boundary within Exchange. In most cases, this is desirable because sites are in different geographic locations with local administrators who want to manage their own Exchange servers. However, the default configuration gives you the same level of permission to all objects within that part of the Exchange organization, so it's difficult to assign permission for specific activities to individual users. There is no easy way, for example, to give users permission to monitor mailbox size (which requires little administrative expertise) and not give them permission also to modify connector properties (which requires a much higher level of expertise). Every object in the Exchange directory has an ACL, so you can configure the permissions at an individual object level, but the process of doing so is complicated.

NOTE: *The following description of administrative groups and routing groups is accurate when the Exchange organization is running in native mode. Before you switch to native mode, there is a stronger one-to-one relationship between administrative groups and routing groups with less flexibility when configuring the administrative options, and no option to move servers between routing groups. The limitations of running in mixed mode and the process of switching to native mode will be covered in detail in Chapters 9 and 10.*

Administrative groups in Exchange 2000 are designed to make configuration and delegation of administrative rights easier. An *administrative group* is a group of Exchange objects grouped together to administer them the same way or have them administered by the same people. An administrative group is more sophisticated than a site because you can control what types of objects are put into an administrative group.

In an Exchange 4.0/5.x site, all the objects are grouped in one site container and you cannot move objects, such as the Connections container, into a different container. Exchange 2000, however, is flexible in what an administrative group can contain. For example, you can create an administrative group that contains all the servers in a location, but does not contain the routing groups for the organization. In this way, you can configure one group of administrators with permission to manage the servers, while another group manages the routing groups and connectors. You also can configure an administrative group that contains all your public folders and then assign the correct permissions to that administrative group. By default, any permission set at the administrative group level is inherited by all new and existing objects in the administrative group.

Exchange 2000 also improves the management of permissions in an administrative group through Exchange Administration Delegation wizard. Rather than going directly to the ACL and configuring permissions on an object in the System Manager, you can run the Exchange Administration Delegation wizard to configure permissions on an administrative group. For example, you might create an administrative group that contains the public folders for the entire organization and move all the public folder trees into that administrative group. You can then use the wizard to assign full control to a Public Folder Admins group while giving everyone else read-only permission to the public folder hierarchy.

When running the Exchange Administration Delegation wizard, you can assign three levels of administrative permissions:

▲ **Exchange View Only Administrator.** This administrator has read-only permission to all objects in the administrative group. To create mailboxes on an Exchange server, you need at least Exchange View Only Administrator permissions to the administrative group that contains the Exchange server.

▲ **Exchange Administrator.** This administrator has full control of all objects in the administrative group, but does not have the right to change permissions on objects.

▲ **Exchange Full Administrator.** This administrator has full control of all objects in the administrative group, plus the right to change permissions on objects.

Configuring Administrative Groups

Different companies can have different Exchange administration strategies, and Exchange 2000 provides the flexibility needed to carry them out. One corporation, for example, might have a centralized administrative model in which one group of administrators must perform all administration. This corporation can implement a single administrative group with all the Exchange objects in that one group. Another corporation might have a decentralized administrative model, and create multiple administrative groups to distribute the administration in each location.

The real power of the administrative group model is that you can easily mix the models. For example, suppose your corporation wants to distribute responsibility for all administrative tasks *except* system policy management and routing group management. Because you can move objects between administrative groups, you can easily configure the administrative structure to fit this requirement.

To create and configure administrative groups, use the following procedure:

1. To create an additional administrative group, right-click the Administrative Groups container in the System Manager and select New/Administrative Group.

2. Type a descriptive name for the administrative group and click OK.

3. To create container objects in the administrative group, right-click the administrative group and select New/*Containertype* where *Containertype* is the type of container object you want.

   When you create a new administrative group, there are no objects in the container. Before you can move objects (such as routing groups) into the administrative group, you must first create a container for the types of objects you want to move. For example, if you wanted to place all the routing groups into this administrative group, you would select New/Routing Groups Container. You also can create System Policy Containers, and Public Folder Containers.

4. To create objects in the container you just created, right-click the container and select New/*objecttype* where *objecttype* is the object type you want.

   You can create new objects in the container, or you can move objects from other containers. If you create a routing groups container, for example, you can right-click the container and create a new routing group, or you can move a routing group from another administrative group by dragging it into the current container. You can only move objects between containers; you cannot move the containers themselves.

5. To run the Exchange Administration Delegation wizard, right-click the administrative group and select Delegate Control.

   The Delegation wizard runs and you have the choice of adding, editing, or removing groups of users. When you select a user or group to add, you are given a choice of what level of permission to grant the user. Figure 2-9 shows the wizard interface.

Figure 2-9: Running the Exchange Administration Delegation Wizard.

Moving Exchange Servers between Administrative Groups

You cannot move an existing server between administrative groups. When you install Exchange 2000 into an organization with more than one administrative group, Exchange lets you choose which administrative group in which to place the server, and it remains there. You cannot create a Servers container and move a server into it. The early beta versions of Exchange 2000 provided the capability to move servers between administrative groups, but this feature was dropped in the final product because the results of the move were not reliable. It is therefore difficult to change the administrative group configuration for an existing organization in Exchange 2000, and there will be considerable pressure to provide a tool to do this as a service pack or in future versions of Exchange. If Microsoft does not provide such a tool, you can be sure that third-party tools will be available.

Message Routing

From an administrative point of view, message-routing configuration has not changed a great deal in Exchange 2000. Exchange 2000 uses routing groups rather than sites, so you configure routing groups and routing group connectors rather than sites and site connectors, but the process is much the same. However, one of the biggest changes in Exchange 2000 is what happens behind the scenes when messages are routed through the organization. Because it uses the link state instead of the GWART, Exchange 2000 can handle changes in the routing topology much more effectively than Exchange 4.0/5.*x* could.

Sites Versus Routing Groups

In Exchange 4.0/5.*x*, you configure sites based primarily on the bandwidth between company locations. Within a site, all the servers are connected with reasonably fast network connections (at least 128 kbps of available bandwidth). Messages and directory information are sent between servers using a direct connection. To control message delivery and directory replication traffic, you must configure additional sites and then configure site connectors to send the messages when you want. You can control message routing more precisely by assigning costs to different connectors and by configuring bridgehead servers at each of the company locations.

Exchange 2000 uses routing groups in much the same way. You configure routing groups as you would sites to control traffic on a WAN link, and you configure bridgehead servers at company locations. You configure routing group connectors, such as site connectors, with costs based on available bandwidth. Because the preferred protocol is now SMTP, you might be able to combine some sites into fewer routing groups, but the concepts of routing groups and routing group connectors are similar to sites in Exchange 4.0/5.*x*.

 NOTE: *In Exchange 2000, you manage directory information replication through Active Directory. In many cases, the Active Directory site corresponds to the Exchange 2000 routing group, but there is no direct relationship between Active Directory sites and replication and Exchange routing groups.*

Message Routing Administration in Exchange 4.0/5.x

In Exchange 4.0/5.*x*, all messaging and directory replication within the same site is automatically configured and enabled for a new server as soon as you install it into a site. To be in the same site, servers must have direct RPC connectivity with each other. When a message needs to be delivered between servers in the same site, the originating server delivers it immediately and directly to the recipient server, with no transfer through any intermediate servers. While you can configure some of the default behaviors through modifying the Registry, most traffic between Exchange servers in the same site is automatically configured and beyond administrative control.

If you want to control the traffic between Exchange servers, you must configure sites in Exchange 4.0/5.*x*. By default, no e-mail or directory replication traffic moves between servers in different sites until you configure the connections. Exchange 4.0/5.*x* provides four types of site connectors: Site, X.400, Internet Mail Service, and Dynamic RAS. The Site connector is the fastest connector and the easiest to configure, but it requires RPC connectivity. The second-best option is the X.400 connector, which is used to connect Exchange sites but also can be used to connect to other non-Exchange organizations.

If an organization has multiple sites and multiple connections between sites, the Exchange servers determine the best route for a message from one site to another by consulting the Gateway Address Routing Table (GWART). The Routing Information Daemon (RID) on a single server in a site builds and maintains the GWART and then replicates it to all other servers. The RID calculates the GWART based on the available connectors, the address spaces for each of the connectors, the scope of the address spaces, and the cost of the connectors. The GWART contains all the routing information needed for any server in the site to be able to send messages anywhere in the organization as well as to external destinations linked with external connectors.

The GWART works well in stable, reliable networks, but it has no way to automatically detect and deal with failed connectors. For example, suppose you have a site configuration that contains five sites, as illustrated in Figure 2-10. The number next to each route is the cost of that route.

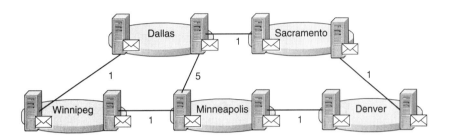

Figure 2-10: Message Routing Topology Scenario.

If a message needs to be sent from Denver to Winnipeg, the bridgehead server in Denver consults its routing table and determines that the lowest-cost route to Winnipeg through Minneapolis. It sends the message to the bridgehead server in Minneapolis, which then continues to route it through to Winnipeg. If the connector between Minneapolis and Winnipeg fails while the message is on its way to Minneapolis, the bridgehead server in Minneapolis checks if there are any alternate routes to Winnipeg. In Figure 2-10, there are two available routes: through Dallas to Winnipeg, or back to Denver, through Sacramento, through Dallas, and then to Winnipeg. The server determines that the route through Denver is the cheaper route, as the link to Dallas is a slow or congested link configured with a higher cost. However, Exchange 4.0/5.x prevents message looping by not sending a message back on a connector that originally sent it. Therefore, the server sends the message via the Dallas route across the higher-cost link — a less-than-ideal resolution.

However, an even bigger problem with message routing in Exchange 4.0/5.x shows up when the server sends another message from Denver to Winnipeg while the link between Minneapolis and Winnipeg is still down. The server in Denver makes the same routing calculation as before and sends the message to Minneapolis, where the server repeats the same retry and recalculation process. The only way to prevent Denver from continuing to route messages through

Minneapolis to Winnipeg is to remove the connector manually from Minneapolis to Winnipeg and then rebuild the routing table in each site by forcing a recalculation. Because of such issues, almost all organizations with several sites implement a hub and spoke topology for Exchange routing, in which one central location has a connector to all the other sites but the other sites do not have connectors to each other.

Message Routing Administration in Exchange 2000

Message routing administration in Exchange 2000 is similar to that in Exchange 4.0/5.*x*, with one important exception: Exchange 2000 replaces the GWART with a link state table. When working with multiple company locations, you create routing groups rather than sites and create and configure routing group connectors rather than site connectors. Exchange 2000 has three routing group connectors:

▲ **Routing group connector.** This is the preferred connector. Its configuration options are similar to those of a site connector, in that you can configure multiple bridgehead servers, configure message scheduling, and specify who is allowed to send messages and what message sizes are accepted. There is also a new option for setting a different schedule for the delivery of oversize messages. Like a site connector, a routing group connector is a one-way connector, so you need to configure a separate connector for each direction. However, after you create the first connector, Exchange 2000 asks whether you want the other connector to be automatically created. The routing group connector can be used to connect only routing groups, not to connect to any external e-mail system. The biggest difference between a routing group connector and a site connector is that the routing group connector uses SMTP as the messaging protocol rather than using RPCs.

▲ **SMTP connector.** This connector replaces the Internet Mail Service in Exchange 4.0/5.*x*. The configuration options when using the SMTP connector to connect routing groups are virtually identical to those for the routing group connector. However, because you also can use the SMTP connector to send e-mail to any SMTP server accessible on the Internet, you have to define the routing groups that are being connected using this connector. As the connector to the Internet, the SMTP connector has many configuration options, such as security for outbound messages, ETRN and ATRN configuration for collecting queued mail from a remote system, and external address space configuration.

▲ **X.400 connector.** This connector is included primarily for connectivity to other X.400 systems. You should use it to connect Exchange 2000 routing groups only if you have an existing X.400 connection or if you have an extremely slow or unreliable network connection. The process of creating and configuring the X.400 connector is similar to that for the X.400 connector in Exchange 4.0/5.*x*. You cannot use the TP4 protocol in Exchange 2000, however, because Windows 2000 does not support it.

Both the routing group connector and the SMTP connector use SMTP and the SMTP virtual servers. If you have multiple virtual servers on a server, you can chose which of the virtual servers should serve as the bridgehead server.

> *NOTE: Exchange 2000 does not provide a Dynamic RAS connector. However, you can configure one of the other connectors to use a demand dial connection provided through Routing and Remote Access in Windows 2000.*

Just like in Exchange 4.0/5.*x*, you can create multiple routing group connectors and assign costs to the connectors in Exchange 2000 so that you can control the movement of mail messages through the organization.

SMTP and E-Mail Security

By default, all SMTP packets are sent in clear text. Because of Exchange 2000's dependence on SMTP as the messaging protocol, you should consider whether you need some type of encryption to increase SMTP security. The best option for providing such security is to use IPSec to encrypt all SMTP traffic between your servers. The encryption and decryption process uses significant server resources, however, so you need to plan this carefully. I cover configuring SMTP to use IPSec in Chapter 10.

Exchange 2000 makes administering routing groups much easier by enabling you to easily move servers between routing groups. To move a server between sites in Exchange 4.0/5.*x*, you had to use the Move Server wizard, because moving a server meant changing the distinguished name for every object on the server. Moving the server to a different site also meant moving it into a different administrative context, not just changing the routing context. In Exchange 2000, moving a server to a different routing group is as easy as clicking the server in the Members container in the current routing group and dragging it into the Members container in the destination routing group. This makes changing your routing topology easy, so if you don't get the planning exactly right initially, you can easily modify your topology later.

Link State Table

As I mentioned earlier, Exchange 2000 replaces the GWART with a link state table. The link state table is built on each Exchange server using a modification of the Dijkstra algorithm, which is similar to the algorithm that the routing protocol Open Shortest Path First (OSPF) uses. When a server boots up, it reads the routing topology information from Active Directory and uses all the available connectors and their associated costs to build the link state table. Each server can then determine the best route for a message through the routing groups. The link state table resides in the server's memory for quick access when the server must make a routing decision.

Because the GWART in Exchange 4.0/5.*x* is static, routing problems ensue when a network link fails. The link state table, which is dynamically updated based on the latest link status information, corrects this problem. In Exchange 2000, when a route between two routing groups fails, the entire Exchange organization quickly learns of the failure and each server routes messages around the failed link if possible, or holds messages in a local queue if there is no alternate route.

Let's return to the example in Figure 2-10 to see how the situation would be handled in Exchange 2000. Assume that the sites have been replaced with routing groups and the connectors have been configured with the same costs.

1. A message is sent from Denver to Winnipeg using the lowest-cost route through Minneapolis.

2. After the message leaves Denver, the connector between Winnipeg and Minneapolis fails.

3. When the message arrives in Minneapolis, it is forwarded to a bridgehead server connecting to Winnipeg.

    The server tries to send the message to a bridgehead server in Winnipeg, but does not receive a response. The server retries sending the message three times, waiting 60 seconds between retries. If the retries fail, the server tries all the other bridgehead servers in Winnipeg before assuming that the connection is down.

4. As soon as the bridgehead server determines that the route is down, it informs the routing group master in the Minneapolis routing group that the route is down.

    The routing group master is a server in each routing group designated as the primary destination for routing updates. The message informing the routing group master is sent on port 691.

5. The routing group master informs all the other bridgehead servers for the other connectors that the route to Winnipeg is down (also using port 691).

6. The bridgehead servers then pass this information on to the bridgehead servers across their connectors. For example, the bridgehead server in Minneapolis for the connector to Denver informs the bridgehead server in Denver.

    This routing update uses SMTP command verbs rather than messages. The bridgehead server sends one packet of information on port 25 to the remote bridgehead server. The packet includes the globally unique identifier (GUID) of the downed link, the GUID of the server that detected the downed link, and the word *Down*. This command verb syntax is much more efficient than a regular message with all its overhead.

7. The bridgehead servers at each routing group pass the information on to the routing group master, which passes it on to all the other Exchange servers in the routing group. This process continues until the entire organization has been updated.

   This whole process occurs before the server that detected the downed link tries to reroute the message, to make sure that all servers have the updated routing information.

8. After the update, the server determines the lowest-cost route to the destination and sends the message using that route.

The link state table's advantage is most apparent when another message needs to be sent from Denver to Winnipeg while the connector is still down. The server in Denver checks the link state table, determines that the lowest-cost route is not available, and chooses the next-lowest-cost route. It sends the message through Sacramento, rather than going through the high-cost Minneapolis link.

The link state table also efficiently deals with situations in which no route is available. For example, suppose that both of the connections to Winnipeg are down. When this information is propagated throughout the organization, any server that has a message intended for Winnipeg holds it in its queue until it receives information that the connection is available again. That server could be the bridgehead server in Minneapolis, the originating server in Denver, or any server in between. If the connection is down for a long time (the default is 48 hours), any server that has a message intended for Winnipeg sends a nondelivery report (NDR) to the sender and drops the message from the queue.

When the connection becomes available, that fact also is replicated throughout the organization. The server that originally detected the downed link tests the connection at the retry interval (15 minutes by default) by trying to establish an SMTP session with a bridgehead server on the other side of the failed connection. When the connection succeeds, the server determines that the connection is once again available and informs the rest of the organization using the same process that it used to report that the link was down.

As you can see, the link state table is much more efficient than the GWART in dealing with changes in the link status. Its increased efficiency gives companies more flexibility in designing the routing topology, because they need not be tied to a hub-and-spoke configuration to ensure smooth routing in the event of a link failure.

Administering External Connectors

If your organization includes other e-mail systems, such as Lotus Notes or Novell GroupWise, you'll find that Exchange 2000 provides most of the same connectors to these organizations that Exchange 4.0/5.x does. The following connectors are provided with Exchange:

▲ Exchange connector for Lotus Notes

▲ Exchange connector for cc:Mail

▲ Exchange connector for Novell GroupWise

▲ Microsoft Mail connector for PC Networks

▲ Microsoft Schedule+ Free/Busy connector

You can configure all these connectors to exchange directory information too, as well as e-mail messages. With exception of the connector for cc:Mail, these connectors also can exchange calendaring and free/busy information. To install these connectors, you simply choose them during a custom Exchange Server installation. You can then configure them in the Connections container in the server's routing group.

NOTE: Exchange 5.5 also included connectors to Systems Network Architecture Distribution System (SNADS), an IBM proprietary standard for e-mail implemented by a variety of e-mail systems, and IBM's Professional Office System (PROFS) e-mail systems. These connectors are not included with Exchange 2000. However, you can maintain an Exchange 4.0/5.x server with the connector to these mail systems in an Exchange 2000 organization to provide the connectivity.

Implementing Routing Groups

To create and configure an additional routing group, use the following procedure:

1. Expand the administrative group where you want to create the new routing group. Then expand the Routing Groups container.

   If the administrative group does not contain a routing group container, right-click the administrative group and select New/ Routing Groups Container.

2. Right-click Routing Groups and select New/Routing Group.

3. Type a descriptive name for the routing group and click OK.

4. Double-click the routing group you just created.

   There are two containers in the routing group: Connections and Members. The Connections container contains any connectors you create in this routing group, and the Members container contains the servers in the routing group.

5. To move a server into the routing group, locate the server in the Members container of its current routing group. Drag the server into the Members container for the new routing group.

   NOTE: *You also can add servers to routing groups by choosing the routing group when you install Exchange.*

Implementing Routing Group Connectors

Creating and configuring routing group connectors is just as easy.

1. Locate the Connection container in the routing group that you are working with.

2. Right-click the Connection container and select New, and then select the type of connector you are installing.

   The list of connectors depends on the options you chose when installing Exchange. You always have the option of configuring a routing group connector, SMTP connector, TCP X.400 connector, or X25 X.400 connector. If you have installed other external connectors, such as the Exchange connector for Lotus Notes, you also have the option to install it.

3. Configure the routing group connector to meet your requirements.

   The options you can configure on the connector depend on what connector you are installing. If you are installing a routing group connector, you can specify which routing group you are connecting to, the bridgehead servers on both sides of the connector, who can use the connection, the maximum message size, and the message delivery schedule. Figure 2-11 shows the dialog box used to configure a routing group connector during installation.

4. To configure the connector after creating it, locate the connector in the System Manager, right-click it, and select Properties.

NOTE: If you are creating an X.400 connector, you must install a transport stack for the protocol you are using before installing the connector. To install the transport stack, right-click the X.400 object under administrativegroup/Servers/servername/Protocols and select New, and then select the transport stack you want to install.

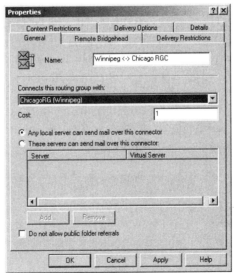

Figure 2-11: Configuring a Routing Group Connector.

Information Store

Exchange 5.5 introduced an enhanced database engine that improved reliability and eliminated the size restriction on the information store (when using the Exchange 5.5 Enterprise Server). However, despite these improvements, the information store still presents a roadblock to configuring large Exchange servers supporting many thousands of users. The problem is not the total size of the database, but rather the amount of time it takes to back up a large database, and more importantly, the amount of time it takes to restore it in the event of a disaster. For many organizations, the time it takes to restore a single large database is prohibitive, so they partition their database into smaller units. In Exchange 4.0/5.x, the only way to partition the information store database is to install additional servers.

Exchange 2000's information store enables you to split a large database into multiple storage groups with multiple mailbox or public folder stores in each storage group. This feature alone makes working with the information store easier. However, Exchange 2000 also has introduced additional changes, such as Exchange System Policies, to make managing stores throughout the organization easier.

Information Store Configuration

As I mentioned in the previous chapter, the information store in Exchange 2000 can be split into multiple storage groups and stores. A storage group is a group of databases that all share a single transaction log. A store is a single database that can be managed as an individual unit for configuration, backup, and restoration purposes. You can configure a store either as a mailbox store for individual mailboxes or as a public folder store.

Because of the storage group configuration, you need to plan the placement of the databases on the physical hard disks on the server carefully. In Exchange 4.0/5.x, the only issue was to separate the databases from the transaction logs and store them on separate hard disks to provide enhanced performance and redundancy. Exchange 2000 still uses essentially the same database technology as Exchange 4.0/5.x, so if you have a single storage group, this is still the best configuration. However, if you create additional storage groups, you need separate hard drives for each of the transaction log. Figure 2-12 illustrates how the databases and transaction logs should be configured if you have multiple storage groups.

You can configure separate hard disk locations for each store within a storage group, or even different locations for the native content store (the .stm file) and the Exchange format store (the .edb file). If you have many hard disks in your server, you might want to separate the stores to optimize performance. However, this does not improve the backup and restore times because the entire store (which includes both files) is backed up and restored at the same time. Most large Exchange servers use a hardware RAID solution for the database files, so put both files on the hardware RAID for optimal performance.

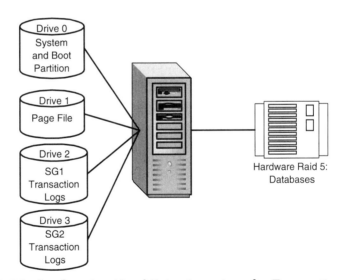

Figure 2-12: Configuring Hard Drive Locations for Transaction Logs and Database Files.

To create and configure storage groups, use the Exchange System Manager snap-in:

1. To locate the storage groups and stores, expand Administrative Groups/*administrativegroup*/Servers/*servername*.

The storage groups are located in the *servername* container, and the stores are located in the storage group.

2. Right-click the storage group and select Properties. Figure 2-13 shows the Properties box for a storage group.

    The configuration options that you are likely to change in the Properties box are:

    ▲ **Transaction log location.** All the stores in the storage group share the same transaction log, so you specify the transaction log location at the storage group level.

    ▲ **Zero out deleted database pages.** This option overwrites with zeroes any pages that have been deleted during backup. This provides some security in case an intruder accesses the backup tapes, but negatively affects server performance during backup.

    ▲ **Enable circular logging.** Circular logging is disabled by default in Exchange 2000. If you have a group of stores that does not require the enhanced recoverability provided by circular logging, you can group all those stores in one storage group and enable circular logging on that storage group.

3. To create a new storage group, right-click the server name and select New/Storage Group. Type a descriptive name for the storage group and select the location for the transaction logs and system files.

4. To configure the store properties, expand the storage group in which the store is located, right-click the store, and choose Properties.

    Many of the configuration options are similar to the options available on the private information store in Exchange 4.0/5.*x*. Figure 2-14 shows the configuration tabs for a mailbox store. Some of the additional configuration options for the mailbox store are listed in Table 2-2.

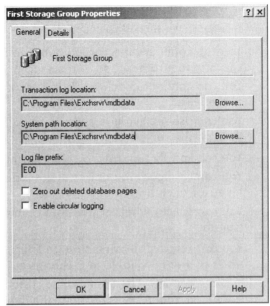

Figure 2-13: Storage Group Properties.

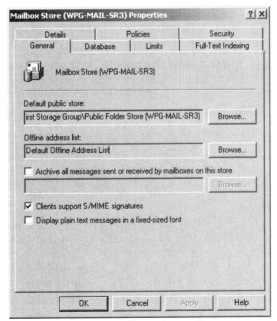

Figure 2-14: Mailbox Store Properties.

Table 2-2: Configuration Options for Mail Stores

Tab	Configuration Options
General	You can configure the default public folder store to point to a specific store rather than to a server. You can configure each mailbox store with an individual offline address list. You can use archiving to save a copy of all messages sent through the server.
Database	You can specify separate locations for the .edb and the .stm files. You can configure the online maintenance to run at different times for each store. You can specify whether the store automatically mounts at startup.
Limits	You can specify the same storage limits and message retention times as were available in Exchange 5.5. You can configure deleted mailbox retention times. When a user is deleted from Active Directory, the mailbox store retains the mailbox for the specified time in case the mailbox needs to be linked to another user account.
Full-Text Indexing	You can specify when the server will update or rebuild the full-text index.
Policies	You can view the policies that are linked to the mailbox store. These can only be used to view, not change the policy links.

NOTE: *Most objects in the System Manager have Details and Security tabs, as shown in Figure 2-14. The Details tab shows when the object was created and modified and provides space for an administrative note for information purposes. The Security tab is the standard Active Directory tab, showing the ACL for the object.*

5. To configure a public folder store, expand the storage group in which the store is located, select the store, and select Properties.

The Database, Full-Text Indexing and Policies tabs are the same for both store types. The public folder store includes several new settings as well, as shown in Table 2-3.

Table 2-3: Configuration Options for Public Folder Stores

Tab	Configuration Options
General	This tab shows the public folder tree associated with the store. Each public folder store must be associated with a unique tree for that server. You can specify whether the public folder clients support S/MIME signatures and whether to display plain text messages in a fixed-sized font.
Replication	You can set the public folders replication schedule and specify the size of replication messages.
Limits	You can set limits on the size of the public folder store, deleted item retention, and age limits for messages in the store can be configured.

6. To create a new store, right-click a storage group and select New and then select Mailbox Store or Public Store. Type a descriptive name for the store; then configure the remainder of the properties.

When you create the additional store, the .edb and .stm files are created in the location you specify. (The default location is the same directory as the transaction log location configured for the storage group.) The .edb and .stm file names are the same as that of the store name.

7. To mount or dismount a store, right-click the store and select Mount Store or Dismount Store.

Each store can be individually mounted or dismounted. This is useful for restoration purposes. For example, to restore just one store, dismount that store while all the others are still mounted, perform the restore, and mount the store again. Only the users on that single store are affected by the restore.

NOTE: *It's so easy to create additional stores that you might be tempted to provide individual users with their own store so that you can restore their e-mail quickly. This is probably not a good idea, however, because Exchange 2000 allocates about 10 MB of RAM for each mounted store. However, creating a store for a small group of top* *executives in a company (including the one who signs your paycheck) might be a great idea.*

If you need to move the database files or transaction logs in Exchange 4.0/5.*x*, you can run the Performance Optimizer and move the files as part of the optimization process. Exchange 2000 does not have an equivalent tool, however. To move the files in Exchange 2000, you access the storage group property sheet to move the transaction logs, or the store property sheet to move the database files, and type (or use Browse to select) a new location for the files. It displays several warning messages and then dismounts the store and moves the files. To move the transaction logs, the server must dismount all the stores in the storage group. I strongly recommended that you perform a complete backup of all the affected files before moving them.

Exchange System Policies

In addition to the architectural change that enables you to create multiple storage groups and stores, Exchange 2000 also includes an important administrative change that makes managing those stores easier. Because you set many of the policies, such as mailbox size limits, retention limits, and maintenance schedules, at the store level, and you now have the option to have many more stores, you could spend much more time administering the store properties. To make administering the store easier, Exchange 2000 includes *system policies*.

When you create an Exchange system policy, you configure a set of properties for a server or store. You can then apply that policy to any server or store in the entire enterprise. This gives you a great deal of administrative power without a lot of complicated administration work. For example, you might implement a separate mailbox store on each server in the organization for the executives and managers, in addition to a mailbox store for other employees. You might want to provide the executives unlimited storage space in their stores but set limits for all the other employees. You can accomplish this goal by creating two system policies: one for the stores containing the executive mailboxes, and the other for the remaining mailboxes. You can then link the Exchange System Policy to any store in the organization, much as you can link the Group Policy Objects to OUs in Active Directory.

You can implement and manage Exchange system policies through the Exchange System Manager. Perform the following steps to create and configure a system policy:

1. To create a system policy, expand the administrative group in which you want to locate the system policy, and locate the System Policies container.

   If the administrative group does not have a System Policies container, right-click the *administrativegroupname* and select New/System Policy Container.

2. Right-click the System Policies container, select New, and then select the type of system policy you want to create.

   You have three choices:

   a. **Server Policy.** The only configuration options are message tracking and subject logging. You can use this policy to enable or disable message tracking on selected servers.

   b. **Public Store Policy.** Configuration options include limits, full-text index scheduling, replication scheduling, and maintenance intervals.

   c. **Mailbox Store Policy.** Configuration options include the default public store and offline address lists, limits, and maintenance and indexing scheduling.

3. Select the tabs that you want to include in the system policy and click OK.

   When you create a new system policy, you can choose the tabs you want to include on the system policy. For example, as Figure 2-15 shows, when you create a new mailbox store, you can choose from four tabs that can be included on the system policy.

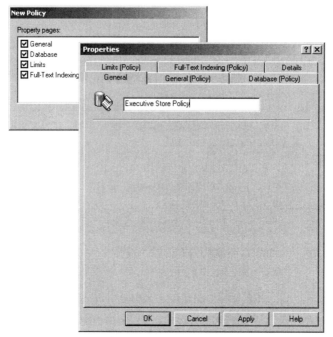

Figure 2-15: Mailbox Store System Policy Configuration.

4. Type a descriptive name for the system policy, and configure the settings on each of the tabs.

   As Figure 2-15 shows, the system policy Properties box includes a General tab for the policy object itself and also a policy configuration tab for each of the tabs you selected in the previous step.

5. After creating the system policy, link the policy to the Exchange objects to which you want to apply the policy by right-clicking the system policy you just created and selecting Add *object* where *object* is the object type.

   For example, if you were adding a new public store, you would select Add Public Store.

6. The dialog box displays all the objects of the selected type. If you created a Public Store Policy, all of the public stores in the organization are listed. Add the stores that you want to link to the system policy.

You can link the system policy to any of the specified objects in the entire organization. After you create the link, the added objects appear the Details pane and the policy is applied to the stores or servers. The tabs in the object's own Properties box become unavailable for changes, since all properties are now inherited from the policy. The Policies tab in the object's Properties box lists the policies that apply to the object.

7. To remove an object from the policy, right-click the object in the Details pane and select Remove from policy.

When you remove an object from a policy, the policy's settings remain applied to it; however, you can once again use the object's own Properties box to change the settings.

You can apply multiple system policies to a server or store, as long as the policies do not overlap in tab coverage. For example, if you have a mailbox store policy that configures the Limits tab but does not configure the Database tab, and a second policy that configures the Database tab, you can apply both policies to a mailbox store. However, if you try to add the mailbox store to a third system policy that also configures the Limits tab, an error message appears indicating that you cannot add this store to the policy until you remove the other policy.

System policies provide a powerful tool for administering the stores in your organization. Because Exchange stores this configuration information in the configuration partition in Active Directory, the information is replicated to all domain controllers in the entire forest, and each Exchange server reads it as it starts.

Public Folders

Public folder administration has not changed as significantly in Exchange 2000 as some of the other components have. However, there are still a few important changes.

Public Folder Trees

The most obvious change is that you can now support multiple public folder trees within the Exchange organization. In Exchange 4.0/5.*x*, you are limited to the default public folder tree. You can create as many public folders as you want underneath the public folder tree, but you cannot create any additional trees. The public folder hierarchy is replicated to every Exchange server in the organization that has a public information store, even if no user on the server needs to access the public folders.

In Exchange 2000, you can create multiple public folder trees, and you can limit the scope of the hierarchy replication for the additional public folder trees. When you create a new public folder tree, only the server on which the public folder has been created has information about the new tree. Exchange does not replicate the information to any other server unless you configure the new tree on the server.

The process of creating additional public folder trees is complicated by several factors. First, each public folder store can be associated with only a single public folder tree, so in addition to creating an additional public folder tree, you must create a public folder store for the tree. Second, the public folder tree is not accessible from MAPI clients (such as Outlook 2000) that can access only a single public folder tree. Clients can access the additional trees using Web or NNTP clients, but even there the server configuration is complicated. The default virtual servers for HTTP and NNTP are associated with the default public folder store, so you must create an additional virtual server for the protocols and then associate it with the new store.

To create additional public folder trees and to make them accessible to clients, use the following procedure:

1. To create a new public folder tree, locate the Folders container in the administrative group, right-click it, and select New/Public Folder Tree. Type a descriptive name for the tree.

2. Create the public folder store to contain the tree using the procedure outlined earlier. When you create the store, select Browse on the General tab and locate the public folder tree that you just created. Configure the remainder of the store properties.

3. If you want this tree to be replicated to another server in the organization, create a public store on that server and then associate the store with this tree. The information for the tree is then replicated to the second server.

4. To make the new public folder tree available to HTTP clients, create a new virtual server in the HTTP container. When you create the HTTP server, choose to associate this virtual server with the public folder tree that you just created.

5. To make the public folder tree available to NNTP clients, create a new NNTP virtual server in the NNTP container. When you create the NNTP server, select the option to use the new public folder tree to store the news group content.

Public Folder Administration

Exchange 2000 has made several other changes to the administration of the public folders:

▲ You can now do most of the public folder administration using the Folders snap-in in the System Manager. In Exchange 4.0/5.x, the only way to create public folders is to use a client such as Outlook. In Exchange 2000, you can create folders that for mail items, assign permissions, and configure all public folder properties using the System Manager. To create public folders for calendar items (or any other items other than mail items), you must still use an e-mail client.

▲ As in Exchange 4.0/5.x, public folders do not appear in the global address list by default. To make a public folder show up in the GAL in Exchange 2000, you must select the option to make it visible in the GAL. You can add this object to distribution lists or use it as a mail recipient when sending mail.

▲ Many types and levels of permissions can be assigned to public folders in Exchange 2000. In Exchange 4.0/5.x, you could assign permissions to public folders based on roles such as Author or Editor. In Exchange 2000, you can still assign permissions in the same way. In addition, you can assign directory rights that determine the level of permissions on the Active Directory object for a mail-enabled folder. You also can assign administrative rights, which control access to the administration of the public folder including assigning limits and message expiration times. You can configure all these options on the Permissions tab in the public folder's Properties box. If you need to assign permissions to individual items in the public store, you can access the items through the drive mapped to the information store (usually the M: drive) and assign NTFS permissions to individual objects.

NOTE: Assigning permissions to individual items in the public folder store falls under the category of: "Just because you can doesn't mean you should." While it can be useful in specific cases, you should normally avoid assigning permissions at this level unless you want to be buried under an avalanche of administrivia.

▲ Exchange 2000 also changes how you configure access to public folders for users in other routing groups. In Exchange 4.0/5.*x*, users do not have access to the public folder contents stored at a remote site until you configure an affinity between the sites. In Exchange 2000, this default behavior has been reversed. Now users are able to access public folders in other routing groups unless you disable the option. In Exchange 2000, you set this option by configuring the public folder referral option on a routing group connector rather than configuring it at the site level.

Conclusion

This chapter has presented an overview of the differences between administering an Exchange 2000 and an Exchange 4.0/5.*x* organization. This was not an exhaustive list of differences, and it did not provide all the details you need to administer Exchange 2000. However, it did introduce you to Exchange 2000 by building on what you already knew about Exchange 4.0/5.*x*.

Chapter 3 introduces you to North American Air, a large company getting ready to migrate from its current e-mail system to Exchange 2000. You learn in Chapter 3 — in a fair bit of detail — about North American Air's current network and messaging configuration. The remainder of the book, then, follows this company as it moves to Exchange 2000.

Chapter 3

Introduction to North American Air

FOR A NETWORK ADMINISTRATOR FACING a major task, such as migrating to a new messaging system, one of the most useful experiences is to watch another organization go through the same process. By watching another company, you can identify the major steps in the process and develop a list of the issues that you need to address as you plan your own migration. Often the most valuable part of watching someone else is seeing what that person or company does and then thinking about how you might do things differently based on the unique network and organizational requirements in your company. I have designed this book to give you just such an opportunity; you will watch another company go through a migration before you have to deal with the same complex issues.

Most Exchange 2000 books focus primarily on the software, with short scenarios or examples to provide illustrations for the concepts. In this book, however, one scenario provides the context for the entire process. In this chapter, I explain my rationale for using this approach, and then I introduce you to North American Air, a medium sized corporation that is beginning the migration to Windows 2000 and Exchange 2000.

Purpose of the Business Scenario

This book revolves around North American Air, a company facing the same situation that you are facing: migration to Exchange 2000. This company is currently running a Windows NT 4.0 network with Exchange 5.5 servers as well as a Domino Server/Lotus Notes and MS Mail servers. The company has grown over time and has acquired other companies as part of this growth, and the Windows NT domain structure has grown in complexity along with the company. Their current Exchange sites correspond to their several locations throughout North America. In other words, this company is similar to many other companies that are beginning to look at their networks in preparation for moving to Windows 2000 and Exchange 2000.

By basing this book on a scenario, I hope to provide you with a context for the technical content. As this book follows a company through migration, you can see the planning and implementation issues involved in the process. These issues can be dealt with abstractly, as they are in most Exchange 2000 books, but observing a company as it deals with issues, such as corporate goals, budgets, and schedules, makes the issues more realistic. As you follow this process, you can think about the issues that you are dealing with in your company, in terms of both how they are similar to the issues faced by North American Air and how they are different.

One of difficulties in learning a new technology or process is that you can get so caught up in learning the details of how to do something that you forget why you are doing it. Therein lies another advantage of using a scenario throughout this book. Each time I introduce you to a new concept or procedure, I also show you how North American Air is implementing the concept or procedure. Placing the new technology within the context of a real-world example helps you to understand why you are learning the technology.

NOTE: In addition to writing and consulting, I also work as a corporate trainer teaching network administrators new technologies. If I tell my students about a complex technology or procedure, I am sure to see many blank looks on their faces. But when I show them how I have used that technology or procedure to solve a complex problem similar to one they are facing, lights go on all over the room.

Placing the content of this book within the context of a scenario also enables you to follow the entire process of migration from start to finish. This chapter introduces the scenario as the starting point for the entire migration process, and then the rest of the book builds from that starting point in logical steps moving toward the final goal of supporting the new Exchange 2000 organization. Understanding the entire process gives you a realistic picture of what is involved from start to finish. If you do not know the complexity of what lies ahead, you cannot be prepared for it.

I have designed the North American Air scenario to be complex enough to deal with most of the issues that you might face as you migrate to Exchange 2000. North American Air is a fairly large company with multiple locations, domains, and sites, similar to many medium and large corporations. A company of this size and complexity needs to plan the migration carefully, as well as perform the migration incrementally. As the scenario unfolds, you will be able to identify components of the scenario that relate to your own corporate environment.

I have broken down the actual migration for North American Air into several steps. This is realistic in that most large corporations are simply too big to migrate the entire organization in one step. This stepped approach can help you work through your own migration as well. The book may cover some topics that you do not need to know anything about because your environment does not require them. For example, this book covers migrating from Domino Server/Lotus Notes to Exchange 2000; if you do not have a Domino Server, you do not need to go through that part of the scenario. While some parts of the migration are required in all cases, such as upgrading to Windows 2000, other parts are optional. But even in this multistep process, the scenario helps you keep the entire context in mind. As you are dealing with one particular issue, you can see how the issue fits into the big picture.

Now that you know why this book uses a scenario as a focal point, it's time you met North American Air.

North American Air Overview

North American Air began 40 years ago as an aircraft manufacturing company based in Dallas, Texas, making structural and engine components used in civilian and military aircraft throughout the world. The corporation later moved into the aircraft maintenance business, maintaining both its own aircraft and aircraft for other airlines and military organizations. While this manufacturing and maintenance business is still the most important one for North American Air, it also has diversified its business over the last 10 years, and now provides overnight airfreight delivery between most major cities in North America.

The corporate headquarters and much of the manufacturing are still located in Dallas. The corporate headquarters, located in a modern building close to downtown, also serves as the operations center for the airfreight business unit. The primary manufacturing center is located near Dallas/Fort Worth International Airport, approximately 25 miles (40 km) from corporate headquarters. A second major manufacturing and maintenance facility is located in Houston, Texas.

North American Air acquired an additional manufacturing and maintenance facility in Winnipeg, Manitoba about 10 years ago, at about the same time that it started the airfreight component of the business. In the last three years, the corporation has been pursuing an aggressive expansion policy. The company has bought five small companies involved in a variety of related businesses, including an avionics manufacturing plant in Atlanta, Georgia and an electronics factory in Chicago, Illinois. North American Air is using these two plants to expand the maintenance and manufacturing services to include aircraft electronics. In addition, the corporation also has acquired two small airfreight companies located in San Diego, California and Vancouver, British Columbia. And very recently, North American Air has acquired a company located in Portland, Oregon that specializes in refitting commercial aircraft interiors.

The management at North American Air is committed to continued growth in the future by expanding the company's presence in current markets and by increasing manufacturing capabilities. They also will continue to acquire additional companies to expand the range of services they provide.

Corporate IT Infrastructure

The current Information Technology (IT) infrastructure reflects the history of the corporation. The IT infrastructure for the core business components is well planned and centralized. The last major IT upgrade to Windows NT 4.0 and Exchange 5.5 occurred three years ago, and the current IT infrastructure has performed well for the company. As the company has expanded over the last three years, however, there have been problems integrating multiple domains and several different e-mail systems and applications into the corporate network. One of the reasons why the company is looking at migrating to Exchange 2000 is to once again standardize the IT infrastructure on a single corporate platform as much as possible.

> **NOTE:** *The details that follow describe the entire North American Air infrastructure, not just the current messaging infrastructure. It deals with some of the business issues and concerns facing North American Air; upcoming chapters address how the company deals with these concerns as part of the migration to Exchange 2000.*

Domain Structure

All the locations are using Windows NT 4.0 as the network operating system, but with a variety of domain designs. The corporate office and the manufacturing plants in Dallas and Houston are configured in a single master domain with three resource domains. The Winnipeg location, on the other hand, is configured as a single domain, as are each of the newer acquisitions. Because all of the domains must share information with each other, two-way trust relationships have been configured between most of the domains. Table 3-1 lists the current domains.

Table 3-1: Domain Structure at North American Air

Location	Number of Employees	Domain Name	Domain Type
Dallas corporate office	8,000	DALLAS_ACCT DALLAS_CORP	Master domain Resource domain
Dallas manufacturing facility	10,000	DALLAS_MANU	Resource domain
Houston manufacturing facility	7,000	HOUSTON_MANU	Resource domain
Winnipeg	3,000	WINNIPEG	Account and Resource domain
Vancouver	300	VANCOUVER	Account and Resource domain
Portland	600	PORTLAND	Account and Resource domain
San Diego	500	SAN_DIEGO	Account and Resource domain
Chicago	800	CHICAGO	Account and Resource domain
Atlanta	1,000	ATLANTA	Account and Resource domain

The domain administration in the Texas locations is centralized. The DALLAS_ACCT domain manages all user accounts, and resources are spread throughout the three resource domains. The domain management of the rest of the company, however, is not centralized. Each of the locations outside of Texas has its own IT staff and manages its networks independently.

The complexity of the trust relationships in the current domain structure is problematic. Each of the manufacturing and maintenance facilities needs access to resources in each of the other locations that work on manufacturing and maintenance. To accomplish this, two-way trusts have been configured between all of those locations along with one-way trusts between the domains containing user accounts and the resource domains in Texas. In each case where there is a one-way trust, the account domain is the *trusted domain*, and the resource domain is the *trusting domain*. The airfreight business operates as an independent business managed from Dallas and does not need access to information in the manufacturing and maintenance locations. However, to help integrate the two new airfreight companies that North American Air has acquired, administrators have configured a two-way trust between the corporate office and the two subsidiaries. As shown in the Table 3-2 and Figure 3-1, the trust configuration is fairly complex.

Table 3-2: Domain Trust Relationships at North American Air

Domain	Trust Relationships
DALLAS_ACCT	Two-way trust with WINNIPEG, VANCOUVER, PORTLAND, SAN_DIEGO, CHICAGO, ATLANTA One-way trust (trusted domain) with: DALLAS_CORP, DALLAS_MANU, HOUSTON_MANU
DALLAS_CORP	One-way trust (trusting domain) with DALLAS_ACCT, WINNIPEG, PORTLAND, CHICAGO, ATLANTA
DALLAS_MANU	One-way trust (trusting domain) with DALLAS_ACCT, WINNIPEG, PORTLAND, CHICAGO, ATLANTA
HOUSTON_MANU	One-way trust (trusting domain) with DALLAS_ACCT, WINNIPEG, PORTLAND, CHICAGO, ATLANTA
WINNIPEG	Two-way trust with DALLAS_ACCT, PORTLAND, CHICAGO, ATLANTA One-way trust (trusted domain) with DALLAS_CORP, DALLAS_MANU, HOUSTON_MANU
VANCOUVER	Two-way trust with DALLAS_ACCT One-way trust (trusted domain) with DALLAS_CORP
PORTLAND	Two-way trust with WINNIPEG, DALLAS_ACCT, CHICAGO, ATLANTA One-way trust (trusted domain) with DALLAS_CORP, DALLAS_MANU, HOUSTON_MANU
SAN_DIEGO	Two-way trust with DALLAS_ACCT One-way trust (trusted domain) with DALLAS_CORP

Table 3-2: Domain Trust Relationships at North American Air (Continued)

Domain	Trust Relationships
CHICAGO	Two-way trust with WINNIPEG, PORTLAND, CHICAGO, ATLANTA One-way trust (trusted domain) with DALLAS_CORP, DALLAS_MANU, HOUSTON_MANU
ATLANTA	Two-way trust with WINNIPEG, PORTLAND, CHICAGO One-way trust (trusted domain) with DALLAS_CORP, DALLAS_MANU, HOUSTON_MANU

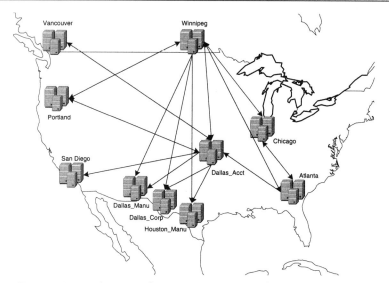

Figure 3-1: The Windows NT Trust Configuration at
North American Air.

WAN Connectivity
All the locations outside of Dallas are linked to Dallas using a variety
of dedicated WAN links. Figure 3-2 shows the WAN connections.

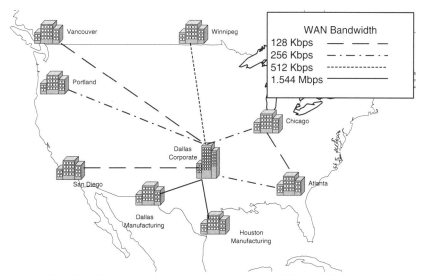

Figure 3-2: North American Air Locations and WAN Connections.

Application Support

The Texas and Winnipeg locations have standardized on a set of corporate applications. They use Office 97 as the productivity suite, and Outlook 98 as the standard e-mail client. In addition, the corporation is running several custom applications based on a three-year-old version of Sybase SQLAnywhere server. These applications support the core business of the corporation, including the manufacturing, maintenance, and airfreight components. The applications worked well before the company began its latest expansion, but are becoming more difficult to upgrade as the corporation grows and adds new business components. The SQLAnywhere servers that support these applications reside in the corporate headquarters, with client software on desktops throughout the organization.

The smaller locations use a variety of software applications and e-mail clients. Most locations are still using the same applications that they were using when acquired by North American Air, but the lack of a corporate standard is becoming increasingly problematic. The avionics company in Atlanta, for example, was using a custom business application before North American Air acquired it. To integrate the electronics factory in Chicago with the avionics component, the company modified the application and then deployed it in Chicago as well. The servers that run these applications are all located in Atlanta. Integrating this custom application with the manufacturing and maintenance application used in the other part of the company has proven to be difficult, and so there is no real integration at this point between the electronics facilities and the maintenance and manufacturing locations.

The airfreight companies in San Diego and Vancouver use a paper-based system and custom Access databases to manage the airfreight business. The IT staff at North American Air would like to integrate the IT infrastructure in these locations with the corporate network so that they can use a single custom application to manage all the airfreight business. The Portland aircraft refitting company also uses a custom application for managing its business. Because the Portland facility was only recently acquired, IT has not yet done any work toward integrating the application into the corporate infrastructure.

Mobile Users

North American Air supports about 200 mobile users. Fifty of these users are salespeople who travel throughout the world selling maintenance contracts to international airlines and components to aircraft manufacturers. All of these salespeople must be able to connect to the corporate network to access manufacturing schedules, price lists, and component availability from anywhere in the world, as well as access corporate e-mail. Most of these users currently connect using dial-up access through one of 10 toll-free numbers in Dallas and Winnipeg. The primary issue in supporting the mobile users is connection bandwidth and availability. Some of the custom applications perform poorly over the dial-up connection, and as the number of remote users increase, the demand for additional phone lines grows.

Another 25 remote users sell airfreight to companies throughout North America. These users need access to the corporate network to check flight schedules and space availability and to place the orders from clients. These remote users also are using the dial-up connections.

The remaining remote users are repair engineers who travel to airports throughout North America to perform minor maintenance and repair tasks. These engineers need access to the corporate network to order aircraft components, update the progress information on their tasks, and check for upcoming tasks. They also occasionally need access to a network archive of technical manuals.

When North American Air adopted Windows NT 4.0 and Exchange 5.5 as the corporate standard three years ago, they expected that the technology would remain in place for 3-5 years. However, the new acquisitions have increased the impetus to move to a new corporate standard.

North American Air Messaging Infrastructure

The messaging infrastructure for North American Air also reflects the corporate history. The Texas and Winnipeg locations have been using Exchange 5.5 as the e-mail server for the last three years, while the newer locations run a mixture of messaging servers.

All the Exchange sites have been integrated into a single Exchange organization called NA_Air_Org. Figure 3-3 gives an overview of the current e-mail configuration.

Texas

When North American Air first deployed Exchange 5.5 three years ago, the WAN links between the Texas locations were limited to 512 Kbps. Because of the amount of network traffic on the WAN links, IT configured the three Texas locations as separate sites so that they could control the messaging traffic on those links. They later upgraded the links to full T-1 capacity (1.544 Mbps).

The corporate IT policy at North American Air specifies that a single Exchange server cannot contain more than 2000 mailboxes. This policy limits the size of the information store so that recovery will be easier in the event of a disaster. In addition to the user mailboxes, North American Air makes limited use of public folders, so each site must provide limited space for 10 public folders. The Dallas corporate site also operates as the hub for connections from all the other sites. Two dedicated servers provide the site connectors to the other sites and the connectors to the non-Exchange e-mail systems. This means that the Texas locations have 16 Exchange 5.5 servers, as shown in Table 3-3.

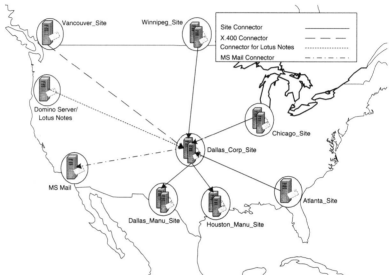

Figure 3-3: Overview of the Messaging Infrastructure at North American Air.

Table 3-3: Exchange Server Configurations for the Texas Locations of North American Air

Site	Exchange Server	Information Store	Bridgehead Server and Connectors
Dallas_Corp_Site	Dal-C-Mail-Svr1	2000 mailboxes 10 public folders	Not applicable
Dallas_Corp_Site	Dal-C-Mail-Svr2	2000 mailboxes	Not applicable
Dallas_Corp_Site	Dal-C-Mail-Svr3	2000 mailboxes	Not applicable
Dallas_Corp_Site	Dal-C-Mail-Svr4	2000 mailboxes	Not applicable

Table 3-3: Exchange Server Configurations for the Texas Locations of North American Air (Continued)

Site	Exchange Server	Information Store	Bridgehead Server and Connectors
Dallas_Corp_Site	Dal-C-Mail-Svr5	0 mailboxes	Connector to all other exchange 5.5 Sites Microsoft Mail connector (for San Diego) Internet mail service for Internet mail
Dallas_Corp_Site	Dal-C-Mail-Svr6	0 mailboxes	Connector to all other exchange 5.5 Sites Connector for Lotus Notes (for Portland) Internet mail service for Internet mail
Dallas_Manu_Site	Dal-M-Mail-Svr1	2000 mailboxes 10 public folders	Not applicable
Dallas_Manu_Site	Dal-M-Mail-Svr2	2000 mailboxes	Not applicable
Dallas_Manu_Site	Dal-M-Mail-Svr3	2000 mailboxes	Not applicable
Dallas_Manu_Site	Dal-M-Mail-Svr4	2000 mailboxes	Not applicable
Dallas_Manu_Site	Dal-M-Mail-Svr5	1000 mailboxes	Connector to Dallas_Corp_Site
Dallas_Manu_Site	Dal-M-Mail-Svr6	1000 mailboxes	Connector to Dallas_Corp_Site
Houston_Manu_Site	Hou-Mail-Svr1	2000 mailboxes 10 public folders	Not applicable
Houston_Manu_Site	Hou-Mail-Svr2	2000 mailboxes	Not applicable

Table 3-3: Exchange Server Configurations for the Texas Locations of North American Air (Continued)

Site	Exchange Server	Information Store	Bridgehead Server and Connectors
Houston_Manu_Site	Hou-Mail-Svr3	1500 mailboxes	Connector to Dallas_Corp_Site
Houston_Manu_Site	Hou-Mail-Svr4	1500 mailboxes	Connector to Dallas_Corp_Site

Internet Mail Service has been configured on the two dedicated connector servers in the Dallas_Corp_Site. This means that the other sites in Texas route their Internet mail through Dallas_Corp_Site.

About 125 remote-access users access the corporate location through an RAS server. The IT staff at North American Air has deployed a single Outlook Web Access (OWA) server on a Windows NT 4.0 server running Internet Information Services (IIS) 4.0, and they have begun to test OWA for remote-access users. However, because the users also need access to other corporate information that is not accessible through a Web client, OWA implementation is limited at this point.

Winnipeg

The messaging infrastructure in Winnipeg provides e-mail connectivity for the 3,000 users in Winnipeg plus approximately 75 dial-up users. Both Exchange servers in Winnipeg are located in Winnipeg_Site. The messaging configuration consists of two servers configured as shown in Table 3-4.

Table 3-4: Exchange Server Configuration in the Winnipeg Location of North American Air

Exchange Server	Information Store	Bridgehead Server and Connectors
Wpg-Mail-Svr1	2000 mailboxes	None
Wpg-Mail-Svr2	1075 mailboxes 10 public folders	Internet mail service for Internet mail Site connector to Dallas_Corp_Site

In addition, to these servers, Winnipeg has been testing an OWA server. Winnipeg also provides its own Internet Mail Service.

Atlanta

The Atlanta location uses a single Exchange 5.5 server located in the Atlanta_Site site. They installed the Exchange server when North American Air acquired the Atlanta company. Table 3-5 lists the details of the Atlanta site.

Table 3-5: Exchange Server Configuration in the Atlanta Location of North American Air

Exchange Server	Information Store	Bridgehead Server and Connectors
Atl-Mail-Svr1	800 mailboxes	Internet mail service for Internet mail Site connector to Dallas_Corp_Site

Chicago

The Chicago location uses two Exchange 5.5 servers located in the Chicago_Site site. They installed the Exchange server when North American Air acquired the Chicago company. Table 3-6 lists the details of the Chicago site.

Table 3-6: Exchange Server Configuration in the Chicago Location of
North American Air

Exchange Server	Information Store	Bridgehead Server and Connectors
Chi-Mail-Svr1	800 mailboxes	None
Chi-Mail-Svr2	200 mailboxes	Internet mail service for Internet mail Site connector to Dallas_Corp_Site

San Diego

The facility in San Diego uses two Microsoft Mail servers. The
Microsoft Mail network name for the San Diego location is SD_Mail.
The Microsoft Mail servers in San Diego are not configured with
Internet Mail connectivity; all Internet mail is routed through the
servers in Dallas. Table 3-7 lists the details for the San Diego site.

Table 3-7: Microsoft Mail Server Configuration in the San Diego Location of
North American Air

MSMail Server	Mailboxes	External Connectors
SD-MSMail-Svr1	300 mailboxes	None
SD-MSMail-Svr2	200 mailboxes	Connector to the Exchange organization through the Microsoft Mail connector on Dal-C-Mail-Svr5

Vancouver

The Vancouver location uses a single Exchange 5.5 server located in
the Vancouver_Site site. The airfreight company in Vancouver was
using Exchange 5.0 when North American Air acquired the company. They upgraded the Exchange server to Exchange 5.5 and
installed Service Pack 2, so that the server could be moved into the
North American Air organization using the Move Server wizard. The
connection between Vancouver and the Dallas Corporate site is the

only X.400 connector used in the organization. Table 3-8 lists the details of the Vancouver site.

Table 3-8: Exchange Server Configuration in the Vancouver Location of North American Air

Exchange Server	Information Store	Bridgehead Server and Connectors
Van-Mail-Svr1	300 mailboxes	Internet mail service for Internet mail X.400 connector to Dallas_Corp_Site

Portland

The company that North American Air bought in Portland runs a single Domino Server with Lotus Notes version 4.5.3 providing messaging services. They have developed a few limited applications for Lotus Notes, but the applications are not critical for the company's operations. Table 3-9 lists the details of the Portland site.

Table 3-9: Domino Server/Lotus Notes Configuration in the Portland Location of North American Air

Domino Server/Lotus Notes	Number of Users	Connections
Portland-Mail	300 mailboxes	SMTP MTA for Internet mail Connection to the Exchange organization using the connector for Lotus Notes on Dal-C-Mail-Svr6

NOTE: *This section has provided a high-level overview of the messaging infrastructure at North American Air. I deal with more specific details about the actual server configurations as necessary in upcoming chapters, as the company begins its migration.*

Conclusion

This chapter explained the rationale for using a scenario-based approach to teach you how to migrate an Exchange 4.0/5.*x* organization to Exchange 2000. The chapter also described the company that will be migrating to Exchange 2000 as this book progresses. This chapter provides a context for the rest of the book.

Now that you have been introduced to North American Air, it is time to begin the process of migration. Planning is the first step in the migration process, so the next chapter introduces the planning that North American Air must go through as it prepares to migrate to Exchange 2000. In Chapter 4, you will see how North American Air determines the business value versus cost of migrating and puts together a project team to gather the information needed for detailed planning.

Part 2

Planning

Chapter 4

Migrating to Exchange 2000: The Planning Phase

LIKE MOST CORPORATIONS, NORTH AMERICAN AIR constantly strives to optimize its business practices to be more competitive and efficient. As in most companies these days, North American Air's IT infrastructure is a crucial factor in the equation. As the corporation has grown, it has faced new IT-related business issues, such as the difficulty and cost of supporting multiple applications and messaging platforms. North American Air now needs to consider whether a major change in the IT infrastructure — such as a company-wide migration to Exchange 2000 — will help achieve overall corporate goals.

This chapter describes the planning process when a large corporation begins an infrastructure migration. The company must first clarify its corporate vision and goals and then explore options for achieving them. When the company is clear on what business problems it expects the technology to solve, it can evaluate the technologies available to deal with the problems, choose one, and then continue planning the migration.

North American Air already uses Microsoft technologies throughout the organization, so one of the options is to use newer Microsoft technologies, such as Exchange 2000, to address new issues. However, before committing to Exchange 2000, the company must go through an extensive evaluation and planning process to make sure that Exchange 2000 is the best way to meet its goals. To manage the planning process, the company must put together a project team with a wide range of IT experience and expertise. This team must collect a great deal of information before it can develop any concrete plans for the migration. This chapter describes the makeup of the team and the types of information that the team must collect.

The corporation also must provide a test lab where the project team can learn the new technology and thoroughly test all the components involved in the migration. The project team might visualize many different ways to use Exchange 2000 to accomplish the corporate goals, but until the team has tested the technology in a lab setting similar to the actual corporate environment, IT administrators can't know for sure whether the technology will achieve those goals. This chapter discusses the lab configuration and provides an overview of the testing process.

> **NOTE:** *This chapter and the next present the two essential components of planning a project of this magnitude. This chapter presents the planning component, which produces several high-level documents that provide an overview of the entire migration project but do not get into a great deal of detail about the actual network design. Chapter 5 provides an overview of the more detailed design process, which deals with issues such as domain design, routing group design, and server placement. Many of the concepts in these chapters are based on Microsoft's Solutions Framework (MSF), which is a set of guidelines for planning IT projects. Information on MSF is available on the Microsoft Web site (www.microsoft.com/msf), as well as through courses developed by Microsoft.*

Corporate Preplanning

A company must do a great deal of preplanning at the corporate/ executive level before assembling a project team and tasking them with IT planning. Although certain key IT professionals should be involved in this phase, the main work in this phase consists of identifying the corporate vision and goals and articulating how technology can help the corporation achieve them.

Identifying the Corporate Vision and Goals

A corporation's vision and goals should drive all the activity in the organization. The corporate vision provides the answer to the question "Why are we doing this?" When the corporate vision and goals are clearly articulated and understood throughout the organization, they provide a clear measuring stick against which all actions can be measured. In most corporations, the Board of Directors and the upper management develop this vision. The upper management then has the task of articulating this vision to all employees of the corporation.

It's essential to have a clear understanding of the corporate vision and goals when beginning a large project such as migrating to Exchange 2000. Everyone involved in the process must understand and be committed to achieving the vision. One of the documents that is produced during the planning process is a vision/scope document for the migration project. This document, which outlines the vision and goals for the project, must reflect the corporate vision and goals. When the project vision is clearly defined, and the vision enhances the chances of the corporation achieving its goals, the project has an excellent chance of succeeding.

In addition, everyone involved in planning the project should know the core products and services the corporation delivers or is planning to deliver. Understanding the core business components provides a focus for the corporate activities, including the adoption of a new technology. The technology might be able to provide some great functionality, but if this functionality does not help the corporation deliver on its core products and services, the technology is of little benefit. Everyone involved in the migration process also should know who the current and future customers are for the organization.

Before the process of evaluating a new technology even begins, everyone involved in the process needs to be able to answer some basic questions:

▲ What is the corporate vision? How is the corporation planning on achieving the vision?

▲ What are the corporate goals? Where is this corporation going?

▲ What are the core products and services that the corporation provides?

▲ Who are the current and potential customers for this corporation's products and services?

Once everyone involved in the pre-planning understands the answers to these questions, the process can continue. Without a clear understanding of the corporate vision and goals, the group cannot articulate how the technology can help the corporation achieve its goals. In other words, until you know where you want to go, you can't really determine the best way to get there.

Identifying Opportunities and Obstacles

Once everyone understands the corporate vision and goals, the next steps are to identify opportunities to achieve that vision and to anticipate the obstacles that might get in the way. It's important that top IT managers and top company executives hammer out a broad picture of the company's success strategy — and how the company expects IT to participate in that strategy — in advance of the main migration planning process.

Intelligent IT implementation can be a powerful tool in helping a corporation take advantage of opportunities and overcome obstacles. IT infrastructure is — or at least should be — at the center of almost any corporate plan, whether the goal is product development, service improvement, or market share gain. In some cases, IT innovation can even create new opportunities. A common example in today's economy is the use of the Internet. Most corporations see the

Internet as an opportunity to reach new markets and to make it easier for customers to contact the corporation. Companies use the Internet to provide sales information, but also to support a product after it has been sold. Many organizations see the Internet as a new tool for reaching their customers, creating a new opportunity to achieve corporate goals.

The IT infrastructure also can provide a means to overcome obstacles that prevent the corporation achieving its goals. One of the most important commodities in a large corporation is information, and that's exactly what the IT infrastructure provides. Whenever there is a decision to be made, the decision-makers need quick access to the right information — without having to wade through a lot of the wrong information. Most companies' IT infrastructures can provide a lot of information quickly, but fewer companies have systems in place that can filter the raw data intelligently and appropriately for a given situation. By developing enhanced options for information management, the IT infrastructure can overcome this obstacle.

Making maximum use of IT to achieve corporate goals requires a good working relationship between the IT staff and upper management. Virtually every business effort now depends on information technology, and nobody understands the technology better than the IT professionals. If the IT staff also understands where the company is going and how it plans to get there, staff members can design all IT projects to help the corporation take advantage of the opportunities and overcome the obstacles.

Choosing the Technology

The next step is to evaluate the information technologies that might be used to achieve the corporate goals. An organization like North American Air will spend considerable time exploring the available technical solutions to the business issues facing the corporation. This process should include researching the options available and doing some preliminary testing to see whether a particular technology can meet the objectives. For example, North American Air is looking for a new messaging system, but also is exploring other options that will improve the corporation's ability to organize information and make it available to a wide variety of people. During the evaluation process, the corporation should explore other messaging systems, such as Domino Server, and test other alternatives such as using a database server connected to a Web server to provide the information. The final choice of technology will come down to a single question: Which technology will best enable the company to achieve its goals?

By approaching technology evaluation from a business standpoint, a company can set realistic goals for its implementation. Over the last few decades, almost every company has gone through a major investment in a new technology, only to find that the new technology could not deliver the expected results, or to find out that achieving the goals identified for the technology would be much more expensive than originally budgeted. Sometimes the problem has been that the IT staff did not understand what problem the technology was supposed to solve. Sometimes the problem has been that the business staff did not understand the limitations of the technology. When both the IT group and the business group understand the corporate goals and the technology, the planning team for the project can set realistic goals that the new technology can help the company achieve.

The goal of this part of the project is to identify the technology that will best solve the business problems for the corporation. After evaluating the alternatives, the corporate executives must make the choice as to which technology to adopt. Once this decision has been made, the process of planning the implementation can continue.

NOTE: Many factors in addition to the purely technical questions need to be addressed when making the choice on what technology to implement. Sometimes a company has too much money or time invested in a particular technology to switch to another, better technology. The IT staff also may have a great deal of expertise using one technology, and may not want to train personnel on a new technology. Or perhaps the company's technical experts do not consider a new technology reliable enough to be adopted even though it has great promise in addressing the company's needs.

Assembling the Project Team

One of the first steps in a migration project is to form a project team to lead the corporation through the planning, design, and implementation. The initial team might be made up of a few people whose first task is to evaluate the various technologies being considered to solve the business problem, as described in the preceding section. As the project moves to the planning phase, the team will likely add additional personnel, each of whom will bring unique expertise and experience to the team.

> **NOTE:** *The team should be managed as a group of peers participating in the planning process. If all members see each other as equals, they will be empowered to act and hold each other accountable.*

For the team to be effective, the members must share the following:

▲ **An understanding of the project vision.** All members of the team must understand and commit to project goals and objectives. This vision provides a purpose for the planning group and can prevent contradictory visions from hijacking the planning process.

▲ **A commitment to the planning process.** All team members must agree to the process that is being followed. This includes being committed to understanding and solving the business problem, aligning the business goals with the technology, involving end users in the entire process, and perhaps most importantly, implementing the best possible solution.

▲ **A willingness to learn.** The team must be ready to try new technologies and procedures and participate in a constant evaluation of what was learned during the planning process.

The project team's makeup is crucial to its success in planning a migration to Windows 2000 and Exchange 2000. Table 4-1 identifies some of the roles and responsibilities that team members need to fulfill. In a smaller organization, one individual might take on multiple roles, while in a large, complex organization a small group of people might take on a single role as a mini-team.

NOTE: *All the team members should have a good understanding of Windows 2000 and Exchange 2000.*

Table 4-1: Team Members' Roles and Responsibilities

Roles	Responsibilities
Executive Sponsor (CIO)	Represents the project to the corporate decision makers Promotes business vision and goals Secures funding
Project Manager	Responsible for the overall Exchange design and implementation Develops the functional design for the project Responsible for scheduling, budget, personnel, and day-to-day project coordination
Windows 2000	
Active Directory Design	Designs the Active Directory structure Understands the implications that planning for Exchange has on Active Directory design
Networking Infrastructure Design	Designs the networking infrastructure components such as DNS, WINS, DHCP and TCP/IP
Desktop Configuration and Support	Designs group policies for desktop configuration Deals with other desktop configuration and support issues
Exchange 2000	
Messaging	Provides overall expertise in messaging design and configuration
Message Routing	Designs the message routing configuration for the Exchange organization Has extensive knowledge of SMTP configuration
Server Configuration and Optimization	Develops and implements the Exchange server hardware configuration

Table 4-1: Team Members' Roles and Responsibilities (Continued)

Roles	Responsibilities
Integration of Messaging Systems	Helps integrate Exchange with other e-mail systems such as Domino Server/Lotus Notes and MS Mail Helps migrate other e-mail systems to Exchange
Testing/Quality Assurance	Designs and manages the testing lab Performs thorough testing of all components before implementation
WAN Configuration	Develops and supports the WAN connectivity between corporate locations Analyzes the WAN traffic implications of implementing Exchange
End User E-mail Support	Designs and supports e-mail client configurations
Training	Develops a training plan for technical and end-user training
Documentation	Develops the documentation needed to implement the project Also might work with the training personnel in developing training materials
Migration	Develops the detailed plans for migrating servers to Exchange
Exchange Application Development	Designs and manages the design of custom applications for Exchange Brings extensive experience in application development to the process
Security	Designs the security configuration for the organization, including internal and Internet security
Internet Information Services	Designs the implementation of the Exchange virtual servers Designs the OWA implementation

 NOTE: *In the scenario used in this book, North American Air has not yet migrated to Windows 2000. Even if a corporation had already*

implemented Windows 2000 and Active Directory, the Windows 2000 expertise would still be required on the project team because of the tight integration between Windows 2000 and Exchange 2000.

It's essential that the team include people who are capable of filling each of these roles. If nobody is available with the needed skills in a certain area, the team leaders should look outside the organization for the required expertise, or provide training for one of the internal people.

Collecting Corporate Information

Once the project team has been assembled, it can begin to gather information about the corporation's IT and messaging infrastructure. This step is extremely important because detailed information is needed to create a detailed migration plan. The needed information includes:

▲ Corporate structure and locations

▲ Current network infrastructure

▲ Current messaging infrastructure

▲ Current business application configuration

▲ Current desktop configurations

▲ Current administrative practices

I briefly address each of these in the following sections.

Corporate Structure and Locations

The team must collect information about the corporation's physical locations. This information includes:

▲ Geographic locations

▲ Business units at each location

▲ Number of users at each location

▲ Number of remote users

▲ Number of client computers

▲ Physical layout for each location

Current Network Infrastructure

The project team also needs to collect detailed information about the current networking infrastructure at all locations. This information includes:

▲ The physical network topologies, including the LAN configurations at each location, hub or switch configurations, and backbone topology

▲ The WAN topology, including a diagram of the WAN topology, total bandwidth and available bandwidth, and router configurations

▲ The remote access configuration, including RAS servers and dial-in and VPN configurations

▲ The DHCP, WINS, and DNS configurations

▲ The Windows NT domain configuration (including trusts), or, if the network has been migrated to Windows 2000, the Active Directory configuration

▲ The conventions used for computer naming

▲ The network administration and support-management procedures, including who is responsible for managing the network infrastructure and what the current management strategies are

▲ The firewall and proxy server configurations

Current Messaging Infrastructure

The project team also needs to collect detailed information about the current messaging infrastructure. The information collected should include:

▲ The high-level Exchange messaging topology, including the site configuration, server location, message routing and site connectors, external connectors, directory replication topology, and Exchange service account for each domain

▲ Any additional messaging servers, including all configurations for the other e-mail servers that are part of the organization

▲ The messaging naming conventions, including the naming conventions for the Exchange users, other messaging users, domain names, additional addresses for specific users, X.400 naming conventions, and server and site naming conventions

▲ Detailed server configuration information, including the server hardware configuration and the messaging configuration on the server. Details for the messaging configuration include the following:

   – The server name and site name

   – The information store configuration such as mailbox size limits, maintenance schedules, circular logging, size of the information store, and so on.

   – The MTA configuration

   – The server and link monitor configuration

   – The number of mailboxes and public folders on each server

   – The backup and restore configuration and procedures

   – Distribution list details, including a list of the distribution lists and specific details such as designated servers for distribution list expansion

▲ Site connectors, including the type of site connectors and detailed information about each site connector such as the following:

   – Message scheduling

   – Bridgehead servers

   – Message size limitations

   – Address spaces configuration

    – Override account configuration

    – Directory replication connector configurations

▲ External connector details, including detailed information about all connectors to any messaging system outside of the Exchange organization. The details are similar to the list above for site connectors, but also should include the directory synchronization details.

▲ Internet mail connections details, including the details of Internet Mail Service configuration for Exchange 5.x as well as any other SMTP connectors used in the organization to send or receive Internet mail

▲ DNS mail record configuration, including all domain names used by the organization and the complete DNS MX record configuration for the mail servers

▲ E-mail usage information, including the average size of the user mailboxes on each server, the average number of messages sent and received by users on a daily basis, the number of messages sent between corporate locations and to the Internet, and any anomalies in e-mail use (for example, one business group that sends much more mail than the average)

Current Desktop Configurations

Ideally, even a large organization should have a limited number of desktop configurations. To make e-mail client implementation more efficient, the team should collect information on the following desktop configuration settings. In each case, the team should include information about how many computers would fall into a certain category and where those computers are located. The information collected should include the following:

▲ Desktop hardware configurations

▲ Operating systems currently supported

▲ Network clients and protocols

▲ Mobile computer configurations

▲ Handheld or Personal Digital Assistant (PDA) configurations

Current Administrative Practices

A successful system migration should cause only minimal disruption in network services. To achieve this goal, the team should collect detailed information about the current network and messaging administrative practices. This information should include both the people who are responsible for a certain procedure and information about the procedure. The information collected should include the following:

▲ User and group administration, including who is responsible for creating, deleting and modifying user accounts, and whether there is a standard procedure for the process

▲ Regular administrative tasks, such as information on backups, restore procedures, anti-virus software implementation, monitoring activities, and who is responsible for performing these tasks

▲ Messaging server administration, including the personnel who manage the e-mail servers, create and delete mailboxes, perform backups, monitor the information stores, and create and manage public folders

▲ Messaging routing administration and monitoring, including the personnel responsible for managing and monitoring the site connectors and the external connectors

▲ Troubleshooting procedures, including how troubleshooting issues are dealt with, what the different levels of support are, and whether there is a clearly defined process for escalating a troubleshooting issue

▲ Disaster recovery procedures, including what plans are in place to recover from a disaster, who is responsible for keeping the procedures up to date, and when the procedures were last reviewed and tested

Current Business Applications

Assessing the current business applications is especially important if the corporation is planning to implement some of them on Exchange or if a new application developed for Exchange needs to share data with one of the existing applications. For example, North American Air will want to test the possibility of migrating the current database applications to Exchange 2000. For North American Air, collecting the current application configuration is essential. Even if this component is not part of the original project plan, the team might still want to collect this information to explore the possibility or for future reference. Here is some information to include:

▲ Application server configuration, including the physical configuration and operating system configuration

▲ A description of what the application does for the organization

▲ The types of client software used to access the application

▲ Current issues, including any problems experienced with the application

Application Development with Exchange 2000

North American Air plans to explore the possibility of developing a custom application based on Exchange 2000 to replace the current database application. Exchange 2000 includes the Web Store, which can be used to store semi-structured data that can be accessed using a variety of programming techniques such as ADO or CDO. If an organization deploys an application using Exchange 2000, a variety of clients can access the application data. If the application is implemented using a public folder, users will be able to access the information through a MAPI client or through a custom interface. In addition, if the corporation implements OWA, the information in the public folders can be accessed from anywhere using a Web browser and a customized Web form. To decide whether such a custom application makes sense, the corporation would need to perform a detailed analysis of the current applications it would replace as well as explore the capability of Exchange 2000 to provide enhanced functionality. A detailed analysis of this topic is beyond the scope of this book. The focus of this book is to provide the Exchange infrastructure that would make the development of this application possible. There are several excellent resources if you need more information on developing applications for Exchange. *Exchange and Outlook: Constructing Collaborative Solutions* (New Riders Publishing) by Joel Semeniuk and Duncan MacKenzie provides an excellent overview of application development and the possibilities for using these tools to create applications to streamline business practices. *Programming Collaborative Web Applications with Microsoft Exchange 2000* (Microsoft Press) by Mindy Martin provides more specific information on application development for Exchange 2000.

The preceding sections provided a preliminary list of all the information that the project team should assemble. Essentially, they should document every piece of information that could in any way affect the migration plan.

Developing the Project Plan

One of the first tasks of the project team is to make the recommendation of what technology the corporation should use to achieve its business goals. Once the organization has made a commitment to implement a particular technology, the rest of the planning can continue. This planning begins concurrently with the information collection I outlined in the preceding section, but continues as the team uses the collected information to put together the final design.

The project plan includes a number of important documents, including:

▲ A planning and scope document

▲ A gap analysis document

▲ A risk mitigation document

I'll discuss each of these documents in the following sections.

Planning and Scope Document

The planning and scope document is a high-level document that provides the outline of the entire project. The document provides a functional overview of the issues facing the corporation and how the company can use the chosen technology to respond to the issues. The team presents this document to the corporate executives who will make the decision about whether the project will continue. Consequently, the planning document must show that the project team is aware of the corporate vision and goals, as well as the opportunities and obstacles in the way of achieving those goals. The document also must explain how the technology being considered can help the organization achieve those goals. If the project is presented in this way, it has a much better chance of getting the complete support of the top decision-makers.

> **NOTE:** *The team should initially present this document as a work-in-progress. Until the IT staff has had a chance to thoroughly test the technology, the document should not make any promises about what the technology can deliver.*

The planning and scope document also should include a preliminary budget for the project. Often the bottom line for the corporation is: "How much will it cost for us to implement this new technology?" Migrating to Exchange 2000 is an expensive process for many corporations so this is an important issue to address up front.

This document also needs to present a clear scope for the project. One single project cannot address all the company's business issues, so this document needs to clearly specify what the project is designed to accomplish as well as define the limits of what the technology can do. Defining what is *not* included in the project is almost as important at this point as defining what is included. As the design phase of a project progresses, it often becomes tempting to include more components in the project, but such additions usually mean that the project will not be done on time, or the project will not be completed within the budget. The scope document can help prevent this by clearly defining what will not be included in the project. The scope of the project also is essential when the project team is testing the technology and designing the network structure. In the testing lab, the team tests only the aspects of the technology that fall within the scope of the project. The scope also describes the boundaries of what is included in the design; this description is useful when the team designs the network structure.

Corporate decision-makers must approve the planning and scope document before any more work is done. Without executive support, the project cannot proceed. The primary job function of any executive is to ensure that the company is profitable; therefore, the planning and scope document should clearly identify how the project will improve corporate profits, at least in the long run. This is important because migrating to Windows 2000 and Exchange 2000 is expensive, especially if all the workstations also are upgraded to run Windows 2000 Professional. The company's executives control the budget, and they need to be assured of future profitability before they will approve the expenditure. Earlier in this chapter I noted that the team should include an Executive Sponsor; if this person does not have the needed decision-making authority, this person should present the document to those who do.

NOTE: The support from the corporate executives also is important to deal with resistance to the new technology. Regardless of how well a project of this magnitude is planned, there will be changes and possible disruptions for network users as the new technology is implemented. These disruptions can create some resistance to the project. Executive support is essential for overcoming the resistance.

Gap Analysis Document

The next step is to perform a *gap analysis*. A gap analysis reviews the current messaging infrastructure and envisions the ideal infrastructure, and then determines what must be done to move from one to the other. To perform the gap analysis, the team must use the detailed information about the current IT infrastructure gathered earlier. It then compares this current configuration to the final goal. The questions that the gap analysis should answer include:

▲ What components have to be changed to achieve the final goal?

▲ Will any current functionality be lost?

▲ Are there any additional functions that are important to include?

▲ Are any of the new functions more difficult or expensive to implement than others?

The gap analysis, together with the planning and scope document, can help the project team establish its priorities. The priorities for the implementation project can be based on a number of factors, including these:

▲ What parts of the project are most urgently required?

▲ What parts of the project can be implemented with the least disruption and cost, while still providing significant value to the business?

▲ What parts of the project can be implemented quickly? What parts will take longer to implement?

▲ What parts of the project will take more effort and money to implement? How much do these components add to the value of the project?

▲ Is there a chronological order that must be followed in the implementation?

NOTE: There is one example of a chronology issue: Before an administrator can install Exchange 2000, Windows 2000 Active Directory must be implemented in at least some part of the organization. There may be other issues as well, depending on the current IT structure and the proposed plan.

Risk Mitigation Document

The project team also needs to do a risk assessment for the project, documenting the possible risks in migration and proposing strategies for mitigating them. A risk assessment document looks at all the things that could possibly go wrong during the implementation of the project and presents a plan to avoid the risks or to alleviate the impact of the risks as much as possible. A project, such as rolling out

Windows 2000 and Exchange 2000, could have number of risks connected to it, including these:

▲ What if key personnel quit during the project?

▲ What if the budget is set too low?

▲ What if the technology cannot deliver the desired functionality?

▲ What if the company decides to reorganize or acquire another company during the project?

▲ If there are other ongoing IT projects in the corporation that this project depends on, what if one of them is delayed or cancelled? For example, if the company is planning to have a new WAN technology in place when the Exchange 2000 rollout takes place, what impact will a delay in the WAN project have on the implementation?

A project of this magnitude has many other risks, both big and small. The project team's goal is to minimize the likelihood that a particular problem will occur and to minimize the damage if it does occur. For example, to minimize the risk of a key person quitting during the project, the project team may propose an incentive program for the personnel who are managing the project. To minimize the damage to the project that might result from a key person quitting, the project team can make sure that several people are trained for each of the tasks and insist on thorough documentation of all current procedures and any modifications being made to the network. If other IT projects might impact the project, the risk assessment document should identify the associated projects and recommend ways to minimize the risk exposure.

The risk assessment document also should present a plan of action to implement in the event that the project exceeds budget expectations. The plan might propose alternative options for funding or outline what should be the first part of the project to be dropped in the event of a cost overrun.

NOTE: The team should find ways to encourage people to identify the risks that they see in the project plan and take those concerns seriously from the beginning rather than sweeping them under the rug. A problem that is relatively easy to fix in the planning stages can become very expensive to fix later.

Another essential component of the planning process is to begin testing the technology as soon and as thoroughly as possible. Thorough premigration testing can minimize the risk that the technology will not deliver as expected. I cover the process of setting up a test lab later in this chapter, but this is an essential part of the planning process. Without a test environment, many of the questions related to the technology's functionality simply cannot be answered.

This entire planning process should include an open exchange between technical professionals and top management. As the project team works on the plan, team members must keep the corporate decision-makers informed on the progress of the plan and milestones achieved. The process also should remain an iterative one, in which the team constantly refines and clarifies the project. For example, as the project team interviews end users, they might identify functionality that creates additional benefits for the organization. Or a new technology might become available during the planning phase that enhances or replaces the technology being evaluated. As the IT staff begins to test the technology in the test lab, they might discover additional functionality in the technology, or they might discover that the technology cannot deliver all the anticipated features. Until the final project has been approved, the project team must always be open to changes to the plan.

The project team's end product should be a detailed document outlining the entire project. It should clearly identify every step in the project and provide detailed information on the implementation of the technology. For a large and complicated project, such as implementing Windows 2000 and Exchange 2000, the planning process might continue even as some parts of the plan are being implemented. As the first part of the project design is finished, the testing and implementation of that part of the project can begin. Often the first implementations provide valuable feedback to the planning process for later components of the project.

NOTE: *The next chapter provides an overview of what the planning document might look like as it describes the design decisions made at North American Air.*

North American Air Business Issues

North American Air is a successful company that over the last few years has identified a clear corporate vision as well as a strategy to achieve that vision. Led by an aggressive board and CEO, North American Air has developed a vision to become a world leader in aircraft maintenance and aircraft manufacturing parts sales. A secondary goal is to expand the airfreight business. To achieve this vision, North American Air plans to continue expanding by buying additional aircraft maintenance and manufacturing companies that complement its current manufacturing capability. In particular, North American Air would like to expand its corporate presence to other parts of the world outside of North America.

In addition to the expansion, North American Air also plans to enhance its reputation as a corporation that provides superb customer service. To do this, North American Air must optimize its information flow throughout the organization. Any person in the organization with sufficient permissions should be able to check the availability of any aircraft component, or check the progress of any aircraft's maintenance report regardless of where the maintenance is taking place. In particular, the external salespeople should be able to access this information quickly from virtually anywhere in the world. In addition, airfreight customer representatives should be able to check the status of any airfreight being shipped throughout the continent.

Several IT-related concerns arise out of the corporate vision and goals:

▲ The company currently uses a variety of custom business applications, and some of the information stored in these applications is not easily accessible to all.

▲ As the company expands further, it will be difficult to integrate additional domains into the current infrastructure. In particular, the current trust configuration is already quite unwieldy.

▲ The cost of supporting the current IT infrastructure is rising due to the following:

  – The lack of an organization-wide corporate standard.

  – Aging and inefficient desktop computer and server hardware.

  – The need to support multiple e-mail systems.

  – The high cost of supporting many medium-sized servers.

  – The IT infrastructure has not adapted well to the corporate expansion, so an important requirement for any new technology must be that it be able to adapt to changing situations with minimal disruption and effort.

To respond to these concerns, and to ensure that the IT infrastructure assists the corporation in achieving its goals, the project group has identified the following issues as the primary focus for evaluation as it explores the migration to Windows 2000 and Exchange 2000:

▲ Reconfiguring the Windows NT domain structure

▲ Using Exchange 2000 to manage information flow

▲ Using Outlook Web Access to make information on the Exchange servers more accessible

▲ Decreasing support costs by decreasing the number of servers and by developing a single corporate messaging system

▲ Accommodating future corporate growth

I discuss these issues in the following sections.

Windows 2000 Domain Structure

The current configuration of Windows NT domains is becoming difficult to manage, and will become increasingly more difficult as North American Air expands and acquires more companies. The corporation did explore the possibility of moving all user accounts into a single account domain in Dallas and then configuring all other domains as resource domains with one-way trusts. However, each location already has a set of skilled administrators with a history of managing all aspects of their domain, so the company would like to explore other options. The Windows 2000 domain structure looks like it will solve the trust issues while still leaving considerable control in the hands of the local administrators. The project team is considering the implementation of a single tree with multiple child domains.

Organizing and Managing Information Using Exchange 2000

The second issue facing North American Air is the efficiency with which the company shares information among locations. The custom applications that worked well when the organization consisted of just the Texas and Winnipeg locations are not proving to be flexible enough to integrate with the applications in use at the more recently acquired locations.

One of the organization's overall goals is to make all the mission-critical information easily accessible from many locations. The project team needs to evaluate whether Exchange 2000's enhanced collaborative solutions can help achieve this goal. Exchange 2000 provides many ways to access and manipulate data in the information store, so the project team should examine the possibility that the business applications that are currently implemented on database servers can be implemented on the Exchange servers instead. If the applications can be implemented in Exchange, the manufacturing and maintenance information on the Exchange servers will be easily accessible to all users through their e-mail client.

In addition, the project team also should evaluate the possibility of using the real-time collaboration tools available with Exchange. Instant messaging and chat services provide options for instant communication throughout the organization. Conferencing services enable online meeting hosting, which can potentially decrease the amount of travel required for corporate executives and increase the opportunities for information exchange.

Outlook Web Access

If the company implements the business applications in Exchange, remote users can access information through a Web browser by using Outlook Web Access (OWA). OWA provides remote users with a single interface for sending and receiving e-mail and accessing the business applications. Exchange 2000's enhancements to OWA provide remote users with application access through a Web form, which uses a public folder on the Exchange servers to store data.

To implement OWA securely, North American Air can use Secure Sockets Layer (SSL) to encrypt all business traffic between the remote users and the OWA servers. However, SSL encryption negatively affects server performance, so the project team needs to test performance levels on a front-end/back-end server configuration with and without SSL in the testing lab.

Consolidating Servers

Because Exchange 2000 can partition the information store into multiple storage groups and stores, more mailboxes can be located on a single server. Splitting up the information store also means that individual stores can be restored more quickly. To take advantage of this enhancement, North American Air will consolidate some of its medium-sized servers into a smaller number of more powerful servers.

The project team should use the test lab to confirm the enhanced scalability of the Exchange 2000 servers. The first step in this testing would be to define a corporate standard outlining acceptable performance levels for the Exchange servers. The acceptable performance standards should include items such as client response times and the amount of time that it should take to rebuild a server in a disaster recovery situation. The project team can then use these performance levels to determine how many mailboxes can be stored on a server and how large the information stores can be. In addition, the project team can determine the optimal hard disk configuration for the

Exchange servers by testing several different options. At the end of the testing, the project team should develop a corporate standard, detailing the number of mailboxes that can be supported on each server and the optimal server configuration.

Lowering Support Costs

Windows 2000 Active Directory provides a number of options to help the North American Air lower support costs. By grouping the users and computers in each location into Organizational Units (OUs), the administrators can centralize desktop management using group policies. Standardizing all the desktops on Windows 2000 Professional with a common set of applications means that the support staff has to support only a single configuration. The project team should test a potential Active Directory configuration in the testing lab to plan the optimal group policy and client configuration.

Implementing Exchange 2000 throughout the organization also should lower support costs. By migrating the Domino Server/Lotus Notes and MS Mail servers to Exchange 2000, the corporation benefits from having to support only a single e-mail server platform, with no inter-organization connectors. As part of the migration to Exchange 2000, the project team also should test several e-mail clients to determine which should be the new company standard.

Future Growth

Throughout the planning phase, the project team needs to keep the corporate goal of continued expansion in mind. Whatever the final configuration looks like, it must be easily extendable to include additional features and additional companies.

NOTE: Some of the advantages listed in the preceding sections are reasons to move to Windows 2000, not necessarily to Exchange 2000. There are many good reasons to determine the advantages of both migrations, but the focus of this book is on the planning and implementation of Exchange 2000. While the next two chapters do discuss migration to Windows 2000, my goal is to provide you with an understanding of the process rather than to provide detailed procedures for the migration to Windows 2000.

Developing a Test Environment

Developing and managing a test environment is an essential part of the planning process. The test lab is used to test all aspects of the Exchange implementation before the actual rollout. Every implementation of Exchange is different, so a company must test whether the specifications outlined for generic implementations also apply to its situation. In this section, I explain how a project team, such as the one for North American Air, can set up and utilize one or more testing labs.

Purpose of the Test Environment

Why create a test environment? There are four reasons:

▲ **To provide an environment in which the network administrators can learn a new technology.** Windows 2000 and Exchange 2000 are different from their predecessors, and network administrators need a place to learn. While a classroom can provide valuable training, a classroom provides a generic, fail-safe environment. In a test lab, administrators work with a configuration that more closely matches their own network. The test lab also provides a safe place in which to make mistakes. People often learn the most by making a mistake and then fixing it. In a test lab, this is a natural part of the process.

▲ **To test all of the components that might become part of the actual deployment.** The initial project plan should list many components that might be of value to the corporation, but until administrators test the actual implementation of the components, they cannot confirm that the components meet company requirements. For example, suppose that a company wants to implement OWA. To test this, administrators would implement an OWA configuration in the lab and test it based on current specifications. One of the most valuable parts of such testing might be to determine ways to optimize the implementation. If the OWA implementation includes many servers with thousands of clients, administrators might test a variety of front-end/back-end server configurations to determine what works best. In addition, as each component is being tested, the administrators are gaining valuable experience with the product.

▲ **To provide an ongoing training and test environment.** Many companies find it advantageous to maintain a basic test environment even after the initial implementation. A company can use a test lab to train new employees or to provide updated training for existing employees. They also can use the test lab to test new releases of software, including service packs and patches. If the corporation is developing its own applications, the test lab is a valuable place to test the applications in an environment that closely matches the production environment. The test lab also provides a natural environment in which to practice disaster recovery procedures, or to confirm that a server backup worked by performing a test restore. Administrators also can use a test computer to perform painful tasks, such as recovering a mailbox that has been accidentally deleted or recovering a specific e-mail message that exists only on a backup tape.

▲ **To provide a demonstration and test platform for end users who will be using the technology.** Successful migration requires buy-in from the end users, not just the administrators. The test lab is a good place to expose the end users to the new technology and give them a chance to see how the new technology will make them more efficient at their jobs.

Test Environment Configuration

The test environment should duplicate the corporate production environment as closely as possible while still operating completely separately. This means that the lab should match the production environment in the following ways:

▲ **Domain structure.** If the organization also is testing the migration to Windows 2000, the lab should duplicate the current Windows NT domain structure. It also should be able to duplicate the domain structure of the final Windows 2000 Active Directory implementation.

▲ **Exchange organization and site configurations.** It's important to test the message flow between different parts of the organization in Exchange, so the test environment should include multiple locations. Administrators can then test the traffic generated between the sites (or routing groups) and the configuration of the various routing group connectors.

▲ **Interoperability configurations.** If the corporate network includes multiple network operating systems or multiple messaging servers, these should be included in the test environment.

▲ **External connectors.** The test environment should include any current external messaging connectors to the Internet or other e-mail systems.

▲ **Server hardware configurations.** As much as possible, the testing lab should duplicate the server hardware in the production environment. This serves two important purposes: It can confirm the functionality of the actual hardware, including options such as backup hardware and software, and it can test the server performance using the actual server.

▲ **Networking infrastructure components.** The test lab should include DNS, WINS, DHCP, firewalls, and proxy servers with similar configurations to the corporate configuration.

▲ **LAN/WAN topologies.** The test environment should duplicate the LAN technologies used in each location. This could include the physical topologies (Ethernet, Token Ring) as well as the hub, switch, and router configurations. To test the WAN configuration, administrators can configure test labs in two or more locations and use the existing WAN links to test the WAN performance. A second option is to simulate the WAN link in a single testing lab. Having multiple test labs allows administrators in other locations to participate in the testing. Simulating the WAN topology in the lab isolates the test environment from the production environment, producing results that are more precise and eliminating the danger of negatively affecting the production environment.

▲ **Client desktop configurations.** The lab should duplicate as many of the client configurations as possible.

▲ **Administrative configurations.** If the production environment includes options, such as system policies or OUs and group policies, administrators should implement them in the testing environment as well.

The lab testing changes as the project changes. The initial lab should duplicate the current corporate environment as closely as possible. However, as the testing progresses, the lab should increasingly resemble the final goal of the migration. For example, a company might start out with only Exchange 4.0/5.x servers in the lab, then move to a mixed environment in which they have both Exchange 4.0/5.x and Exchange 2000 servers, and then do the last major testing in an environment that includes only Exchange 2000 servers.

When setting up a test environment, the planning team should appoint a testing manager or coordinator to oversee the lab and implement an effective change control process. The testing coordinator also needs to implement some means of sharing the information that is collected in the test lab with all project participants. For a project as complex as migrating to Windows 2000 and Exchange 2000, many different groups will use the test lab and perform many different tests. The testing manager maintains a testing schedule that clearly identifies who is using the test lab and what changes the tests are making to the lab configuration. For accurate test results, it is essential that the lab state remain consistent and predictable. For example, one group might be testing the Exchange implementation while another group is testing Active Directory configurations. Installing Exchange introduces almost 1,000 changes to the Active Directory schema, including many changes to the global catalog and configuration containers. If the Active Directory group does not know about the changes made by the Exchange group, the test results will not be reliable.

One way to ensure consistency is to use a backup system or disk-cloning software to create snapshots of the lab at various stages. For example, after configuring the lab to match the current corporate configuration, the testing manager might save the beginning configuration for each computer on a backup tape, or clone the disk and save the drive image on a server hard disk. Then, as the testing progresses, testers can save the configuration again at certain milestones. For example, it might be advantageous to save the configuration after the migration to Windows 2000 and Active Directory, and again right after the Exchange server installation. Each group using the lab can save its configuration at the end of a testing period, so that it can be easily restored when the group gets access to the lab again. This process makes it easy and fast to restore the lab to a particular point.

After planning and implementing the test lab, the next step is to carefully plan the actual tests to perform. This step is as important as setting up the lab because even the perfect test environment cannot provide good results if the tests are not well designed. Before starting a test, the administrator running it should create a test document. This document should clearly identify what is being tested, the starting point for the testing, and the expected result of the test. For example, if an administrator wants to test the implementation and performance of a distributed server configuration for OWA, his test document should clearly identify how the servers should be configured at the beginning of the test. Then he should document how he plans to change the server configuration and how he will be testing the server configuration. The document also should identify the information he expects to gather from the testing.

Some tests are designed to isolate and test a particular component of Exchange 2000. If an administrator wants to test only OWA, she should make sure that nothing else in the testing environment is interfering with the test. Other tests are designed to test the integration of multiple components. For example, an administrator might test the performance of a back-end server in the OWA configuration while the server also is receiving multiple requests from MAPI clients on the network. She also might test the performance of a connector server using a single routing group connector, or when the server also is operating as an Internet mail server. Another test might be to evaluate the performance of a connector server and measure the effect of putting several hundred mailboxes on the server.

Configuring a test lab that can be used to thoroughly test the implementation is expensive and requires a significant time commitment. Ideally, the equipment used in the test environment should be built or purchased to match the desired corporate standard for all components, so that most of the lab computers can eventually be reused in the production environment after the test is complete. While creating and maintaining a test environment is costly, it is inexpensive compared to the potential risk cost of an untested system migration.

The North American Air Test Environment

Early in the process of planning the migration to Exchange 2000, North American Air implemented a test lab to begin testing the new technologies. At first the lab was used to gain some basic experience with Windows 2000 and Exchange 2000. As the planning progressed, administrators used the lab to thoroughly test the options in the project plan and to validate all components.

The management at North American Air decided to provide enough hardware for each corporate location to create its own small Windows 2000 and Exchange 2000 lab. The goal was to provide an environment in which the network administrators in all locations could begin working with the new technologies without impacting the corporate network. Several administrators also received formal training in the new technologies.

As the project progressed, the company set up a more formal testing lab at the corporate headquarters. This lab was used to explore the new product enhancements and test both Windows 2000 and Exchange 2000. The company appointed a test lab manager and implemented a formal testing plan and schedule. After thorough testing in the lab in the Dallas corporate office was complete, North American Air expanded the test to include a lab at Winnipeg. They chose Winnipeg because it is the largest location outside of Texas and because it will be the first domain migrated to Windows 2000 and Exchange 2000. Expanding the test to an additional location gave the test team the opportunity to test the effect of Exchange 2000 on the WAN links between Winnipeg and Dallas.

The formal testing lab in Dallas was configured to match the corporate environment as closely as possible. Figure 4-1 and Table 4-2 provide the details of the testing configuration.

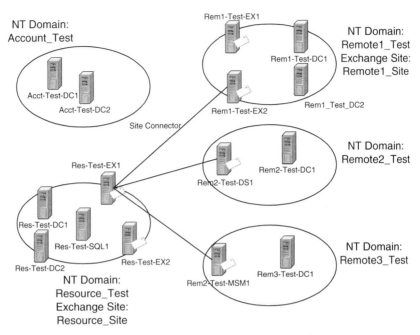

Figure 4-1: The Test Lab Configuration at North American Air.

Table 4-2: Test Lab Server Configuration at North American Air

Server Name	Server Function
Acct-Test-DC1	Primary domain controller for Account_Test domain
Acct-Test-DC2	Backup domain controller for Account_Test domain
Res-Test-DC1	Primary domain controller for Resource_Test domain
Res-Test-DC2	Backup domain controller for Resource_Test domain
Rem1-Test-DC1	Primary domain controller for Remote1_Test domain
Rem1-Test-DC2	Backup domain controller for Remote1_Test domain
Rem2-Test-DC1	Primary domain controller for Remote2_Test domain
Rem3-Test-DC1	Primary domain controller for Remote3_Test domain
Res-Test-Ex1	Exchange server in Resource_Site, connector server to other sites, Lotus Notes connector, connector for MS Mail
Res-Test-Ex2	Exchange server in Resource_Site, Mailbox server

Table 4-2: Test Lab Server Configuration at North American Air (Continued)

Server Name	Server Function
Res-Test-SQL1	SqlAnywhere server in Resource_Test domain, loaded with the business applications
Rem1-Test-Ex2	Exchange server in Remote1_Site, connector server to Resource_Site
Rem1-Test-Ex1	Exchange server in Remote1_Site, Mailbox server
Rem2-Test-DS1	Domino server in Remote2_Test domain
Rem3-Test-MSM1	MSMail server in Remote3_Test domain

> **NOTE:** *Because North American Air is testing the migration to Windows 2000 and Exchange 2000 at the same time, the test lab includes multiple domain controllers in several domains. If your company has already migrated to Windows 2000, you could use a single domain controller in some of the domains.*

The trusts were configured to correspond to the trusts in North American Air. Test administrators configured a two-way trust between each of the remote domains and the account domain, and a one-way trust from the Account_Test, Remote1_Test, and Remote2_Test (trusted domains) with the Resource_Test (trusting domain).

To create the accounts on the domain controllers and mailboxes on the e-mail servers, the lab manager created a set of scripts that create 2000 accounts and mailboxes in the Resource_Test and Remote1_Test domains. The Domino Server and MS Mail Server also were configured with mailboxes equivalent to those in the actual North American Air domain. As an alternative to using the scripts, the lab manager could have used a backup tape from the actual production servers in North American Air and created the lab using the same domain and computer names as the production environment and then just restored the data and the configuration from tape. (In that case, the test lab would have had to be completely isolated from the production environment for the entire testing period.) However, because North American Air planned to expand the test lab to include other locations where the WAN connections will be shared, the lab manager decided to create a fresh test environment.

In addition to the servers, each domain also included a variety of client computers, including Windows 95, Windows 98, and Windows NT Workstation. The client computers were loaded with the client applications used on the network.

The first part of the testing at North American Air was devoted to testing the migration from Windows NT to Windows 2000. They tested a variety of migration paths and tools as well as a number of possible Active Directory configurations. Testing also explored the client configuration and support options available with Active Directory. In addition, the team tested the configuration options for the Active Directory connector, which operates as the connection between the Exchange 4.0/5.x directory and Active Directory for the entire migration period. The lab also was used to test a variety of network infrastructure configurations, including DNS, DHCP, and WINS. For most of the tests, these components were implemented on one of the domain controllers. However, when the test was designed to specifically test the performance of these components, additional servers were added to the lab environment for that particular test.

Once the project team was comfortable with the Windows 2000 migration testing, the next step was to test the migration to Exchange 2000. Again, they tested a variety of approaches, including the effects that different Windows 2000 Active Directory configurations might have on the Exchange 2000 implementation. A crucial part of this testing was to test the interoperability between Exchange 4.0/5.x and Exchange 2000. The entire migration of North American Air to Exchange 2000 was projected to take more than a year, so testing how well the different e-mail systems interoperate with each other was an essential part of the testing procedure.

After the lab team thoroughly tested the migration to Exchange 2000, the next phase was to test Exchange's performance and scalability options. To test this, the lab team used tools such as LoadSim to create a load on the Exchange servers to test the individual servers and the flow of messages between the servers. At that point, they installed more Exchange servers in the test environment to test additional options such as OWA and remote user connectivity. They used the lab to test the Exchange sever interaction with domain controllers, global catalog servers, and VPNs.

> **NOTE:** *LoadSim is available for download from the Microsoft Exchange site. Although LoadSim was developed to test the scalability of Exchange 5.x servers, it also can be used to test Exchange 2000 servers. The LoadSim tool uses a MAPI client to connect to the Exchange server and then simulates the load that a configured number of users would put on the server.*

An essential testing component for North American Air was the testing of applications for Exchange 2000. Early in the planning and testing process, they configured a separate lab devoted to application testing. This lab started out as a single Exchange 2000 server in a single domain. As the application was developed, administrators expanded the application-testing lab to include multiple Exchange servers and domains, as well as OWA servers. As the application neared completion, they implemented it in the primary test lab, where they could test it in an environment closely modeled on the anticipated production network after migration.

Conclusion

This chapter provided an overview of the planning process that an organization such as North American Air goes through as it prepares to migrate to Exchange 2000. It began by discussing the importance of developing a corporate vision and goals and then using the technology to help the corporation achieve the goals. Then the chapter discussed the make-up of a project team, the information the team must gather, and the planning documents the team must draft, including a project overview, gap analysis, and risk mitigation plan. The last part of the chapter discussed the importance of having a testing lab and how such a lab should be configured.

The next chapter presents the next step of the process, which is the design phase. The planning process has produced a planning document, a high-level document identifying general concepts and components of the migration process. The design phase focuses on the detailed design of Active Directory domains and sites and the Exchange organization. The next chapter describes the project plan developed for North American Air detailing the migration process that the company will follow as North American Air moves toward adopting the new technology.

Chapter 5

Completing the Planning Process

THE MIGRATION PROJECT TEAM'S FINAL PROJECT in an organization such as North American Air is a document that details the migration process for the entire corporation. This document, which can take months to complete, details the major components and milestones for the project and describes all the steps needed to complete the migration.

This chapter provides an overview of North American Air's final planning document. The planning in this chapter is not as detailed as would be required in an actual project plan, but instead presents a high-level view of the planning involved, with particular focus on *why* a particular decision is made. Detailed information about the implementation process follows in later chapters.

The first section of this chapter describes North American Air's Windows 2000 Active Directory deployment plan. With previous versions of Exchange, Windows NT domain planning and Exchange planning could happen almost in isolation from each other. As a result, Exchange administrators had little input into the domain design, and did not always understand all the details. However, Exchange 2000 uses Active Directory as its directory services component, and therefore the domain design is much more important in Exchange 2000. Many of you, as Exchange administrators, have not worked with domain design before and have not been exposed to the basics of Active Directory. Therefore, this chapter reviews the basic components of Active Directory and then focuses on the implications for the Exchange implementation for each component.

The second part of the chapter details the Exchange 2000 deployment planning. The project team must make many decisions as it implements Exchange 2000, such as determining the basic structure of the administrative and routing groups and the server locations. Again, this chapter focuses on the deployment decisions to be made rather than on the actual technology implementation.

> **NOTE:** *The first part of this chapter goes into some detail on Windows 2000 Active Directory concepts and planning. If you are familiar with this information, you can skim through this section and move quickly to the section on the Exchange design issues.*

Windows 2000 Deployment Planning

The migration process at North American Air consists of two main activities: migrating the existing Windows NT network to Windows 2000, and migrating the existing Exchange 5.5 organization to Exchange 2000. The two migration plans are separate, but decisions made in one plan affect the other. For example, the Active Directory structure must be planned prior to migration to Windows 2000, and this structure impacts the Exchange 2000 implementation.

> **NOTE:** *Planning for Windows 2000 migration is a major project on its own. It includes many components, one of which is Active Directory planning. This chapter focuses on Active Directory structure planning because it has a great impact on Exchange migration planning.*

Should You Migrate to Windows 2000 and Exchange 2000 at the Same Time?

"It depends…". This is my standard response whenever people ask me planning-related questions. Planning questions rarely have simple answers and require a great deal of background information to answer correctly.

To answer this question, there are a number of related questions that you need to answer first:

▲ **What are the most urgent requirements in your organization?** This question goes back to why you are migrating in the first place. If the primary goal in migrating is to take advantage of the benefits provided by Windows 2000, then you should complete the migration to Windows 2000 first and work on Exchange 2000. If the primary goal for the migration is to take advantage of some new feature in Exchange 2000, you can migrate part of the organization to Windows 2000 Active Directory and then begin the migration to Exchange 2000. Exchange 2000 provides many benefits for North American Air, so migrating to both Windows 2000 and Exchange 2000 at the same time is the right decision for them.

▲ **Are you planning to migrate to Exchange 2000 in the near future?** If you know that you will be moving to Exchange 2000 soon, at least the planning portions of the two migrations should be integrated. Some of the decisions you make when designing Active Directory are influenced by the choice to implement Exchange.

▲ **Do you have the personnel to manage two projects at the same time?** If you are migrating one part of your organization to Windows 2000 while at the same time migrating another part to Exchange 2000, you need at least two highly skilled teams to manage the migrations, plus personnel to continue to support the existing network. If you do not have the personnel to manage two complicated projects along with your regular operations, take it one step at a time.

▲ **What is your timeline?** Do you have enough time to perform the migrations sequentially? Large organizations can take many months or even years to complete a migration project, so if you perform the migrations sequentially, it will be a long time before everyone experiences the benefit of the new technology.

Performing both migrations at the same time requires many people dedicated to the task. As a general rule, the smaller the company, the more likely it is that the migration should be done separately. If you have a single domain, it is relatively quick to upgrade the domain to Windows 2000 Active Directory and then begin the Exchange migration. If you have many domains and locations, however, and you require the enhancements offered by Exchange, you can begin the migration by upgrading one domain to Windows 2000 and then beginning the migration to Exchange 2000 in that domain while the migration to Windows 2000 continues in another domain.

Active Directory Planning

Windows 2000 marks a dramatic departure from Windows NT in the way that a network is organized and administered. With Active Directory, Windows 2000 has moved away from a flat directory structure with scalability limitations, to a hierarchical directory structure that can be scaled to almost any size. This new directory structure has a great impact on all network systems, including Exchange 2000.

This section presents a brief discussion of Active Directory concepts and planning practices and explains the implications of Active Directory design for Exchange planning.

Domains

Domains are still the basic building blocks for the directory structure. A domain in Windows 2000 Active Directory refers to a group of objects, such as computers and users, that share a common directory database. The domain also serves as a security boundary so that permissions, policies, and trusts are configured at a domain level and do not automatically transfer to other domains. Because a domain is a logical grouping, it can span more than one physical location; actual physical configuration of the network has limited impact on domain design. Domains use DNS naming; for example, the domain name for North American Air might be NA-Air.com.

Most organizations can implement their networks using a single Active Directory domain. A single domain can theoretically contain several million objects, but a realistic limit when implementing a domain is 100,000 users per domain.

There are a number of advantages to using a single domain. First, it requires only one team of domain administrators. Each additional domain requires an additional domain administrator group. Second, it requires only one group of domain controllers. Additional domains require more domain controllers, resulting in extra costs. For example, if you set up a single domain with 5,000 users, you could use two domain controllers. (The second controller is for redundancy.) Creating two domains would require at least four domain controllers. Third, it makes it easier to make changes when users move within the company. Moving users from one domain to another is a much more difficult task than moving the users between OUs.

You should use a single domain in Active Directory unless there are good reasons to implement multiple domains. Here are some reasons to implement multiple domains:

▲ **To decentralize administration.** In a single domain, the Domain Admins group has complete administrative control over the entire domain. Some organizations might need separate administrative control for different parts of the company; you can achieve this by implementing multiple domains.

▲ **To isolate domain replication traffic.** If a slow network link connects two locations, you might not want the replication traffic between the domain controllers to cross that slow link. To circumvent this, you can create two separate domains, so that only the global catalog replication traffic crosses the link.

▲ **To separate two locations with large numbers of users in each location.** Even if the network connection between two locations is relatively fast, the replication traffic between locations with large user populations can still be significant. If the domain contains many objects — over 100,000 or so — you should look at multiple domains.

▲ **To define separate domain-level policies.** Some policies, such as account policies, can be configured only at a domain level. If the organization requires multiple policies at this level, you must create multiple domains.

▲ **To deal with differing requirements for different countries.** International organizations might need to separate administration due to language or business practice differences.

▲ **To make the migration from an existing multiple domain NT 4.0 network easier.** The easiest way to upgrade an existing NT domain structure is to upgrade each NT domain into a Windows 2000 domain.

▲ **To minimize the potential effects of disaster.** Active Directory is designed to be fault-tolerant, but disasters can still occur. For example, if an administrator accidentally deletes a large organizational unit with thousands of users, and this change is replicated to all the domain controllers in the organization before the error is detected, restoring the OU from a backup tape and replicating the information throughout the domain would take a significant amount of time. Using multiple domains decreases the scale of such a situation.

Trees

When an Active Directory structure contains multiple domains, one of the options is to form a tree of domains. A *tree* is a group of domains under a single root. Figure 5-1 illustrates an Active Directory tree.

Active Directory trees have the following characteristics:

▲ **All domains in the tree share a common and contiguous namespace.** In other words, the root domain name is identical for all domains. For example, if you configure an additional domain in the NA-Air.com domain, it is assigned a name like Winnipeg.NA-Air.com.

▲ **All domains share a common schema.** The schema is the configuration information for Active Directory that defines what types of objects can be created in Active Directory and what properties each object can be assigned.

▲ **All domains share a common global catalog.** The global catalog is a subset of the information in each Active Directory domain database. Every object that exists in any domain in the forest also exists in the global catalog database. However, only some of the properties for each object are replicated to the global catalog. The first server to be installed in a forest is the only default global catalog server in the forest, but other domain controllers can be configured as global catalog servers too.

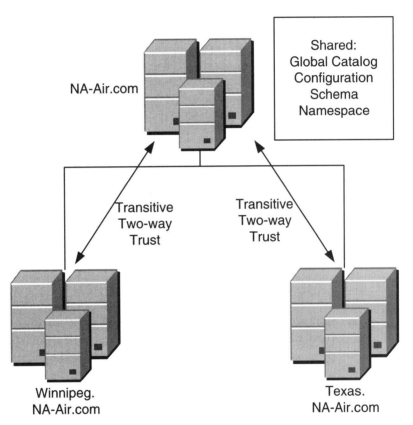

Figure 5-1: An Active Directory Tree.

▲ **All domains have an automatic two-way transitive trust relationship with all other domains in the tree.** This is an important change from Windows NT, in which trusts had to be manually configured and were always one-way, nontransitive trusts. When you install a child domain in a tree, it is automatically configured with a two-way transitive trust with the parent domain. A transitive trust creates a trust path that includes all the domains that trust a common domain. For example, if Winnipeg.NA-Air.com trusts the parent domain (NA-Air.com), and Texas.NA-Air.com trusts the same parent domain, the Winnipeg domain and the Texas domain also trust each other. This makes assigning permissions across domains much easier than in Windows NT, and users can log on to their home domain from any of the other domains.

▲ **Each of the domains in the tree is a parent domain, a child domain, or both.** At the top of the tree is the *root domain*, which is the parent domain for each child domain created below it. Each child domain can have only one parent domain, but parent domains can have multiple child domains. A child domain also can be a parent domain for a child domain created below it. There are no theoretic limitations to how many layers the domain structure can contain in Active Directory. However, you should limit the number of domain levels in the tree because of the length of time it could take to traverse a trust path if you have many domain levels. When you log on to a domain that is not your home domain, the domain controller you are logging on to must determine that a trust path exists to your home domain. This path is traversed from child domain to parent domain, up to the root of the tree, and then from parent to child domain until a trust path is established to your home domain.

▲ **Although each domain is connected to other domains in its tree, there is a definite boundary between domains.** For example, domain-level policies, such as password policies, apply only within the domain in which they were created. Domain controllers replicate complete domain information only with other domain controllers in the domain. In addition, domain administrative permissions are applied at the domain level. Even though you have domain administration permissions in your domain, you do not have any permissions in other domains unless those permissions have been explicitly granted to you.

NOTE: *When you install the first domain in an organization, you create a domain, a tree, and a forest. The simplest tree configuration is a single domain, and the simplest forest configuration is single* *domain in a single tree. Installing the first domain controller creates the schema and configuration partitions that become the standard for the entire forest.*

If your organization decides to implement a tree of domains, you must then decide how to configure the root domain. The root domain can be implemented using two different models.

The first is to create an empty or dedicated root domain that does not contain any user or computer accounts (other than the built-in accounts) and serves primarily as a placeholder for the root domain name. This scenario might be implemented if two companies merged and decided that they wanted to use a single DNS name, but continue to operate as separate companies with completely separate network administration and corporate identities. In this case, you could create an empty root domain with the common DNS name and create a child domain for each company. This model also might appeal to organizations migrating domains from NT 4.0 in which none of the domains could logically be created as the root domain.

This first model has a number of advantages. One is that only the root domain contains the Enterprise Admins and Schema Admins groups. These groups have a great deal of power throughout the entire tree. The Enterprise Admins group is automatically part of every Domain Admins group in every domain in the tree, and therefore has administrative rights throughout the tree. The Schema Admins group is the only group that has the right to change the schema for the tree. Because these groups are so powerful, you need to strictly control membership in the groups. When these groups are located in a separate domain — such as the root domain — they are easier to administer. A second advantage is that you can easily replicate the root domain to multiple locations because it is essentially empty. Additionally, a well-chosen root domain never becomes obsolete and never needs to be changed. A final advantage is that this model might be the best political option in a company that cannot agree on which part of the company should form the root domain.

There are two disadvantages to this model. First, all the DNS names and domain names become longer because of the addition of a root domain name. Second, the empty root domain is still a domain that requires domain controllers and some administrative effort. Because of the importance of this domain, you must have at least two domain controllers in case of computer failure. You might even want to have domain controllers in multiple locations to protect against network failure.

> **NOTE:** *The root domain in a tree (and in a forest) is an extremely important domain even if it is empty. If the root domain is ever destroyed with no way to recover it, you have to rebuild the entire tree structure. At this point there is no way to promote another domain to be the root domain, or to join existing domains to a new root domain.*

The second model is to use one of the regular domains that includes user, group, and computer objects. This might be a good choice for organizations that have one central location with multiple branch offices or locations. In this case, the root domain might contain most of the users and resources and require the most administration.

The advantage of this model is that there is no extra domain to administer. If an organization's corporate structure follows the head office/branch office structure, creating child domains at the branch offices is useful in clearly identifying users and resources by their branch locations. In addition, the DNS namespace also is shorter at the root domain, which, as mentioned earlier, might contain most of the users.

Forests

A second option when creating a group of domains is to form a forest. A *forest* is a collection of trees that do not share a contiguous namespace but do share a common schema and global catalog and participate in trust relationships. Figure 5-2 illustrates an Active Directory forest. Forests have the following characteristics:

▲ **The trees in a forest do not share a contiguous namespace**. For example, if North American Air wanted to configure a completely separate tree structure for the airfreight business, they could use a name, such as NA-Freight.com, as shown in

Figure 5-2. This domain could be in the same forest as NA-Air.com, but because it has a different namespace, it would have to be a separate tree.

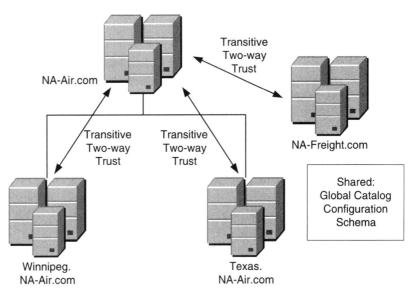

NA-Air.com

Transitive Two-way Trust

NA-Freight.com

Shared:
Global Catalog
Configuration
Schema

Transitive
Two-way
Trust

Transitive
Two-way
Trust

Winnipeg.
NA-Air.com

Texas.
NA-Air.com

Figure 5-2: An Active Directory Forest.

▲ **The first domain installed in the forest is the forest's root domain.** Only the first domain contains the Enterprise Admins group and the group that has administrative rights throughout the forest. You cannot remove the root domain from the forest. If the root domain is ever lost, you must rebuild the entire forest.

▲ **All domain controllers in the forest share a common schema.** One of the reasons to create multiple trees is to separate two parts of an organization. However, any changes made to the schema (such as installing Exchange 2000) are replicated throughout the entire forest.

▲ **All domain controllers in the forest receive a common Active Directory configuration container.** The *configuration container* is one of the partitions in Active Directory; it contains configuration information for the entire forest. For example, the configuration container stores information about sites and domains; domain controllers use this information to automatically configure replication connections. You can design an application to write information to the configuration container; that information is then accessible on all domain controllers in the forest. Exchange 2000 also writes configuration information to the configuration container in Active Directory.

▲ **A transitive two-way trust is established between the root domains for all the trees in the forest.** That means that all domains in the forest participate in this trust, and users and groups from any domain can be included in the ACL of any object in the forest.

▲ **The domains share a single global catalog.** This enables fast and efficient searching of the entire forest. The global catalog makes the domain and tree structure almost irrelevant to users who are looking for resources anywhere in the forest. By using one consistent interface, such as the Find option in My Network Places in Windows 2000, a user can search an entire forest without being aware of the underlying Active Directory design.

▲ **The global catalog enables users to log on to any domain in the forest.** When a user logs on using her user principal name (UPN) (for example, Alias@NA-Air.com), the global catalog determines in which domain the user's account resides and passes the authentication to that domain.

NOTE: UPNs are useful for logging on in a multi-domain or multi-forest environment. By using a UPN, a user can log on to any domain in the forest without regard for his home domain name. If the UPNs are the same as the users' e-mail addresses, you can direct users to log on using their e-mail address and they can log on anywhere in the entire forest.

Need for more than one namespace is the most common reason that an organization might implement a forest of multiple trees. A single tree is scalable to any size by adding more child domains, but all the domains become part of the root domain namespace. If you need more than one DNS name, you must create separate trees.

Multiple Forests
In some cases, an organization also might decide to implement multiple forests. When an organization implements multiple forests, no information is shared between the forests. One of the advantages of using multiple forests is that each forest can have different schema. However, no trusts are automatically created between the forests and the forest cannot share global catalog information. You can configure trusts between domains in separate forests, but the trusts are one-way and nontransitive.

Multiple forests are needed in the following situations:

▲ **You need a complete separation of network information except for manually configured trusts between domains within a forest.** Because the global catalog is not replicated between the domains, one forest cannot see information in another.

▲ **A unique schema is required.** If two parts of the organization require a unique schema due to administration differences, or different applications that require schema changes, you must create separate forests. It's important to consider this issue when implementing Exchange 2000. As I mentioned earlier, Exchange 2000 makes about 1,000 changes to the Active Directory schema, and this schema must be the same throughout the forest. If you are planning to install Exchange 2000 in only a single domain in the forest, you have to change the schema for the entire forest.

▲ **You must limit the scope of trust relationships.** Within a forest, all domains share a transitive trust with all other domains, and there is no way to break or limit these trusts. If your network environment requires a more limited trust configuration, you must use multiple forests.

▲ **An organization needs a close working relationship with another company.** Suppose, for example, that due to a business agreement, one company needs access to resources on another's networks. You can keep strict control over resource access by creating a trust between only the domains that need to be involved.

Exchange 2000 and Active Directory Planning

Exchange 2000 can operate in just about any Active Directory configuration. All the Exchange servers can be located in a single domain, or every domain can contain Exchange servers. The only important limitation is that an Exchange organization cannot include more than one Active Directory forest.

If you implement multiple forests, you also have to configure multiple Exchange organizations. This places some serious limitations on e-mail service interoperability between the different parts of the organization. For example, you cannot combine the Exchange servers from different organizations into administrative or routing groups. The Exchange servers cannot share configuration or link state table information, so there is no dynamic routing between the organizations. You cannot share schedule information between the organizations, and directory information, such as the global address list, is not automatically available in both domains. When you create multiple forests, you are essentially creating a completely separate Exchange organization as well. While you can exchange e-mail between the organizations using an SMTP connector, it is difficult to replicate any other information between the organizations.

> **NOTE:** *Tools, such as Microsoft Metadirectory Services (MMS), are available to help integrate multiple directories. Most of these tools are difficult to configure, however, and provide only directory synchronization; they do not address the other compatibility issues.*

North American Air Domain Planning

One of North American Air's first decisions must be what the domain structure will look like. North American Air faces two important issues when designing the structure. The first is whether to combine some or all the Windows NT domains into a smaller number of Active Directory domains. The second is how the forest root domain would be configured if the company decides to implement a tree of multiple domains.

The project team at North American Air first considered combining all domains into a single domain. This approach would have enabled them to centralize administration of the entire domain. Since North American Air has just over 30,000 user accounts, the total number of objects in the Active Directory database would have been well below the maximum number of objects for a single domain. In addition, the network connections between the company locations would have had enough bandwidth to support domain controller replication, especially if the sites were configured correctly.

However, the project team decided not to combine all the domains into a single domain. Instead, they decided to combine some of the domains but leave most of the current domains in place as child domains. They based this decision on several factors, including these:

▲ **Each of the corporate locations already has skilled IT personnel to manage the network.** Each location has a history of managing its own network, and administrators would resist giving up too much control to the central office.

▲ **A tree with multiple domains offers more expansion potential than a single domain does.** One of the corporate goals is to expand rapidly over the coming years, particularly outside of North America. If the expansion does happen, the company might require child domains to manage the requirements for some locations. The project team decided that it would be easier to deal with the expansion if the organization already included multiple domains in a tree.

▲ **The transitive trusts in Active Directory make managing the trusts between domains much easier.** This removes one of the major drawbacks to multiple domains in Windows NT.

▲ **Maintaining most of the current domains as child domains makes the Windows 2000 migration easier to manage.** Upgrading a domain to Windows 2000 is much quicker and less problematic than combining domains before, during, or after the migration.

The project team did decide to change the current domain configuration in two cases, however. First, they decided to move all the resource domains in Texas into the account domain in Dallas. Each of the resource domains will become a high level OU in the Texas domain. Because these locations are already centrally administered, the history of separate administration is not as important in these locations as it is in other locations. In addition, the resource domains contain only computer accounts and resources, not user accounts, so migrating the accounts into the master domain should be easy.

Second, the project team decided to combine the Chicago and Atlanta domains into a single child domain. These two locations are both working with aircraft electronics, and they require access to the resources at each other's location, so combining them is advantageous for users as well as administrators. There also is some discussion that a major component of the Chicago business unit might be merged with a similar business unit in Atlanta. If this happens, several hundred employees will be moved to Atlanta. Moving objects between OUs is much easier than moving them between domains. In addition, the two locations are connected with an existing WAN link that can be upgraded to a faster speed if needed.

The team also faced the important question of how to configure the tree root domain. They could either configure a dedicated root domain or configure the Texas domain as the root domain. In this case, the project team decided to implement a dedicated or empty root domain. Here are their reasons:

▲ **A dedicated root domain is easier to administer.** The corporation would like to strictly limit the membership of the Enterprise Admins and Schema Admins groups so that only a limited number of people can change the domain configuration and schema.

▲ **Migration to Windows 2000 is easier to manage with a dedicated root.** The Texas domain is by far the largest domain in the organization, and the project team decided that it would like to test the migration to Windows 2000 in a smaller domain before migrating the larger domain. None of the smaller domains would be appropriate as the root domain.

▲ **Migration to Exchange 2000 is easier when at least one domain has been switched to native mode.** Migration to Exchange 2000 requires a native mode domain to correctly migrate distribution lists. This means that at least one domain in the forest must be configured in native mode. The project team decided that it did not want to switch the Texas domain to native mode so soon in the migration, so creating a root domain that could be configured in native mode was the best decision.

Figure 5-3 provides the details on the planned Active Directory domain structure for North American Air.

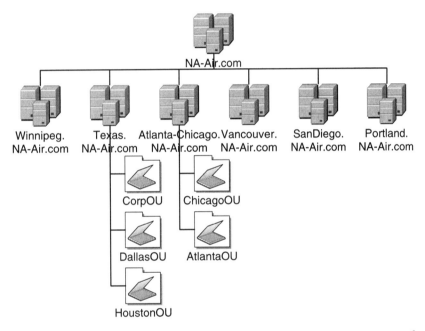

Figure 5-3: The Windows 2000 Active Directory Domain Design for North American Air.

The project team decided not to configure multiple trees within the forest initially. While some of the smaller subsidiaries do have separate DNS names registered, they decided to create only a single internal namespace. The distinct DNS names will be maintained for the subsidiaries, but only for the Internet presence. If some of the users require e-mail addresses based on the alternative domain names, they can be configured from within Active Directory and Exchange. However, there is nothing in the current design that would prevent the organization from adding an additional tree or trees to the forest later. If North American Air bought another company and there were important reasons to maintain a distinct namespace for it, they could add a separate tree to the forest.

Active Directory OU Design and Exchange

When designing a domain structure, the project team also should design an OU structure for each domain. In Active Directory, OUs are designed entirely for administrative purposes. Whenever you have a group of users or computers that you want to administer the same way, or by the same group of administrators, you can create an OU and then use the Active Directory Delegation of Control wizard to assign the appropriate level of permissions. You also can assign group policies to OUs.

OUs are not security principals in Active Directory. That means you cannot use an OU to assign permissions to other objects and then have all the users in the OU inherit that permission.

The only direct link between OU design and Exchange 2000 design occurs when you want to delegate administrative rights in both Exchange and Active Directory. To create user accounts in an OU and mailboxes on an Exchange server in a particular administrative group, the administrator must have sufficient rights to create the users in the OU and at least Exchange View-only Administrative rights for the administrative group.

DNS Planning

An essential component in Active Directory planning is DNS planning. Exchange administrators are accustomed to thinking about DNS only in reference to Internet mail and the MX records required for Internet mail functionality. However, Windows 2000 Active Directory requires extensive DNS planning because the domain and DNS zone configurations overlap extensively.

NOTE: The requirement for the MX records for Internet mail is the same in Exchange 2000 as it was in Exchange 5.x. You still need to configure the zone information for your domain with MX records pointing to your Internet mail servers. Exchange 2000 also uses SMTP to deliver mail internally, and you can use MX records internally as well. However, every Exchange server should have a host name registered in DNS so you don't have to use MX records for internal mail server name resolution. More on this in Chapter 11.

Windows 2000 Active Directory depends on DNS. Without a DNS server, Active Directory cannot be implemented and Windows 2000 clients cannot log on to the network. This is because Windows 2000 has moved away from using NetBIOS names and now uses host names instead.

When a user logs on to a Windows NT network, the user's computer locates a domain controller by using a NetBIOS name on the network. All Windows NT domain controllers register a NetBIOS name that consists of the domain name with a <1C> as the 16th character. For example, a domain controller in the Dallas_ACCT domain registers the name "Dallas_Acct   1C" on the network. In most cases, the client computer queries the WINS server for the IP address of a computer with this name registered and then contacts the domain controller to log on.

In Windows 2000, client computers use host names rather than NetBIOS names and the DNS server rather than WINS for name resolution. A client computer still needs to identify which computers on the network are domain controllers, however. Windows 2000 uses SRV resource records in DNS to provide that information. Here's an example of an SRV resource record that identifies DC1 as a domain controller for the NA-Air.com domain:

```
_kerberos._tcp.NA-Air.com 600 IN SRV 0 100 88 DC1.NA-
   Air.com
```

When a client logs on to a Windows 2000 domain, this record identifies the domain controller. The client uses Kerberos to log on to Active Directory. This record indicates that when logging on to the NA-Air.com domain, the client computer should contact DC1.

NOTE: Kerberos is the protocol that Windows 2000 computers use when authenticating Windows 2000 domain controllers. It replaces the NTLM authentication used in earlier versions of Windows NT. Kerberos, which is based on an open Internet standard, is a faster, more versatile, and more secure authentication protocol than NTLM.

SRV resource records can be used to identify many services on a network. All SRV records follow the same format. For example, Table 5-1 describes the preceding SRV resource record example.

Table 5-1: SRV Records in WIndows 2000 DNS

Component	Example	Explanation
Service	_Kerberos	The type of network service this resource record identifies. For a DC, this is identified as Kerberos because the client computer uses Kerberos to log on to Active Directory. Domain controllers also register other SRV records, such as LDAP services, to indicate that if you want to search for information in Active Directory using LDAP, you must contact the domain controller.
Protocol	_tcp	The protocol used for this service, usually TCP or UDP.
Name	NA-Air.com	The domain name to which this resource record refers.
TTL	600	Time to Live; how long the record stays current.
Class	IN	The standard DNS "IN" Internet class.
Priority	0	The priority for the client. For example, if there is more than one similar record and one has a lower priority than the other, the client tries to contact the server with the lowest priority number first. This number ranges from 0 to 65,535.

Table 5-1: SRV Records in WIndows 2000 DNS (Continued)

Component	Example	Explanation
Weight	100	A second method of setting a priority for a record. If two records have the same priority, the weight for each record is examined and the load is balanced based on the relative weight numbers. This number ranges from 0 to 65,535.
Port	88	The port number used for this service. The common port number for Kerberos is 88.
Target	DC1.NA-Air.com	The host and domain name of the computer to which the record refers.

When designing the Active Directory structure, you also must plan the DNS structure and the location and configuration of the DNS servers. The DNS structure does not directly affect the Exchange implementation, but it affects the naming scheme. For example, North American Air has registered the DNS name NA-Air.com on the Internet and has decided that all users in the organization will have an SMTP address of *alias*@NA-Air.com. North American Air has decided to implement child domains so the DNS name for the domain in Winnipeg is Winnipeg.NA-Air.com. When they assign the SMTP address to the users in Winnipeg, they can use *alias*@NA-Air.com or they can use *alias*@Winnipeg.NA-Air.com. So while DNS configuration is essential for Active Directory design, the implications for Exchange 2000 are limited.

NOTE: *You can actually use any domain name as the domain part of the SMTP address. With Exchange 2000, you can configure multiple SMTP addresses to individuals or groups of individuals. Also note that we are discussing SMTP addresses, not UPNs. You probably want the UPN and SMTP address to match, but they do not have to match.*

Active Directory Site Planning

The project team also needs to determine how to configure the organization's Active Directory sites. Windows 2000 defines a *site* as an area of the network in which all domain controllers are connected by a fast and reliable network connection. In most cases, a site is one or more IP subnets connected on a LAN or high-speed WAN and connected to the rest of the network via routers and slower WAN connections.

A site has no direct correlation to the logical domain and forest structures, so the site design can be different from the logical domain design. For example, one site might contain multiple domains or one domain might span multiple sites. One site might contain some of the domain controllers of multiple domains, with the other domain controllers scattered throughout other sites.

Sites are used to control network traffic within a Windows 2000 network in three ways:

▲ **Replication.** Sites optimize network performance by managing the replication traffic between domain controllers and global catalog servers. Directory information replication within a site is handled differently than between sites. Table 5-2 shows some of the differences between intra-site and inter-site replication.

Table 5-2: Comparing Intra-Site and Inter-Site Replication Traffic

Category	Intra-Site Replication	Inter-Site Replication
Replication traffic	Replication traffic is not compressed due to the extra load compression would put on the processor.	Replication traffic is compressed to save bandwidth. This compression is efficient, compressing the amount of data up to 90 percent.
Latency	Replication partners notify each other when changes to the Active Directory have occurred, thus minimizing replication latency.	Replication partners contact each other only during scheduled times; there is no change notification.
Protocols	Replication uses the RPC transport.	Replication uses either RPC over TCP/IP or SMTP.

Table 5-2: Comparing Intra-Site and Inter-Site Replication Traffic (Continued)

Category	Intra-Site Replication	Inter-Site Replication
Replication connections	Replication connections can be created between any two domain controllers in the site.	Replication connections can be created only between bridgehead servers in each site.
Connection configuration	The Knowledge Consistence Checker (KCC) automatically creates multiple connections between domain controllers.	The Knowledge Consistence Checker (KCC) creates connections only between bridgehead servers, using the lowest-cost route.

NOTE: You can use SMTP to replicate information between sites that have a slow connection, or that do not have a permanent connection. SMTP can be used to replicate GC and forest information (such as the configuration and schema partitions), but cannot be used to replicate between domain controllers in the same domain.

▲ **Authentication.** When a client computer logs on to an Active Directory domain, it tries to log on to a domain controller in the same site. If the domain is configured for native mode, the computer also tries to contact a global catalog server in the same site during the logon process. The client determines which domain controllers are in the same site by querying the DNS server for site-specific SRV records. Two of the SRV records registered with the DNS server by a domain controller are:

```
_ldap._tcp.sitename._sites.domainname 600 IN SRV 0 100
    389 servername.domainname.com

_kerberos._tcp.sitename._sites.dc._msdcs.domainname
    600 IN SRV 0 100 88 servername.domainname.com
```

The first record identifies the server as an LDAP server located in the specified site, and the second record identifies the server as the Kerberos authentication server in the same site. When the client logs on to the network, it queries the DNS server and receives these two responses. Afterward, the client contacts the server on the local site, thus preventing the logon traffic from crossing a WAN link.

NOTE: If the client computer can't locate a domain controller in its site, either because the domain controller is down or because there is no domain controller, the client computer attempts to contact any other domain controller listed in DNS, regardless of the domain controller's location. This can have serious repercussions for network traffic if the domain controller is across a slow WAN link.

▲ **Active Directory Network Services**. Microsoft has designed the site concept to optimize access to network services. For example, an administrator can use Distributed File System (Dfs) to create multiple replicas of a folder in various sites on the network. Because Dfs is designed to be aware of the site configuration, client computers always try to access a Dfs replica in their own sites before crossing a WAN link to access the information in another site. When designing applications for Windows 2000, it's advantageous to make the applications site-aware so that they also help to optimize network traffic.

Exchange 2000 and Site Design

Good site design plays an important part in successfully implementing Windows 2000 Active Directory to manage WAN link traffic between corporate locations. You must make sure that a domain controller and global catalog server are on the same fast network segment as the Exchange server. This means that every site that includes an Exchange server also includes a domain controller and a global catalog server. Exchange uses the Active Directory sites like any other Active Directory client. The Exchange server frequently has to look up information both in Active Directory and in the global catalog, and the Exchange server uses a DNS query just like any other client to locate these servers in its site.

There is no direct correlation between sites and routing groups. An Exchange routing group might have the same boundaries as an Active Directory site because the reasons for creating them are similar. Configuring a routing group reduces messaging traffic on the WAN connection, while creating sites reduces Active Directory replication traffic on the same connection.

North American Air Site Design

North American Air has a simple Active Directory site design. Each domain and each location consist of a single site, with two exceptions. One exception is the combined Atlanta and Chicago domain, which has a site for each location. The other exception is the Texas domain, where the corporate location, the Dallas manufacturing location, and the Houston location are separate Active Directory sites in the Texas domain.

Locating Domain Controllers and Global Catalog Servers

Planning the location of domain controllers and global catalog servers is an important issue when designing the Exchange organization because of the number of directory lookups associated with mail delivery. As a rule, every site in a domain must have at least one domain controller that also is a global catalog server. However, a location with fewer than 50 users can get by without having its own, as long as it has a fast network connection to a site that contains a domain controller. As the number of client computers in a site increases, a site might need additional directory servers.

When a messaging client connected to an Exchange 2000 server needs to access an address list, it sends a query to the Exchange server. Because the Exchange 2000 server does not store the directory information, it forwards the query to a domain controller or a global catalog server. In most cases, the global catalog server deals with an address lookup, because the global catalog stores most of the messaging directory information. However, if the address list includes a global or domain local group that has been mail-enabled, a domain controller must respond to the request to expand the list.

The Exchange server responds differently to client requests for directory information depending on the type of client making the request. If the client is a pre-Outlook 2000 MAPI client, the client requests the directory information from the Exchange server. The Exchange server uses a process called Directory Service Proxy (DSProxy) to accept the client request and forward the request to a local global catalog server using port 3268. The global catalog server responds back to the Exchange server, which then forwards the requested information to the client. If the client is an Outlook 2000 MAPI client, the first query from the client also is sent to the Exchange server. In this case, however, the Exchange server responds to the client with a referral indicating the host name for a global catalog server that the client should use for all future directory lookups. The name of the global catalog server is stored as part of the MAPI profile in the Registry on the client computer. From then on, the messaging client directly queries the global catalog, reducing the load on the Exchange server. If the server to which the MAPI client was referred is not available when the client tries to do a lookup, the client goes back to the DSProxy process on the Exchange server and a new global catalog server becomes part of the profile.

In addition to responding to the directory lookups for messaging clients, the Exchange server also frequently queries Active Directory. Whenever the server needs routing information to route a message through the organization, it queries the domain controller for the Exchange organization configuration. The configuration partition in Active Directory stores the Exchange configuration information. If the Exchange server needs to expand a mail-enabled group, it queries a global catalog server (for universal groups) or a domain controller (for domain local or global groups). To optimize the query process, each Exchange server uses a Directory Access (DSAccess) cache. By default, the DSAccess cache stores directory information for a maximum of 10 minutes, using a maximum cache size of 4 MB. (These settings can be changed through the Registry.) The cache stores information that the server has resolved from a domain controller or global catalog server. Any information that the Exchange server resolves from the Active Directory server can be cached except the information collected for MAPI clients using the DSProxy process.

Because of the amount of traffic between the Exchange server and the Active Directory servers, every Exchange server must have a fast network connection to both a domain controller and global catalog server. In addition, if an Active Directory site contains an Exchange server, you must ensure that the domain controllers and global catalog servers in the site have the capacity to handle the additional load that the Exchange server places on the servers when querying the domain controllers for configuration and user information.

In some situations, you might decide to locate the Exchange server on a domain controller that is also a global catalog server to minimize network traffic. However, this configuration also creates some complications. First, if there are many users in a site and the server is the only domain controller and global catalog server, there is already a significant drain on the server's resources without adding the Exchange Server service. Second, running many critical services on a single computer is risky because that server becomes a single point of failure. Because of these drawbacks, in most cases the Exchange server should not be located on a domain controller or global catalog server except in sites where there are a limited number of users (less than 100).

The project team at North American Air tested the domain controller and global catalog location issue carefully. The corporate standard they created as a result of their testing requires all sites to have at least two domain controllers and two global catalog servers, to allow for redundancy. In addition, sites that include more than 5,000 users must have an additional domain controller for each 5,000 users over the initial 5,000. Sites that include more than 7,000 users must have an additional global catalog server for each 7,000 users over the initial 7,000. Table 5-3 shows North American Air's configuration for each domain.

Table 5-3: Domain Controllers and Global Catalog Servers in the North American Air Active Directory Tree

Domain/Site	Number of Domain Controllers	Number of Global Catalog Servers
Texas/Corporate	3	3
Texas/Dallas	4	3
Texas/Houston	3	3
Winnipeg/Winnipeg	2	2
Atlanta_Chicago/Atlanta	2	2
Atlanta_Chicago/Chicago	2	2

Table 5-3: Domain Controllers and Global Catalog Servers in the North American Air Active Directory Tree (Continued)

Domain/Site	Number of Domain Controllers	Number of Global Catalog Servers
Vancouver/Vancouver	2	2
Portland/Portland	2	2
San-Diego/San-Diego	2	2

The corporate project team also decided not to install Exchange on any domain controllers. Their primary reason for not doing so in the smaller locations was to limit the effects of a single server failure. In these locations, they will use domain controllers to provide networking infrastructure services (such as DNS, DHCP).

Server performance is an issue in this configuration only in the Texas locations. In these locations the domain controllers and global catalog servers will be configured as dual processor machines, with a minimum of 512 MB of RAM and a hardware RAID 5 disk subsystem for the Active Directory databases.

The Effect of Exchange 2000 on the Global Catalog

As I mentioned earlier, installing Exchange into an Active Directory forest adds over 1,000 new objects to the schema. In addition, installing Exchange 2000 also significantly increases the number of attributes that are replicated to the global catalog. Before installing Exchange 2000, the global catalog partition for a domain is approximately 50 percent of the size of the domain database. After the schema changes, the global catalog is about 60 percent of the size of the global catalog.

This is an important issue in large organizations with multiple domains. Recall that the global catalog contains information from every domain in the entire forest. If you have 10 domains with an average Active Directory database size of 100 MB (about 7,000 users per domain) the global catalog database approaches 600 MB. In addition, because the global catalog server also must be a domain controller, the entire directory database on the server could be 700 MB. As the number of domains increases, the size of the global catalog increases rapidly.

Group Planning and Implementation

The last important Active Directory planning issue is how to implement groups in Active Directory. Because Exchange 2000 allows you to mail-enable any of the security groups, group implementation is much more important in Exchange 2000 than it was in Exchange 4.0/5.*x*.

Two types of groups are available in Active Directory; Table 5-4 lists them.

Table 5-4: Group Types in Active Directory

Group Type	Description
Security groups	Used to assign permissions to objects in Active Directory. Any security principal, including other groups, can be added to security groups.
Distribution groups	Used to group users together for e-mail distribution lists, but cannot be used to assign permissions to objects. Security groups can be added to distribution groups, but distribution groups cannot be added to security groups.

Because you can mail-enable security groups, you do not need distribution groups in Exchange 2000. This means that you work primarily with security groups. You can define security groups with any of three scopes, as described in Table 5-5. The scope of a group determines who can belong to it as well as where that group can be granted permissions.

 NOTE: *Universal groups and the nesting of security groups are enabled only when you have switched the domain to native mode. You can switch your domain to native mode only when all domain controllers are running Windows 2000 Server.*

Table 5-5: Group Scopes in Active Directory

Group Scope	Group Membership	Access Resources
Domain local group	Can contain user accounts, global group accounts, and universal group accounts from any domain in the forest, and nested domain local groups in the domain where the group is located.	Can be used to assign permissions only in the domain where the group is located. The membership of these groups is not replicated to the global catalog.
Global group	Can contain user accounts and global groups from the same domain.	Can be used to assign permissions anywhere in the forest. These groups are listed in the global catalog, but the group membership is not.
Universal group	Can contain user accounts, global groups, and universal groups from any domain in the forest.	Can be used to assign permissions anywhere in the forest. The members of the groups are listed in the global catalog.

Using security groups as mail-enabled groups has important implications for the Exchange deployment when the organization includes more than one domain. Domain local groups and global groups are listed as objects in the global catalog, but the group membership is not. Instead, the membership of a group is listed in the domain partition for the domain in which the group is located. When you mail-enable one of these groups, a user can send mail to the entire group at once. When a user does so, the Exchange server needed to expand the group must be able to connect to the domain controller rather than the global catalog server.

Consider the following example. Both the Winnipeg.NA-Air.com and the Texas.NA-Air.com domains have a global group called Sales_GG, and both groups have been mail-enabled so they show up in the GAL in both domains. When a user connected to an Exchange server in the Winnipeg domain sends a message to the Winnipeg Sales_GG group, the Exchange server must connect to a domain controller in the Winnipeg domain when expanding the group. The Exchange server connects to the domain controller, gets the list of the group members, and then forwards the message to each group member. If, however, a user from the Texas domain sends a message to the Sales_GG in the Winnipeg domain, the Exchange server in the Texas domain contacts a global catalog server. The global catalog does not contain the members for the global group, so the global catalog query cannot provide the list of members. The Exchange server assumes that there are no members in the Sales_GG group and does not send the message anywhere.

There are two potential solutions to this problem. First, the project team at North American Air can use universal groups for all distribution lists. Because the global catalog contains complete membership for all universal groups, any Exchange server in any domain can connect to a global catalog server and determine the group membership. However, because the entire membership list is published in the global catalog, changes to the membership of a universal group can cause considerable replication traffic. Active Directory replication is done on a per-attribute basis, but the group membership of a universal group is stored as a single attribute of the group. Therefore, whenever the membership of a universal group changes, the entire membership list must be replicated to all other global catalog servers.

To optimize the use of universal groups, the project team at North American Air can nest universal groups. For example, if they want a universal group that includes all the employees in a corporation, they can create an All_Employees universal group, and then create smaller universal groups for each department or domain. These smaller universal groups can then be added to the All_Employees group. This decreases the amount of global catalog replication that results from adding a member to the smaller universal groups.

NOTE: *Microsoft recommends that the membership of any group never exceed 5,000 people. One of the reasons for this recommendation is so that the entire membership list can be replicated in a single transaction.*

Second, North American Air can configure an expansion server for each global group. To use global groups as mail-enabled groups, they must make sure that the group's expansion server is located in the same domain as the global group. As with distribution lists in Exchange 4.0/5.x, they can configure which server expands the group membership. If the expansion server is in the same domain as the global group, it connects to the domain controller, expands the group, and sends the mail. In the preceding scenario, the expansion server for the Sales_GG in the Winnipeg domain should be an Exchange server in the same domain. Then when the user from the Texas domain sends a message to the Winnipeg Sales_GG group, the message is forwarded to the Exchange server in the Winnipeg domain, and the group membership is expanded. The primary problem with this approach is that it might put a significant load on that server. If the server fails, users cannot send mail to that global group until it is restored.

The project team at North American Air decided to use universal groups for the mail-enabled groups. They will create a universal group in each domain for the different business units in that domain. They will then nest these universal groups inside a universal group for each business unit. This means, for example, that the Winnipeg domain will have a Wpg_Sales_UG group nested in the Corp_Sales_UG group. Replication traffic between their global catalog servers is not a great concern because there is adequate bandwidth connecting corporate locations.

Migration Process and the Active Directory Connector

After planning what the final configuration will look like, you can then plan how to migrate the current Windows NT domains to Windows 2000 Active Directory. When you begin the migration to Windows 2000 Active Directory, you also must configure the Active Directory Connector (ADC) that serves as the connector between the Exchange 4.0/5.x directory service and Active Directory. I'll discuss the options and techniques for migrating to Windows 2000 and configuring the ADC in Chapter 6 and Chapter 7.

Exchange 2000 Deployment Planning

Once the Windows 2000 Active Directory planning is complete, you're ready to move on to the actual Exchange migration planning. Your team faces a number of important choices as it plans the Exchange organization, in the areas of administrative, message routing, and server planning. I address each of these separately in the following sections.

Administrative Planning

To begin, you need to plan an administrative structure for the Exchange organization. When you create a new Exchange organization, all Exchange servers are installed into a single administrative group by default. A single administrative group is adequate for most small or medium-sized companies and for companies with centralized messaging administration.

Larger corporations, however, might decide to implement multiple administrative groups. If your corporation has a distributed model for network administration, you might decide to distribute the Exchange administration to match the network administrative structure. In a corporation that crosses national boundaries, you might split the administrative groups along national lines. As I mentioned earlier, administrative groups in Exchange 2000 are not limited to geographic regions or to the Exchange 4.0/5.x sites (at least after switching the Exchange organization into native mode). You can configure administrative groups based on Exchange functions, rather than just geographic locations. This means that you can create an administrative group that contains all the routing groups, or you can create an administrative group that contains all the public folders. After creating the administrative group, you can use the Exchange Delegation wizard to assign the permissions that you want to each routing group.

When you are migrating an organization from Exchange 4.0/5.x to Exchange 2000, you can't take advantage of all the administrative options during the migration process. When you upgrade an existing Exchange 4.0/5.x organization, each site is converted into an administrative group and all the servers in that site are located in that routing group. As long as the Exchange organization is running in mixed mode (which means that you are still supporting Exchange 4.0/5.x servers), you cannot change this default configuration. After you have migrated all the Exchange 4.0/5.x servers, you can switch the organization to native mode and then move servers between routing groups. However, you cannot move servers between administrative groups.

The project team at North American Air decided to maintain the distributed configuration for messaging administration to match the current Exchange 5.5 site configuration closely, for several reasons. First, the Exchange administrators in each location are capable and experienced and want to manage their own Exchange servers. Second, the upgrade from Exchange 5.5 is significantly easier if the current site configuration is maintained and migrated into administrative groups. The only way to change the administrative group structure would be to move all the existing Exchange 5.5 servers into a common site by using the Move Server wizard in Exchange 5.x, and then upgrade the servers.

The project team also plans to take advantage of some of the new functionality. The central messaging administration group in Dallas is the only group that manages routing groups and routing group connectors, so they will create an administrative group for the routing groups. Until the Exchange organization is switched to native mode, the routing groups must remain in the administrative group that corresponds to the existing site. Once the organization has been switched to native mode, they plan to move all the routing groups and server objects into the routing group container in the routing administrative group. This will centralize the message routing management in a single location. North American Air also is planning to use public folders a great deal as the new business applications are developed. This means that public folder administration will assume an essential role in the organization. The project team therefore plans to centralize the public folder management in a single administrative group. The corporation also plans to use instant messaging, a chat server, and a conferencing server to enhance communication between users. To centrally manage these services, they will create a separate administrative group to store these configuration objects.

The Exchange administrators at the corporate location will be tasked with managing Exchange system policies to configure mailbox stores, public folders stores, and servers. They will configure an administrative group containing the Policies container and limit permissions to the group to administrators at the corporate location in Dallas. All the administrators in the other locations will assign the system policies to the correct objects in their own domains. Table 5-6 shows what the administrative group structure will look like at the corporate headquarters when the migration is complete.

Table 5-6: Administrative Group Configuration at the Texas Location in North American Air

Administrative Group	Containers	Function
Dallas-Corp-AG	Servers	Manages all Exchange servers in Corporate location.
Dallas-AG-Manu-AG	Servers	Manages all Exchange servers in the Dallas manufacturing location.
Houston-Manu-AG	Servers	Manages all Exchange servers in the Houston manufacturing location.
Routing_Group_AG	Routing Groups	Manages the routing groups and routing group connectors for the entire organization.
Texas_PubFolder_AG	Folders	Manages all public folders in the entire organization.
Texas_Collab_AG	Instant messaging Chat server Conferencing	Manages the instant messaging, chat server, and conferencing server configuration for the entire organization.

Each of the other locations will be configured with a single administrative group. During the migration, the administrative group will contain the server container for managing the local servers and the routing group container to manage the routing group connectors. After the migration is complete, the routing groups will be located in the administrative group at corporate headquarters.

Message Routing Planning

The second important component to plan is the routing group and routing group connector configuration. In a new organization, every server is in the same routing group by default. When upgrading an existing organization, the routing group is located in the administrative group that was an Exchange 4.0/5.x site and cannot be moved or changed until the organization is switched to native mode. After switching to native mode, you can create or delete routing groups and easily move servers between routing groups.

You can use routing groups to manage message routing and delivery times. To provide the best performance across WAN links, the North American Air project team decided to maintain the default routing groups created when the sites are upgraded for all locations except those in Texas. Even though they plan to allow message delivery across the WAN link at all times of the day, using multiple routing groups rather than a single group still provides some benefits. If the entire organization were configured as a single routing group, all messages would be delivered from the originating server directly to the destination server. This means that if a user in Vancouver were to send a message to a mail-enabled group and the group had members with mailboxes on five servers in Dallas, the Vancouver server would send five copies of the message across the WAN link. In contrast, if they create a routing group in each location and configure the bridgehead server(s), a single message can be sent to the bridgehead server and then distributed to the five servers in Dallas. In addition, if the network bandwidth does become an issue, the separate routing groups enable the routing administrators to schedule mail delivery or to set a different schedule for large messages.

The project team decided to move all servers in Texas into a single routing group. The locations in Texas are connected with adequate bandwidth to enable direct SMTP messaging between all the Exchange servers, and a single routing group configuration ensures the fastest message delivery times. Most importantly, one of the corporate goals in the migration is to decrease the number of Exchange servers in the organization. By creating a single routing group, they can remove some of the servers from service that were formerly used for site connectors and perhaps reuse them as public folder servers or collaboration servers.

The project team decided to use routing group connectors for all connections between routing groups. Unless bandwidth is an issue (such as a WAN link of less than 56 Kbps between two locations), Microsoft recommends using routing group connectors. In North American Air's case, bandwidth is not an issue so there is no reason not to use routing group connectors. The routing group connectors will be configured to permit messaging traffic all day and to deliver messages every 15 minutes. As they implement Exchange 2000 throughout the organization, the project team will keep a careful eye on the WAN utilization for messaging. The effect of implementing a new network system, such as Exchange 2000, on network traffic is one of the most difficult items to test thoroughly in a lab environment, so the team plans to monitor this carefully as the implementation proceeds.

The project team also is responsible for planning Internet Mail connectivity for the new Exchange organization. The current configuration includes a connector for SMTP mail to the Internet at each location except San Diego. The team explored the possibility of centralizing all Internet mail access and creating a single SMTP connector to the Internet in the Texas routing group. This would have simplified administration because only one firewall would need to be configured to support SMTP mail, and any filtering or virus scanning could be configured on just one server. However, the project team decided to maintain the current configuration and maintain an SMTP connector at each location as well as implement an SMTP connector in San Diego after the migration of the MS Mail servers to Exchange 2000. Employees in all locations use the Internet extensively, so the corporation needs to maintain a connection to the Internet at all locations. Because the connection already exists, the project team decided to use the connection for Internet mail connectivity. In addition, each location already has network administrators with the expertise needed to manage the Internet connection, and the routing group administrators from the Texas location will manage the SMTP connectors.

NOTE: Every Exchange 2000 server includes an SMTP virtual server by default and is capable of sending and receiving e-mail from the Internet without any additional configuration (assuming the server can connect to a DNS server that can resolve Internet addresses). If the default behavior is acceptable, you do not have to configure any additional SMTP servers. However, if you want to change the default configuration, you can create and configure SMTP connectors to deliver Internet e-mail.

Server Planning

The project team also is responsible for planning the Exchange server hardware configuration. The best way to configure Exchange servers in a location with multiple servers is to set each of them up as a dedicated server for a specific function. For example, you might configure one or more servers as mailbox servers and configure others as connector servers or OWA front-end servers. The type of task to which the server is dedicated determines the server's optimal hardware configuration.

For a mailbox or public folder store server, the most important hardware components are the hard disk and RAM. If the server hosts more than 2,000 mailboxes, it should have at least one gigabyte (GB) of RAM installed. The hard disk configuration should consist of a hardware RAID configuration for the message databases and a separate mirrored drive for the system files and for each set of transaction logs. (Remember, each storage group has its own transaction logs.) The size of the database depends on the amount of space provided for each individual mailbox and whether full-text indexing is enabled. If you are going to use full-text indexing, the index will be about 20-30 percent of the size of the database.

For a connector server, processing speed has the greatest effect on performance. While a connector server requires a certain amount of hard disk space for queuing messages and for temporary storage while converting messages, the actual sizes of database and transaction logs on a connector server are relatively small. To optimize the performance of a connector server, use a multiple processor server with at least 512 MB of RAM. If you are using multiple connectors on the server — such as routing group connectors, SMTP connectors for Internet mail, or connectors to other messaging systems — you can locate the directories for each connector on a different hard disk to optimize the disk access time for all connectors.

> **NOTE:** *The Microsoft Exchange 2000 Server Resource Kit from Microsoft Press includes detailed information about the hardware requirements for Exchange 2000 servers with various configurations. Hardware manufacturers, such as Compaq, Hewlett-Packard, and IBM, also provide detailed information on recommended hardware configurations.*

After testing, the project team at North American Air decided on a corporate limit of 3,000 mailboxes per Exchange server. This means that the total database on an Exchange server can now be 50 percent larger than the previous standard for Exchange 5.5. The primary reason for limiting the database size in Exchange 5.5 was the amount of time it took to recover the database from a backup. By splitting the information store into multiple stores, the recovery time for individual stores is greatly reduced. The Exchange 2000 server could support even more mailboxes, but the project team decided to set this limit to maintain high performance and to decrease the impact if one server did fail. This new standard means a slight decrease in the number of mailbox servers, but the real decrease in the number of servers is gained by combining all the servers in Texas into a single routing group, thus eliminating four connector servers.

Since North American Air is planning to use public folders to store the data for the new corporate applications, there will be more demand for public folders. The project team decided to dedicate a single server as a public folder server in each of the Texas locations. As they complete the application testing and implement it across the organization, the project team will monitor the server load on the public folder servers to determine when an increase in the number of public folder servers might be required. These public folders also will be accessed through OWA, so the team installs OWA front-end servers at the Dallas Corporate location and in Winnipeg. Table 5-7 lists the servers at each of the Texas locations after migration.

Table 5-7: Exchange 2000 Servers in the Texas Routing Group

Server Name	Administrative Group	Routing Group	Functionality
Dal-C-Mail-Svr1	Dallas_Corp_AG	Texas_RG	Mailbox server (3,000 mailboxes)
Dal-C-Mail-Svr2	Dallas_Corp_AG	Texas_RG	Mailbox server (2,500 mailboxes)
Dal-C-Mail-Svr3	Dallas_Corp_AG	Texas_RG	Mailbox server (2,500 mailboxes)
Dal-C-PF-Svr1	Dallas_Corp_AG	Texas_RG	Public folder server
Dal-C-Con-Svr1	Dallas_Corp_AG	Texas_RG	Connector server
Dal-C-Con-Svr2	Dallas_Corp_AG	Texas_RG	Connector server
Dal-C-OWA-Svr1	Dallas_Corp_AG	Texas_RG	OWA front-end server
Dal-C-Col-Svr1	Texas_Collab_AG	Texas_RG	Instant messaging test server Conferencing test server
Dal-M-Mail-Svr1	Dallas_Manu_AG	Texas_RG	Mailbox server (2,500 mailboxes)
Dal-M-Mail-Svr2	Dallas_Manu_AG	Texas_RG	Mailbox server (2,500 mailboxes)
Dal-M-Mail-Svr3	Dallas_Manu_AG	Texas_RG	Mailbox server (2,500 mailboxes)
Dal-M-Mail-Svr4	Dallas_Manu_AG	Texas_RG	Mailbox server (2,500 mailboxes)
Dal-M-PF-Svr1	Dallas_Manu_AG	Texas_RG	Public folder server
Hou-Mail-Svr1	Houston_Manu_AG	Texas_RG	Mailbox server (3,000 mailboxes)

Table 5-7: Exchange 2000 Servers in the Texas Routing Group (Continued)

Server Name	Administrative Group	Routing Group	Functionality
Hou-Mail-Svr2	Houston_Manu_AG	Texas_RG	Mailbox server (3,000 mailboxes)
Hou-Mail-Svr3	Houston_Manu_AG	Texas_RG	Mailbox server (1,000 mailboxes) and public folder server

Table 5-8 lists the Exchange servers that will be configured at each of the other locations.

Table 5-8: The Exchange Servers in the Other North American Air Locations

Server	Administrative Group	Routing Group	Functionality
Wpg-Mail-Svr1	Winnipeg_AG	Winnipeg_RG	Mailbox server (3,000 mailboxes)
Wpg-Mail-Svr2	Winnipeg_AG	Winnipeg_RG	Mailbox server (100 mailboxes) Public folder server
Wpg-Con-Svr1	Winnipeg_AG	Winnipeg_RG	Connector server
Wpg-OWA-Svr1	Winnipeg_AG	Winnipeg_RG	OWA server
Van-Mail-Svr1	Vancouver_AG	Vancouver_RG	Multiple functions
Por-Mail-Svr1	Portland_AG	Portland_RG	Multiple functions
SD-Mail-Svr1	San_Diego_AG	San_Diego_RG	Multiple functions
Chi-Mail-Svr1	Chicago_AG	San_Diego_RG	Multiple functions
Atl-Mail-Svr1	Atlanta_AG	Atlanta_RG	Multiple functions

Conclusion

This chapter discussed the completion of the planning process for an Exchange 2000 migration. Before beginning Exchange planning, the project team must understand and plan for the migration to

Active Directory. The fact that the organization is migrating to Exchange has a direct impact on the Active Directory structure. After planning the Active Directory structure, the project team can plan the Exchange migration. This planning begins by designing the organizational structure for the Exchange organization, including the design of the administrative groups and routing groups. The planning also includes the configuration and placement of individual Exchange servers throughout the organization.

In the next chapter, the project team at North American Air starts working on the actual migration. The first part of the migration is the implementation of Windows 2000 and Active Directory. The next chapter discusses the options that North American Air has in migrating the Windows NT domains to Active Directory and covers the actual procedures for doing the migration to Active Directory.

Part 3

Migrating to Windows 2000 Active Directory

Chapter 6

Migrating to Active Directory

NOW THAT THE PLANNING PHASE IS COMPLETE, the project team at North American Air is ready to move forward with the implementation. Exchange 2000 requires Active Directory in order to install the Exchange servers, so the first essential step in a migration to Exchange 2000 is to create an Active Directory forest and domain structure.

Some organizations might create the required Active Directory structure without any reference to the existing Windows NT domain structure. For an organization like North American Air, however, the better option is to migrate the current Windows NT environment to Windows 2000. The organization already has a Windows NT directory structure that includes all the users, groups, and resources in the organization, and moving that information into an Active Directory structure is preferable to recreating it.

This chapter details the process of migrating a Windows NT domain structure to a Windows 2000 Active Directory structure. One way to accomplish the migration is to upgrade the current Windows NT domains. Upgrading a domain consists of installing Windows 2000 on the domain controllers in a Windows NT domain, starting with the primary domain controller. After the operating system upgrade is complete, the Active Directory Installation wizard runs automatically to upgrade the Windows NT domain to an Active

Directory domain. Each Windows NT domain becomes a new Windows 2000 domain. The second option is to restructure the Windows NT domains as part of the migration. This involves creating a Windows 2000 Active Directory structure separate from the Windows NT domain structure and copying the security principals from the existing Windows NT domains into the new Windows 2000 domains. This method enables several Windows NT domains to be combined into a single Active Directory domain.

An organization like North American Air might use a combination of both methods. The project team at North American Air has decided to retain most of the current domains after the migration, and those domains will be upgraded to Windows 2000. However, the project team also has decided that some of the domains should be restructured to take advantage of the new network administration options in Windows 2000. This chapter will detail the procedures required both when upgrading an individual Windows NT domain and when restructuring domains.

In practice, most Exchange administrators are not deeply involved in Active Directory migration; they merely need to understand the process. Consequently, this chapter does not deal with all of the complexities of migrating to Active Directory, but instead provides an overview of the planning and the procedures involved.

Migration Options

As stated earlier, one option for migrating to Exchange 2000 is to upgrade the existing domains. This is the easiest migration to implement and causes the least amount of disruption for the users on the network. When upgrading a domain, you upgrade the domain controllers to Windows 2000, starting with the primary domain controller (PDC) and then the backup domain controllers (BDCs).

Alternatively, you can restructure the existing Windows NT domains when you migrate them to Active Directory domains. This is the preferred option when the current domain structure is no longer appropriate for your company. The company may have reorganized since the initial NT implementation or grown to the point where the current domain structure is difficult to manage. In this case, you might reorganize the domains by creating a Windows 2000 domain structure and then moving security principals (users, groups, and computers) from one or more Windows NT domains into the new Active Directory domains.

The first step in the migration process is to choose how you will migrate your domains. To make the right decision, you must have completed the preparatory steps outlined in previous chapters. You must have gathered detailed information about the current networking infrastructure and domain configurations in your organization, and you must know what the new Active Directory domain structure will look like. If the Active Directory structure will contain the same domains as in Windows NT, then you will probably choose to upgrade the domains. If the planned Active Directory structure has a different domain configuration, however, then you will need to restructure at least some of your domains.

Many organizations decide to upgrade their current Windows NT domains to Active Directory domains. The domain upgrade option is the best choice if:

▲ Your current domain structure is very close to the planned Active Directory domain structure. If only minor modifications to the domain structure are required, you can upgrade the domains and then restructure.

▲ You want to maintain the current IT administrative structure at the domain level. You can change the way you administer the objects in a domain by using OUs and group policies without changing the domain administration.

▲ You have a significant investment in the current domain controllers, and the machines are capable of functioning as domain controllers in Active Directory.

▲ You want a quick and easy migration.

If the current domain structure is acceptable, or if the effort required to change the structure does not yield sufficient benefit, upgrading the current domains is the best option in your organization.

197

For many companies, however, the domain restructuring option makes more sense. The domain restructuring option is the best option if:

▲ Your current domain structure does not match your corporate structure. Many corporations extensively reorganize their business divisions and geographic locations from time to time, such that the existing Windows NT domain structure might no longer reflect the current corporate structure.

▲ You want to restructure the current domain administration model. For example, if you have several domains in the organization and you want to centralize the administration of those domains, you might combine the domains into a single domain with multiple OUs. By combining the domains, you also can have a single group of domain administrators and delegate some of the administrative tasks at an OU level.

▲ Your current Windows NT domain structure was limited by the maximum size of the directory database in Windows NT. Because Windows NT domains are limited to approximately 40,000 objects in the directory, some organizations have had to create additional domains just to stay below this limit. In Active Directory, however, you can have well over 100,000 objects in the directory. This means that you can combine the Windows NT domains into fewer Active Directory domains.

▲ You want to combine the Windows NT account and resource domains. Many organizations have used a Windows NT domain model with one or more account domains and several resource domains. This model overcomes the size restriction for the directory database and separates the administration of the user accounts from the administration of the resources on the network. In Active Directory, you can replace the resource domains with an OU structure that maintains the separation of administration within a single domain.

You also can combine these two approaches. For example, you might upgrade all your organization's domains and then restructure them. This can be a good solution in many cases, but keep in mind that you are performing two major operations on your network in a short time. You must plan carefully to minimize the procedures' impact on network activity. Another option is to upgrade some of the domains and restructure the other NT domains.

Upgrading a Domain

If you are running Windows NT 4.0 Server or Windows NT 3.51 Server on your domain controllers, they can be directly upgraded to Windows 2000 Server or to Windows 2000 Advanced Server. The domain upgrade process consists of upgrading the PDC in a Windows NT domain to Windows 2000 and then running the Active Directory Installation wizard to upgrade the Windows NT domain information to Active Directory. After upgrading the PDC, you also have the option of upgrading each of the backup domain controllers using the same procedure.

Disaster Recovery Planning

An essential preliminary step is to prepare for a failure in the upgrade process. If something goes wrong during the upgrade, you must be able to restore your system to a pre-upgrade state. To protect yourself from disaster, use the following steps:

1. Document the services and applications running on all your domain controllers. For example, if one of your domain controllers is also the DHCP server, document the DHCP configuration. You also should document any special configuration options for the domain controllers.

2. Designate one BDC as a domain recovery computer. You take this computer offline during the upgrade process, so add another BDC to the domain if needed before the upgrade.

3. Back up all the domain controllers. Test the backup by performing a test restore on a machine that is not connected to the network.

4. Use Server Manager to synchronize all the domain controllers.

5. Take the domain recovery BDC offline. If the upgrade fails, you can bring this computer back online, promote it to be the PDC, and get your domain back. You might want to keep this domain controller available after the upgrade is complete, bringing it back online occasionally to synchronize with the rest of the domain. A backup server such as this can provide a quick way to restore the domain database if the upgrade fails.

The Upgrade Process

Once your backup and recovery plan is in place, you can begin the upgrade by installing Windows 2000 Sever or Advanced Server on the Windows NT PDC. After the Windows 2000 installation is complete and the server reboots for the last time, the Active Directory Installation wizard runs and installs Active Directory. During the Active Directory installation, you can choose to create a new forest, create a new tree in an existing forest, or create a new domain in a tree.

NOTE: If you want to perform a domain upgrade, but also want to use new computers as the domain controllers, you can install Windows NT 4.0 on a new computer and install it as a BDC in the existing domain. Then you can promote the computer to be the PDC, and then upgrade the computer. Once you have upgraded the domain controller, you can add additional Windows 2000 domain controllers to the domain, and then decommission the old BDCs.

Upgrading the PDC configures it as the first domain controller in the new domain. The upgrade process moves the user and group accounts from the Registry's Security Accounts Manager (SAM) database to the Users container in Active Directory. It moves computer accounts into the Computers container, and maintains any existing trust relationships. If the domain that you just upgraded is a child domain in an Active Directory tree, the upgrade process configures a transitive two-way trust with the parent domain.

The upgraded PDC also assumes the role of PDC emulator, relative identifier (RID) master, and infrastructure master for the domain. (See the sidebar on Flexible Single Operations Masters

[FSMO] for an explanation of these roles.) If this server is the first domain controller in the forest, the domain controller is also the global catalog server, the schema master, and the domain naming master.

Flexible Single Operations Masters (FSMOs)

In Active Directory, all domain controllers are equal and the roles of PDC and BDC have been replaced by multimaster domain controllers that all contain writeable copies of the domain database. However, some functions must still be performed on a single domain controller. Microsoft developed the Flexible Single Operations Masters (FSMOs) to deal with this. There are five FSMOs:

▲ **Schema master:** The schema master is the only computer on which changes can be made to the forest's schema. To change the schema for the forest, you must connect to the schema master and be logged in as a member of the Schema Admins group. There is one schema master for the entire forest.

▲ **Domain naming master:** The domain naming master is the only computer on which domains can be created or removed. When you create a new domain, the domain naming master must be accessible using an RPC connection. The same applies when you remove a domain by uninstalling Active Directory from the last domain controller. If the domain naming master is not available, the process fails. Only the members of the Enterprise Admins group have permission to add or remove domains. There is one domain naming master for the entire forest.

▲ **RID master:** The relative identifier (RID) master ensures that no security principals receive the same security identifier (SID). When you create a new security principal in Active Directory, the object is assigned a SID based on the domain SID and a relative identifier (RID). Because objects can be created on any domain controller, there has to be some way to prevent the creation of two objects with the same SID. The relative identifier master guarantees that this duplication does not occur. Every domain controller queries the RID master to get a list of RIDs that it can assign to security principals.

When that list of RIDs is depleted, the domain controller must create an RPC connection to the RID master and request a new set of RIDs. If the RID master is not available, no new security principals can be created on that domain controller until the connection is reestablished. There is one RID master in the domain.

▲ **PDC emulator:** While the domain is in mixed mode and there are still Windows NT BDCs in the domain, the BDCs depend on the PDC emulator to perform the duties that the PDC performed in the Windows NT domains. For example, no domain changes can be made on the BDCs; they must all be made on the PDC emulator. The changes then replicate to the BDCs. If the PDC emulator is not available, users who are not using the Active Directory client in Windows 9x, or who are using Windows NT, cannot change their passwords. Even after you switch a domain to native mode, the PDC emulator still performs specific functions. For example, whenever a user changes her password (which can be done on any domain controller in Windows 2000), the domain controller on which the change was made replicates the changed password to the PDC emulator. If a user tries to log on with an unrecognized password, the domain controller queries the PDC emulator to see whether it has a more recent password. There is one PDC emulator in the entire domain.

▲ **Infrastructure master:** The infrastructure master updates group membership lists between domains whenever a user account is renamed. For example, if you rename a user account, and that user is a member of a group that is assigned access to resources in another domain, it takes some time for the name change to be replicated to the other domains.

The infrastructure master first updates all the local domain controllers with the changed name and then replicates this information to other domains. If the infrastructure master is not available, the updates take longer to replicate between domains. This delay does not affect the user's permissions, however, because permissions are based on the SID rather than on the user name. There is one infrastructure master in the entire domain.

> By default, the first computer installed in a forest is the schema master and the domain naming master. The first computer installed in a domain is assigned the domain-specific roles, but you can change which servers fulfill each function.

After upgrading the PDC, you should ensure that the network is stable and that migrating to Windows 2000 has not caused any unexpected problems before continuing with the upgrade. Once you are satisfied that the network is stable, you can continue the migration by upgrading the BDCs in any order.

Domain Upgrade Issues

In most cases, upgrading a domain is much more complicated than just upgrading the domain controllers. Many of the infrastructure and security configurations are significantly different in Windows 2000 than they are in Windows NT. Here are some issues to think about before you upgrade the first domain controller.

Network Infrastructure Components

In Windows NT 4.0, the primary means of name resolution were NetBIOS and WINS. In Windows 2000, this responsibility has shifted to host names and DNS. In Windows NT, most of the network connectivity was based on NetBIOS names and many Windows NT networks could not function without a WINS server. Most Windows NT networks did not use a DNS server because DNS was not required in a Windows NT domain. However, Active Directory requires DNS in order for clients to locate domain controllers, so it's essential to have a DNS infrastructure.

When you install or upgrade the first domain controller in an Active Directory domain, the installation process attempts to locate a DNS server that is authoritative for the DNS domain and configured to accept dynamic updates of host information. If either of these conditions is not met, you can install DNS on the computer as part of the upgrade. If you choose to install DNS at this point, the installation process configures the zone for the domain name on the domain controller and adds all the SRV records to the zone files. If you chose not to install DNS at this point, you can continue with the installation, but no Windows 2000 clients can connect to the domain controller and you cannot install a second domain controller in the domain until you configure a DNS server with the domain information. The DNS server need not be a Windows 2000 DNS server, but it must support SRV records and should support dynamic updates.

In small to midsize networks, accepting the default of installing DNS during the upgrade is a good option. You also can configure the zone to be an Active Directory integrated zone, so that the DNS information resides in the Active Directory database rather than in the zone files. If you use Active Directory integrated zones, any domain controller can be a DNS server and each server has a read-write copy of the zone information, rather than the single primary name server in a standard zone. In addition, the zone information is replicated as part of the Active Directory replication rather than using the zone transfer process. In a large corporation, however, you should test the DNS server performance on the domain controller before choosing Active Directory integrated zones. If the domain controller does not have sufficient resources to operate as both a domain controller and a DNS server, install the DNS service to a separate computer and use a standard zone instead of the Active Directory integrated zone.

If you have non-Windows 2000 clients, you also must continue to support WINS servers. Windows 2000 domain controllers, member servers, and workstations can all function as WINS clients, just like Windows NT or Windows 9x clients. If you are using a Windows NT server as a WINS server, the WINS configuration and database is retained when you upgrade the server. Before starting the upgrade, you should disable the WINS service so that the WINS database can be converted to Windows 2000 format during the upgrade. After the server has rebooted for the final time after the upgrade, you can restart the WINS service and configure it to start automatically.

Windows 2000 also implements the DHCP service in much the same way as Windows NT did. Windows 2000 clients can receive their IP configurations from a Windows NT 4.0 DHCP server, and Windows NT 4.0 or Windows 9x clients can receive their configuration from a Windows 2000 DHCP server. However, any Windows 2000 server that is a member of a domain and runs the DHCP service must be authorized in Active Directory before the DHCP service can begin to assign IP addresses. This provides some protection from rogue DHCP servers on the network.

Security Issues

Most of a Windows NT domain's security-related information is automatically migrated to the Windows 2000 domain during an upgrade. The upgrade maintains the SIDs assigned to users, groups, and computers, as well as the ACLs and permissions to all resources in the domain. This means that the upgrade should not affect network resource access. If you have upgraded the PDC to Windows 2000, and a user logs on to the domain controller, the user gets the same SID as part of the access token that the user received before the upgrade. All the resources that were shared on a server before the upgrade continue to be shared with the same permissions, and trusts between domains stay the same. The NT domain's groups move into Active Directory, retaining all the group memberships.

> **NOTE:** *A number of other issues can be important as you migrate the domain to Windows 2000. For example, Windows 2000 does not support LAN Manager Replication, which is often used to replicate logon scripts between domain controllers. Therefore, you must configure a manual or scripted process to replicate the information until you have upgraded all the domain controllers to Windows 2000. In addition, RAS dial-in permissions are configured differently in Windows 2000 than in Windows NT, so you might want to upgrade your RAS server as soon as possible. For a detailed discussion of these and other issues, consult the Windows 2000 Server Resource Kit.*

Integration with Exchange 5.x

In Windows NT, the domain controllers and Exchange 5.*x* servers each managed their own directory service. In Exchange 2000, the directory service is Active Directory. That means you must configure some way for the Exchange servers to connect to Active Directory so that the two directories can share information. The connecting point between Exchange 5.*x* and Active Directory is the Active Directory Connector (ADC), which can be configured to replicate Windows 2000 information into the Exchange directory and Exchange information into Active Directory. During the migration to Active Directory, you can use the ADC to replicate all the rich directory information that you have in the Exchange directory into Active Directory so that you do not have to enter all the information again. The ADC is discussed in detail in Chapter 7.

Switching to Native Mode

To gain the full benefit of Active Directory, you must switch the domain to native mode. When you upgrade the first domain controller, the domain is running in mixed mode, and it continues to do so until you make the switch to native mode. A domain running in mixed mode can continue to employ Windows NT BDCs on the network. After all the BDCs have been upgraded to Windows 2000 or removed from the network, you can switch the domain to native mode.

To switch a domain currently running in mixed mode to native mode, open Active Directory Users and Computers from the Administrative Tools. Right-click the domain name and select Properties. Select the option to Change Mode. Figure 6-1 shows the interface where you change the domain to native mode.

You can leave the domain running in mixed mode indefinitely, but you miss some of the benefits that you might get from Active Directory. The most important benefits from an Exchange administrator's point of view are the capabilities to use universal groups and to nest groups inside other groups.

As soon as you upgrade the first domain controller, you can begin to create OUs and move the domain objects into the OUs. You also can use group policies, but they are applied only to Windows 2000 clients. In addition, only Windows 2000 clients will use Kerberos to authenticate, while the other clients continue to use NTLM.

NOTE: As long as you have any Windows NT BDCs in the domain, the SAM database has a 40MB limit. Once you have upgraded all the domain controllers to Windows 2000, this limitation no longer applies, even if you are still operating in mixed mode.

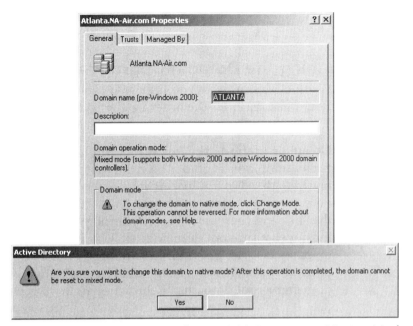

Figure 6-1: Changing a Windows 2000 Domain to Native Mode.

As long as you need to support Windows NT BDCs, you must leave the domain in mixed mode. Until you have made the switch, you can add new Windows NT BDCs to the domain. The procedure for adding the domain controller is the same as adding the BDC to a Windows NT domain, except you must create the computer account in the domain before installing the BDC. Once you have switched the domain to native mode, you can no longer create or employ any Windows NT BDCs in the domain.

In most cases, once you have upgraded all the domain controllers to Windows 2000, you should switch the domain to native mode. However, remember that switching the domain to native mode is an irreversible process. Once the domain has been converted to native mode, it remains that way. Before you make the switch make sure that you test all the network functionality in a test lab. In particular, if you are running any network applications on a BDC, ensure that the application functions on a Windows 2000 domain controller or member server. In addition, if you want to retain the option of going back to the Windows NT domain, do not convert the domain to native mode.

Planning the Domain Upgrade Order

One of the decisions that you have to make as you upgrade a multi-domain organization is the order in which you upgrade the domains. Here are some guidelines:

▲ **Create or upgrade the forest root domain first.** If one of your current domains is going to be the root domain, you must upgrade this domain first. If your Active Directory tree calls for a dedicated root domain, or if you want to create a new domain as the root and then move security principals into the domain, you must create the root domain first. This is a very important domain, as it can never be removed from the forest. All the other domains in the forest become either child domains to this root domain or root domains in a new tree in the forest.

▲ **If you have a master domain and resource domain model, upgrade the account domains before upgrading the resource domains.** If you have multiple account domains, you might want to upgrade one of the domains and then restructure the other account domains to become part of this domain to take advantage of the increased scalability of Windows 2000.

▲ **If you have created a dedicated domain as the root domain in your forest, upgrade a small domain first.** Regardless of how carefully you have tested the upgrade procedure, the upgrade of the production environment can reveal new issues and risks. To minimize the risk of major problems, upgrade a small domain first, so that if the upgrade fails, fewer users are disrupted and you can more quickly roll back to the previous configuration than if you had begun with a large domain.

▲ **After upgrading the account domains, upgrade the resource domains.** When upgrading the resource domains, you should again upgrade a small domain first to confirm the upgrade path. Then, once you are confident that the upgraded system is working, continue the upgrade with the domains that will realize the greatest benefits from the upgrade. For example, if you upgrade a resource domain that contains many workstations, you can quickly begin to take advantage of some of Active Directory's features for managing computers on the network.

Domain Restructuring

The alternative to upgrading the existing domains is to restructure the current domain configuration as part of the domain migration process. While upgrading the domains is generally easier and less disruptive, restructuring the domains may be necessary in order to take full advantage of some of the enhanced features of Active Directory. For example, if one of your company's objectives is to centralize the network administration, it might be advantageous to combine several Windows NT domains into a single Active Directory domain, perhaps moving some resource domains into account domains as OUs.

The process of domain restructuring consists of creating the domain structure that you want and then cloning or moving security principals from one domain to another. Users, groups, and computers can all be moved between domains in the same tree and cloned between domains in separate trees or from Windows NT domains to Active Directory domains. When you have removed all the security principals from a domain, you can remove the domain from the network.

When to Restructure

If you decide to restructure your domains, you must decide *when* you are going to restructure them. You have two options:

▲ **Upgrading and then restructuring.** You can upgrade all the domains to Windows 2000 and then restructure the domains afterward. This requires a two-step migration process, which increases the complexity of the migration. The restructuring can come immediately after the upgrade of the domains, or it can come time later as the corporate structure changes. You can use migration option to move security principals between Windows 2000 domains in the same forest.

▲ **Restructuring instead of upgrading.** Instead of upgrading a domain, you can clone the security principals from one or more Windows NT domains directly into a Windows 2000 domain. You create the Windows 2000 domain structure to fit the corporate goals and then clone the security principals to the new domain. The destination domain must be a Windows 2000 domain running in native mode, but the source domain can be a Windows NT domain or a Windows 2000 domain in a different forest.

Migrating Security Principals

Restructuring a domain consists of moving security principals from one domain to another and moving resource permissions between domains. To move or clone the security principals, you can use the Active Directory Migration Tool or one of the other tools discussed later in this chapter.

When you restructure a domain, you want to avoid having to reassign all the permissions on all resources in the domain. For example, if you have a file server that contains thousands of folders with permissions configured at several levels in the file structure, you do not want to start all over again with assigning permissions. Not only would this be time consuming, but also the probability of making an error in the configuration is high.

To maintain the permissions to resources in the new domain, you must ensure that the new user accounts have access to the same SID in the new domain as they did in the old domain. The user's permission to a resource is determined by the user's security identifier (SID) and the resource's discretionary access control list (DACL). Every security principal has a SID. The SID is made up of a domain identifier, which is the same for all security principals in a particular domain, and the relative identifier (RID), which must be unique for the each security principal. As a user completes the logon to the network, the logon server sends the user an access token. This access token consists of the user's SID, the SIDs for all the groups that the user belongs to, and the system rights granted to the user. The DACL is connected to the resource and is made up of a series of access control entries (ACEs). Each ACE consists of a SID and the level of permission that is granted or denied the group or user identified by the SID. When the user tries to access a file, the SIDs in the access control packet are compared to the permissions assigned to the SIDs in the DACL, and the user is granted appropriate permissions.

When you move or clone a user between domains, however, the SID for the user must change. The user is now part of a new domain, so the domain-specific part of the SID must reflect the new domain. The RID also changes. If you don't have a way to refer back to the original SIDs, you have to recreate the DACLs on all the network resources to reflect the new SIDs.

Fortunately, the domain restructuring process retains an attribute on the user object called sIDHistory. When you move a user between domains, the user is assigned a new SID and the SID from the previous domain is moved to the sIDHistory attribute for the user account. The access token contains both the new SID and the SIDs listed in sIDHistory, so an object's DACL can provide the appropriate level of access to the user.

> **NOTE:** *The sIDHistory attribute is available only when the target domain for the restructuring is a Windows 2000 Active Directory domain running in native mode. This means that you must create the new domain (or upgrade an existing Windows NT domain) and configure it to run in native mode before you can retain the sIDHistory when moving or cloning the security principals.*

Intra- and Inter-Forest Restructuring

One way to restructure a forest is to move security principals between domains within that forest. Intra-forest restructuring might be advantageous for a company that is migrating to Windows 2000 and would like to change the domain structure after the migration. Intra-forest restructuring also is useful when an organization's administrative structure changes such that a new domain model would make more business sense.

When performing an intra-forest restructure, you move, rather than copy, the security principals between the domains. This is because SIDs in a domain, including the SIDs listed in the sIDHistory attribute, must be unique within the forest. When you move a security principal, its account is copied and then deleted. In addition, because the built-in accounts and groups have well-known SIDs that are the same in all domains, the built-in security principals cannot be moved. For example, the Domain Admins group has the same SID in all Windows 2000 domains, and therefore the Domain Admins group cannot be copied between domains.

When you restructure a domain by moving security principals, you must move certain objects as part of closed sets. For example:

▲ When you move a user that is part of a global group, you must move the user and the group at the same time.

▲ When you move a global group, you must move all the members of the global group at the same time.

▲ If you move a global group that has nested groups in it, you must migrate all the groups and all members of the groups at the same time.

If you do not want to move all the objects as a closed set (for example, you want to move the users but not the groups), you must recreate the groups in the target domain and assign the memberships and permissions again in the new domain. The other alternative is to use universal groups (discussed in Chapter 5) during the restructuring process.

Inter-forest restructuring consists of cloning security principals between domains that are *not* in the same forest. The target domain must be an Active Directory domain running in native mode, but the source domain can be a Windows NT domain or an Active Directory domain in a separate forest. You can use this option during the migration process to restructure the existing Windows NT domains.

One of the most important advantages of inter-forest restructuring is that the security principals are copied (cloned) between the domains, rather than moved. The process creates a new account in the destination domain with the SIDs from the previous domain listed in the sIDHistory attribute. This means that you can extend the restructuring period over a longer timeframe. You can create the destination domain, switch it to native mode, and then migrate a small group of test users to the new domain. As long as the two domains are configured to trust each other, the users are able to continue accessing resources in either domain. After thorough testing, you can complete the migration process in stages until all security principals have been moved to the new domain. You can then decommission the old domain by removing the domain controllers from the network. It is also very easy in this scenario to roll back to the previous domain structure at any point. The restructuring process does not directly affect the source domain, so you can cancel the restructuring at any time.

When you clone users between domains, they retain their group memberships even if you do not clone the users and groups at the same time. If you migrate the users to the new domain, and then migrate the Windows NT groups later, the users are automatically added to the group when you clone the groups. If you copy the groups first, the group members are added as the user accounts are cloned to the new domain.

Domain Restructuring Tools

Windows 2000 provides a number of tools that you can use when restructuring domains. The specific tool you should use depends on whether you are performing an inter-forest or an intra-forest restructuring. The following sections outline some of the tools at your disposal.

Active Directory Migration Tool

The Active Directory Migration Tool (ADMT) is the most flexible and easy-to-use tool for migrating the domains. The ADMT supports both inter-forest and intra-forest migration. The ADMT includes an MMC snap-in and you can configure the migration options using wizards. I'll provide a detailed description of the procedures and capability for this tool later in this chapter, when discussing North American Air's migration path.

ClonePrincipal

ClonePrincipal is a script-based tool that you can use only to clone users and groups between domains in different forests. You'll find the ClonePrincipal files on the Windows 2000 Server CD in the Support Tools folder. You can use the ADMT to perform the same tasks as ClonePrincipal for inter-forest migrations, but because ClonePrincipal is a script-based tool, it provides more options for automating and customizing user account migration. The ADMT is much easier to use, but in a large domain environment, you might save time overall by using ClonePrincipal. The scripts that come with Clone-Principal are only samples, and must be modified to fit your specific situation.

To use ClonePrincipal, your configuration must meet the following requirements:

▲ The target domain must be running Windows 2000 Active Directory in native mode.

▲ The source domain must be a Windows NT 4.0 domain (Service Pack 4 or later), or a Windows 2000 mixed mode or native mode domain in a different forest.

▲ If you are cloning the security principals from a Windows NT domain, the scripts must be configured to use the PDC.

▲ A trust must be configured between the domains.

▲ You must be a member of the Domain Admins group in the target domain and a member of the Administrators group in the source domain.

▲ The Registry on the source Windows NT PDC must be modified to include the following DWORD value with the value set to 1:

```
HKLM\SYSTEM\CurrentControlSet\Control\LSA\TcpipClient
Support
```

▲ A local group must exist in the source domain called *Domain-Name$$$*, where *DomainName* is the name of the source domain.

▲ Auditing for success and failure of account management operations must be enabled in both the source and target domains.

NOTE: This list also describes the requirements to run the ADMT when cloning accounts between domains. The only exception is that the ADMT automatically creates the Registry value and local group as well as configures auditing. Another distinction between the ADMT and ClonePrincipal is that only users and groups (global, local, domain local, and universal) can be cloned using ClonePrincipal, while the ADMT also can clone computer accounts.

If your configuration meets these prerequisites, you can modify and run the VBScript scripts that make up ClonePrincipal. Before running the scripts in a production environment, however, ensure that the scripts are working properly in the test lab.

Netdom

Netdom is a command-line utility that you can use to move computer accounts between domains, both within forests and among them. You can also use Netdom to determine the current trust configurations in your domain and manage the trusts.

The ADMT provides a graphical interface to accomplish the same tasks as Netdom. However, if you are using ClonePrincipal or MoveTree to move users using a script, you can use Netdom to move computer accounts as part of the migration.

MoveTree

MoveTree is a Support Tools utility that you can use to move users, groups, and OUs between domains in the same forest. When you move a user between the domains, the user's password and GUID are retained. However, since local groups and global groups must be empty to be migrated, and the groups must be repopulated in the new domain, MoveTree is not very helpful in most cases.

NOTE: This chapter covers upgrading the domain structure to Windows 2000 — in other words, the domain controllers in the domains. Obviously, the migration to Windows 2000 is more than just a migration to Active Directory; you also must move other services to Windows 2000 and implement Windows 2000 Professional on client PCs.

However, other migrations do not directly affect Exchange 2000, so the focus here is on domain migration.

Migrating North American Air to Windows 2000

North American Air plans to use both the domain upgrade and the domain restructuring procedures to complete the migration to Windows 2000. As outlined in the last chapter, the project team at North American Air decided to create a dedicated root domain called NA-Air.com and then create child domains for most of the other corporate locations. For example, the Winnipeg domain will be upgraded to Windows 2000 to become the Winnipeg.NA-Air.com domain. The resource domains in Texas will be restructured to become high-level OUs in the Texas.NA-Air.com domain. In addition, the Atlanta and Chicago domains will be restructured to form a single domain. Here's an outline of the steps, many of which I'll discuss in the next several sections of the chapter:

1. Install the root domain.

    Creating the root domain must be the first step. The project team will create their root domain on a new domain controller at the corporate headquarters in Dallas.

2. Upgrade the domain in Winnipeg.

    The project team will upgrade the domain controllers for Winnipeg to Windows 2000. They have chosen Winnipeg for a number of reasons. First, the domain administrators in Winnipeg have been involved in testing Windows 2000 from the beginning and are very knowledgeable. In addition, by choosing a small domain to upgrade first, the team hopes to minimize the recovery time if the upgrade fails. The experience gained in upgrading the Winnipeg domain will be valuable when the time comes to upgrade the account domain in Texas.

3. Upgrade the Atlanta domain.

   The Atlanta domain will be the second domain upgraded to Windows 2000, primarily because it will be the destination domain for the domain restructuring of the Chicago domain.

4. Restructure Chicago domain into the Atlanta domain.

   The Chicago domain will be restructured to be part of the Atlanta domain using the ADMT. Again, this is a smaller scale restructuring that can be used to test the restructuring procedures before restructuring the resource domains in Texas.

5. Upgrade the Texas account domain.

   Upgrading this domain affects the largest number of users, which is both positive and negative. If there are serious problems during the upgrade, 25,000 users might be affected. However, upgrading this domain also moves 25,000 users into Active Directory, where the advanced management tools can be used to ease the administrative tasks.

6. Migrate the Texas resource domains into the upgrade account domain as OUs.

   One of the goals of the migration is to centralize the administration of all the resources in Texas in a single domain. To accomplish this, the project team will restructure the Texas resource domains into the Texas domain using the ADMT. The project team has decided not to upgrade the resource domains first, but rather to clone the computer accounts and groups in the resource domains in the Texas domain.

7. Upgrade the other domains.

   Once the larger domains have been upgraded, the smaller domains will be upgraded one at a time. In each case, the domain controllers will be upgraded to migrate the domain.

   These steps provide an overall view to the process. The following sections look at each of the procedures in more detail.

Installing the Root Domain

The first step in migrating North American Air to Windows 2000 Active Directory is to install the root domain at corporate headquarters. This root domain will be a dedicated root that is essentially empty except for the built-in accounts, the most important of which are the Enterprise Admins group and the Schema Admins group.

Active Directory Installation Requirements

Active Directory installation requires the following:

▲ The computer must be running Windows 2000 Server, Advanced Server, or Datacenter Server.

▲ The computer must have a partition that is formatted with NTFS 5. The Sysvol folder, created during the installation of Active Directory, must be put on an NTFS 5 partition to support the File Replication Service.

▲ The computer must have network connectivity that includes the TCP/IP protocol. The server should have a static IP address. If the computer is joining an existing tree or forest, or if it will be an additional domain controller in an existing domain, it must have network connectivity to the existing domain controllers.

▲ The DNS configuration must be correct.

  – If this is the first domain controller being installed, the Active Directory Installation wizard can install and configure the DNS.

  – If there are already other domain controllers in the domain or tree, the TCP/IP properties on the server can be configured to point to a DNS server that is the authoritative name server for the installation domain.

▲ If the installation must create a new domain, the Domain Naming Master server for the forest must be available through a Remote Procedure Call (RPC) connection.

▲ An account with sufficient permission must initiate the installation.

- If this is the first computer in the forest, a local Administrator account must be used.

- If this is an additional domain controller in an existing domain, an account from the Domain Admins group must be used.

- If this is a child domain, an account that is a member of the Enterprise Admins group must be used, or a member of the Enterprise Admins group must first create the domain in Active Directory using the Ntdsutil utility.

- If this is a new tree in a forest, an Enterprise Admins account must be used.

Installing Active Directory

To install Active Directory on a Windows 2000 server, a North American Air administrator runs Dcpromo from the Run command. This starts the Active Directory Installation wizard. Figure 6-2 shows the first set of screens, used to choose the role that the new domain controller plays in the Active Directory configuration.

The administrator must first specify whether the computer is the domain controller in a new domain or an additional domain controller in an existing domain. For example, if he has already created a domain called NA-Air.com by installing a domain controller, the computer can become an additional domain controller in the domain. To do this, the administrator selects Additional domain controller for an existing domain. The wizard then prompts him for the account and password of an account with sufficient permissions to add a domain controller to the domain he chooses. In contrast, if the domain does not yet exist, he chooses Domain controller for a new domain to create a new domain with the installation of this domain controller.

If the administrator is creating a new domain, his next choice is whether the computer forms a new domain tree or whether the new domain is a child domain in an existing tree. If the computer being upgraded is the first domain controller in the domain NA-Air.com, he would select the option Create a new domain tree to install the domain controller as the root domain in a new tree. However, if the computer being promoted forms a child domain in an existing tree, he would select Create a new child domain in an existing domain tree. This is the case when creating a domain called Winnipeg.NA-Air.com under the NA-Air.com domain. When creating a child domain, the wizard prompts for an Enterprise Admins account and password and then displays the parent domain.

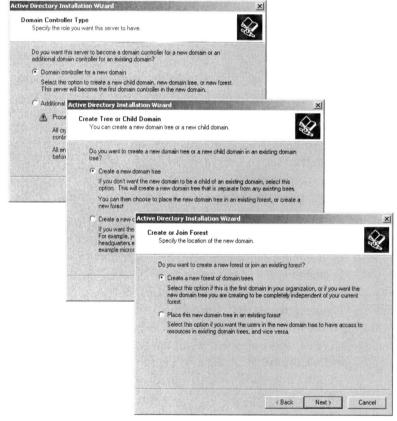

Figure 6-2: The Forest Configuration Options When Installing Active Directory.

When creating a new domain tree, the next option is whether the new domain tree joins to an existing tree and forest, or whether this is the first tree in a new forest. For example, if this domain controller is the first domain controller in the NA-Air.com domain and there are no other trees in the organization, the administrator would choose Create a new forest of domain trees. This installs the domain controller as the root domain in the tree as well as the root for a new forest.

The administrator would choose Place this domain tree in an existing forest option if the domain were being created in an already existing forest. For example, if North American Air decided to separate the manufacturing component of the business from the air-freight component by creating two separate trees, the NA-Freight.com domain could be installed as a second tree in the NA-Air.com forest. The trees would share a common schema and global catalog, as well as a transitive trust relationship between the two trees.

After configuring the domain controller's role in the forest, the Active Directory installation process continues. The administrator must provide the following additional information during the installation:

▲ **Domain name and NetBIOS name.** When creating a new domain, the wizard prompts for a domain name and a domain NetBIOS name. The domain name should be the same as the domain name choice made during the DNS planning. The NetBIOS name is used for backward compatibility for clients such as Windows NT 4.0 clients, who need a NetBIOS name to connect to the domain controller. The NetBIOS name is, by default, the first part of the DNS name, but it can be changed. The NetBIOS name must be unique on the network.

▲ **Location for the Active Directory database and log files.** Active Directory information is stored on the Active Directory database. The *%systemroot%*\NTDS directory is the default location, but it can be changed. For performance and redundancy reasons, the log files and the database should be located on separate hard drives.

▲ **Location of the shared system volume.** All the data replicated between domain controllers resides on the shared system volume. The default volume is called Sysvol, and must be located on an NTFS 5 partition.

▲ **Default permissions to user and group objects in Active Directory.** One of the choices made during Active Directory installation is the level of permissions assigned to the Active Directory information. Figure 6-3 shows the options.

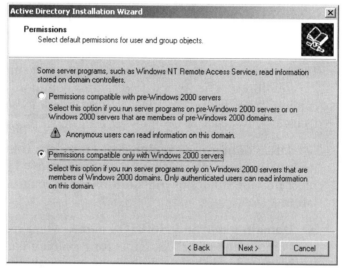

Figure 6-3: Default Permission Configuration When Installing Active Directory.

By default, Windows 2000 does not allow users logged in with the Anonymous account access to any Active Directory objects. Some applications, such as NT 4.0 RAS and some SQL and third-party applications, require anonymous access to the Active Directory. You can enable this access during or after the installation process. To enable this option after installation, add the Everyone group to the Pre-Windows 2000 Compatible Access group in Active Directory Users and Computers.

▲ **Directory Services Restore Mode Administrator Password.** One of the important installation options is the Directory Services

Restore Mode password. The installation screen is shown in Figure 6-4.

This password is stored in the SAM database and is used only when you need to repair Active Directory. This password will be used when you choose Directory Services Restore Mode from the Windows 2000 Startup menu. If the domain controllers are not physically secure, choose a complex password for this account.

After the administrator provides the information that the wizard needs to complete the installation of Active Directory, the installation process begins. It creates the default Active Directory database, schema, and configuration partitions, and configures Registry security.

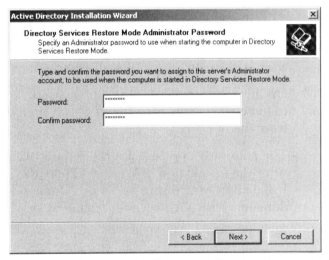

Figure 6-4: Configuring the Directory Services Restore Mode.

Upgrading an Existing Domain

The procedure for upgrading an existing domain is similar to the procedure for installing a new domain. In this case, the administrator installs Windows 2000 on a Windows NT Primary Domain Controller. After completing the upgrade to Windows 2000 and rebooting the server, the Active Directory Installation wizard automatically starts. The options available during the Active Directory

223

installation are identical to those for a fresh install of Active Directory, except that there is no option for creating a new domain controller in an existing domain.

North American Air has decided to upgrade the Windows NT domain in Winnipeg first. The Winnipeg domain currently has a PDC and two BDCs. The project team has determined that the current PDC and one of the BDCs can be upgraded to Windows 2000, while the second domain controller should be removed from the network due to hardware limitations and reliability issues. The project team laid out the following procedure for upgrading the Winnipeg domain to Windows 2000:

1. The administrator first installs an additional BDC in the domain. This BDC is a server class computer that provides good hardware redundancy.

2. The administrator performs a complete backup of all the domain controller and then tests the backup of the servers by performing a test restore on an additional server.

3. On the additional BDC, the administrator uses Server Manager to force replication with the PDC and then disconnects the BDC from the network.

4. The administrator then upgrades the PDC to Windows 2000. After the installation of Windows 2000, the Active Directory Installation wizard runs and a new domain is created as a child domain in the NA-Air.com domain, as shown in Figure 6-5.

5. After upgrading the PDC, the administrator thoroughly tests all domain functions. The administrator tests whether all clients log on to the network and whether all network applications still work and confirms that changes to the domain database on the Windows 2000 domain controller are being replicated to the Windows NT BDCs.

6. The project team then allows the network to function for several days. At least once a day, they connects the offline BDC to the network again, force replication, and then disconnect the server again.

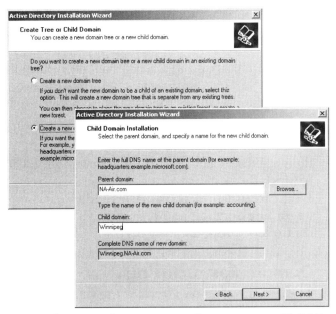

Figure 6-5: Configuring the Winnipeg Domain as a Child Domain in the NA-Air.com Domain.

7. The administrator upgrades the production BDC to Windows 2000. After the Windows 2000 installation, the Active Directory Installation wizard runs and the server is installed as an additional domain controller in the Winnipeg.NA-Air.com domain.

8. Again, the team tests the network and confirms that the network is stable.

9. The administrator installs a new Windows 2000 computer and promotes it to be the third domain controller in the domain.

    Because one of the BDCs will be removed from service, the project team considered a couple of options to provide a third domain controller. One option was to use the temporary BDC — to connect it to the network and then upgrade it to Windows 2000. The project team decided, however, to do a clean install of Windows 2000 on an additional server, and then install Active Directory on it and configure it as an additional domain controller in the domain. In most cases, it is preferable to perform a clean install of an operating system rather than upgrade an existing operating system.

10. Once all three domain controllers are installed and the network is stable, the administrator removes the two BDCs from the network and switches the domain to native mode.

The administrators can use this domain upgrade procedure in most of the other domains at North American Air. The only exceptions are the Texas resource domains and the Chicago domain, both of which they will restructure as described in the following section. In every case, the project team uses additional computers as BDCs when upgrading domains and performs consistent backups of all domain controllers throughout the upgrade process.

Domain Restructuring

The restructuring required for the Chicago domain and the resource domains in Texas is significantly more complicated than the upgrading of the other domains. Administrators must upgrade the Atlanta domain and configure it as child domain in the NA-Air.com domain before tackling Chicago. The project team must then decide how to restructure the Chicago domain. One option is to upgrade the Chicago domain as a child domain in the same tree and then migrate the security principals to the Atlanta domain. Another option is to perform an inter-forest migration that does not upgrade the Chicago domain but instead clones the security principals to the new domain using the Active Directory Migration Tool.

The team chose this second option because it allows for the creation of the security principals in the new domain without removing them from the Chicago domain. If the trusts are configured properly, the users can log on to either domain and access all resources. This option also provides the easiest rollback option if the restructuring fails.

The project team developed the following procedure to restructure the Chicago domain:

1. Upgrade the Atlanta domain to be a child domain in the NA-Air.com domain using the same procedure outlined in the preceding section for the Winnipeg domain.

   The domain must be completely upgraded to Windows 2000 and switched to native mode before proceeding.

2. Configure a two-way trust between the Atlanta domain and the Chicago domain.

   The trust is a standard Windows NT trust. To configure the trust from Windows 2000, open Active Directory Domains and Trusts from the Administrative Tools folder and right-click the domain name. Select Properties and click the Trusts tab. To create a two-way trust, add the Windows NT domain to both the trusted and trusting domain list. Figure 6-6 shows the interface for adding the trusts. The trusts also must be configured from the Windows NT PDC.

3. Enable account management auditing in both the target and destination domains.

   To enable account management in Windows 2000, open Domain Controller Security Policy from the Administrative Tools folder and expand Security Policy/Local Policies/Audit Policy. Then double-click Audit account management and select the check boxes for Success and Failure. In Windows NT, account management auditing is enabled through User Manager for Domains.

4. Install the ADMT.

   The ADMT can be downloaded from the Microsoft Windows 2000 site and installed on a domain controller in the target domain or any computer running Windows 2000. Installing ADMT on a domain controller minimizes network traffic but adds a significant load to the domain controller. In most cases, it is preferable to install the ADMT on a member server that has a fast network connection to a domain controller and global catalog server in the target domain.

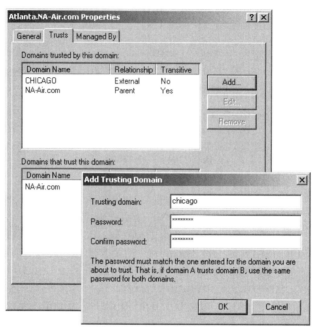

Figure 6-6: Configuring Trusts with Windows NT Domains in Windows 2000.

5. Open the Active Directory Migration Tool from the Administrative Tools folder.

 NOTE: *The rest of the steps describe the process of migrating groups from the source domain to the target domain, including the migration of group members.*

6. Right-click Active Directory Migration Tool and select Group Migration Wizard. The Group Account Migration wizard starts.

7. Chose whether to test the migration only or to perform the migration now.

For all the wizards that come with the ADMT, the migration process can be tested without actually performing the migration. Figure 6-7 shows the options at this point. Regardless of the option chosen on this screen, the rest of the wizard goes through the same procedure.

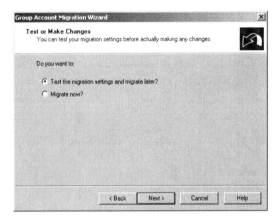

Figure 6-7: The ADMT Can Be Used to Test the Migration Procedure.

8. Choose the source domain and the target domain.

9. Choose the groups to be migrated to the target domain.

    Click Add and then select the groups the groups to be cloned in the target domain. The project team at North American Air decided to migrate the Domain Users group so that all the users in the domain will be cloned. Figure 6-8 shows the interface used to migrate the groups.

10. Choose the Destination OU for the groups that are being migrated.

11. Chose the options for the migration (see Figure 6-9).

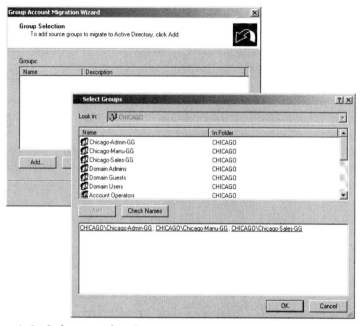

Figure 6-8: Selecting the Groups to Migrate to the Target Domain.

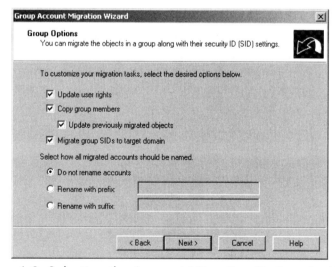

Figure 6-9: Selecting the Account Migration Options in ADMT.

The project team at North American Air decided to select the first four options:

▲ **Update user rights.** Copies any rights assigned to the user to the target domain.

▲ **Copy group members.** Copies the members of the selected groups to the target domain.

▲ **Update previously migrated objects.** Adds previously migrated user accounts into the same groups they were in before the migration.

▲ **Migrate group SIDs to target domain.** Copies the SIDs for the users and groups that you are migrating to the new account in the target domain.

The other selections on the dialog box configure whether the wizard should rename any of the migrated accounts.

12. Chose the option to allow the ADMT to create the *domainname*$$ group in the source domain and add the TcpipClientSupport value to the Registry on the PDC in the source domain. After the Registry value has been added to the PDC in the source domain, it reboots to change the Registry.

13. Type in the user name and password of an administrator account in the source domain.

14. Choose how to deal with conflicting accounts in the target domain if a user or group with a duplicate name is cloned.

    The options available include to not upgrade accounts with duplicate names, or replace the account in the target domain with the account from the source domain. The last option is to rename all duplicate accounts. Figure 6-10 shows the dialog box.

15. Choose how the wizard creates the user passwords and whether to enable or disable the accounts. See Figure 6-11.

    You can use the wizard to generate complex passwords or to assign passwords that are the same as the user names. In either case, the wizard writes the password to a file.

The wizard can disable the source account, disable the target account, or leave both accounts active, and can be configured with an expiration date.

A roaming user profile from the source account with the target account can be migrated with the account.

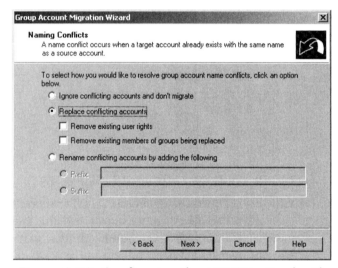

Figure 6-10: Configuring the ADMT to Deal with Duplicate Accounts.

16. Review the summary of the configuration options and then complete the migration process.

   After running a test migration, examine the log file that is created to determine how the migration would have worked if you had performed the actual migration.

   The preceding steps outlined the procedures for cloning groups and users from a Windows NT domain to a Windows 2000 Active Directory domain. The ADMT includes several other wizards that can be used to migrate other domain information to the target domain:

▲ **User Migration Wizard.** Used to migrate users between domains. It also can be configured to migrate group accounts.

▲ **Computer Migration Wizard.** Used to migrate computer accounts from Windows NT domains to Windows 2000 Active Directory.

▲ **Security Translation Wizard.** Used to update the access control lists for resources on computers that have been migrated to a Windows 2000 domain. This wizard should be run just before the Windows NT domain is decommissioned. The wizard replaces the user and group SIDs for accounts from the source domain with the new SIDs from the accounts in the target domain. The sIDHistory attribute can then be cleaned up on the target accounts by using a script.

▲ **Reporting Wizard.** Used to create reports on the migration process.

▲ **Trust Migration Wizard.** Used to migrate trust configurations from the source domain to the target domain.

▲ **Group Mapping and Merging Wizard.** Used to merge groups from the source domain with groups in the target domain. It also can create a custom mapping to identify the target groups for specific source groups.

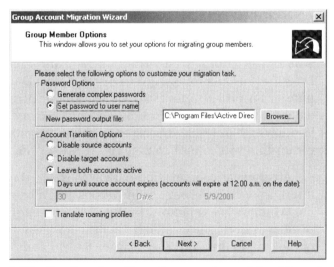

Figure 6-11: Configuring User Passwords and Enabling Accounts.

233

Exchange Server and the ADMT

There are two Exchange-specific issues that can arise from running the ADMT to clone users in a new domain: Exchange-specific permissions for Windows NT accounts, and migrating the Exchange service account.

The ADMT includes an Exchange Directory Migration wizard that changes the Exchange-specific permissions. In Exchange, you can set permissions in many places, including mailboxes, distribution lists, organization, sites, and containers. In addition, every Exchange mailbox must be associated with one Windows NT account. The ADMT can change the SIDs for these permissions if the Exchange Administrator program is running on the same computer that is running the ADMT and if the account that is used for the migration has Permissions Admin rights to the Exchange site.

The Exchange service account is migrated using the Service Account Migration wizard. The wizard asks which computers it should scan for service account information and then presents a list of accounts that can be migrated.

Conclusion

This chapter describes the process of migrating Windows NT domains to Windows 2000 Active Directory. The easiest way to perform this migration is to upgrade the domain controllers in the Windows NT domains to Windows 2000 and then run the Active Directory Installation wizard to install Active Directory on the computer. This process moves all the security principals from the SAM database in Windows NT to the Active Directory database in Windows 2000. While this is the simplest migration path, it also means that you cannot change the Windows NT domain structure.

An alternative migration path is to create the Windows 2000 forest according to your specifications and then restructure the existing Windows NT domains. In this case, you migrate the security principals from one domain to another. Microsoft provides a number of tools to do this, and this chapter looked at the Active Directory Migration Tool, as the easiest tool for completing this process.

This chapter described the first major step that North American Air had to take to begin the migration to Exchange 2000. Before even starting the implementation of Exchange 2000; however, North American Air must begin the implementation of Windows 2000. This chapter described that step in the process. Because the directory service is now Active Directory, there has to be some way for Exchange 4.0/5.*x* and Active Directory to communicate. The tool that makes this possible is the Active Directory Connector (ADC), which synchronizes Active Directory information and Exchange 4.0/5.*x* information. The next chapter discusses the ADC in detail.

Chapter 7

Using the Active Directory Connector

IN COMPANIES RUNNING WINDOWS NT and Exchange 4.0/5.*x*, there are two directory services: one in Exchange and one in Windows NT. In Windows 2000 and Exchange 2000, however, there is only one directory service — Active Directory. Both directory services must be migrated to Active Directory to complete the upgrade.

This chapter describes the first step in merging the directories — installing and using the Active Directory Connector (ADC). The ADC is the connector between the Exchange 4.0/5.*x* directory and the Windows 2000 directory. It's used to populate Active Directory with user information from Exchange and to keep the two directories synchronized. Deploying the ADC is a temporary measure when an organization is migrating to Exchange 2000. The ADC is needed only when the organization is running Exchange 4.0/5.*x* and has migrated at least one domain to Active Directory. As soon as all the servers have been upgraded to Exchange 2000, the need for the ADC disappears.

In a single domain and single-site environment, deploying the ADC is fairly easy. As you move into larger environments where you have multiple domains and sites, however, ADC configuration becomes much more complicated.

Preparing the Exchange Organization for Migration

Before implementing any information sharing between the Exchange directory and Active Directory by installing ADC, you need to resolve a couple of issues.

The first is whether you want to redesign the Exchange sites before you migrate. This is an important issue because when you upgrade an existing Exchange organization to Exchange 2000, each site becomes an administrative group that also contains a routing group with all the servers from the site. You can move servers between routing groups after you migrate to Exchange 2000 and switch the Exchange organization to native mode, but there is no way to move servers between administrative groups. This means that if you want to change the administrative structure of your Exchange organization, you must change the site configuration *before* migrating. Exchange 5.5 Service Pack 2 includes a Move Server wizard that you can use to move servers between sites.

> **NOTE:** *Moving servers between sites is a major task. If you are planning on redesigning your sites, be prepared to spend a significant amount of time, planning, testing, and implementing the process.*

The second issue that you need to investigate is the mailbox permissions. In Exchange 4.0/5.*x*, you could identify a single user as the primary Windows NT account for more than one mailbox. For example, a user might have both a personal mailbox and a general information mailbox and use the same Windows NT account name to gain access to both. In Exchange 2000, however, each user account can be associated with only one mailbox. When you replicate the mailbox information from Exchange 4.0/5.*x* to Active Directory, only one mailbox can be associated with each user account. If you do not create a one-to-one association between user accounts and mailboxes before you run the ADC, you get inconsistent results. Since only one of the mailboxes associated with the user's account can be assigned to the user in Active Directory, the ADC associates one of the mailboxes with the user account and creates a new Active Directory object for the other(s). To ensure a smooth migration between the Exchange directory and Active Directory, you should make sure that each user account is associated with only one mailbox.

> **NOTE:** *Another essential step in the migration process is to prepare the Windows 2000 forest for Exchange 2000 by running the Exchange setup with the /forestprep and /domainprep options. When you are migrating an existing Exchange organization, you should first configure the ADC and then prepare the forest. I cover the /forestprep and /domainprep options in the next chapter.*

The Active Directory Connector

In a Windows NT and Exchange 4.0/5.*x* environment, there is little connection between the Windows NT domain directory and the Exchange directory. The only connecting point between the two directories is the primary Windows NT account that is associated with each Exchange mailbox. The two directories can be administered separately. If you run the Exchange Administrator and User Manager for Domains on the same computer, the Mailmux.dll creates a link between the two administration programs so that you can create a mailbox whenever you create a user, or create a Windows NT account every time you create a mailbox. Other than that, there is no shared information between the two directories. Part of the reason for this is that the two directories store different information.

The Windows NT directory (stored in the SAM database) includes basic information about a user, such as the username and a short description of the user, plus security related information such as SID, group membership, home directory, dial in rights, and so on. The Exchange directory, with its richer selection of data, is a more useful directory if you are looking for particular users on the network. For example, you can include the users' phone numbers, addresses, supervisors, departments, and so on. Many organizations store a great deal of user information in the Exchange directory and enable users to search it for people meeting specific criteria.

When the Exchange 4.0/5.*x* server operates in a Windows 2000 environment that includes Active Directory, however, this configuration changes. Active Directory can contain the same rich information about each user that was maintained by the Exchange directory. When you are looking for a user in Active Directory, you can search on any attribute associated with the user object, just like you can in Exchange 4.0/5.*x*.

Many organizations have invested significant time in entering employee data into the Exchange directory and would like to be able to migrate that information into Active Directory without having to retype all the information. When you upgrade a domain, or clone security principals into a new domain, only the information from the Windows NT domain database transfers with the user account, but you can use the ADC to migrate all the information from the Exchange directory to Active Directory as well.

> **NOTE:** *If you have a single Exchange site and a single Windows 2000 domain, and you are not planning to implement Exchange 2000, you do not have to install ADC. When you create a mailbox on the Exchange 4.0/5.x server, you can create a user in the domain just like you could in a Windows NT environment. You can create a user account in Active Directory and associate the account with a mailbox in Exchange. However, none of the rich information about users flows between the two directories. Essentially, you are administering a Windows 2000 domain just like you administered a Windows NT domain, thus losing some of the benefit of moving to Windows 2000.*

After the initial synchronization, it's helpful to be able to keep the two directories synchronized, such that when a change is made in one directory, the change is automatically replicated to the other directory. Because both directory services enable you to enter rich data for every user, you can administer the same information from either the Exchange Administrator or Active Directory Users and Computers. If you want to continue to administer the user information using the Exchange Administrator, you can configure the ADC so that all changes from the Exchange Administrator are replicated to Active Directory. You can also use Active Directory Users and Computers, and replicate the changes to the Exchange directory. If you want to use both tools, you can configure a two-way synchronization in which any change made in either directory is replicated to the other directory.

There are two versions of the ADC. One version is included with Windows 2000 Server, while the second comes with Exchange 2000. The Windows 2000 version can only replicate user information between the two directories (that is, only the information in the Recipients container). The Exchange directory contains considerably more information than just user information, however. It also includes information about public folders that you might want to replicate between the two directories. In addition, the directory contains the topology information about the entire organization, including information on the Exchange sites and servers and the connectors between sites. Exchange uses this information when it makes message routing decisions and to determine the directory replication topology. If Exchange 2000 is to seamlessly fit into the Exchange 4.0/5.x organization, it needs some way of exchanging this topology information with the Exchange 4.0/5.x servers. The Exchange version of the ADC enables this. It can be configured to replicate public folder and organizational information with Exchange 4.0/5.x servers.

If you are not planning to migrate the Exchange 4.0/5.x servers to Exchange 2000 right away, the Windows 2000 version of the ADC is all you need to replicate the user information between the directories. When you do install Exchange 2000, ADC is updated to the Exchange 2000 version. However, if you are planning on upgrading to Exchange 2000 soon, you should start with the Exchange 2000 version of the ADC.

NOTE: *This chapter discusses the ADC as a means to replicate user information. In later chapters, when I discuss the coexistence of Exchange 4.0/5.x and Exchange 2000, I explain the role of the ADC in synchronizing topology information and show you how to use it to replicate public folder information.*

To use the ADC, you must first install it on a Windows 2000 server. The ADC does not replicate any information until you configure a connection agreement between the two directory services. A connection agreement defines how you want synchronization to occur. You can configure a number of options when you create a connection agreement, including:

▲ **The containers to replicate.** For example, you can configure a specific recipient container in Exchange as the source directory and an OU in Active Directory as the destination directory.

▲ **The Exchange objects and AD objects to replicate.** For example, from Exchange, you can choose to replicate mailboxes, custom recipients, and distribution lists. From Active Directory, you can replicate users, groups, and contacts.

▲ **The direction of data flow and the schedule for synchronization.** You can configure the synchronization information to flow from Exchange to Active Directory, or Active Directory to Exchange, or both ways. You can also configure a schedule for the synchronization so that you can control what time of day the synchronization takes place.

▲ **Rules for creating and deleting objects.** When you configure the connection agreement to replicate mailboxes from Exchange, you can configure how the ADC deals with the replication when there is no matching user in Active Directory. It creates a disabled user account by default, but you can change the default to create an enabled account or to create a contact. When you delete a mailbox or user object, the corresponding object in the other directory is also deleted. However, you can change that default so that the deletion information is written to a file instead. You can then manually import the change into the directories after an administrator has examined the file.

You can configure multiple connection agreements for a single ADC running on a server. For example, if you have multiple Exchange sites that need to be replicated with one Active Directory domain, you can install the ADC on one computer and then configure multiple connection agreements to replicate the different sites. If you want to configure a different destination OU for Custom Recipients than you use for the regular mailboxes, you can also configure separate connection agreements using the same ADC to replicate the two types of objects.

ADC Synchronization Overview

When you first configure the ADC and connection agreements, a complete replication of all the information in both directories takes place (assuming that you configured a two-way connection agreement). When replicating objects from the Exchange 4.0/5.*x* directory to Active Directory, the following rules apply:

▲ Exchange 4.0/5.*x* mailbox objects that are mapped to Active Directory user accounts appear in Active Directory as mailbox-enabled users. The *msExchHomeServerName* attribute on the Active Directory user object identifies the Exchange server on which the mailbox exists, the *Object-GUID* attribute on the mailbox is set to the GUID of the user object in Active Directory, and the *legacyExchangeDN* attribute on the Active Directory user object is set to the distinguished name of the mailbox object. (See the Microsoft Exchange *2000 Server Resource Kit* for a complete listing of the attribute mappings.)

▲ Exchange 4.0/5.*x* mailbox objects that are mapped to Windows NT user accounts appear in Active Directory as disabled user accounts. This situation might arise if you had a single Exchange site with multiple domains and you had not upgraded all the domains to Active Directory. You can change the default behavior on the connection agreement so that either enabled user accounts or contacts are created.

▲ Exchange 4.0/5.*x* custom recipient objects are created as contact objects in Active Directory.

▲ Exchange 4.0/5.*x* distribution lists are created as mail-enabled universal distribution groups in Active Directory if the destination domain is not running in native mode. If the destination domain is running a native mode, the ADC checks whether the distribution list is used to assign permissions anywhere in the Exchange organization. If not, it creates a universal distribution group. If the destination domain is running in native mode and the distribution list is used to assign permissions, it creates a universal security group. (For more information, see "Planning and Deploying the ADC" later in the chapter.)

If you configure a two-way replication, or replication from Active Directory to Exchange only, the following rules apply:

▲ Mailbox-enabled users in Active Directory appear as mailboxes in Exchange 4.0/5.x.

▲ Mail-enabled users in Active Directory appear as custom recipients in Exchange.

▲ Mail-enabled contacts in Active Directory appear as custom recipients in Exchange.

▲ Mail-enabled groups in Active Directory (either distribution or security) appear as distribution lists in Exchange.

▲ Any objects in Active Directory that are not mail-enabled or mailbox-enabled do not appear in the Exchange directory.

The computer running the ADC connects to a domain controller using an LDAP connection on port 389. The LDAP port is also used to connect to the Exchange server. It accesses the global catalog service on port 3268.

The ADC computer must also have RPC connectivity to the Exchange server. The RPC connection is used only when you create a new user in Active Directory Users and Computers and assign the user a mailbox on an Exchange 4.0/5.x server. During the next ADC cycle, an LDAP write creates a new mailbox for the user on the Exchange server, but to create the proxy addresses, such as the SMTP or X.400 address, an RPC connection on port 135 must be established with the Exchange server. This is an important issue only if your network configuration requires a firewall between the ADC computer and the Exchange server.

Once the ADC has been installed and connection agreements configured, the ADC begins keeping the directories synchronized. The following steps describe the process of synchronization:

1. At the scheduled time, the ADC performs an LDAP query to collect the information about what has changed in each directory. If the connection agreement is a two-way agreement, it polls the Exchange directory first, followed by Active Directory. The ADC

uses Update Sequence Numbers (USNs) to determine whether changes have been made to each directory. Both Active Directory and the Exchange 4.0/5.*x* directory service use the USNs to manage directory updates. The USN is incremented every time a change is made to either directory. By examining the USN, the ADC can determine whether any changes have been made to either directory. The ADC maintains two USN attributes: *MSExchServer1HighestUSN*, which tracks the latest changes received from Active Directory, and M*SExchServer2HighestUSN*, which tracks the latest changes received from the Exchange server.

2. The ADC retrieves any changed object from both directories and stores them in the memory of the server on which the ADC is running. It then compares the attributes of the objects and writes any changed attributes to the destination directory.

3. The ADC updates the USN for each server.

The ADC queries each directory every five minutes for changes by default. If you set a schedule specifying when the ADC runs, it queries the directories every five minutes during that time. By default, the ADC also runs for a maximum of five minutes at a time, followed by a five-minute break. In a large organization, where there might be many changes to the directories, the ADC process can place a significant load on the Active Directory domain controller to which it connects. This slows down other operations that also need access to Active Directory. The five-minute break enables any backlogs to clear.

You can configure both the frequency with which the ADC runs and the length of time it runs continuously by editing the Registry. Use the Registry Editor and locate the following key:

```
HKEY_LOCAL_MACHINE\System\CurrentControlSet\Services\
MSADC\Parameters
```

To change how frequently the ADC runs, add the following value to this key:

Value Name: `Sync Sleep Delay` (secs)

Data Type: `REG_DWORD`

Value: The length of time between syncs in seconds

To change how long the ADC runs continuously, add the following value:

Value Name: `Max Continuous Sync` (secs)

Data Type: `REG_DWORD`

Value: The length of time in seconds

In most cases, the default values are appropriate. However, you might want to have the ADC running all day, but not running every 5 minutes because of the load it places on the domain controller. You could then configure the ADC to replicate every 10 or 15 minutes. To set the Sync Sleep Delay to 10 minutes, set the value of the Registry key to 600 seconds.

Installing and Configuring the ADC

You can install the ADC on any Windows 2000 server that is part of an Active Directory domain. When you configure a connection agreement, you must choose an Active Directory domain controller and an Exchange server that will operate as the replication bridgehead servers. The server that is running the ADC should be connected to both of these computers, as well as to a global catalog server with a fast network connection. To decrease the amount of network traffic, you can install the ADC on a domain controller and global catalog server. However, you should do this only if the domain controller is powerful enough to handle the extra processor and memory requirements for running the ADC. The Exchange server that is operating as the synchronization bridgehead server must be running Exchange 5.5 with Service Pack 2 or greater. Other Exchange servers in the site can be running Exchange 4.0 or 5.x.

To install the Exchange 2000 version of the ADC, you must be logged in with an account that is a member of the Schema Admins and Enterprise Admins groups. The installation process makes extensive changes to the Active Directory schema, so you must have permission to do this, as well as be able to connect to the schema master for the domain.

NOTE: If you are not a member of the Schema Admins group or do not have access to the schema master, a member of the Schema Admins group can change the schema on the schema master in the root domain by running the ADC setup on the schema master using the setup /schemaonly command from the ADC\I386 directory on the Exchange 2000 CDROM. Running setup with this option makes the required changes to the schema but does not install the service.

ADC Installation Procedure

If you are planning on migrating to Exchange 2000, you should install the Exchange version of the ADC. The following procedure describes the installation and configuration procedure to install this version.

1. Run setup.exe from the Exchange 2000 CD in the \ADC\I386 folder. The Microsoft Active Directory Connector wizard starts.

2. Choose whether you want to install just the service component, or the management component, or both. See Figure 7-1.

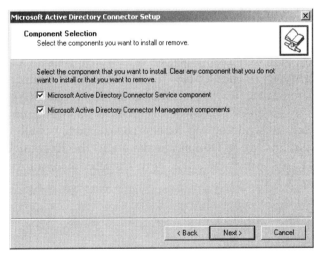

Figure 7-1: Installing the ADC Service or Management Components.

You can install the ADC service on one computer and then install the administration tools on another computer. The service must be installed on a Windows 2000 server, but the management components can be installed on a Windows 2000 Professional computer.

3. Choose the directory where the program will be installed.

4. Choose the service account under which the ADC runs. See Figure 7-2.

The default account is the user account under which you are running the installation. You might want to configure a different default account, however. This default account must have the right to log on as a service on the computer where the ADC is running and must be a member of the built-in Administrators group in the domain where ADC is installed.

If this is the first copy of ADC to be installed in the forest, the installation process modifies the schema. The schema update process can take a long time, especially if you are not installing the ADC on the Schema Master. See Figure 7-3.

After changing the schema, the program files are installed.

The ADC runs as a service on the Windows 2000 server and appears in the services list as MSADC. Installing the ADC also adds the Active Directory Connector Management MMC snap-in and creates an Active Directory Connector Management tool in the Administrative tools folder. In addition, installing the ADC creates the Exchange Domain Servers and the Exchange Services groups in Active Directory and assigns the user account used by ADC as the only member.

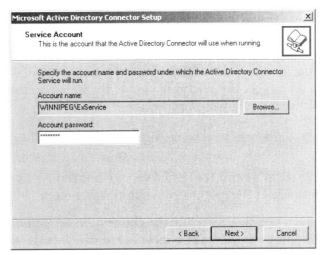

Figure 7-2: Choosing the Active Directory Account Used by the ADC.

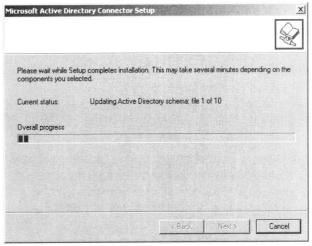

Figure 7-3: Changing the Schema as Part of the ADC Installation.

Configuring Connection Agreements

Installing the ADC adds a service to the Windows 2000 server, but does not actually begin any replication. To configure replication, you must configure connection agreements between the Exchange organization and the Active Directory domain. Once the ADC is installed, you can configure connection agreements on the server using the following eleven-step procedure.

1. Open Active Directory Connector from the Administrative Tools folder.

2. Right-click Active Directory Connector and select New, and then select Recipient Connection Agreement.

3. Type the name for the connection agreement, select the direction for the synchronization, and select the server where the ADC will run. See Figure 7-4.

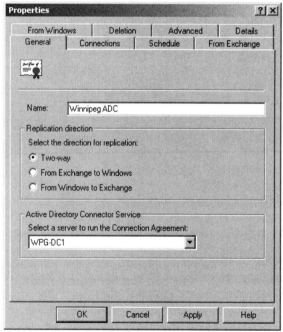

Figure 7-4: Configuring the General Tab for the Connection Agreement.

4. Click the Connections tab to configure the Windows 2000 server and the Exchange 5.5 server that will be the ADC bridgehead servers. See Figure 7-5.

The accounts that you choose for each connection must have at least read and write permission for each directory that will be written to. If you are configuring this connection as a two-way agreement, both accounts must have read and write permission for the objects that will be replicated. The default authentication option is Windows Challenge/Response. The other options are Basic (Clear-text) using SSL and Windows Challenge/Response using SSL.

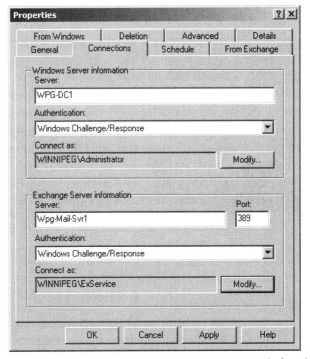

Figure 7-5: Configuring the Connections Tab for the Connection Agreement.

251

NOTE: *If the Exchange Server is installed on a Windows 2000 domain controller, you must change the port number for the Exchange server. By default, the ADC uses port 389 to query the Exchange server. Port 389 is the default LDAP port, but both Active Directory and Exchange 4.0/5.x use the LDAP port as well, so the two services conflict on a domain controller. Because the Active Directory service starts before the Exchange directory, the Active Directory service blocks the Exchange server from using the port. You must change the port number to avoid a conflict. Microsoft recommends using port 390, but you should confirm that the port is not used for any other application on the network. You also must change the port number for the Exchange server using the LDAP configuration settings for the server in Exchange Administrator. To avoid this problem in the first place, many people simply avoid installing Exchange 4.0/5.x on a Windows 2000 domain controller.*

5. Click the Schedule tab to configure when the replication occurs. See Figure 7-6.

   By default, the ADC runs from midnight to 6 A.M. every day. During the times selected on the Schedule tab, the ADC polls the source directory (or directories if the connection agreement is a two-way agreement) every five minutes for new updates. If you select Always on this tab, the ADC polls the source directory every five minutes for changes throughout the entire day.

   The Replicate the entire directory the next time the agreement is run option results in a complete synchronization of the directory. It replicates the entire directory by default the first time the agreement is run, but only changes are replicated after that. Use this option only when you need to rebuild the entire directory.

   If you want to initiate a replication outside of the regular schedule, right-click the connection agreement in Active Directory Connection Manager and select Replicate Now.

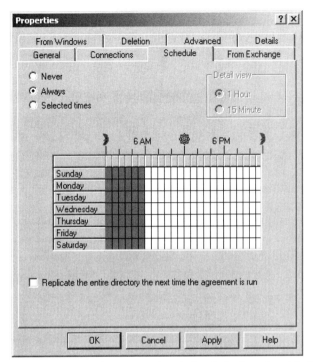

Figure 7-6: Configuring the Schedule for the ADC.

6. Click the From Exchange tab and configure the synchronization of Exchange objects. See Figure 7-7.

You can configure what types of objects are replicated, as well as the source and destination containers for the replication. All object types are replicated by default. The source container you select depends on the purpose of this connection agreement. If you have additional recipient containers in addition to the default Recipients container, you can select any of the containers as the source container. The easiest way to configure the source directory in Exchange is to use the site as the source container. By using a higher-level container, you can make sure that all objects of the selected types are replicated.

You can also configure the destination container. You can choose any container or OU in the Active Directory domain. You can also configure the domain as the destination container in Active Directory.

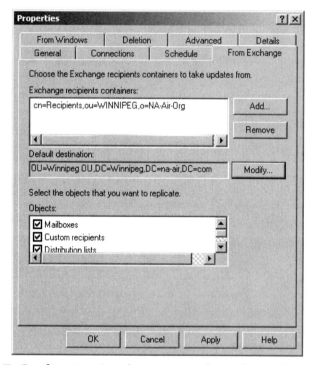

Figure 7-7: Configuring Synchronization from the Exchange Server.

7. Select the From Windows tab to configure the replication from Active Directory. See Figure 7-8.

The configuration options shown in Figure 7-8 are similar to those on the From Exchange tab (Figure 7-7). You can choose the types of objects to be replicated as well as the source and destination containers.

You can also enable the Replicate secured Active Directory objects to the Exchange Directory option. A secured Active Directory object is any object that has an explicit access control entry (ACE) denying permission to that object. Because

Exchange does not support the option to deny permissions, these objects are not replicated by default.

You can also configure the Create objects in location specified by Exchange 5.5 DN option. This option requires that every object in Active Directory have a value for the *legacyExchangeDN (Distinguished Name)* attribute. If an object does not, the ADC cannot determine where the object should be created, and the creation fails. When you create a new object in Active Directory, it does not have a value for this attribute, so you should accept the default of not creating objects in the location specified by the Exchange DN.

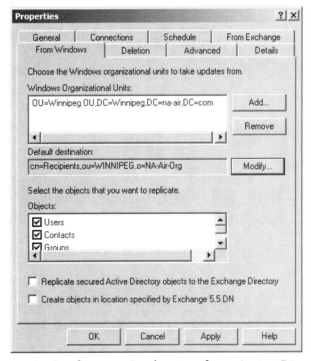

Figure 7-8: Configuring Replication from Active Directory.

8. Click the Deletion tab to configure how the ADC handles deletions from either directory. See Figure 7-9.

When you delete an object in Active Directory, you can configure the ADC either to delete automatically the corresponding object in the Exchange directory or to write the deletion information into a .csv file instead. If you choose to write the information to a .csv file, you can examine the content of the file to confirm that you want to delete the objects, and then you can use Directory Import from Exchange Administrator or the Admin /i command from the command line to import the .csv file into Exchange and delete the object.

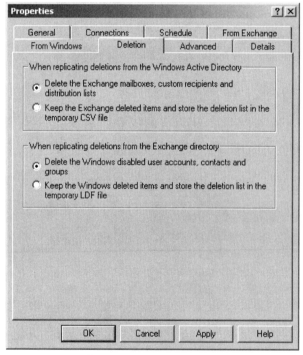

Figure 7-9: Configuring the Deletion Tab in the ADC.

You have a similar option for objects that have been deleted from the Exchange directory. When you delete an object like a mailbox from Exchange, the ADC can delete the corresponding user account in Active Directory or write the information to a LDAP data interchange format file (an LDIF file with an .ldf extension).

You can then examine the content of the file and use the LDIFDE command line utility to import the content into Active Directory.

9. Click the Advanced tab (Figure 7-10) to configure performance settings, choose the type of connection agreement, and specify how the connection agreement handles replication of objects that do not exist in Active Directory.

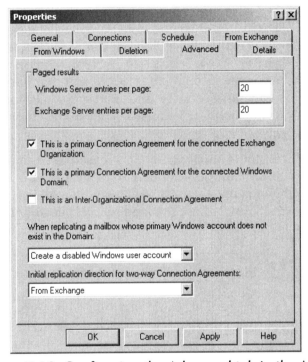

Figure 7-10: Configuring the Advanced tab in the ADC.

The Paged results settings configure the performance of the connection agreement. The Windows Server entries per page and the Exchange Server entries per page define how many entries are transmitted at one time between servers. To improve performance, you can increase the number of entries per page. This requires more memory on the servers. You should not set

Exchange Server entries per page higher than the number of entries returned for an LDAP search on the Exchange server. (The default is 100.)

The options that define the primary connection agreements also determine whether this connection agreement can create objects in the destination directory. For example, if you have defined this connection agreement as the primary connection agreement for the connected Exchange organization, creating a new contact in Active Directory also creates a new custom recipient in Exchange. If you do not configure the agreement as a primary agreement, the agreement can modify properties of objects that already exist, but cannot create new objects. This option requires some planning in an environment that has multiple sites and domains. For more information, see "Primary Agreements and Connection Agreements" later in the chapter.

The option to configure this connection agreement as an inter-organizational agreement is used to configure replication of information from one Exchange 4.0/5.*x* organization to another Exchange 4.0/5.*x* organization in a different Active Directory forest. You can use this option to replicate some of the user attributes, but not security-related information.

You can also configure what the connection agreement should do if a mailbox is replicated to Active Directory and the primary account associated with the mailbox does not exist in Active Directory. This could occur if you had one Exchange organization with multiple domains and one of the domains had been upgraded to Windows 2000, while the other domains had not. You can configure the connection agreement to create a disabled Windows user account, create an activated user account, or create a contact.

The Initial replication direction for two-way Connection Agreements setting specifies which directory is updated first when the connection agreement runs. By default, the information from Exchange is replicated to Active Directory first to make sure that the Exchange objects are created in Active Directory and to populate the attributes for the Active Directory objects with the attributes from Exchange.

10. Click the Details tab to configure an administrative note for the connector.

11. When you are finished configuring the ADC, click OK to save the configuration. An information dialog box appears stating that the ADC is designed as a temporary step in migrating to Exchange 2000. If the Active Directory domain that you have chosen is running in mixed mode, a warning dialog box suggesting that you should use a domain running in native mode also appears, shown in Figure 7-11.

When the ADC replicates distribution lists from Exchange into Active Directory, it attempts to create matching universal security groups, which can be created only in native mode domains. If you do configure the ADC to use a mixed mode domain, it creates universal distribution groups instead of universal security groups. See the section on Exchange 4.0/5.*x* distribution lists and universal groups later in this chapter.

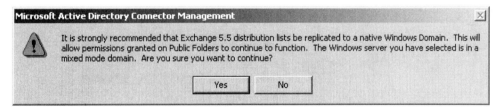

Figure 7-11: Warning Dialog Box When the ADC Is Configured to Use a Mixed Mode Domain.

After you have configured the connection agreement, the computer running the ADC immediately begins the first replication and performs a complete two-way replication (if the connection agreement is configured for two-way replication). After this initial replication, only changes are replicated between the two directories.

By default, the values for all attributes are replicated between the two directories. If you want to change this, you can configure which attributes the ADC replicates and how the ADC matches objects between the two directories To do so, right-click Active Directory Connector Management in the Active Directory Connector Management console, choose Properties, and click the From Exchange or From Windows tab. Figure 7-12 shows the default attribute replication configuration as well as how to configure additional attribute matching rules.

You can configure which attributes are replicated between the two directories. If you are using only a selection of the attributes in Active Directory and Exchange, replicate only the attributes you are using.

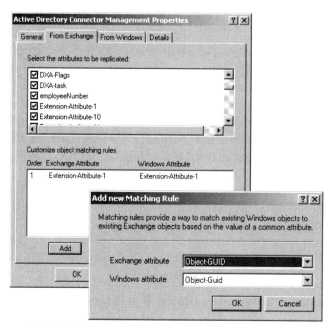

Figure 7-12: Configuring the Default Attribute Replication in the ADC.

When the ADC runs for the first time, it searches Active Directory for objects that it can match with the Exchange mailbox information. For example, if you use the ADMT to clone users from one domain to another and then use the ADC to synchronize the Exchange information with the Active Directory information, the ADC locates the

Active Directory account linked to each mailbox and synchronizes the information between the two objects.

By default, the ADC tries to locate objects with the same globally unique identifier (GUID), legacyExchangeDN, and primary Windows NT account attributes (such as the SID). You can add additional attributes to this list. For example, if you have used one of the Extension Attributes (Custom Attributes in Exchange) to assign employee numbers, you can match the Exchange object to the Active Directory object using this attribute.

NOTE: *If you modify the settings on the From Exchange tab, make sure you make the same modification on the From Windows tab.*

After you configure a two-way connection agreement, you can administer the directory information from either Exchange Administrator or Active Directory Users and Computers.

Planning and Deploying the ADC

The ADC is a powerful and useful tool to ease the transition to Exchange 2000, but it also requires careful planning. There are a number of issues you must address before implementing the ADC. The following sections discuss some of them.

Exchange 4.0/5.x Distribution Lists and Universal Groups

When migrating Exchange 4.0/5.*x* information to Active Directory, you must plan how to handle distribution lists. In Exchange 4.0/5.*x*, the members of a distribution list can include mailboxes, distribution lists, and custom recipients from anywhere in the entire Exchange organization. The Windows NT accounts associated with the mailboxes in the organization can come from any domain. The primary purpose of a distribution list is to group multiple mailboxes to make it easier to send mail to a group of recipients. However, distribution lists can also be used to assign permissions to Exchange objects, such as public folders, on any Exchange server in any domain in the organization.

The fact that members of a distribution list can come from any domain in the organization, and that the distribution list can be used to assign permissions to any Exchange object in the organization, makes migrating distribution lists to Active Directory complicated. Any security group in Active Directory can be mail-enabled, such that it functions as a distribution list on an Exchange server. The only security group in Active Directory that shares the distribution list characteristics of having members from any domain, and being available to assign permissions anywhere in the forest, is a universal security group. This means that to duplicate the complete functionality of the distribution list in Active Directory, the distribution list must appear as a universal security group in Active Directory.

This is an important issue if you have more than one domain in your organization and if you use distribution lists to assign permissions to public folders. When you configure the ADC to replicate distribution lists to Active Directory, the type of object created in Active Directory depends on the whether the distribution list appears in any ACL in the Exchange organization (for example, on the permissions list on a public folder) and on whether the destination domain runs in native mode. If the distribution list appears in an ACL and the destination domain is running native mode, a universal security group is created. If the destination domain runs in mixed mode, a universal distribution list is created. You can use this group in Exchange 2000 as a mail recipient, but not as a security principal, which means you cannot use it to assign permissions to public folders on Exchange 2000 servers. If the distribution list does not appear in an ACL in Exchange 4.0/5.x, a universal distribution list is created. If you add this group to an ACL on an Exchange 4.0/5.x public folder after the ADC has been implemented, it changes the group to a universal security group during the next synchronization cycle.

You might run into a problem with the default configuration if you are using the Exchange 4.0/5.x distribution lists to assign permissions to Exchange objects, and you have one or more domains that are still running in mixed mode. There are two ways to deal with this situation. The preferred way is to convert at least one of your domains to native mode and then migrate the Exchange distribution lists into the native mode domain. For example, if North American

Air did not want to convert all the child domains to native mode, they could set the root domain (NA-Air.com) to native mode. Then, they could configure separate connection agreements for the distribution lists in the child domains so that the distribution list information was replicated to the root domain. Any distribution lists could then be replicated to the native mode domain as either security or distribution groups. This method provides the most seamless migration of both distribution lists and permissions to Active Directory. The second way is to leave the domains in mixed mode and then have the ADC create only universal distribution groups for the distribution lists. Distribution groups can have members from any domain even when the domain is running in mixed mode, but a distribution list cannot be used to assign permissions to resources in Active Directory domains. While you can still use the group to assign permissions to objects in Exchange 4.0/5.x, you cannot use them to assign permissions in Exchange 2000.

Replicating Multiple Recipient Containers

Another issue to address when you configure connection agreements is how the ADC should handle additional recipient containers in the Exchange 4.0/5.x organization. By default, only a single Recipients container is created in every Exchange 4.0/5.x site, but you can configure additional recipient containers. For example, if you wanted to create a separate container for each department such as Sales, you could create the container and then create all the sales mailboxes in the container. One of the limitations of Exchange 4.0/5.x is that it is very difficult to move mailboxes between containers, so companies rarely implement this option. However, some companies do create additional recipient containers for objects such as Custom Recipients or Distribution Lists.

If a company does have additional recipient containers, there are two ways to configure the replication to Active Directory. The first is to select the Site container as the Exchange source container for the replication and select the Active Directory domain as the destination container. When the connection agreement runs, a Recipients OU is created in Active Directory containing all the user accounts for the mailboxes under the Recipient container. An additional OU is created for each additional recipients container that you created in Exchange, and all the objects from each container are replicated to the destination OU.

The second way is to configure replication for each of the Exchange subcontainers separately. You can use this option to merge all the subcontainers into a single Windows 2000 OU. In this case, you would select each of the containers in Exchange as a separate replication source, and configure each container to replicate with the same Active Directory OU. For example, if you had a Recipients container and a Custom Recipient Container in the Winnipeg site, you could configure the connection agreement so that both recipient containers replicated to the Winnipeg OU.

If you want to configure additional connection agreements, you can also use this option to replicate each additional container to different OUs in Active Directory. To have two separate OUs in Active Directory as the replication targets, you can configure two connection agreements each with one of the recipient containers as a replication source and a separate OU as the replication target.

The process also works the same way for replication from Active Directory to Exchange. If you choose an OU with a child OU as the source container, the same child OU configurations are reflected as subcontainers in the destination container in Exchange.

NOTE: Until you migrate your Exchange servers to Exchange 2000, using multiple containers, particularly multiple OUs in Active Directory, is not a seamless operation. For example, any OUs that you created before enabling the connection agreement are replicated only as additional recipient containers after you create an additional mail-enabled user in the OU. If you move a user from one OU to another in Active Directory after you have configured the connection agreement, the change is not reflected in the recipient containers in Exchange. If you are planning to migrate to Exchange 2000 soon after implementing Active Directory and installing the ADC, you should wait until you have migrated before modifying the default user configuration from the upgrade to Windows 2000. If you are going to be waiting several months before upgrading, you should carefully test the effects of moving objects between Active Directory containers and of changing the Active Directory structure.

Migrating User Information to Active Directory

Another planning issue is how to use the ADC to migrate the information from the Exchange directory into Active Directory. There are several different approaches you can take:

▲ Upgrade the Windows NT domain and then use the ADC to migrate the user information.

▲ Use the Active Directory Migration Tool (ADMT) to clone the user accounts in a Windows 2000 domain, and then use the ADC to migrate the user information.

▲ Run the ADC first and configure it to create disabled user accounts in a transition domain, and then upgrade the source domain to Active Directory. Then use the Active Directory Cleanup wizard to merge the disabled account information with the upgraded account.

▲ Run the ADC first and configure it to create disabled user accounts in a permanent domain, and then use the ADMT to clone the users from the Windows NT domain to the Active Directory domain.

▲ Run the ADMT without the sIDHistory option, and then recreate the DACLs for network resources including Exchange. Then run the ADC to populate the user attributes.

I'll explain each of these options more thoroughly in the following sections.

Upgrade the Domain; Then Run the ADC

This is the easiest method to implement. You begin by upgrading the domain controllers, which upgrades the Windows NT domain to Active Directory. The user SIDs do not change, so the users can access their mailboxes on the Exchange 4.0/5.*x* servers after the upgrade. After you have upgraded all the domains controllers to Windows 2000, you can switch the domain to native mode.

Next, you install the ADC service on a server in the Active Directory domain. After installing the ADC, you configure a connection agreement to replicate information between the Exchange directory and Active Directory. When the connection agreement runs for the first time, the ADC compares the SIDs of the mailbox primary Windows NT accounts with the SIDs of the Active Directory user objects. It then migrates the user information from the Exchange directory to the user object in Active Directory.

Run the ADMT with sIDHistory; Then Run the ADC

A second scenario is to restructure a domain with the ADMT and then run the ADC to populate the attributes. In many ways this is similar to the previous method, in that you are first creating the user accounts in Active Directory and then using the ADC to migrate the information. This scenario is different, however, in that you first must create the Windows 2000 domain, clone the security principals to the new domains from the Windows NT domain, and then use the ADC to synchronize the user information.

This process works because the ADC can use the sIDHistory attribute to match user accounts. When the user accounts are cloned to the Active Directory domain, the user gets a new SID, but the SID from the Windows NT domain is stored in the sIDHistory attribute. When the ADC tries to find a match for the primary NT account for an Exchange mailbox, it examines both the SID and the sIDHistory attribute for user objects in the destination domain. When the ADC finds a matching SID, it migrates the mailbox information to the Active Directory account.

Run the ADC; Then Upgrade the Domain

The third method is to create a transition domain first to use as the destination domain for the ADC. This transition domain must be a part of the same Active Directory forest as the production domains, and can be either one of the permanent domains or a temporary domain. After you select the transition domain, you use the ADC to create disabled user accounts in the transition domain with all the Exchange attributes. Then you upgrade the Windows NT domain to Windows 2000 and add it to the corporate forest. Finally, you use the

Active Directory Cleanup tool to merge the disabled user accounts with the upgraded user accounts.

You might want to use this procedure if you need to upgrade to Exchange 2000 before upgrading a particular domain to Windows 2000. When you run the ADC, it creates a disabled user account in the transition domain for each Exchange mailbox and copies all the Exchange information to the disabled account. It also migrates the mailbox permissions to the new account. Each of the disabled accounts has an msExchMasterAccountSid attribute that identifies the Windows NT account that serves as the primary account for the mailbox. You can then install Exchange 2000 into this environment by upgrading the Exchange 4.0/5.x servers to Windows 2000 and Exchange 2000 or by installing an Exchange 2000 server into the site and moving the mailboxes to the new server. Because of the way the SIDs are linked between the disabled account and the Windows NT account, users can access the mailboxes on the Exchange 2000 server using their Windows NT accounts.

For example, North American Air could use this option to upgrade a domain such as Winnipeg. They would first create a domain to be used as a transition domain. The transition domain could be the root domain, or a temporary domain created at the Winnipeg location. To avoid using the bandwidth between Winnipeg and Dallas for the ADC, the best option would be to create a temporary domain.

Here's the process you would use as a North American Air administrator for Winnipeg:

1. Create a temporary domain at Winnipeg. The domain must be a child domain of NA-Air.com and you must switch it to native mode to support the correct migration of the distribution lists. For example, you could create the domain Wpg-Temp.NA-Air.com in Winnipeg.

2. Install the ADC on one of the servers in the Wpg-Temp domain. Configure a connection agreement by which the Winnipeg site will be replicated with an OU in the Wpg-Temp domain. The replication direction for the agreement depends on how long

this ADC is used. If this is a temporary configuration, you should use a one-way replication from Exchange. If you plan to manage the directories using this configuration for some time, you should configure a two-way agreement. When the connection agreement runs for the first time, disabled user accounts are created in the Wpg-Temp domain.

3. When you upgrade the regular Winnipeg domain, join it to the NA-Air.com domain as a child domain. This procedure creates users in the Winnipeg.NA-Air.com domain that have the same SID that they had in the Winnipeg Windows NT domain. This SID is also the same as the SID assigned to the msExchMasterAccountSid attribute on the disabled user account created by the ADC.

NOTE: *The next step must be completed immediately after the previous step, as Exchange 2000 server does not operate until the two accounts have been merged.*

4. Next, use the Active Directory Cleanup wizard to merge the two accounts. The Active Directory Cleanup wizard goes through the Active Directory forest and tries to locate accounts in which the SID on the upgraded account is the same as the SID linked to the disabled user account. When the wizard locates a duplicate, it merges the attributes from the disabled user account to the upgraded account and then deletes the disabled account.

The Active Directory Cleanup wizard is included with Exchange 2000. To install the wizard, you must run the Exchange 2000 setup and install the Administration Tools.

Run the ADC; Then Use the ADMT

This method is much the same as the preceding one. Again you need to create a Windows 2000 domain to be the destination container for the ADC. In this case, however, you should use a domain that is part of the corporate forest instead of using a transition domain. After running the ADC, you can install Exchange 2000 and it functions using the disabled account in Active Directory. Then when you are ready to clone the user accounts from the Windows NT domain, you can choose the option in the ADMT to replace the disabled Active Directory account with the cloned account from Windows NT. In this way, you do not have to run the Active Directory Cleanup wizard to merge the two accounts.

North American Air could use this option when working with the Atlanta and Chicago domains. Here's the process you would use as a North American Air administrator for Atlanta and Chicago:

1. Upgrade the Windows NT domain at Atlanta to Windows 2000, and then convert the domain to native mode.

2. Run the ADC at Atlanta to merge the Exchange 5.5 attributes with the Active Directory accounts and to migrate the distribution lists and custom recipients into Active Directory.

3. Create an additional connection agreement on the server running the ADC between the Chicago Exchange site and a Chicago OU in the Atlanta domain. Configure the connection agreement to create disabled user accounts in the Atlanta domains.

4. Upgrade the current Exchange 5.5 organization to Exchange 2000. The users in Atlanta will use their Windows 2000 accounts to access the Exchange server, while the users in Chicago will continue to use the Windows NT accounts.

5. Use the ADMT to clone the security principals from the Chicago domain to the Atlanta domain. Make sure that the ADMT is configured to replace any user accounts that it finds with duplicate SIDs. Replacing the accounts moves the additional attributes from the disabled accounts to the enabled accounts and then deletes the disabled accounts.

You can also use the ADMT to rename any account for which it finds a duplicate SID. If you chose this option, you can specify how the new account is renamed. Then you need to run the Active Directory Cleanup wizard to merge the two accounts.

Run the ADMT without sIDHistory; Then Run the ADC

In some cases, you might not want to migrate the sIDHistory when you clone a user from one domain to another. For example, if you are using the migration as an opportunity to redesign the existing file structure and resource permissions, you can use this method to migrate the user information into Active Directory but not migrate the SIDs with the users. To do so, run the ADMT without migrating the SID from the Windows NT domain into the sIDHistory attribute and then use the ADC to migrate the user information.

To implement this method, you must first create a destination Active Directory domain running in either native mode or mixed mode. Then you clone the user accounts from the Windows NT domain into the Active Directory domain without cloning the security information for the users. As a result, the user accounts in the new domain do not have access to any resources because the new SIDs have not been assigned any permissions, including permission to the mailbox on the Exchange server.

Before running the ADC, you must re-establish the link between the mailboxes and the user accounts. You can do this manually, but this would be a long and tedious task in a large organization. The ADMT includes the Exchange Directory Migration wizard, which automates the task of reassigning the primary account for the Exchange mailbox.

After you have assigned the new account as the primary Windows NT account for the Exchange mailbox, you can run the ADC to migrate the user information to the new account. The ADC uses the user name of the account to determine which account from the Windows NT domain to associate with the account in the Active Directory domain.

NOTE: *An important limitation of this last approach is that because no SID information is migrated with the account, you have to reassign permissions to every resource in the new domain, not just the Exchange mailboxes. Use this option only if you want to totally rework your resource permissions.*

Designing ADC Connection Agreement Scenarios

When designing the connection agreements within your organization, there are a number of questions that you need to answer, including these:

▲ What tools will you use to perform the user and mailbox administration? You can perform the administration from Exchange Administrator, from Active Directory Users and Computers, or from both places. The tool you choose determines the direction of the connection agreement replication.

▲ What are the source and destination containers for each direction of the connection agreement?

▲ How many sites and domains will you include in your ADC planning?

This last question is addressed in more detail in the following sections.

Single Domain, Single Site

If your organization includes only one Active Directory domain and only one Exchange site, the connection agreement configuration is fairly straightforward. The simplest option is to configure a single two-way connection agreement that synchronizes the Active Directory domain with the Exchange site. You can use a single two-way connection agreement if you have a one-to-one relationship between a domain and a site. For example, even though the Winnipeg location of North American Air includes one domain that is part of a larger forest and one site that is part of a larger Exchange organization, the connection agreement really has to deal with only a one-to-one scenario. This means you can create a connection agreement that has the Winnipeg domain as the Windows source and destination container and the Winnipeg Exchange site as the Exchange source and destination container.

The first question in this scenario is which tool you want to use to administer the user information. If you want to continue to use the Exchange Administrator, you can configure a one-way connection agreement from Exchange to Active Directory. Any change you make in the Exchange directory is replicated to Active Directory, but changes you make in Active Directory are not replicated back. Alternatively, you can also use Active Directory Users and Computers as your management tool. In this case, you can configure a one-way connection agreement from Active Directory to Exchange. If you want changes to flow both ways or if you want the initial population of user attributes from Exchange while administering from Active Directory, you can configure a two-way agreement.

Another question is what to use as the source and destination locations for the connection agreement. The easiest option is to select the Exchange site as the source for the Exchange replication and as the destination for the Windows replication. Then you configure the Active Directory domain as the source for the From Windows replication and as the destination for the From Exchange replication. If you choose this option, the Exchange recipient containers are duplicated in Active Directory. As an alternative, you can configure a separate connection agreement for each container in Exchange so that it replicates with a specific Active Directory OU. For example, if you have a Custom Recipients container in Exchange and you want to replicate the objects in the container with a Contacts OU in Active Directory, you must configure a separate connection agreement between these two containers, replicating only custom recipients from Exchange and only contacts from Active Directory.

Single Domain, Multiple Sites

Many organizations have multiple sites and a single Active Directory domain. In this scenario, configuring the connection agreements becomes more complicated. The configuration depends on what tool you want to use to manage the directory information.

▲ To manage the directory information from Exchange Administrator, configure a single connection agreement between one of the sites and the Active Directory domain. Because the directory in each site contains the directory information for the entire Exchange organization, you can copy all the Exchange information from one site to Active Directory. Any changes made to the directory in any Exchange site are replicated through the

Exchange 4.0/5.*x* directory replication process to the site with the connection agreement, and then to Active Directory.

▲ To manage the directory information from Active Directory, configure two connection agreements. You must configure a connection agreement for every site to which you want to write information. In this case, you set up a two-way connection agreement so that the initial information can be replicated from Exchange. You can then manage the objects from Active Directory. When you configure multiple connection agreements you must specify which connection agreement is the primary agreement for the Exchange organization and the Windows domain. (See "Primary Agreements and Connection Agreements" later in this chapter for details.)

▲ To manage the directory information from both directories, configure two connection agreements, one between each site and the domain.

This scenario can become much more complicated if you configure separate replication containers for each site. For example, if you have a Distribution List container in one site that you replicate with a specific container in Active Directory, you must configure an additional connection agreement with that site.

Multiple Domains, Single Site
A third scenario includes multiple Active Directory domains with a single Exchange site. The Exchange site contains mailboxes for user accounts located in multiple domains. The configuration of the connection agreement again depends on what tool you use to administer the domain information.

▲ To administer the domain from Exchange only, configure two one-way connection agreements. Each connection agreement uses the Exchange site as the source container and one of the Active Directory domains as the destination container. This scenario is complicated by the requirement of having only a single primary connection agreement for the Windows domain. (See the following section for details.)

▲ To administer the domain from Active Directory only, or from either Active Directory or Exchange, configure a two-way connection agreement between each domain and the Exchange site.

Primary Agreements and Connection Agreements

When you set up connection agreements that include more than one Active Directory domain or Exchange site, you must plan your configuration of the connection agreements carefully so that you do not create duplicate objects in either directory. The most important settings for the connection agreement configuration can be found on the Advanced tab, where you configure primary agreements. (The configuration options are shown in Figure 7-13.)

When a connection agreement is a primary agreement, it can create objects in the destination directory. For example, when you select the This is a primary Connection Agreement for the connected Windows Domain option, you configure the agreement to create new objects in the Windows domain. When the connection agreement runs and detects a new object in the Exchange directory, it checks to see if a matching object exists in the destination Windows container. If no matching object exists, the ADC creates a new object. For example, if you create a new custom recipient in the Exchange 4.0/5.*x* container, a new contact is created in the destination Active Directory container as well.

To see how this works, suppose North American Air had a single Exchange 5.5 site, Site1, with mailboxes for two Active Directory domains, Dom1.NA-Air.com and Dom2.NA-Air.com. See Figure 7-13.

To administer the directory information from Exchange or Active Directory, you must install the ADC in both domains and then configure it with two connection agreements: a two-way agreement between Site1 and Dom1, and another two-way agreement between Site1 and Dom2. If you configure both agreements as primary agreements for the Windows domain, and then you create a custom recipient in Exchange, a contact with the same properties as the custom recipient is created in both Windows domains. If you create a distribution list in Exchange, a universal group is created in both domains. To avoid this, you must configure one of the agreements as a nonprimary agreement. A nonprimary agreement can replicate changes to existing objects in the destination domain, but it cannot create new objects.

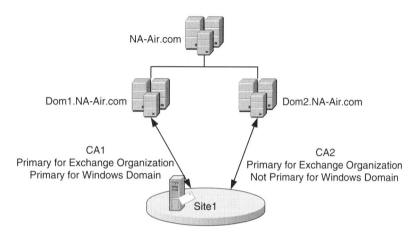

Figure 7-13: Configuring Primary Connection Agreements.

NOTE: *This issue does not affect the ability to create user accounts and mailboxes. When you create a new mailbox in Exchange, you can choose in which domain the account is created. The object is created directly in that domain.*

You also must think about this if you are working with a single domain and multiple sites. If you had a single domain (Dom1) and two Exchange sites (Site1 and Site2), you would have to configure two connection agreements. In this case, you would configure only one of the agreements as a primary agreement for the Exchange organization. If you configured both agreements as primary, and you created a contact in Active Directory, a custom recipient would be created in both sites.

If your network configuration is more complex and includes multiple domains and multiple Exchange sites, the planning becomes even more difficult. Again, you must make sure that you are not replicating the same information across more than one primary agreement.

Multiple Domains, Multiple Sites

Setting up connection agreements in a more complicated environment that includes multiple domains and multiple sites makes the configuration of the connection agreements even more difficult. Consider the example illustrated in Figure 7-14. The organization has two Active Directory domains that contain users with mailboxes in three different Exchange 5.5 sites.

In this case, you would have to install the ADC in both domains and then configure the connection agreements as outlined Table 7-1.

This scenario assumes that each connection agreement is configured with the source containers as the Recipients container in Exchange and a single OU in Active Directory, and that you are replicating all the possible objects (mailboxes, custom recipients, distribution lists) with a single connection agreement. If you want to configure subcontainers as the replication containers, or if you want to replicate different objects in different ways (for example, if you want to replicate custom recipients from Site3 to the West domain while replicating mailboxes and distribution lists with the East domain), you would have additional connection agreements to configure.

As mentioned earlier, this configuration does not affect the creation of mail-enabled user accounts and mailboxes. When you create a new mailbox in Site3, for example, you can select the domain in which to create a new account, or the domain in which to search for an existing account (assuming you have permission to create an account in the domain). All other types of objects that you create in Site3, such as distribution lists and custom recipients, are created in the East domain, but this does not apply to mailboxes and user accounts. When you create a new user account in the West domain, you can choose to create the mailbox on any server in any site, not just in Site1.

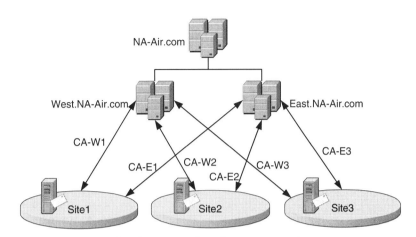

Figure 7-14: Configuring the Connection Agreements in a Complex Environment.

Table 7-1: Connection Agreements

CA Name	Primary CA for Exchange	Primary CA for Windows	Explanation
CA-W1	Yes	Yes	Any new object created in the West domain should be replicated to Site1. Any new object created in Site1 should be replicated to the West domain.
CA-W2	No	Yes	Any new object created in the West domain should not be replicated to Site2. (The object is created in Site1.) Any new object created in Site2 should be replicated to the West domain.
CA-W3	No	No	Any new object created in the West domain should not be replicated to Site3. (The object is created in Site1.) Any new object created in the Site3 should not be replicated to the West domain. (The object is created in the East domain.)

Table 7-1: Connection Agreements (Continued)

CA Name	Primary CA for Exchange	Primary CA for Windows	Explanation
CA-E1	No	No	Any new object created in the East domain should not be replicated to Site1. (The object is created in Site3.) Any new object created in the Site1 should not be replicated to the East domain. (The object is created in the West domain.)
CA-E2	No	No	Any new object created in the East domain should not be replicated to Site2. (The object will be created in Site3.) Any new object created in the Site2 should not be replicated to the East domain. (The object will be created in the West domain.)
CA-E3	Yes	Yes	Any new object created in the East domain should be replicated to Site3. Any new object created in Site3 should be replicated to the East domain.

Implementing the ADC at North American Air

As part of the migration to Windows 2000 and Exchange 2000, North American Air needs to implement the ADC to migrate the Exchange information to Active Directory and keep the two directories synchronized. The project team at North American Air decided on the following outline for implementing the ADC.

The ADC in the Winnipeg Domain

The Winnipeg domain was the first domain to be upgraded to Windows 2000, so it will also be the first place where the ADC is implemented. The implementation is straightforward because there is a one-to-one relationship between the domain and the site.

This situation requires only a single connection agreement between the Exchange site and the Winnipeg domain. The project team decided to allow administration of the directory from both Exchange Administrator and Active Directory Users and Computers initially, so they configured the connection agreement as a two-way agreement. Later, as the Exchange administrators become more comfortable with Active Directory Users and Computers, the project team plans to change the configuration of the connection agreement to one-way from Active Directory to Exchange.

The project team also decided to keep the configuration of connection agreements as simple as possible and therefore selected the Exchange site as the replication container for Exchange and the Winnipeg domain as the replication container for Windows. This means that the team can not make use of some of the advanced options for managing Active Directory until the migration to Exchange 2000 is complete and moving users between OUs does not affect the Exchange Recipient containers.

The second important decision facing the project team was how to handle the distribution lists. Essentially the team had two options. One option was to upgrade all the domain controllers to Windows 2000 and convert the domain to native mode before installing the ADC so that the distribution lists could be replicated as universal security groups. The other option was to use the root NA-Air.com domain as the group management domain and set up a separate connection agreement to replicate the distribution lists to the root domain. The project team decided to implement the first option, primarily because it's the easiest. A gap of a few days between the upgrade to Windows 2000 and the implementation of the ADC is not a problem for them. When the domain is upgraded, the Exchange users continue to be able to access their mail without any interruption. The project team did not identify any issues that would require a significant delay in moving the domain to native mode, so they will convert the Winnipeg domain to native mode within days of upgrading the last Windows NT domain controller, and then they will install the ADC.

The ADC in the Atlanta-Chicago Domain

Configuring the ADC in the Atlanta and Chicago domains is slightly more complicated because the two Windows 2000 domains will be combined as part of the upgrade to Windows 2000. In this case, the project team decided to upgrade the Atlanta domain to Windows 2000 and convert it to native mode. As soon as the domain is converted, the team will install the ADC and create a single connection agreement between the Atlanta site and the Atlanta domain.

The project team is planning to use the ADMT to clone security principals from the Chicago domain to the Atlanta domain. However, team members plan to maintain a separate Exchange site in Chicago, so the configuration for these two locations will be a single domain in Atlanta and two Exchange sites — one in Chicago and the other in Atlanta.

The project team considered two options for migrating the Exchange information into Active Directory. One option was to run the ADMT to clone the security principals from the Chicago domain to the Atlanta domain, and then use the ADC to merge the user information. The other option was to run the ADC first and create disabled user accounts for the Chicago users in the Atlanta domain, and then use the ADMT to clone the users. Then the team would use the Active Directory Cleanup wizard to merge the user accounts. The second option would be a good choice if the project team planned on implementing Exchange 2000 in Atlanta before it ran the ADMT. However, the team decided to clone the user accounts first and then run the ADC. This meant that the team had to manage only two procedures, rather than three, and the team decided to finish the Windows migration before starting the migration to Exchange 2000 in the Atlanta domain.

While the security principals are being migrated to the Atlanta domain, the current Exchange configuration will not be affected. The users in Atlanta log in to Windows 2000, but their user accounts give them access to the Exchange server because their SIDs do not change during the upgrade. The users in Chicago that have been cloned in Atlanta also log on to Active Directory, but the sIDHistory attribute for the cloned accounts still give them access to the

Exchange server. The users in Chicago that have not been cloned, or are not yet using their cloned accounts, access the Exchange server the same way they always have.

The team must then move the Exchange servers from Chicago to the Atlanta domain. The ADMT provides several tools for making this move easy. They can use the Service Account Migration wizard to migrate the Exchange service account to the new domain, and use the Computer Migration wizard to move the Exchange servers to the new domain. They can also use the Exchange Directory Migration wizard to set the SID for each mailbox for the cloned users to the new primary SID so that the sIDHistory attribute can be cleaned up.

When they have moved all the components to the new domain, the team removes the Chicago domain from the network. This leaves the ADC configuration with a single domain and two Exchange sites. Because most of the users are in Atlanta and the administration of the domain has been centralized there, the team configures the connection agreements so that the agreement between the Atlanta domain and site is a primary agreement for both Exchange and Active Directory. They configure the connection agreement between the Atlanta domain and the Chicago site as a primary agreement for Windows, so that any objects created in the Chicago site are replicated to the domain. This agreement, however, is not a primary connection for Exchange; therefore any changes made in Active Directory are replicated to the Atlanta site, but not to Chicago.

The ADC in the Texas Domains

Configuring the ADC in the Texas domains is simple because the domains are configured as a single account domain with multiple resource domains. Because all the user accounts already exist in the account domain, the ADC needs to be configured for only the one domain. In this case, the team upgrades the domain to Windows 2000, and then configures the ADC to replicate user information to Active Directory.

The project team decided to merge the Texas domains so that all the resource domains are OUs in the Texas domain. The team uses the wizards from the ADMT to accomplish this. After the migration, there will be only one domain in Texas, but three Exchange sites. Just like in the Atlanta domain, this means that the connection agreements are not all primary agreements in both directions. In this case, the team decided to configure the connection agreement to the corporate site as a primary connection in both directions, but the other connection agreements with the Dallas manufacturing site and the Houston manufacturing site as primary for Windows only, so that changes made in that site are replicated to Active Directory.

NOTE: The North American Air project team will configure the other company locations running Exchange the same as the Winnipeg domain after the domain is upgraded to Active Directory. The only difference will be that in some of the smaller sites, the ADC server might also be one of the domain controller/global catalog servers, because the load on the servers is not as great as in larger sites.

Conclusion

After migrating to Windows 2000 and Active Directory, the next major step is to implement the Active Directory Connector, as you learned in this chapter. The ADC replicates user information between the Exchange directory and Active Directory and prepares the organization for the next step, which is the installation of the first Exchange 2000 servers in the domain.

This chapter discussed the implementation of the ADC and applied the discussion to North American Air. In the next chapter, I explain the issues and procedures involved in upgrading one of the current Exchange sites to Exchange 2000.

Part 4

Migrating to Exchange 2000 Server

Chapter 8

Migrating a Single Site to Exchange 2000

NOW THAT THE PLANNING PHASE IS COMPLETE, and Active Directory has been installed in part of the organization, North American Air is finally ready to upgrade or install the first Exchange 2000 servers on its network. This chapter describes the options and procedures for upgrading the first site to Exchange 2000 by upgrading one of the current Exchange 4.0/5.x servers or installing a new Exchange 2000 server into the site.

Before you implement the changes described in this chapter on your own network, you must prepare your environment for the installation of Exchange 2000. In particular, your domain must be upgraded to Windows 2000 Active Directory and you must have installed the ADC to migrate the user information from Exchange 4.0/5.x to Active Directory. These procedures were described in the preceding chapters. Then you can upgrade your existing Exchange servers or install a new server and move the mailboxes to the new server. As you upgrade the site, you must make sure that all essential components are successfully migrated from your old system, including public folders and external connectors. And finally, if you are retiring the first Exchange server in the site, you must make sure that you have moved all of the site-specific information off the server.

So far, this book has focused on the planning and implementation of Exchange 2000 in an enterprise environment. However, most of the procedures discussed in this chapter are equally effective whether you are upgrading an organization that consists of a single domain and a single site or upgrading a single site in a much larger Exchange organization. I clearly highlight any differences along the way.

Preparing the Forest for Exchange 2000

Before you install Exchange 2000 in your organization, you must prepare the forest by adding the Exchange 2000 classes and attributes to the Active Directory schema and modifying the schema to include additional attributes in the global catalog. To make these modifications to the forest, you must run the Exchange 2000 setup using the /forestprep switch.

Using /forestprep

Running Exchange 2000 setup with the /forestprep switch runs the forestprep utility, which makes the needed changes to the schema and assigns one Exchange administrator account full control of the Exchange organization. Because the installation changes the schema, you must be a member of the Schema Admins group to run the installation. In addition, because this installation writes information into the configuration container in Active Directory, you also must be a member of the Enterprise Admins and the local Administrators groups. By default, the Schema Admins and the Enterprise Admins groups exist only in the root domain for the entire forest and contain only the administrator account that was used to create the domain.

Running the forestprep utility performs all the Exchange installation actions that require Schema Admins and Enterprise Admins level permissions. As part of the installation, one account is assigned Exchange Full Administrator rights to the entire Exchange organization. This user can then install the Exchange servers in the organization or use the Exchange Administration Delegation wizard to give other users the same level permissions to install Exchange.

NOTE: Like in Exchange 4.0/5.x and Windows NT, administrative rights in Exchange 2000 and Windows 2000 are configured sepa-

rately. The administrator account designated during the installation has complete administrative rights to the Exchange organization but does not have any rights in Active Directory to perform tasks such as creating users. Therefore, if you are going to use this account to create users, or modify user settings in Active Directory, you also have to make the account a member of the Account Operators group or at least give permissions to create user accounts in a specific OU.

When you run the forestprep utility, you also either create an Exchange organization or join an existing organization. If you already have an organization, in which case you join the Exchange 2000 servers to the existing organization, you should run the forestprep utility after you have installed the ADC. You can run forestprep either before or after you configure the connection agreements, but the connection agreements must be in place before you install the first Exchange 2000 server. The following requirements apply to the forestprep utility:

▲ You must run the utility in the domain where the schema master is located. (Recall from Chapter 6 that the schema master is the only computer from which changes can be made to the forest's schema.)

▲ The account you are using must have both Schema Admins and Enterprise Admins permissions as well as local Administrator rights.

▲ To join an existing organization, you must:

  – Know the name of one of the Exchange servers in the existing Exchange organization. You are asked for this information during the install process.

  – Know the service account name and password for the organization.

  – Verify that the account used to run forestprep has at least Exchange Admin permissions to the site you are joining and to the configuration container in the site.

- Verify that the Exchange version of the ADC is installed. (Refer back to Chapter 7 for an explanation of the differences between the Exchange and Windows versions of the ADC.)

- Verify that the Exchange 5.5 server that you choose to connect to during the install is running at least Service Pack 3.

- Verify that the display name in Exchange Administrator for the existing organization and any sites in the organization are less than 64 characters long and do not contain any special characters. For example, the underscore in NA_Air_Org is an invalid character. Changing the display name to NA-Air-Org allows forestprep to run.

▲ To create a new organization, you need to know the name of the organization that you are creating and the name of the administrator who has full Exchange permissions. By default, the administrator running the forestprep utility is given Full Exchange Administrator rights. You can choose any other account from Active Directory.

NOTE: You do not have to run the forestprep utility if you have only a single site and domain. If you are a member of the Schema Admins group, the Enterprise Admins group, and the Domain Admins group for the domain where you are installing Exchange, if you are a local Administrator, and if you are installing Exchange in the domain that contains the schema master, you do not have to run the forestprep setup. When you install the first Exchange 2000 server, forestprep (and the domainprep) are run as part of the Exchange installation and the user who is running the install is given the full Exchange administrative permissions.

To run the forestprep utility, perform the following seven steps:

1. Insert the Exchange 2000 installation CD-ROM, open a Run box, and enter the following command, where D: is the letter of your CD-ROM drive:

```
D:\setup\i386\setup.exe /forestprep
```

The Microsoft Exchange 2000 Installation Wizard starts.

2. Read and accept the license agreement and type in the product identification number.

3. Accept the default options on the Component Selection dialog box and click Next. (See Figure 8-1.)

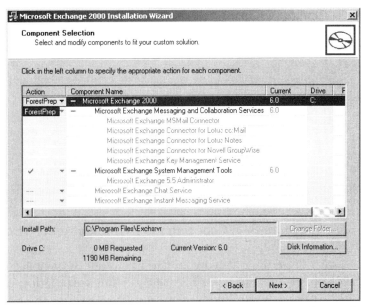

Figure 8-1: Selecting the Exchange 2000 Forestprep Setup Option.

Because you used the /forestprep switch, the only option available is the forestprep option for the Microsoft Exchange 2000 component.

4. Select Join or upgrade an existing Exchange 4.0/5.*x* Organization and click Next.

5. Type the name of the Exchange 5.5 server in the site that you are joining and click Next.

6. Type the domain and the name of the account to be given full Exchange Administrator permissions for the organization. (See Figure 8-2.)

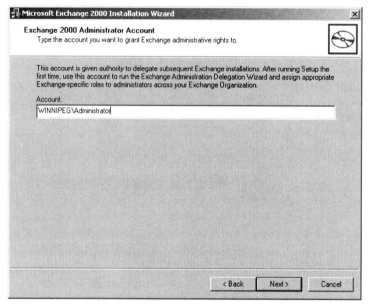

Figure 8-2: Choosing the Exchange Administrator Account.

7. Type the password of the Exchange service account for the existing domain. (See Figure 8-3.) The installation process runs. The
   process can take several minutes because the schema is extensively modified.

*NOTE: Because the /forestprep utility is being used to join an existing
organization, the utility automatically enters the name of the site service account for the site of the designated Exchange 5.5 server.*

After running the forestprep installation, allow time for the
schema changes to replicate to all the domains and sites. Do not run
the domainprep installation in any domain until the information has
been replicated to the domain controllers in the domain.

*NOTE: To determine whether the schema changes have replicated,
you can use the ADSIEdit.msc snap-in from the Windows 2000 Support Tools or use the Active Directory Schema snap-in to check for the
schema changes on the domain controllers. The default Windows*

2000 Active Directory schema contains 1006 items (class objects and attributes). After running the ADC setup with the /schema only option, the schema contains 1194 items, and after running the forest-prep installation, the schema contains 2018 items.

Running the forestprep utility not only makes over 1000 changes to the schema, but also adds a number of additional attributes to the global catalog. The schema changes must be replicated to all domain controllers in the forest, and the entire contents of the global catalog must be replicated to all global catalog servers. In a large organization this results in a large amount of replication traffic. Ideally, you should run the forestprep utility during nonbusiness hours so that this initial replication can occur when the network is less busy.

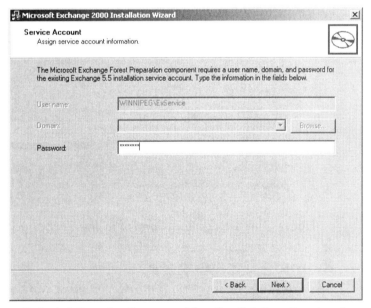

Figure 8-3: Adding the Password for the Existing Service Account.

After you run the forestprep utility, the administrator designated as the Exchange Full Administrator during the forestprep setup can use the Exchange Delegation wizard to give other administrators the permission needed to install other Exchange servers. To do so, open the Exchange System Manager, right-click the organization name, and choose Delegate Control. The Exchange Administration Delegation wizard enables you to assign Exchange administrative permissions to any user or group. See Figure 8-4.

In Exchange 4.0/5.*x* you have to set additional permissions at the site and configuration level to have full control throughout the organization. In Exchange 2000, however, permissions are inherited from the organization level through the whole organization. If you want to assign permissions at an administrative group level, you can run the Exchange Administration Delegation wizard at that level.

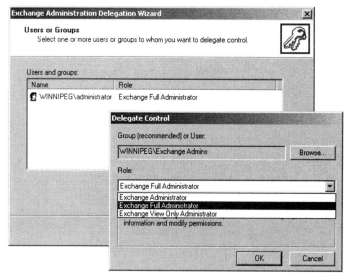

Figure 8-4: Delegating Control to the Exchange Organization.

Running Domainprep

After you run the forestprep utility, you must run the Exchange 2000 setup with the /domainprep switch in every domain in which you are installing Exchange 2000 and in every domain in which there are users connecting to Exchange mailboxes. The domainprep utility creates the groups and permissions needed for the Exchange servers to read and modify user attributes in Active Directory.

To run the domainprep utility, you must be logged as a member of the Domain Admins group (as well as a member of the local

Administrators group). The domainprep utility creates two new groups in Active Directory: the Exchange Domain Servers global group and the Exchange Enterprise Servers domain local group. As you install Exchange servers in the domain, the computer accounts are added to the Exchange Domain Servers group. The Exchange Enterprise Servers group contains all the Exchange Domain Servers groups from all the domains in the organization where the domain-prep utility has been run. This group gives the servers permission to read and modify specific attributes on user accounts. The Recipient Update Service uses this permission when it creates and modifies address lists or modifies user e-mail addresses.

Running the domainprep utility also creates a new container object in Active Directory: Microsoft Exchange System Objects. This container stores the Active Directory information about the system public folders as well as any public folders you create.

To run the domainprep utility, perform the following steps:

1. Insert the Exchange 2000 installation CD-ROM, open a Run box, and run the following command, where D: is the letter for your CD-ROM drive:

    ```
    D:\setup\i386\setup.exe /domainprep
    ```

    The Microsoft Exchange 2000 Installation Wizard starts.

2. Read and accept the license agreement and type the product identification number.

3. Accept the domainprep installation option on the Component Selection dialog box. The installation process begins and creates the groups and containers in Active Directory.

Once you have run the forestprep and domainprep utilities, the forest and domain are prepared and you can install your first Exchange 2000 server. However, before you install the first Exchange server, you must decide how to move your current Exchange site to Exchange 2000. I discuss this topic in the following section.

Upgrading the Exchange Site

There are three ways to upgrade an existing site to Exchange 2000:

▲ Perform an in-place upgrade of the current Exchange 5.5 servers to Exchange 2000.

▲ Install one or more Exchange 2000 servers into the current site and then move the mailboxes from the Exchange 4.0/5.x servers to the new server(s).

▲ Use a *leapfrog upgrade,* in which you install a temporary Exchange 2000 server and move all the mailboxes from the Exchange 4.0/5.x servers to the new server. Then you upgrade the hardware on the original server (if needed) and install a clean copy of Windows 2000 and Exchange 2000 on the server. Then you move the mailboxes from the temporary server back onto the production server.

In some organizations, the best option might be to combine two or more of these. For example, you might decide to upgrade one of your current servers, but then move the mailboxes from another existing server to a new server.

Upgrading an Existing Exchange 5.5 Server

The easiest option is to upgrade a current Exchange 5.5 server to Exchange 2000. In this scenario, you upgrade your current server to Windows 2000 and then upgrade the Exchange server to Exchange 2000. This process upgrades the database format to ESE98 from ESE97, but maintains all the mailboxes and public folders as well as any connectors on the server. While this option is the easiest to perform, it is also the highest risk option because if the upgrade fails, the entire server has to be restored before the messaging services are again available to clients.

The process involves two steps: upgrading the Windows NT servers to Windows 2000 and upgrading Exchange 5.5 to Exchange 2000. I discuss each of these steps individually in the following sections.

In-Place Upgrade of Windows NT Servers to Windows 2000
Exchange 2000 can be installed only on Windows 2000 servers, so you must upgrade the current servers running Exchange 5.5 to Windows 2000 before you install Exchange 2000. Even if you plan to continue running Exchange 5.5 for several months before you upgrade to Exchange 2000, you might want to upgrade the servers to Windows 2000 right away to take advantage of Windows 2000's new features. You can upgrade the Exchange server to Windows 2000 at any time, either before or after you upgrade the domain to Active Directory. You have to upgrade to Active Directory only when you are ready to install Exchange 2000.

On the other hand, you may have some good reasons *not* to upgrade all your Windows NT Exchange 5.5 servers to Windows 2000 right away. For example, if the server hardware is not compatible with Windows 2000, the cost of upgrading it (if upgrade components are even available) may make the upgrade impossible or impractical. If a server is more than a couple of years old, you might want to use the migration as an opportunity to upgrade to new hardware, or to do away with that server altogether and consolidate its functionality with that of another server.

Here are some issues to keep in mind if you do plan to run Exchange 5.5 on Windows 2000:

▲ Only Exchange 5.5 with Service Pack 3 (either Standard Edition or Enterprise Edition) runs on Windows 2000. Earlier versions of Exchange are not supported.

▲ If you are running Exchange 5.5 on a Windows NT PDC or BDC, you can upgrade the server to Windows 2000 as you upgrade your domain to Active Directory. If you maintain the server as a domain controller in the Windows 2000 domain, however, you need to modify the LDAP port number in Exchange. You might want to take advantage of the upgrade to change this server into a Windows 2000 member server. One of the benefits of Windows 2000 is that even if the computer was a domain controller in Windows NT domain, you can run the Active Directory Installation wizard on the computer after the upgrade and demote the server to a member server.

▲ If you are running the Internet Mail Service on the Exchange 5.5 server, you must disable (or not install) the SMTP service from IIS 5.0 in Windows 2000. The two services both use port 25, and the IIS SMTP service blocks the Exchange server's use of the port. If the SMTP is not installed in the current version of IIS, it will not be included in the upgrade.

▲ After you upgrade to Windows 2000, the service account used by Exchange 5.5 must be in the local Administrators group or the Exchange services do not start.

▲ Plan your upgrade so that the downtime for the users is minimized. In most cases, this means you must perform the upgrade after regular working hours.

▲ Back up the Exchange server before you start the upgrade. Make sure the backup worked by performing a test restore. If the upgrade fails, you must be able to roll back to the original configuration quickly and with no loss of data. You can also use disk-cloning software to create an image of the server as a backup.

The actual upgrade of Windows NT to Windows 2000 is a straightforward procedure. To upgrade to Windows 2000, perform the following steps:

1. Insert the Windows 2000 Server CD-ROM into the CD-ROM drive. Open a Run box and run this command, where E: is your CD-ROM drive:

```
E:\i386\winnt32.exe
```

2. Accept the default Upgrade to Windows 2000 option.

3. Read and accept the license agreement.

4. Enter your product key.

   The installation process copies the setup files to the hard disk and then restarts the computer. When the computer reboots, Windows 2000 Setup starts and copies more setup files from the CD-ROM and then reboots the computer again.

When the computer reboots, the GUI component of the setup begins.

Because this is an upgrade of the current operating system, many of the configuration options that you would see as part of a clean install do not appear. The settings are copied from the Windows NT server configuration. After the install is done, the computer reboots again.

5. Before moving on, verify that the upgrade to Windows 2000 was successful.

   Use the Services tool to confirm that all the services, especially the Exchange services, started properly. Check the event logs to check for any warning or error messages.

6. Back up the Exchange server again.

7. Test messaging connectivity by confirming that messages can be sent between two mailboxes on the server as well as between users on other servers. If this server is a messaging or directory bridge-head server to another site, confirm that mail and directory replication messages are flowing between the sites. In addition, if the server is running as an OWA server or Internet Mail server, confirm the functionality of these services.

   NOTE: *Exchange 2000 requires that Windows 2000 Service Pack 1 be installed on all domain controllers and on the servers where Exchange 2000 is installed. Before you can upgrade to Exchange 2000, you must install the latest Service Pack for Windows.*

   The upgrade to Windows 2000 should have little effect on Exchange 5.5. If the upgrade completed without any problems, all the components on the server should continue to work without requiring any reconfiguration.

In-Place Upgrade of Exchange 5.5 Servers to Exchange 2000
After upgrading the server to Windows 2000 and confirming that everything still works, you are ready to upgrade to Exchange 2000.

The in-place upgrade has a number of advantages:

▲ It is the least expensive option because it does not require any additional hardware. If you cannot acquire new servers, it is your only option.

▲ It is the least complicated option if all your hardware is on the Windows 2000 Hardware Compatibility List (HCL).

▲ You can perform the upgrade in two steps: first upgrading to Windows 2000, and then upgrading to Exchange 2000.

The in-place upgrade option also has some disadvantages:

▲ The server is unavailable to messaging clients during the upgrade to Windows 2000 and during the upgrade to Exchange 2000. This means that the upgrade should probably be done outside regular working hours.

▲ If the upgrade fails, this is the most difficult scenario to recover from. You must rebuild the entire server as an Exchange 5.5 server.

▲ The upgrade process includes updating the database format from ESE97 to ESE98. While earlier updates of the Exchange database required a complete restructuring of the entire database, the upgrade to Exchange 2000 changes only some key components of the database. The actual content of the databases is upgraded as it is accessed during Exchange's normal operation. However, any time you upgrade a database of any size, there is a risk of database corruption.

▲ You cannot upgrade Exchange Server 4.0 or 5.0 using this method unless you first upgrade it to Exchange 5.5 Service Pack 3.

▲ You cannot take advantage of consolidating servers unless you move mailboxes to or from other servers as a separate operation.

The in-place upgrade is the best option for a small company that has a limited number of users and in which the current hardware can support the installation of Windows 2000 and Exchange 2000. Making sure that the server is backed up at every step of the upgrade process can mitigate the risk of an upgrade failure. This is also a good option if you are upgrading a smaller site that is part of a larger organization. You cannot use this method if you need to upgrade your hardware to run Exchange. This is also not a good option if you cannot take the Exchange server offline for the time that it would take to upgrade to Windows 2000 and to Exchange 2000. While the upgrade of the database is fast (up to 30 GB per hour), a large server still takes considerable time to upgrade.

> **NOTE:** *One of the important differences between Exchange 2000 and Exchange 4.0/5.x is that Exchange 2000 requires IIS to be installed on the server, including the SMTP and NNTP components of IIS. If these components are not installed, the Exchange 2000 setup does not complete successfully. Before starting the installation, make sure that the SMTP and the NNTP services are both installed with the IIS component. If these components are not installed, you can add them through Add/Remove Windows Components under Add/Remove Programs in the Control Panel.*

The procedure of upgrading is straightforward:

1. Insert the Exchange 2000 installation CD-ROM, open a Run box, and run this command, where D: is the letter of your CD-ROM drive:

   ```
   D:\setup\i386\setup.exe
   ```

   The Microsoft Exchange 2000 Installation Wizard starts.

2. Read and accept the license agreement and type in the product identification number.

3. Accept the default options on the Component Selection screen. See Figure 8-5.

   At this point you cannot change the components that are installed on the computer; you can upgrade only the existing components. If you want to add or remove components, you must run the Microsoft Exchange 2000 Installation wizard again after the upgrade.

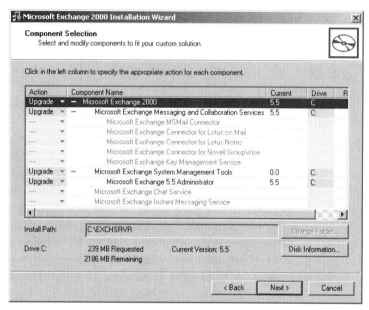

Figure 8-5: Upgrading Components to Exchange 2000.

4. Type the password for the service account.

5. Accept the default installation options and begin the upgrade.

Upgrading the server to Exchange 2000 has little impact on the operation of the server within the site. Because the computer name configuration has not changed, the messaging clients need not be reconfigured. Clients using public folders on the server can continue to use them. External connectors, such as the Internet Mail Service or Site Connectors, continue to function. The most important changes are from an administrative point of view. You can now administer some components differently, and you have more options in the administration. For example, after upgrading the server, you can configure additional storage groups and stores and then move mailboxes to the newly created stores.

NOTE: If you upgrade one Exchange 5.5 server to Exchange 2000 and other Exchange 4,0/5.x servers still exist in the site, the ADC automatically creates a configuration connection agreement that repli-

cates configuration information among the remaining Exchange 4.0/ 5.x servers and Active Directory. This configuration information includes directory information on connectors, bridgehead servers, directory replication, and so on. For the Exchange 2000 server to participate in the site, this information must be replicated to Active Directory, where the Exchange 2000 server can gain access to it. I cover the configuration connection agreements in detail in the next chapter.

Upgrading the Site with a Move Mailbox Upgrade

The second option for upgrading the Exchange 4.0/5.x site is to install one or more Exchange 2000 servers into the site and then move the mailboxes from the Exchange 4.0/5.x servers to the new server(s). This is a good option if the current server does not meet the minimum requirements for running Exchange 2000 or is an older server that you would like to remove from the network or use for another purpose.

Before installing Exchange 2000 on a server, you must meet the following requirements:

▲ The computer must be running Windows 2000 Server.

▲ The SMTP and the NNTP components must both be installed with IIS 5.0. The SMTP component is installed by default, but the NNTP component is not.

▲ You must be logged in using the account identified when you ran the forestprep utility or with an account that has been given the necessary permissions.

The move mailbox upgrade has these advantages:

▲ This option has the least impact on users. You can install the new server without interrupting the mail service. The only time that a specific user cannot access mail is while that mailbox is being moved.

▲ If you need to replace the server hardware, this is the best option.

▲ You can use a server that contains a clean installation of Windows 2000 and Exchange 2000 rather than an upgrade.

▲ You can move the mailboxes into multiple stores on the new server, rather than upgrading and then moving them.

▲ The user migration can be spread over multiple days because there is no problem with the servers coexisting.

▲ The recovery from a failed migration is relatively easy because you are affecting only a few mailboxes at a time and you are not modifying the database versions. At the most, you may need to recover a single mailbox if the upgrade fails while the mailbox is being migrated.

The move mailbox upgrade also has some disadvantages:

▲ This option requires that you invest in new hardware.

▲ Moving many users with large mailboxes can take a long time. If both servers are high-end servers (PIII processors, at least 256 MB RAM), you can expect to move about 100 MB of the information store per hour.

▲ This option is more complicated than just upgrading a single server because you are working with multiple servers.

▲ If you are removing the original server from the site, you must move the site-specific folders and roles to the new server as well. You also must recreate all the connectors on the new server.

The move mailbox upgrade is the best option in most situations where you are planning to replace the server hardware. If you are going to replace the server, you can install the new server into the site and then move mailboxes over to the new server as time permits. The end users in this scenario experience very little disruption, and as long as you regularly back up both servers during the migration, there is little chance of lost data. The only drawbacks to this method are that you must buy new hardware and that the actual migration can take some time to complete.

To install Exchange 2000 on a Windows 2000 computer, perform the following steps:

1. Insert the Exchange 2000 installation CD-ROM, open a Run box, and run the following command, where D: is your CD-ROM drive:

    ```
    D:\setup\i386\setup.exe
    ```

    The Microsoft Exchange 2000 Installation Wizard starts.

2. Read and accept the license agreement and type in the product identification number.

3. Select the components that you want to install.

4. Select I agree that:... to signify that you agree to the condition that Exchange 2000 supports only Per Seat licensing.

5. Type the name of an Exchange 5.5 server in the site you want to join.

6. Type the password for the Exchange service account.

7. Review the Component Summary screen to ensure that all the components you want to install are selected.

The installation process runs, installing all the components you selected.

When installing an Exchange 2000 server into an existing Exchange 4.0/5.*x* site, the setup program offers to install both the Exchange 2000 System Manager and the Exchange 5.5 Administrator. To administer both versions of Exchange from one computer, you must install both administration programs. While both types of servers are visible in both administration programs, they can be administered only with the administration program designed for that version of Exchange Server.

Before you move any mailboxes onto the new server, you should confirm the success of the Exchange 2000 installation. Create several test mailboxes on the server, and send messages between those mailboxes, as well as to mailboxes on other servers. If this server operates as a bridgehead server for Internet Mail, or for other connectors, create the connectors on the server and test messaging connectivity before removing the connectors from the other servers. Install and test the backup application on the server to ensure that you can recover the information stores if the server fails while moving mailboxes.

After installing the Exchange 2000 server in the site, you can move the mailboxes to the new server using Active Directory Users and Computers, as described in the following steps:

> **NOTE:** *The users should not have their mailboxes open while the mailboxes are being moved. If the user is accessing the mailbox, the mailbox move fails. Before moving the mailbox, you can ensure that the user is not logged on to the mailbox by checking the Mailbox Logons in the Exchange Administrator.*

1. Open Active Directory Users and Computers and select the user account for the mailbox that you want to move.

2. Right-click the user account and select Exchange Tasks.

3. The Exchange Task wizard starts. See Figure 8-6.

4. Select the Move Mailbox option.

5. On the next screen, select the destination Exchange server for the mailbox. See Figure 8-7.

    If the destination server is an Exchange 2000 server, you can choose which storage group and which mail store to which the mailbox will be moved.

    The wizard connects to the source and destination computer and moves the mailbox to the new server.

> **NOTE:** *You can select multiple mailboxes using the Control or Shift key and move them to the destination server using the same process.*

When the user logs on to the Exchange server using a MAPI client, the client is redirected to the new Exchange server and the user's profile changes to reflect the new location for the mailbox. Even if you move all the mailboxes from the Exchange 4.0/5.x server, you should still leave the server on the network for several days until all the client profiles have been updated.

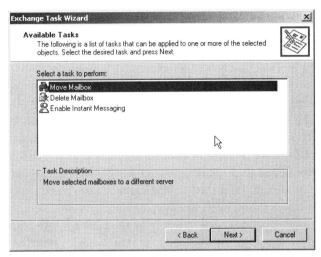

Figure 8-6: Changing Exchange Settings on a Mailbox.

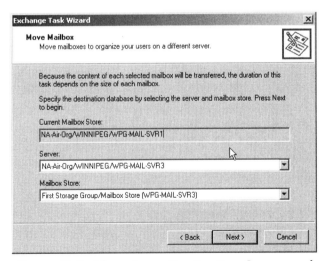

Figure 8-7: Choosing a Destination Server and Mailbox Store for a Mailbox.

In most cases, it's preferable to perform the mailbox migration in stages. After you have confirmed that the server is correctly configured and is providing messaging connectivity for the test accounts, move a small group of mailboxes to the new server. Use this move to determine the speed with which the data is transferred, and then estimate the amount of time it will take to migrate the remainder of the users. If the server is still functioning, begin moving additional mailboxes. If you plan to take several days to move the mailboxes, migrate all the users in a department or workgroup at the same time. These users usually send more messages to each other than they do to users in other departments, so you can gain network and server efficiency by moving these users as a group. In addition, if you have multiple mail stores on the destination server, move the mailboxes for the department to the same store. Exchange still uses single instance message storage, in which only a single copy of a message is stored on a server even if there are multiple recipients on the server. In Exchange 2000, however, the single instance message store applies to mailbox stores rather than the entire information store.

> **NOTE:** *When you move mailboxes to another server, Exchange retains the single message store feature. If you move 10 mailboxes to the same mailbox store and they all contain the same message, only a single copy of the message is stored in the mailbox store.*

As you move mailboxes, continue to perform regular backups of the destination server. As you move each mailbox, all mailbox content is written to the transaction log files on the destination server, and the log files grow rapidly. If they are not removed regularly with a full or differential backup, you may fill the hard disks with the log files.

Leapfrog Migration

The leapfrog migration is a modification of the move mailbox option. In this case, you install a new Windows 2000 server and Exchange 2000 server into the site and use this new server temporarily while you rebuild the original server as an Exchange 2000 server. Then you move the mailboxes back to the original server. This is a good option if you want to reuse the original server, but you also would like to have a clean install of Windows 2000 and Exchange 2000 rather than an upgrade from Windows NT and Exchange 5.5. This is also a good choice if the server that you are upgrading is running Exchange 4.0 or Exchange 5.0 and cannot be upgraded in place to Exchange 2000.

The leapfrog approach has these advantages:

▲ Like the move mailbox method, this method does not affect the users except that the mailboxes must be moved twice. Because users cannot be logged into Exchange while their mailboxes are being moved, this can cause some inconvenience.

▲ This is the best option if you want to reuse the same hardware but want to upgrade some components and install a clean copy of Windows 2000 and Exchange 2000.

The disadvantages of the leapfrog option are as follows:

▲ This option requires extra hardware. Although the hardware can be reused when the migration is complete, you still need a powerful temporary server to maintain performance during the upgrade.

▲ This option requires the most complicated planning, especially if you have only one server in the site and you must move the site-specific folders and roles between the two servers.

The leapfrog upgrade is the best option only if you want to be able to reuse the existing server hardware but you must upgrade some components that require a clean installation of Windows 2000 server. In any other situation, use either of the other two options.

To upgrade a server to Exchange 2000 using the leapfrog approach, perform the following steps:

1. Install a new Exchange 2000 server into the same site as the existing servers.

2. Move all the mailboxes from the Exchange 4.0/5.x server to the new server, as described in the preceding section.

3. Remove the original server from the Exchange site.

NOTE: If this is the first server in the site, make sure that you move the site folders and site-specific tasks to another server in the site before you remove the server. (That procedure is described later in this chapter.)

4. Shut down the server and upgrade the hardware if necessary. Reformat the hard disks.

5. Install Windows 2000 Server and install Service Pack 1. Join the computer to the domain.

6. Install Exchange 2000 on the computer and join it to the existing site.

7. Move the mailboxes from the temporary server back to the original server, along with any other components that you moved to the temporary server earlier.

8. Remove the temporary server from the site.

If you are upgrading multiple Exchange servers in the site, you can use the temporary server to upgrade other servers. You also can uninstall the Exchange server and reinstall Exchange in a different site to use the computer to migrate multiple sites.

Upgrading Public Folders

For the most part, upgrading public folders from Exchange 4.0/5.x to Exchange 2000 is similar to upgrading mailboxes. While some aspects of public folder access and configuration are handled differently in Exchange 2000 than in Exchange 4.0/5.x, the essential concepts have not changed. Public folders still store information and make it available to a variety of messaging clients. When you upgrade the public folder servers, the configuration information for the public folders is automatically replicated to Exchange 2000.

The public folder hierarchy and content replication works the same in Exchange 2000 as it does in Exchange 4.0/5.x. The public folder hierarchy is a listing of all the public folders in the organization, including top-level folders and all child folders. In Exchange 4.0/5.x, you can create only one public folder hierarchy, and all folders must appear in that one hierarchy. This public folder hierarchy is accessible from any client that supports public folder access, including MAPI, IMAP, and OWA clients. The public folder hierarchy is automatically replicated to all servers in the organization that have a public information store. Exchange 2000 supports the default public folder hierarchy in the same way. The default hierarchy is replicated to all public folders servers, and the content of the hierarchy is accessible by the same clients, as well as other clients, such as Office 2000, through the Exchange 2000 Installable File System (ExIFS).

> **NOTE:** *Exchange 2000 also supports additional public folder hierarchies. When you create an additional public folder hierarchy, you must create a dedicated public store for the new hierarchy and its content. The folders in the public folder hierarchy are not accessible to MAPI clients, but users can access them through OWA clients or NNTP clients, as well as through clients using the ExIFS. To make the folders accessible by OWA or NNTP clients, you must configure a specific virtual HTTP or NNTP server for the public folder. The fact that Exchange 2000 supports multiple public folder hierarchies is not an issue during the upgrade process because Exchange 4.0/5.x does not support this option. You must create the additional hierarchies after the upgrade.*

While the public folder hierarchy is automatically replicated to all public folder servers, the actual content of the folders is not replicated in Exchange 4.0/5.x unless you manually configure the replication. You configure replication on a per-folder basis. This has not changed in Exchange 2000. For the actual content of the public folder to be stored in the public folder store, you must create a public folder on the server or configure the folder to be replicated to the server.

One of the public folder configuration options that has changed in Exchange 2000, however, is the way permissions are assigned to public folders. In Exchange 4.0/5.x, permission to public folders is granted to individual mailboxes or distribution lists. In Exchange 2000, only security principals (users, groups, or computers) can be granted permissions to public folders. A second change is the way Exchange 2000 deals with public folder access between routing groups. In Exchange 4.0/5.*x*, users cannot access public folders in other sites unless you enable affinity between the sites. You can control which sites the clients check first for public folder replicas by configuring costs for each affinity. In Exchange 2000, however, users can access public folders in any routing group unless you prevent them from doing so. To change the default behavior, you must reconfigure the option to allow public folder referrals on the routing group connectors. To control which routing group is searched first for public folder replicas, you configure the cost on the routing group connector. When a client tries to connect to a public folder in another routing group, the lowest cost connectors are used first. Exchange 2000 also supports multiple public folder stores per server and full-text indexing, but these do not directly affect the upgrade process.

When planning the upgrade of public folders in your site to Exchange 2000, you must plan for these three issues:

▲ The replication of public folder objects to Active Directory. This is an issue because all permissions to public folders are set in Active Directory. For the public folders to appear in the Public Folders container in Exchange System Manager, they must appear in Active Directory.

▲ The replication of the default public folder hierarchy from the Exchange 4.0/5.*x* servers in the site to Exchange 2000.

▲ The replication of the actual content of the public folders into the information store of the Exchange 2000 servers.

These topics are dealt with in the following sections.

Public Folder Connection Agreements

Public folder connection agreements, which are configured in the ADC, replicate the public folder directory information into Active Directory. When you create a public folder in Exchange 4.0/5.*x*, no corresponding object is created in a Windows NT directory. The public folder exists in only the Exchange directory, and when you assign permissions to a public folder, you use Exchange mailboxes and distribution lists. In Exchange 2000, however, all permissions must be granted using Active Directory security principals, so the public folders must have a corresponding Active Directory object to configure permissions to the object. In addition, when you install Exchange 2000 in the site, the public folder objects must exist in Active Directory.

A public folder connection agreement is similar to a recipient connection agreement with the following exceptions:

▲ You can configure the connection agreement only as a two-way agreement.

▲ You cannot modify the source and destination containers for the connection agreement.

▲ The connection agreement is always a primary connection agreement for the Exchange organization. You can configure it as a nonprimary agreement for the Windows domain.

▲ Only public folder directory items can be replicated using the agreement.

After the connection agreement is configured the public folder objects are replicated to Active Directory and appear in the Microsoft Exchange System Objects container. See Figure 8-8.

After configuring the public folder connection agreements, you can begin upgrading the public folder information in your site. The options for doing this are similar to those for upgrading mailbox servers. You can perform an in-place upgrade, or you can install a new Exchange 2000 server into the site and replicate the contents of the public folders to the new servers.

NOTE: Before you upgrade the public folders to Exchange 2000, you should run the Exchange 4.0/5.x DS/IS Consistency Adjuster on the server that you are upgrading. When running the Consistency Adjuster, select the option to verify that users deleted from the Exchange directory do not retain any permission to mailboxes and public folders. To do this, open the Server Properties dialog box for the server on which you are working and select the Advanced tab. Select the Adjust option under the DS/IS Consistency Adjuster and then select the Remove unknown user accounts from public folder permissions option. If you do not do this, any public folder that includes an unknown user account is accessible only by the folder owner until you manually remove the unknown account.

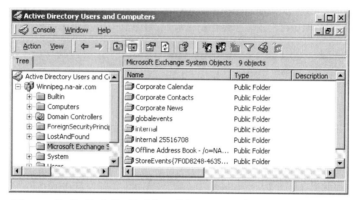

Figure 8-8: Public Folder Objects in Active Directory.

In-Place Upgrade of Public Folder Servers

Every Exchange 4.0/5.x server in a site has a copy of the public folder hierarchy. When you perform an in-place upgrade of the server to Exchange 2000, the public folder hierarchy is automatically updated. In addition, any replica of a public folder that is stored in the public folder store is upgraded with the server.

Installing a New Exchange 2000 Server

Installing an Exchange 2000 server into an Exchange 4.0/5.x site creates few issues with public-folder management. When you install a new Exchange 2000 server into a site that already has an Exchange 4.0/5.x public folder server, the public folder hierarchy is automatically replicated to the Exchange 2000 server. However, before any of the actual messages in the public folder are replicated to the new server, you must configure the folder with a replica of the server. In addition, the ADC public folder replication agreement must be in place before you install the server if you are going to assign permissions to public folders in Exchange System Manager. If the objects have not been replicated to Active Directory, you can only assign permissions through the Exchange 4.0/5.x Exchange Administrator.

Administering Public Folders in Exchange 2000

One of the advantages of managing public folders in Exchange 2000 over Exchange 4.0/5.x is that you can perform all public folder administration, including creating new public folders, from Exchange System Manager. In Exchange 4.0/5.x, you must use a messaging client to create additional public folders. To create a new public folder in Exchange 2000, open the Exchange System Manager and expand the administrative group. Then expand the Public Folders container. Right-click the parent container for the folder (either the Public Folders container or an existing public folder) and choose New/Public Folder.

> **NOTE:** *You can create only public folders that contain mail items using Exchange System Manager in Exchange 2000. If you want to create public folders that contain other items, such as contacts or calendar information, you must still create this folder using a messaging client, as in Exchange 4.0/5.x.*

As mentioned earlier, before you can copy the actual content of the public folder to the Exchange server, you must configure public folder replication. There are two ways to do this in Exchange 2000. The first is to open the public folder in the Public Folders container and access the properties of the public folder. Next, select the Replication tab, click Add, and then select the destination server for the public folder replication. Figure 8-9 shows this interface.

You also can configure public folder replicas by accessing the public folder in the Public Store on the server that currently has a replica of the public folder. To access the folder this way, expand the *administrative group*/Servers/*servername*/*storagegroup*/*public store*. Figure 8-10 shows the location of the public folders in the public folder store.

Right-click the folder and choose Folder Properties and configure the public folder replicas.

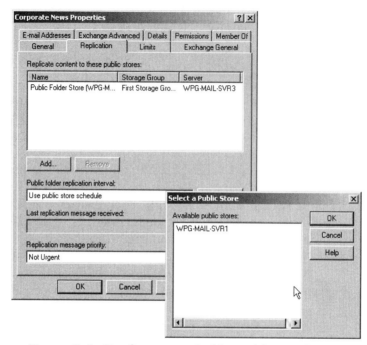

Figure 8-9: Configuring a Public Folder Replica in
Exchange System Manager.

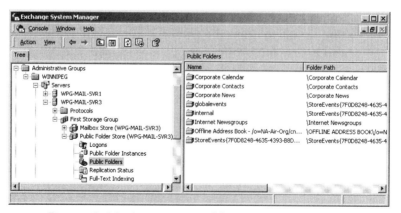

Figure 8-10: Accessing Public Folder Replicas in
the Public Folder Store.

Exchange 2000 is also different in how it assigns permissions to public folders. To configure public folder permissions, access the folder properties through Exchange System Manager and select the Permissions tab. Figure 8-11 shows the Permissions tab.

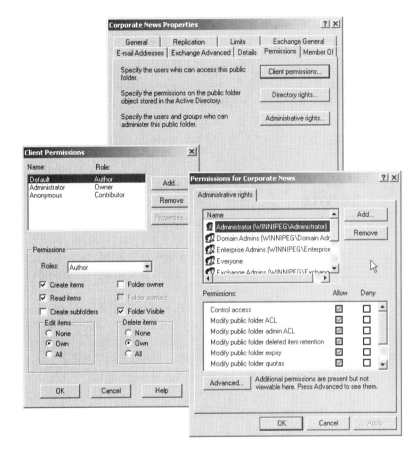

Figure 8-11: Configuring Permissions to Public Folders in Exchange System Manager.

Configuring permissions for public folders is quite a bit more complicated in Exchange 2000 than in Exchange 4.0/5.*x*. Three types of permissions can be configured in Exchange 2000. The first type is Client Permissions. Client Permissions are the same permissions as in Exchange 4.0/5.*x*, and they are used to configure user access to the content of the folder. The second type of permission is Directory Rights. Selecting this configuration option opens the standard Security tab for all Active Directory objects, which you can use to configure access to the public folder object in Active Directory. The third type of permission is Administrative Rights, which you can use to configure the rights that users have to modify the properties of the public folder in Exchange 2000.

As with public folders in Exchange 4.0/5.*x*, public folders created in Exchange 2000 do not appear in the GAL by default. To configure a public folder to appear in the GAL, access the public folder's properties, display the Exchange Advanced tab, and clear the Hide from Exchange address lists check box.

Upgrading and Managing the Internet Mail Service

When you perform an in-place upgrade on an Exchange 5.5 server that has Internet Mail Service configured on it, the Internet Mail Service is upgraded to Exchange 2000. Any configuration options migrate automatically to the Internet Mail Service in Exchange 2000.

> **NOTE:** *The SMTP Connector has replaced the Internet Mail Service in Exchange 2000. When you upgrade a server from Exchange 5.5, the service is still called Internet Mail Service but the configuration options are identical to those for the SMTP Connector. I explain the SMTP connector in more detail in Chapter 10.*

After upgrading the server, you can configure the Internet Mail Service using the Exchange System Manager. Many of the configuration options are the same as they were in Exchange 5.5, but there are a few important modifications. To access the Internet Mail Service properties, expand the routing group, expand the Connections container, and right-click the Internet Mail Service, and choose Properties. The configuration options are described in Table 8-1.

Table 8-1: Configuring the Internet Mail Service After an Upgrade

Exchange 2000 IMS Tab	Configuration Options
General	Configure message delivery using DNS or smart hosts. Configure the bridgehead server or servers that are running the IMS. You can configure any virtual servers in the site. See Figure 8-12.
Content Restrictions	Configure the type and size of messages that can be sent through this connector.
Delivery Options	Configure when messages will be sent using this connector. You can configure a different schedule for sending messages larger than a specified size. Configure this server to queue mail until it receives a TURN or ATRN command from another server. You also can configure which accounts are authorized to issue the TURN/ATRN commands. See Figure 8-13.
Advanced	Configure this connector to operate as a TURN/ETRN client, including the connection times, and security settings. See Figure 8-14.
Details	Configure an administrative note for the connector.
Address Space	Configure the DNS domains to which this connector sends mail. Configure the connector as available either for the entire organization or just for the routing group.
Connected Routing Groups	Configure the routing groups that will be using this connector as a routing group connector.
Delivery Restrictions	Configure which users have permission to send mail using this connector.

NOTE: *You can configure the IMS to use any SMTP virtual server in your site. By default it uses the default SMTP virtual server on the upgraded server. However, you can create additional virtual servers on this computer or use any other virtual server in the site to replace this server as the bridgehead server, or you can configure multiple virtual servers to act as the bridgehead server for this connector. I cover virtual server configuration in Chapter 11.*

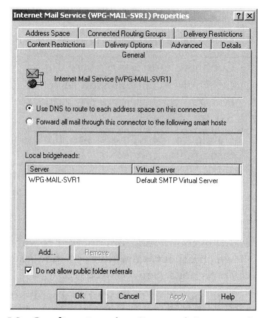

Figure 8-12: Configuring the General Settings for the IMS.

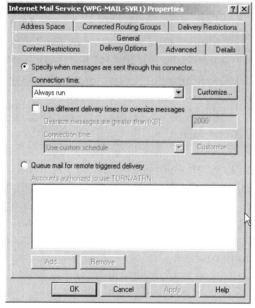

Figure 8-13: Configuring the Delivery Options for the IMS.

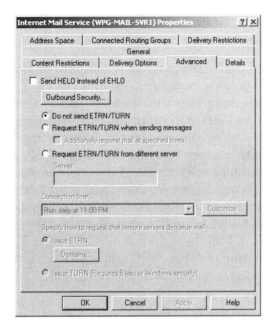

Figure 8-14: Configuring the Advanced Options on the IMS.

Upgrading Outlook Web Access

Many organizations run Outlook Web Access (OWA) in Exchange 5.*x* and would like to upgrade it to Exchange 2000 as well. Upgrading OWA is more complicated than upgrading some of the other components because Exchange 2000 implements OWA differently than in Exchange 5.*x*. In Exchange 5.*x*, OWA uses Active Server Pages running in IIS to create RPC connections to the Exchange server. In Exchange 2000, OWA uses HTTP and connects to the Exchange server through the Exchange Interprocess Communication (EXIPC) layer. In a distributed services environment, the front-end Exchange 2000 server connects to the back-end server using HTTP and WebDAV.

If you are running OWA on the Exchange 5.5 server, it is upgraded when you perform an in-place upgrade of the computer. The new OWA is the Exchange 2000 implementation of OWA, however. This means that if you have customized the Active Server Pages on the OWA server, the customized pages are no longer used. If you want to continue to use the customized pages, you cannot upgrade the server.

In most cases, the OWA component in Exchange 5.x is installed on a separate computer running IIS 4.0. This computer functions as a front-end server with a specific Exchange Server identified as the back-end server. To upgrade this type of configuration, you must upgrade the back-end server first, because you cannot have a front-end OWA server running Exchange 2000 while the back-end server is running Exchange 5.x. You can use the Exchange 5.5 OWA front-end server to connect to an upgraded Exchange 2000 back-end server. If you are using customized .asp pages, you can continue to use these pages in this environment. However, if you use this configuration, keep in mind that you are using the Exchange 5.x implementation of OWA. You cannot take advantage of the scalability and enhancements available in Exchange 2000 OWA.

Upgrading Other Connectors

Performing an in-place upgrade of an Exchange 5.5 server upgrades almost all the connectors configured on the server. For example, if you have Connector for MSMail running on the server, it is upgraded and its configuration remains unchanged. Connectors to host-based messaging systems, such as SNADS or PROFS, are not upgraded because Exchange 2000 does not include connectors to these systems. If you need to maintain a connection to one of these systems, you must maintain an Exchange 5.5 server in your site.

If you chose to perform a move mailbox migration of your site, you also must ensure the connectors on the Exchange 4.0/5.x servers are reproduced on the new Exchange 2000 servers. You cannot move the connectors to the new server, so you must recreate the connectors. To do so, follow these steps:

1. Install and configure the connectors on the new servers before taking the old servers offline.

2. Set the cost of the connector lower than that of the connectors on the old servers, and force a recalculation of the routing information for the site.

3. Monitor the delivery of messages through the connector on the new server. When the messages are moving through the new server and you have removed all the mailboxes from the old server, shut down the old server or set the cost of the connectors on the server to 100 (which means that the connector is used only if the other connector is not available).

4. Verify that the messages are still flowing through the connector on the new server. Then remove the first 4.0/5.x server from the site, as described in the following section.

Removing the First Exchange Server in the Site

During the course of the migration from Exchange 4.0/5.x to Exchange 2000, you eventually remove the first Exchange 4.0/5.x server from the site. This server, because it was the first server in the 4.0/5.x site, has some site-specific functions, and removing it requires some special planning.

The first step in removing the server is to move all the mailboxes, public folders, and connectors off the server. Then you must move the site system folders to another Exchange server. These folders include the Offline Address Book (OAB) folder, the Schedule+ Free/Busy Information folder, and the Organizational Forms folder. By default, the first server in the site is responsible for keeping these folders updated and making them available to other servers. The first server in the site is also the routing calculation server for the entire site. When the Gateway Address Routing Table (GWART) is recalculated, the first server in the site recalculates the GWART and then replicates the information to the other servers in the site.

Before removing the first server from the site, you need to move all its roles to another server in the site. To ensure that you have completed all the required tasks, use the following checklist:

▲ Move all the mailboxes from the server to another server in the site.

▲ Replicate all the public folders on the server to another Exchange server in the site. Each public folder is configured with a home server, which by default is the first server where the folder was created. If this server is identified as the home server for any public folders, you should rehome the public folder to another server in the site by configuring a new home server.

▲ Confirm that this server is not designated as the expansion server for any distribution lists. If it is, designate another server or allow any server to expand the distribution list.

▲ Ensure that all the connectors on the server have been duplicated on other servers in the site. If not, configure the connectors on another server.

▲ Depending on what types of connectors you have installed on the Exchange servers, you also need to replicate system folders to another server in the site. If you have a Schedule+ Free/Busy Information folder (if you are still using it) an Organizational Forms folder, an Offline Address Book, or a OAB Version 2 system folder, replicate the contents of these folders to another server in the site.

▲ Configure another server in the site as the Offline Address Book Server. In Exchange 4.0/5.*x*, you can configure this settings on the DS Site Configuration object using the Exchange Administrator. In Exchange 2000, you can configure this setting on the Offline Address Lists object in the Recipients container in Exchange System Manager. Right-click the Offline Address Lists option and select an Exchange 2000 server as the offline address list server.

▲ Configure another server as the routing calculation server in the site. In Exchange 4.0/5.*x*, you can configure the routing calculation server on the Site Addressing object. In Exchange 2000, the function of the routing calculation server has been distributed to each Exchange server in the site. Each Exchange 2000 server calculates the link state table for itself, using updates from the routing group master. If there are not other Exchange 4.0/5.*x* servers in the site after you remove this server, you do not need to assign another server as the routing calculation server.

Before you remove the Exchange 4.0/5.*x* server from the site, disconnect it from the network for a few days to make sure that all messaging connectivity is maintained in the site. When you are sure that all the messaging functionality provided by this server has been duplicated on another server, remove Exchange 4.0/5.*x* server from the Exchange organization by deleting it either from the Servers container in the site or from the administrative group.

> **NOTE:** *If you delete the first server from the site before moving the first server folders and roles, you can recover the system folders, but the process is pretty painful. It is much easier to move the folders before removing the server. For more information, see the Microsoft Knowledge Base article Q152960 XADM: Rebuilding the Site Folders in a Site.*

Upgrading the Winnipeg Site at North American Air

North American Air will use the procedures described in this chapter to upgrade the Winnipeg location to Exchange 2000.

Winnipeg currently has two Exchange servers. One server, Wpg-Mail-Svr1, is used as a mailbox server and contains about 2,000 mailboxes. The other server, Wpg-Mail-Svr2, is used as a combination of mailbox and connector server. It contains just over 1,000 mailboxes and the Internet Mail Service and functions as the bridgehead server for the site connector to the Dallas corporate site.

The project team has decided to take advantage of the improved scalability options in Exchange 2000 by using a single mailbox server in the Winnipeg location and putting all 3,000 mailboxes on the single server. Wpg-Mail-Svr1 is a three-year-old server, so planning team has decided to replace the server with a new one. This new server holds all 3,000 of the mailboxes, leaving Wpg-Mail-Svr2 free to become a dedicated public folder server. Since Wpg-Mail-Svr2 is fairly new, the team has decided to keep its hardware as-is and perform an in-place upgrade on it.

In addition, the planning team has decided to install a new dedicated connection server to be configured with an SMTP connector for Internet e-mail and to serve as the bridgehead server for the routing group connector with the Texas routing group. One of the key objectives in the upgrade to Exchange 2000 is the implementation of OWA for all the remote users. The planning team has therefore decided to install a dedicated OWA server as a front-end server in the Winnipeg location.

NOTE: More details on the implementation on the Routing Group Connectors follow in Chapter 11. OWA configuration is described in Chapter 12.

The following outlines the steps the planning team will take as a result of these decisions.

NOTE: These steps assume that the ADC is already configured as described in Chapter 7.

The first part of the process is to prepare the domain for the installation of Exchange 2000.

1. Run the forestprep utility in the NA-Air.com domain. A member of the Schema Admins and Enterprise Admins group must run the installation because of the permissions required. The person selects the option to join the existing NA-Air-Org organization during the installation.

2. Use the Exchange Administration Delegation wizard to give the members of the Exchange Administrators group from the Winnipeg.NA-Air.com domain permissions to install the Exchange servers in the Winnipeg location.

3. After the changes to the schema have replicated to the Winnipeg domain, run the domainprep utility in the Winnipeg domain.

4. Use the DS/IS Consistency Adjuster to remove any unknown user accounts from the ACLs of public folders.

Once the domain has been prepared, the next part of the process is to install the first Exchange 2000 server and move the existing mailboxes to the new server.

1. Install a new Exchange 2000 server, Wpg-Mail-Svr3, into the existing Winnipeg-Site. Configure the server to connect to Wpg-Mail-Svr2 during the installation.

2. Design and configure the storage group and store configuration on the new server.

3. Create several test mailboxes on the new server (at least one in each store) and confirm the mail connectivity with the rest of the organization. Back up the server and confirm the success of the backup.

4. Move a test mailbox from Wpg-Mail-Svr1 to the new server. Confirm the success of the mailbox move.

5. Move a group of mailboxes to the new server. Again test the success of the move.

6. Back up the server and test the backup.

7. Move the remainder of the mailboxes from Wpg-Mail-Svr1 to the new server. Move the mailboxes in groups based on departments, and move all the mailboxes for each department to the same mailbox store on the new server. Continually test for messaging connectivity and back up the server regularly.

8. Move the mailboxes from Wpg-Mail-Svr2 to the new server using the procedure outlined in steps 5-7.

Once the first server has been installed, the project team verifies that the messaging system is stable by monitoring the Exchange servers and messaging connectivity for several days. The last part of the process is to install a new connector server, move the existing connectors to the new server, and then install the last servers in the Winnipeg location.

1. Install the new Exchange 2000 connector server, Wpg-Con-Svr4, into the site.

2. Configure an SMTP connector to the Internet on the server, and make the server a messaging bridgehead server for the site connector to the Dallas site. Configure the cost of the connectors on the new server with a lower cost than the connectors on Wpg-Mail-Svr2.

3. Confirm messaging connectivity to the Internet and to the rest of the organization. Use message tracking to confirm that the lower-cost connectors on Wpg-Con-Svr4 are being used.

4. After all the mailboxes have been removed from Wpg-Mail-Svr2, perform an in-place upgrade of the server to Exchange 2000. This server is to be a dedicated public folder server. Because the server already has the public folder hierarchy and replicas of the current public folders, these components will be upgraded as the server is upgraded.

5. Install the new Exchange 2000 server, Wpg-OWA-Svr5, into the organization, and configure it as an OWA front-end server.

6. Before removing Wpg-Mail-Svr1 from the network, move any site-specific roles and system folders to the Wpg-Mail-Svr3.

7. Remove the connectors from Wpg-Mail-Svr2.

 NOTE: *If the Winnipeg-Site were the only site in the NA-Air-Org organization, the organization could be switched to native mode at this point.*

Conclusion

This chapter covered the process of upgrading a single site from Exchange 4.0/5.*x* to Exchange 2000. Before installing the first Exchange 2000 server into the site, you must prepare the forest and the domain for the upgrade. Once all the preparation is complete, the actual upgrade of the Exchange 4.0/5.*x* components can begin. This is not a complicated process. The primary issue is whether to perform an in-place upgrade of the current Exchange servers or install new servers into the site and move the mailboxes, public folders, and connectors to the new servers. An in-place upgrade can take place only if the current Exchange server is version 5.5 with Service Pack 3 installed.

As soon as you install the first Exchange 2000 server into an existing Exchange 4.0/5.x organization, you are working in an environment in which the Exchange servers need to coexist. Exchange 2000 interacts with other servers in the organization differently than Exchange 4.0/5.x servers do. For example, Exchange 4.0/5.x servers in the same site exclusively use RPCs to communicate with each other, while Exchange 2000 servers use SMTP.

The next chapter addresses the coexistence issues that begin when you install the first Exchange 2000 server into your organization and persist until you remove the last Exchange 4.0/5.x server. While many of the coexistence issues are handled automatically by the upgrade process, you need to understand the issues in order to troubleshoot the coexisting server environment.

Chapter 9

Coexisting with Exchange 4.0/5.x Servers

WHEN YOU INSTALL THE FIRST EXCHANGE 2000 server into an Exchange 4.0/5.*x* organization, you begin dealing with coexistence issues, and you continue to face them until the last Exchange 4.0/5.*x* server is removed from the network and the entire organization is running only Exchange 2000 servers. In a large organization, such as North American Air, this coexistence period will span at least several months.

One of the most important goals for the migration must be to ensure that messaging functionality is disrupted as little as possible. The work of the corporation must continue during the migration, and e-mail plays a very important role in that work.

This chapter discusses coexistence issues you must address, including basic messaging functionality and directory replication between the versions of Exchange Server. It also addresses some coexistence-specific problems that might arise as Exchange 4.0/5.*x* sites become Exchange 2000 administrative and routing groups.

Coexistence Issues

In most organizations, e-mail is a mission-critical component of the business. Any disruption in messaging can mean lost revenue or opportunities. As an organization moves to a new messaging system, the risk of disruption is increased considerably, especially if the old and new messaging systems do not coexist well with each other.

The optimal coexistence scenario is one where messaging functionality within the organization is not disrupted at all during the migration period. Ideally, the e-mail users should not even be aware of the migration, or at least it should not disrupt their ability to send and receive e-mail. For this to happen, a number of components have to be present:

▲ **Messaging coexistence.** To coexist, the different versions of Exchange must be able to send messages between them. Users on each version should be able to send messages to users anywhere in the organization without disruption.

▲ **Global address list (GAL) replication.** The users should be able to connect to the Exchange server and see the entire GAL, including users on either version of Exchange. In addition, the GAL should be accurate, so that when a user selects a recipient for the message, the message is delivered to the correct user.

▲ **Configuration replication.** One of the components in the Exchange 4.0/5.x directory service is the Configuration container. It contains all the information about the structure of the Exchange 4.0/5.x organization, including the sites, servers, and connectors in the organization. The Exchange 4.0/5.x servers use this information when routing messages throughout the organization and to external connectors. Exchange 2000 uses the configuration partition in Active Directory for the same purpose. For the two versions of Exchange to coexist, this configuration information must be replicated between the two versions of Exchange so that messages can be correctly routed through the organization.

▲ **Site, administrative group, and routing group coexistence.** Exchange 4.0/5.x sites are replaced by administrative groups and routing groups in Exchange 2000. When the two Exchange versions must coexist, the Exchange 4.0/5.x servers use the site, while the Exchange 2000 servers use routing groups and administrative groups.

▲ **Site service account coexistence.** Exchange 4.0/5.x servers use a site service account to start the Exchange services on the server, as well as to authenticate connections between servers. Exchange 2000 uses the Localsystem account for the same purpose. In order for them to coexist, the Exchange 2000 server must use the site service account when connecting to an Exchange 4.0/5.x server.

As an organization, such as North American Air, migrates to Exchange 2000, the coexistence issues change depending on how many of the Exchange 4.0/5.x servers have been replaced by Exchange 2000 servers. The coexistence scenarios begin with a single Exchange 2000 server in a site with the existing Exchange 4.0/5.x servers. As whole sites are upgraded to Exchange 2000, the coexistence issues change to focus more on the coexistence between the sites rather than within a site. Coexistence issues persist until the last Exchange 4.0/5.x server is removed from the network.

> **NOTE:** *When working in a mixed-mode organization, it is important to use the Exchange management tools intended for the server version that you are administering. If you are using the Exchange System Manager, Exchange 4.0/5.x servers appear as transparent objects in both the administrative group and the routing group. You can view some properties on the servers, but cannot modify any settings.*

If you are using the Exchange Administrator, the Exchange 2000 servers appear in the Servers container as regular Exchange 4.0/5.x servers. You can also configure the Exchange Administrator to connect to Exchange 2000 servers. You can view many of the properties for the servers, and it appears that you can modify some of the settings through the interface. However, the modifications made in Exchange Administrator do not actually change the configuration on the Exchange 2000 servers. This means that in a mixed environment you must use the administration tools that were designed for each version of the server.

Sites, Administrative Groups, and Routing Groups

As North American Air moves forward with its migration to Exchange 2000, the Exchange organization operates in mixed mode until all the Exchange servers have been migrated. Operating in mixed mode places some restrictions on how the organization is administered as well as on its organizational structure.

When you install the first Exchange 2000 server, the Exchange organization runs in mixed mode, whether you are joining an existing Exchange 4.0/5.x organization or installing an Exchange 2000 server into a new organization. Mixed mode enables servers of various Exchange versions to coexist. As long as you are running in mixed mode, you can continue to have Exchange 4.0/5.x servers in the organization. You can even install new Exchange 4.0/5.x servers into the organization.

> **NOTE:** *While the concepts of mixed mode and native mode are similar in Exchange and Active Directory, there is no direct correlation. You can have a mixed-mode Exchange organization in a native-mode Active Directory domain, or you can have a native-mode Exchange organization in a mixed-mode Active Directory domain. They can also both be mixed mode or native mode.*

When the Exchange organization operates in mixed mode, the following restrictions apply:

▲ The Exchange 4.0/5.x sites must be directly mapped to administrative groups, and all the servers in the site must remain part of the administrative group.

▲ You cannot move mailboxes between administrative groups.

▲ All servers in an administrative group must belong to a routing group that is in the administrative group. If you have only one Exchange 2000 server in a site, you can have only one routing group. As you add Exchange 2000 servers to the administrative group, you can create additional routing groups in the administrative group and move the Exchange 2000 servers between the routing groups. However, you cannot move servers to routing groups in other administrative groups.

To illustrate this last point, consider the following example. North American Air plans to create a single routing group in Texas with administrative groups for each of the current sites. The project team alternatively could have chosen to combine all the sites into a single site before upgrading to Exchange 2000. This would have meant that all the Texas locations would have been in a single administrative group after the upgrade.

When North American Air installs the first Exchange server into the site, the server is automatically placed in the first routing group for the organization. That routing group must be in the Texas site. As administrators install more Exchange 2000 servers into the administrative group, they can group the Exchange servers into separate routing groups in the same administration group. For example, when they install the first Exchange 2000 server in Houston (after at least one Exchange 2000 server is installed in one of the Dallas locations), they can create a Houston routing group and move the Exchange 2000 server for Houston into that routing group. As administrators add Exchange 2000 servers to the various locations, the routing group structure might resemble the structure shown in Figure 9-1 when the migration is partially done.

If you configure multiple routing groups per site in a mixed-mode organization, you can start taking advantage of some of the advanced routing capabilities of Exchange 2000 earlier in the migration process. If you have multiple locations in one site, you can configure multiple routing groups and set up routing group connectors to control the routing of messages between the Exchange 2000 servers. There are two limitations to this configuration, however. First, because the Exchange 4.0/5.x servers cannot use the routing group information, all messages from an Exchange 4.0/5.x server to any other Exchange server in the same site (including any Exchange 2000 servers in a different routing group) will be delivered using the intra-site single hop routing. Second, all the routing groups in the original site must remain in the site and can contain only servers from that site until the domain is switched to native mode.

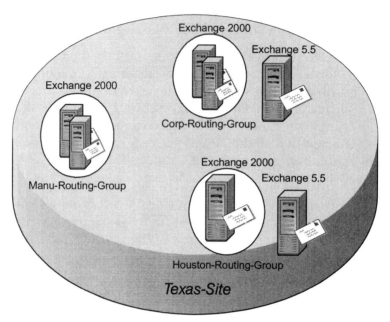

Figure 9-1: Configuring Routing Groups in Mixed Mode.

Messaging Coexistence

For Exchange 4.0/5.x servers and Exchange 2000 servers to coexist, the two Exchange versions must be able to send mail to each other. The process for sending mail has changed between the two versions, however. Exchange 2000 uses SMTP for almost all messaging, including messaging between servers in the same routing group and between servers in other routing groups. When a message is delivered between servers, the message is sent to the SMTP message categorizer, which determines which connector to use to send the message. In Exchange 4.0/5.x, however, RPCs are used. When the information store on the server receives a message destined for another computer, it delivers the message to the Message Transfer Agent (MTA), and the MTA determines how the message is routed to the other server.

Exchange 2000 is able to deliver messages to Exchange 4.0/5.x servers by using its own version of the MTA. The Exchange 2000 server processes the message through the SMTP message categorizer, which determines that the message destination is an Exchange 4.0/5.x server. It then sends the message to the Exchange 2000 MTA for delivery. The MTA on an Exchange 2000 server is virtually identical to the MTA on the Exchange 4.0/5.x server. The only difference is that the MTA on Exchange 2000 uses LDAP for directory lookups, whereas the Exchange 4.0/5.x MTA uses the directory application programming interface. When the MTA on the Exchange 2000 server connects to the MTA on an Exchange 4.0/5.x server, it uses an RPC connection identical to the RPC-based communication between Exchange 4.0/5.x servers.

When more than one Exchange 2000 server exists in the same site, they detect each other and use SMTP for messaging rather than the MTA. When all servers in a site are upgraded to Exchange 2000, all messaging operations use SMTP.

If an organization has more than one site, the Exchange 2000 servers can operate as bridgehead servers in one or more sites. The bridgehead server in one site might be running Exchange 2000 while the bridgehead server in another site is running Exchange 4.0/ 5.x — the Exchange 2000 server is backwards compatible. In Exchange 4.0/5.x, the preferred connector for inter-site messaging is the Site Connector, which uses RPCs to communicate between bridgehead servers. When one of the bridgehead servers for a site connector is upgraded to Exchange 2000, the site connector is upgraded to an X.400 RPC-based connector on the Exchange 2000 server. The upgraded Exchange 2000 server determines that the destination server for the connector is an Exchange 4.0/5.x server, so it uses RPCs for message delivery.

In Exchange 4.0/5.x, you can also use an X.400 connector to connect sites. When you upgrade a bridgehead server for an X.400 connector, the X.400 connector continues to be used to deliver messages between the servers. In addition, Exchange 4.0/5.x can use the Internet Mail Service (IMS) as a connector between sites. The SMTP connector in Exchange 2000 has replaced the IMS, but the functionality remains similar. When you upgrade an IMS bridgehead server to Exchange 2000, the IMS connector continues to function.

In an Exchange 4.0/5.x site, you can use the Dynamic Remote Access Service (Dynamic RAS) connector. Exchange 2000 does not support an equivalent inter-site connector, however, so this configuration must be changed when you upgrade your first server to Exchange 2000. If you require a dial-up connection for connectivity between sites, you can upgrade both bridgehead servers to Exchange 2000 and then configure a routing group connector between the sites. Then you can create a demand dial interface in Routing and Remote Access (RRAS) so that any IP traffic intended for the remote site can initiate a dial-up session with the remote server.

> **NOTE:** *The next chapter goes into more detail about how Exchange 4.0/5.x connectors are upgraded to Exchange 2000 and about configuring the Exchange 2000 connectors.*

Exchange 4.0/5.x servers and Exchange 2000 servers use different information to make message-routing decisions. When an Exchange 4.0/5.x server prepares to deliver a message to another site, it consults the GWART to determine the best route. Exchange 2000, however, uses a link state table for the same purpose. As described in Chapter 2, Exchange 2000's link state table is much more efficient than the GWART in detecting and routing around unavailable links. Because of this, you might want to upgrade the messaging bridgehead servers between sites to Exchange 2000 server before upgrading the mailbox store servers. The bridgehead servers can then take advantage of the link state table. As soon as you upgrade both bridgehead servers for a connector to Exchange 2000 server, the servers can use the Exchange 2000 connectors for message delivery and the link state table for routing information.

Directory Coexistence

Successful multiversion coexistence requires that you make provisions for directory replication. This includes maintenance of the GAL, which contains the information about recipients in the organization. During the transition period, users should be able to connect to either version of Exchange server and access the same GAL. The Active Directory Connector maintains the GAL in a multiple site environment just as it does in a single site. In each site and domain, the ADC synchronizes the Exchange 4.0/5.*x* GAL with the list of mail recipients in Active Directory. As you upgrade additional domains to Windows 2000 Active Directory, you must install and configure the ADC in each domain. You must also configure new recipient connection agreements in each domain to maintain the recipient information in both directories.

You must also ensure that configuration information replicates between the Exchange organizations. In Exchange 4.0/5.*x*, the site Configuration container contains the information about how the site is configured, including information such as the servers in the site, the connections to other sites and external addresses, and the intrasite and inter-site directory replication configuration. In contrast, Exchange 2000 servers store their configuration information in the configuration partition in Active Directory. For Exchange 2000 to coexist with Exchange 4.0/5.*x* servers, this configuration information must be replicated between the different versions of Exchange.

Configuration connection agreements and the site replication service synchronize the configuration information between the two versions of Exchange. The ADC automatically creates configuration connection agreements and uses them to replicate the configuration information from the Configuration container in the Exchange 4.0/5.*x* directory to the configuration partition in Active Directory. The site replication service (SRS) emulates the Exchange 4.0/5.*x* directory replication process on the Exchange 2000 server so that configuration information can be exchanged between the two Exchange server versions.

Configuration Connection Agreements

As you install Exchange 2000 servers into Exchange 4.0/5.*x* sites, the ADC automatically creates the needed configuration connection agreements. Earlier, I discussed recipient connection agreements, which synchronize the information in the Recipients container in Exchange 4.0/5.*x* with the mail recipient information in Exchange 2000. The configuration connection agreement serves a similar purpose, except that it synchronizes the contents of the configuration partition between the two directories.

The configuration connection agreement is created as a two-way agreement. Table 9-1 lists the default containers for the replication.

 NOTE: *Table 9-1 illustrates one of the difficulties an Exchange 4.0/ 5.x administrator might experience during the migration to Active Directory and Exchange 2000. Both the Exchange 4.0/5.x directories are based on X.500 so the terminology and abbreviations are similar but not identical. In the following table, cn stands for common name in both Exchange 4.0/5.x and Active Directory. However, an ou in Exchange 4.0/5.x identifies a site while an ou in Active Directory is an organizational unit. The o in Exchange 4.0/5.x identifies the Exchange organization and the dc in Active Directory stands for domain component and identifies the Active Directory domain name.*

Table 9-1: The Replication Containers for a Configuration Connection Agreement

Replication Direction	Originating Container(s)	Destination Container
From Exchange	cn=Configuration ou=*sitename* o=*organizationname* (One or more sites can be included as the originating container)	cn=*organizationname* cn=Microsoft Exchange cn=Services cn=Configuration dc=*domainname*
From Windows	cn=Recipient Policies cn=*organizationname* cn=Microsoft Exchange cn=Services cn=Configuration dc=*domainname* cn=*sitename* cn=Administrative Groups cn=*organizationname* cn=Microsoft Exchange cn=Services cn=Configuration dc=*domainname*	o=*organizationname*

When you upgrade the first server to Exchange 2000, a configuration connection agreement is created automatically that replicates information for the entire Exchange organization into Active Directory. For example, as Figure 9-2 shows, when the first Exchange 2000 server is installed into the Winnipeg site at North American Air, the source container for the configuration connection agreement includes all the Exchange sites in the entire organization.

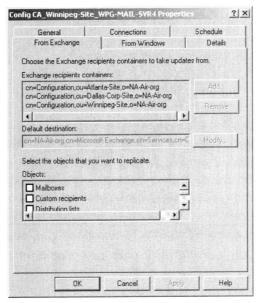

Figure 9-2: The From Exchange Source Containers for the First Configuration Connection Agreement at North American Air.

The destination container for each site's information is the configuration partition in Active Directory. Once the information about the Exchange 4.0/5.x organization has been replicated into this container, the Exchange 2000 servers can read this information.

The information from the Active Directory configuration partition also replicates to the Exchange directory. As Figure 9-3 shows, the source containers for the replication from Windows include the Recipient Policy container and the Exchange 2000 Administrative group information. This means that any recipient policy configuration information can be replicated to the Exchange 4.0/5.*x* organization, as well as any changes to the administrative groups in Exchange 2000.

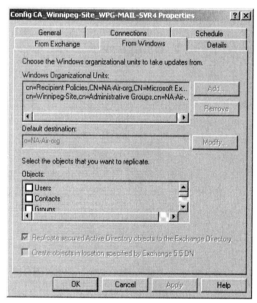

Figure 9-3: The From Windows Source Containers for the First Configuration Connection Agreement at North American Air.

As you upgrade Exchange servers in other sites to Exchange 2000, the process automatically creates additional configuration connection agreements and modifies the configuration of the existing connection agreements. For example, when administrators upgrade one of the Exchange servers in the Dallas Corporate site for North American Air, a new configuration connection agreement is configured. This new connection agreement replicates the configuration information for the Dallas-Corp-Site to Active Directory, and the Dallas-Corp-Site information is removed from the connection agreement that formerly replicated the information.

NOTE: *I present more details about creating and modifying the configuration connection agreements later in this chapter.*

You cannot change the default containers in the configuration connection agreements. You can modify the configuration connection agreement in the following ways:

▲ You can configure the ADC server that hosts the configuration connection agreement. By default, the ADC runs on the first ADC server that the Exchange 2000 setup detects.

▲ You can configure the Windows bridgehead server for the connection agreement. The bridgehead servers are automatically configured, but you can change the Windows 2000 server to use a different domain controller either in the same domain or in a different domain in the forest. The Exchange bridgehead server is the Exchange 2000 server that is running the Site Replication Service. The fact that the Exchange bridgehead server is an Exchange 2000 server is significant in that the configuration connection agreement does not actually replicate information directly with the Exchange 4.0/5.x server. Instead, the Site Replication Service replicates the Exchange 4.0/5.x information to an Exchange 2000 server, and then the information replicates to Active Directory through the configuration connection agreement.

▲ You can configure the accounts that the ADC uses when authenticating to the directories.

▲ You can configure the synchronization schedules between the directories. Like the user connection agreement, the server polls for changes in both directories every five minutes during the selected times.

As long as the connection agreement is required, you cannot delete the configuration connection agreements.

Site Replication Service

The Site Replication Service (SRS) replicates information between Exchange 4.0/5.x servers and Exchange 2000 servers.

The SRS is installed as a component on all Exchange 2000 servers. However, the SRS is activated only on the first Exchange 2000 server in a site, or on Exchange 2000 servers that are configured as directory bridgehead servers. All other Exchange 2000 servers have the SRS installed but not activated.

The SRS emulates the Exchange 4.0/5.x directory service on an Exchange 2000 server in order to replicate configuration information between Exchange 4.0/5.x servers and Exchange 2000 servers. To replicate directory information between servers in the same site, Exchange 4.0/5.x servers use the directory service directly. The directory service on one server uses an RPC connection with another server to request updated directory information. When you upgrade one of the Exchange servers to Exchange 2000, the SRS operates just like the directory service. It uses RPCs to request updated information from Exchange 4.0/5.x servers, and it accepts RPC connections from Exchange 4.0/5.x servers. When replicating directory information between Exchange 4.0/5.x sites, the directory replication service prepares a message containing the directory updates and forwards the message to the MTA, which in turn forwards the message to the remote site. When one of the directory bridgehead servers is upgraded to Exchange 2000, the SRS can send and receive directory replication information in the same way.

NOTE: *The SRS includes a database (Srs.edb) and the database transaction logs located in the \Exchsrvr\Srsdata directory. The SRS database is essentially the same database as the Exchange 4.0/5.x directory services database (dir.edb).*

The SRS replicates directory information in both directions between Exchange 2000 servers and Exchange 4.0/5.x servers. When the first SRS is enabled, the configuration information for the entire Exchange 4.0/5.x organization replicates to the Exchange server running SRS, and then replicates into Active Directory using the configuration connection agreement. At the same time, the Exchange 2000 server running SRS reads the Exchange 2000 configuration information from Active Directory and replicates the information to the Exchange 4.0/5.x servers.

NOTE: *When you upgrade an Exchange server or install a new Exchange server into a site, you can view the Exchange 2000 server properties from within the Exchange Administration program. As Figure 9-4 illustrates, the server container includes two new objects. The Microsoft Exchange Site Replication Service replaces the Directory Replication object, and its properties include the option to update directory information within the site. The X.400 object, which replaces the Message Transfer Agent object, is the representation of the X.400 RPC connection used on the Exchange 2000 server to communicate with the Exchange 4.0/5.x servers.*

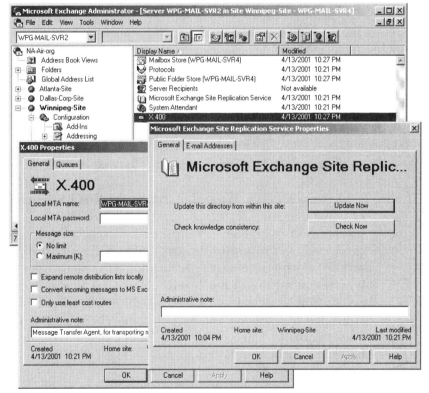

Figure 9-4: The SRS and X.400 Objects in the Exchange 2000 Server Container.

To understand how the ADC and the SRS work together to keep both directories synchronized, consider the following example. The Winnipeg location is the first site at North American Air to be upgraded to Exchange 2000. After the first Exchange 2000 server is installed in Winnipeg, the Winnipeg site has two Exchange 4.0/5.*x* servers and one Exchange 2000 server, as shown in Figure 9-5.

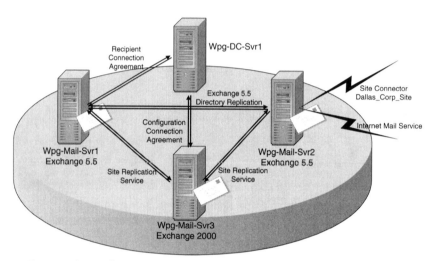

Figure 9-5: The Site Replication Service in the Winnipeg Site.

In this example, Wpg-Mail-Svr3 is the first Exchange 2000 server installed into the site, so it operates both the SRS and the configuration connection agreement for the ADC to keep both directories synchronized. As the administrators make changes to the directory service information in this site or in other sites, the ADC and the SRS keep the information synchronized between all the Exchange servers. As well, as additional Exchange 2000 servers are added to the Winnipeg site, the way the SRS operates changes. The following points illustrate some of the directory changes that can happen and how the information is replicated:

▲ When an administrator makes a change to an attribute on one of the mailboxes in Wpg-Mail-Svr2, the Exchange 4.0/5.*x* replication process replicates the change to Wpg-Mail-Svr1. The information then replicates to Wpg-DC-Svr1 through the recipient connection agreement. Wpg-Mail-Svr3 can then read the information from Active Directory. Recipient information replicates from the Exchange 4.0/5.*x* servers to Active Directory, not directly to Exchange 2000 servers.

▲ When configuration changes occur in the organization (for example, when an administrator configures a new directory bridge-head server in the Corporate site), that information replicates to Wpg-Mail-Svr2. This information then replicates to Wpg-Mail-Svr1 using the normal Exchange 4.0/5.*x* inter-site replication mechanism. The information also replicates to Wpg-Mail-Svr3, which is running SRS to emulate the Exchange 4.0/5.*x* directory service. The new configuration information then replicates from Wpg-Mail-Svr3 to Wpg-DC-Svr1 using the configuration connection agreement.

▲ When all the mailboxes have been removed from Wpg-Mail-Svr1, administrators remove it from the site. All replication between the remaining servers (Wpg-Mail-Svr3 and Wpg-Mail-Svr2) is through the SRS.

▲ When a new Exchange 2000 connector server (Wpg-Con-Svr4) is installed in the Winnipeg location, the connectors are switched from Wpg-Mail-Svr2 to the new server. After administrators implement this, the SRS on Wpg-Con-Svr4 is activated automatically to replicate information with remote sites as well as with Exchange 4.0/5.*x* servers in the same site. In addition, a new configuration connection agreement is automatically configured between Wpg-DC-Svr1 and Wpg-Con-Svr4 to replicate the Exchange information to Active Directory. While this connector is not necessary (because all the information could be replicated from Wpg-Mail-Svr3), the Site Consistency Checker creates the additional configuration connection agreement to optimize replication. At this point, the Winnipeg location's configuration resembles Figure 9-6.

▲ When Wpg-Mail-Svr2 is upgraded to Exchange 2000 and implemented as a public folder server, the SRS configuration is not affected. When administrators upgrade the server, the upgrade disables its SRS. After administrators upgrade all the servers within the site to Exchange 2000, no more Exchange 4.0/5.*x* directory replication occurs in the site. The only replication is

Active Directory replication. The instances of the SRS on Wpg-Mail-Svr3 and on Wpg-Con-Svr4 are still active, but only the SRS on the Wpg-Con-Svr4 is used for directory replication with the Texas site.

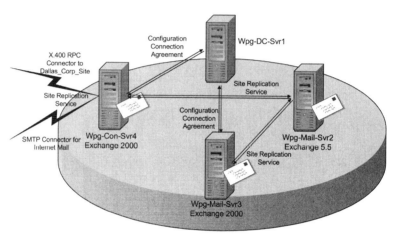

Figure 9-6: The SRS in the Winnipeg Location After the Migration Is Partially Completed.

It might appear that the SRS is not necessary to replicate to the configuration information, since the ADC handles replication between Active Directory and the Exchange 4.0/5.x directory. Any recipient information replicates from the Exchange 4.0/5.x server directly to Active Directory using a recipient connection agreement. You could also use the ADC to replicate the configuration information directly from an Exchange 4.0/5.x server to Active Directory rather than using the SRS to replicate the information to an Exchange 2000 server and then using the ADC to replicate to Active Directory. However, the ADC cannot function in all environments. The ADC uses LDAP to query both the Exchange directory and Active Directory, so direct network connectivity is required between all the servers. In a situation in which the remote Exchange site is connected using an Internet Mail Service site connector, this LDAP connectivity might not be available. The SRS must therefore replicate to an Exchange 2000 server, and then the ADC must connect to that Exchange 2000 server to replicate the information to Active Directory.

As you continue to upgrade or install Exchange 2000 servers in additional sites, the number of configuration connection agreements automatically increases. When you install the first Exchange 2000 server into a site, the SRS is enabled on the Exchange server and a configuration connection agreement is configured for that site, so that any configuration changes in the site can replicate to Active Directory. When you upgrade a directory bridgehead server to Exchange 2000, the process configures an additional SRS and configuration connection agreement for the site. To simplify the configuration, you would normally upgrade the connector servers in each site first, so that you would have only a single instance of SRS running in the site and only a single connection agreement.

Active Directory Replication and Exchange Directory Replication

Implementing Exchange 2000 significantly decreases the amount of replication traffic on the network. Exchange 4.0/5.x servers must replicate directory information with each other, both within a site and between sites. In addition, the Windows NT PDC must replicate any changes to the domain database to all BDCs. When the organization has been completely upgraded to Exchange 2000, the only replication that occurs is Active Directory replication. Table 9-2 contrasts Exchange 4.0/5.x directory replication with Active Directory replication.

The increased efficiency of Active Directory replication means that as more and more Exchange servers are upgraded to Exchange 2000, the amount of replication traffic significantly decreases.

Table 9-2: Comparing Exchange 4.0/5.x Replication and Active Directory Replication

Characteristic	Exchange 4.0/5.x Directory Replication	Active Directory Replication
Replication scope	All the Exchange servers share one directory database, which means that replication traffic is sent between all Exchange servers.	Replication is only sent between domain controllers.
Multiple domain replication	Each Exchange server still receives the entire directory database.	The only replication traffic between domains is global catalog replication, and the replication of the schema and configuration partitions.
Replication traffic on WAN links	Controlled by configuring Exchange sites.	Controlled by configuring Active Directory sites.
Traffic compression	Only replication traffic sent using SMTP is compressed between sites.	All replication traffic between sites is compressed.
Replication granularity	Replication is on a per object basis. If one attribute on any object is changed, the entire object must be replicated.	Replication is on a per attribute basis. If one attribute is changed, only that attribute is replicated.

Implementing the SRS at North American Air

As an organization like North American Air continues to migrate more of the current sites to Exchange 2000, the possibility exists for duplicate replication links to be created. To prevent this duplication from happening, the SRS also includes the Site Consistency Checker (SCC). The functions of the SCC are to check for additional sites that have been upgraded to Exchange 2000, to create new configuration connection agreements as needed, and to disable duplicate connection agreements. The SCC's role is similar to that of the Exchange 5.5 Knowledge Consistency Checker (KCC) in that it ensures that all the directory information is correctly replicated throughout the organization.

In a large organization, the SRS, the ADC, and the SCC are essential in maintaining an optimized configuration replication topology. As North American Air progresses through the migration to Exchange 2000, the SRS, the ADC, and the SCC maintain accurate configuration information on both Exchange servers and in Active Directory.

All three of these components are important as North American Air completes the migration of its Exchange 5.5 sites to Exchange 2000. Figure 9-7 illustrates what the Exchange organization looks like as North American Air completes the migration of the Winnipeg site to Exchange 2000 but has not yet implemented Exchange 2000 anywhere else.

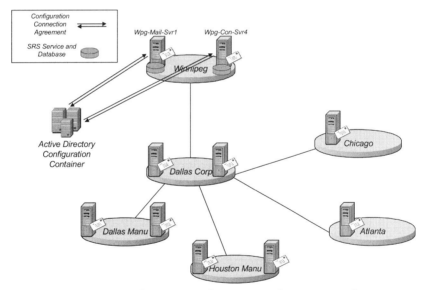

Figure 9-7: The SRS and ADC Configuration After Upgrading the Winnipeg Location.

NOTE: *To make the diagrams used for this scenario easier to understand, I have shown only a single domain controller. In addition, to keep the diagrams simple, I have shown only the Winnipeg, Chicago, Atlanta, and Texas locations. The diagrams are still conceptually accurate, however, because the configuration connection agreements* *replicate information to the configuration partition in Active Directory and all domain controllers in a forest have exactly the same configuration partition information. As North American Air upgrades multiple locations to Exchange 2000, the bridgehead servers for the configuration connection agreements will be domain controllers in the locations being upgraded, but the configuration information will be replicated to all domain controllers.*

In Figure 9-7, there are two active instances of SRS and two configuration connection agreements on Wpg-Mail-Svr2 and Wpg-Con-Svr4. The SRS gathers information about the entire Exchange 5.5 organization, and the ADC replicates this information into Active Directory.

Next, North American Air plans to upgrade the Atlanta and Chicago locations to Exchange 2000. Atlanta has only a single Exchange 5.5 server, so when administrators upgrade it, or when they install a new Exchange 2000 server into the site, another instance of SRS is enabled. The SCC automatically configures a new configuration connection agreement with a domain controller in the Atlanta domain. In Chicago, when administrators upgrade the server currently hosting the connector to the Dallas corporate site, the process enables another instance of SRS and configures a new configuration connection agreement. When administrators upgrade the second server in Chicago, however, the SRS is not enabled on the server and no new configuration connection agreements are needed. Figure 9-8 illustrates the configuration.

As each of these locations is upgraded, the configuration connection agreement in each location assumes responsibility for keeping the configuration information updated for its site. Before the Atlanta site was upgraded, the configuration connection agreements in Winnipeg provided the configuration information for the entire Exchange 5.5 organization to Active Directory. After Atlanta is upgraded, the configuration agreement in Atlanta replicates the configuration information for the Atlanta site to Active Directory. Because there are now configuration connection agreements from two sites, the configuration information from other sites can be replicated through two different connection agreements to Active Directory. The SCC determines that this situation exists and ensures that the information from each site replicates only once to Active Directory. The SCC automatically defines which sites should be replicated to Active Directory through which connection agreement. For example, the Winnipeg connection agreement might replicate the configuration information for the Winnipeg location and the Houston site, and the Atlanta connection agreement might replicate the other sites. The SCC automatically configures the connection agreements, and there is no way to modify how the SCC configures them.

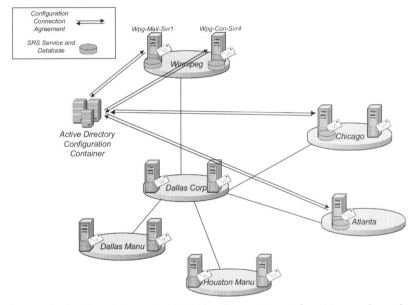

Figure 9-8: The SRS and ADC Configuration After Upgrading the Atlanta and Chicago Locations.

The next step in the migration project is to upgrade the Corporate site in Dallas. Again, the best way to optimize the use of the SRS and the ADC is to upgrade the connector servers first. This way, only two instances of the SRS are running in the Dallas Corporate site as well as one single configuration connection agreement. Figure 9-9 shows the configuration after administrators have upgraded the bridgehead servers in the Corporate site to Exchange 2000.

This process is repeated again as administrators upgrade the connector servers in the Dallas Manufacturing site and the Houston Manufacturing site to Exchange 2000. When they have upgraded all the directory bridgehead servers, the amount of inter-site replication traffic decreases significantly. Because each site then uses Exchange 2000 servers as the bridgehead servers, there is no more Exchange 5.5-based replication traffic, and in fact, no Exchange replication traffic between the sites at all. This means that the SRS is no longer used for inter-site replication — only for replication with Exchange 5.5 servers in each site. In each site, the ADC configures a configuration connection agreement that replicates the configuration information to Active Directory. The regular Active Directory replication replicates this information to all the domain controllers in the entire organization, and the Exchange 2000 servers in each site use the information to determine the organization's configuration.

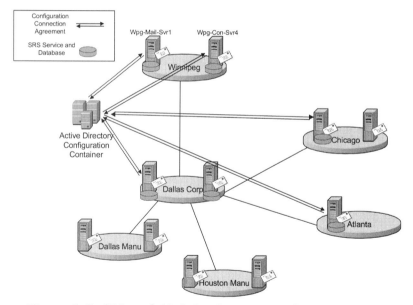

Figure 9-9: SRS and ADC Configuration After Upgrading the Corporate Site.

GWART and the Link State Table Coexistence

An important question when addressing coexistence between Exchange 4.0/5.x servers and Exchange 2000 server is how the two versions make routing decisions. Exchange 4.0/5.x servers make message routing decisions between sites based on the GWART. The GWART is a list of all the connected sites within the organization as well as any external connectors. When a server needs to send a message to a remote site, it consults the GWART and selects the lowest-cost route to the destination site. Under Exchange 4.0/5.x, one server in each site maintains the GWART. The first server in the site is the routing calculation server by default. Once a day, this server recalculates the GWART and replicates the information to all other Exchange servers in the site.

In contrast, Exchange 2000 uses a link state table to make routing decisions. Each server calculates its own link state table. Each routing group has a routing group master that ensures that all the servers in the site have accurate routing information. For example, when one of the bridgehead servers in a routing group detects that one of the links is down, it informs the routing group master and the routing group master informs all the other servers in the routing group.

Because the two versions of Exchange handle the routing information so differently, the coexistence issue is an important one. The Exchange 2000 SRS replicates the routing information between the different server versions. The GWART replicates from the Exchange 4.0/5.x routing calculation server to Exchange 2000 with an active SRS. The ADC configuration connection agreement then replicates this information into Active Directory as the LegacyGWART object in the configuration partition. The Exchange 2000 routing group master monitors this object, and when it detects changes, it replicates them as link state updates to the other Exchange 2000 servers in the site. At the same time, it also replicates the link state table information to the Exchange 4.0/5.x routing calculation server through the SRS so that any changes in the link state table are also reflected in the GWART.

When the Exchange 4.0/5.*x* routing recalculation server is upgraded to Exchange 2000, the upgraded server becomes the routing recalculation server. You can also configure any Exchange 2000 server to operate as the routing calculation server through the Exchange 4.0/5.*x* Administration program. If an Exchange 2000 server is the routing calculation server, it consults the LegacyGWART object in Active Directory and replicates that information to the other Exchange 4.0/5.*x* servers in the site.

Other Coexistence Issues

The most obvious coexistence issues between Exchange 2000 and Exchange 4.0/5.*x* servers are the issues of message flow and directory replication. However, there are a number of other issues that you must also deal with when your organization includes both versions of Exchange.

Proxy Address Coexistence

Every new mailbox created in an Exchange 4.0/5.*x* site is assigned a number of different proxy addresses, including an X.400 address and an SMTP address. You can configure the format of the addresses on the Site Addressing tab on the properties for the Site Addressing object in the site's Configuration container.

When you join an Exchange 2000 server to the Exchange 4.0/5.*x* site, the same proxy address is applied to all mailboxes created on the Exchange 2000 server. This happens because the proxy address-generation rule is migrated from the Exchange 4.0/5.*x* servers into the Exchange 2000 organization and applied as a recipient policy. You can view this recipient policy in the Exchange System Manager, as shown in Figure 9-10. The inherited policy must be configured with the highest priority so that all the users in the site get the same proxy addresses. You can create additional recipient policies in Exchange 2000, but the inherited policy must always have highest priority and cannot be deleted. As shown in Figure 9-10, the filter rule for the policy applies to all objects with a mailNickname and a legacyExchangeDN equal to the name of the Exchange 4.0/5.*x* site. All objects in the site, even mailboxes created on the Exchange 2000 server, fall into this category, and therefore all objects receive the same proxy address.

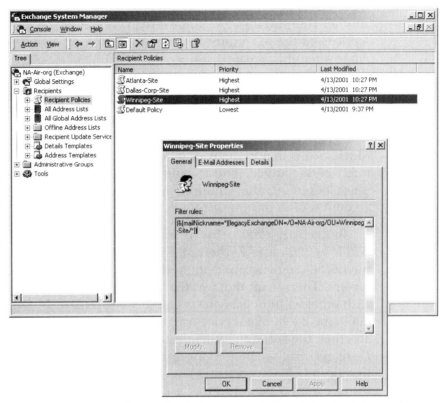

Figure 9-10: The Default Recipient Policy Inherited from the Exchange 4.0/5.x Site.

Site Service Account Coexistence

In an Exchange 4.0/5.*x* organization, every Exchange server must have a site service account. This account authenticates the Exchange services as they start and authenticates connections between Exchange servers. Exchange 4.0/5.*x* servers must use a site service account because the LocalSystem account cannot be used for authentication between two servers in Windows NT. The LocalSystem account is a regular user account, and it has a token that can be used when authenticating with the domain, but it has a flag that prohibits it from being used when authenticating to another computer. Most services in Windows NT use the LocalSystem account when starting because the account is secure (since the password is automatically changed every 7 days) and because it cannot be used to access another computer. In Exchange 4.0/5.x, however, the directory service and the MTA must be able to authenticate with another computer when they create a connection.

The problem with the site service account in Exchange 4.0/5.x is that it has a very high permission level in the Exchange organization, which means that the account is a likely target for attacks. In addition, changing the password for the account involves several steps, which means that in many organizations the account's password rarely gets changed. The account is also usually configured so that it is not locked out after multiple bad logon attempts, making the account is even more susceptible to attack.

In Exchange 2000, this configuration has changed. Because Windows 2000 uses Kerberos for authentication rather than NTLM, the LocalSystem account can now be used to authenticate between servers. This means that two Exchange servers can authenticate with each other without using a special service account. In Exchange 2000, the Exchange services can start using the LocalSystem account and then the account authenticates the service with another server. Using a LocalSystem account rather than a service account provides significantly better security. The account is automatically configured with a complex password that is changed every 7 days so the password for the account remains secure.

When you join an Exchange 2000 server with an Exchange 4.0/5.x site, you must know the service account password for the site. This is because the Exchange 4.0/5.x servers in the site still expect the service account to be used for authentication between servers. After the installation, you can configure the service account information in Exchange System Manager. To access the service account configuration, right-click the administrative group and choose Properties. (See Figure 9-11.)

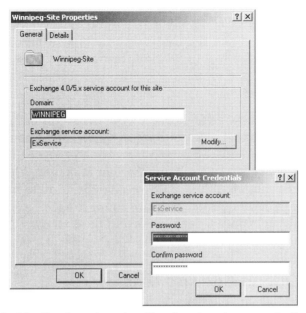

Figure 9-11: Configuring the Site Service Account in Exchange System Manager.

Address Book Views and Address Lists

In Exchange 5.0 and 5.5, you can partition a large GAL into smaller, more usable components by creating address book views. To create an address book view, you can sort the GAL based on one or more attributes and then display the result of the sort as a subset of the GAL. For example, you can create an address book view that sorts your GAL based on the City attribute, and then the Department attribute. When users view the address book from within a MAPI client, they would see a city container for each city in the organization, and inside each city container would be a department container for each department.

In Exchange 2000, address lists have replaced address book views. When you install Exchange 2000, a default set of address lists are configured. These include address lists such as All Contacts, All Groups, and All Users. An address list creates a subset of the GAL based on an LDAP query. For example, you might create an address list based on the City attribute equal to Winnipeg and a Department attribute equal to Sales. When the users open the address book from a MAPI client, they see only a single custom address list. Rather than automatically grouping all the mailboxes based on the selected attributes, Exchange 2000 displays just the address list that matches the query.

Because address book views are so different from address lists, the address book views are not upgraded when you upgrade a server. Consequently, all the address book views need to be recreated as address lists in Exchange System Manager. While working in a mixed environment, the clients receive the address information based on the server to which they are connecting. The Exchange 4.0/5.*x* clients get the address book views and the Exchange 2000 clients get the address lists.

Offline Address Lists

In Exchange 4.0/5.*x*, you can create an offline address book for mobile clients. This means that laptop users can download the entire GAL, or a specified part of the GAL, to the local computer and then access the address while disconnected from the network. By default the offline address book is created for the Recipients container in the site, but you can create additional offline address lists using other recipient containers or using the GAL. When a user downloads the offline address book using a newer Outlook client (Outlook 97, version 8.03 or later), the client is presented with a list of all the offline address lists and given the choice of which list to download.

Exchange 2000 implements offline address books in much the same way. A single Default Offline Address List is created for the organization and includes the entire GAL. You can create additional offline address lists or add any of the address lists to the existing Default Offline Address List. To do this, expand the Recipients container in Exchange System Manager and then expand the Offline Address Lists container. Right-click Default Offline Address List and select Properties. Figure 9-12 shows the configuration options.

To add additional address lists, click Add and select any of the address lists for the organization, including custom address lists. These address lists are then available for download for the clients.

In Exchange 2000, you can associate a particular offline address book with a mailbox store. This might be useful if you were hosting two separate business divisions on one Exchange server and you wanted to make sure that the users in each division access only the offline address book for their division. For example, North American Air might decide to implement this in their Exchange organization to separate the maintenance and manufacturing component from the airfreight component.

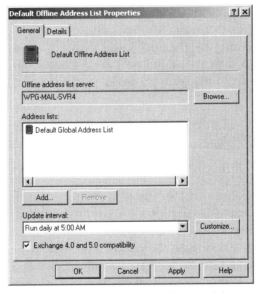

Figure 9-12: Configuring the Offline Address Book in Exchange System Manager.

To accomplish this, the administrators at North American Air would perform the following steps:

1. Create two address lists that sort the GAL based on a particular attribute.

For example, at North American Air the users in the maintenance and manufacturing component could sort the GAL with the Company attribute set to Manufacturing, while the users in the airfreight component could sort the GAL with Company set to Airfreight. Administrators would then create two lists based on the Company attribute.

2. Create two groups in Active Directory — one for each of the divisions — and put all the users from each division into the appropriate groups.

3. To ensure that the users from each division cannot read the address lists for the other division, configure the address list security settings.

   For example, on the Airfreight address list, administrators would configure the Airfreight group with at least read permissions, and deny the Maintenance group read permission. They would also deny both groups read permission to the default address lists.

4. Configure two separate offline address lists in Exchange System Manager, one based on each division's address list.

5. Configure the default offline address list for each division.

   To do this, administrators would configure a separate mailbox store for each division and associate one of the offline address lists with the mailbox store. To configure the default offline address list for the mailbox store, access the mailbox store properties and select the General tab. Click Browse beside Offline address list: and select the appropriate offline address list. Figure 9-13 shows the interface.

   When the clients from each of the departments configure their offline address list, the only option they have is the offline address book that is configured for their information store.

NOTE: *When you create the offline address list, a warning appears that the public folder that will contain the new offline address list will not be created until the next time the information store maintenance runs and that the offline address list will not be available until that* *time. By default the information store maintenance runs between 1 A.M. and 5 A.M. every day.*

The Exchange 4.0/5.x offline address book configuration does not migrate to Exchange 2000. Clients connecting to an Exchange 4.0/5.x server get the Exchange 4.0/5.x offline address book options, while clients connecting to the Exchange 2000 server get the Exchange 2000 options.

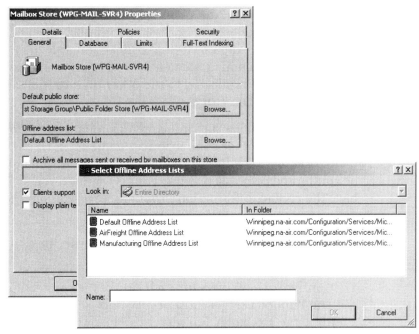

Figure 9-13: Configuring the Default Offline Address List for a Mailbox Store.

Coexistence with Another Organization

In some cases, a company running an Exchange 2000 organization may need to coexist with another Exchange organization. For example, instead of upgrading an Exchange 4.0/5.x organization to Exchange 2000 as North American Air did, a corporation may decide to create an Exchange 2000 organization and then move the users from the Exchange 4.0/5.x organization to the Exchange 2000 organization. A company might choose this option if they planned to extensively reorganize the site configuration rather than upgrade each site. A company might also want to do this if it had an existing Exchange 2000 organization and then acquired a company currently running Exchange 4.0/5.x.

In either case, the two Exchange organizations should share as much as information as possible. At the very least, there should be a connection agreement so that user information is replicated between the organizations and the GAL in both organizations includes the messaging recipients from both. To accomplish this goal, you can configure an inter-organizational connection agreement in ADC. Using this connection agreement, the user objects from each of the organizations are replicated to the other organization as contact objects in Active Directory.

You can configure an inter-organizational connection agreement the same way as other connection agreements in the ADC management interface. The inter-organizational connection agreement can be configured only as a one-way connector, however, so if you want to have the contact information flow both ways, you have to configure two one-way connection agreements.

To configure the connection agreement, perform the following steps:

1. Configure the servers for each side of the connection agreement. The Windows server must be a Windows 2000 domain controller, while the Exchange 5.5 server can be any server in the site that you want to replicate.

2. Configure the source and destination containers for the replication in each direction. You can choose the Exchange site as the Exchange source location, and then specify a particular OU as the destination container in Windows. You can also chose the domain, or a particular OU as the Windows source container, and the Exchange site as the destination container. See Figure 9-14.

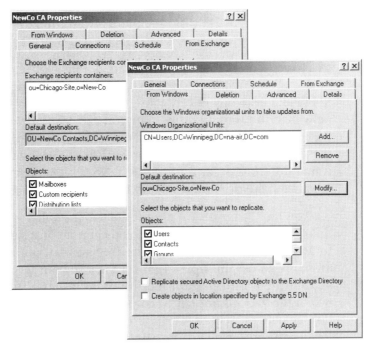

Figure 9-14: Configure the Source and Destination Containers for an Inter-Organizational Connection Agreement.

3. Configure the types of objects the ADC will create if it does not detect an equivalent object in the destination container. In most cases, you should select the option to create a contact item rather than a disabled user account. However, you might choose to create disabled user accounts if you were planning to migrate the users into the Exchange 2000 organization.

4. Configure the types of objects to be replicated, including contacts (custom recipients), mailboxes (users) and groups (distribution lists). If you want to duplicate the GAL in the destination organization, accept the default of replicating all three types of objects.

Once the connection agreement is configured, the ADC begins replication and creates the objects in the destination directory as configured. If you chose to create contacts, the ADC creates a contact for each of the replicated objects. This means that the mailboxes, distribution lists, and custom recipients from the Exchange 4.0/5.x directory all appear in Active Directory as contacts.

To send mail between the organizations, you then must configure an SMTP connector or X.400 connector. If you are configuring an SMTP connector, you can configure the connector to use DNS to deliver to the remote domain or you can configure it to use one of the Exchange servers in the remote domain as a smart host to deliver the messages directly to that server. Because the destination domain is in a different organization, the DNS server must have the MX record for the domain if you do not use a smart host.

You lose a significant amount of functionality when operating in this environment. For example, you cannot configure access to public folders. In addition, the calendar free and busy information is not available across multiple organizations, so your users cannot access appointment information. Additionally, because the users from the two organizations appear as contacts in both organizations, they are not security principals, and therefore you cannot use these accounts for assigning permissions to any resources.

Conclusion

Running Exchange 4.0/5.x and Exchange 2000 servers in the same organization raises a number of coexistence issues, including e-mail access and directory information sharing. This chapter provided an overview of the coexistence issues that an organization, such as North American Air, experiences as it moves through the migration to Exchange 2000. For the most part, the Exchange 2000 servers are backward-compatible and can operate in an Exchange 4.0/5.x organization with little difficulty, if configured correctly. The next chapter goes into more detail about North American Air's specific coexistence issues as the company finishes its migration to Exchange 2000. In addition, the next chapter looks at some of the configuration options that change as more and more Exchange 4.0/5.x servers are upgraded to Exchange 2000. The final section in the next chapter also describes how North American Air's Domino Server and MS Mail messaging systems are migrated to Exchange 2000.

Chapter 10

Completing the Migration

AFTER YOU'VE MIGRATED THE FIRST SITE to Exchange 2000 and managed the coexistence issues between Exchange 4.0/5.*x* and Exchange 2000, the next step is to complete the migration to Exchange 2000. At this point in the North American Air project, the first site in Winnipeg has been upgraded to Exchange 2000 and most of the coexistence issues have been dealt with. They are now ready to upgrade the other Exchange 4.0/5.*x* sites to Exchange 2000, beginning with the Atlanta and Chicago sites and then proceeding to the central sites in Texas. The final part of their migration process is to migrate the smaller Exchange 4.0/5.*x* sites and to migrate the Domino Server/Lotus Notes and MS Mail systems.

This chapter describes the remaining steps and issues in the migration of North American Air to Exchange 2000. The primary issues that remain are the migration of the Exchange 4.0/5.*x* site connectors to Exchange 2000 routing group connectors and the migration of the non-Exchange messaging systems. By the end of this chapter, North American Air will have completed its migration to Exchange 2000.

Upgrading the Site Connectors

As with most large organizations, North American Air's migration to Exchange 2000 will take several months. In some cases, such as at the Winnipeg site, administrators will migrate an entire site before moving on to the next site. In other cases, such as in the Texas location, they will migrate several sites at the same time. Administrators have decided to migrate the connector servers in Texas first to take advantage of the enhanced message routing in Exchange 2000 and then upgrade the mailbox servers there.

One of the most important remaining issues is the upgrade of the site connectors from Exchange 4.0/5.x to Exchange 2000. At North American Air, every site has one or more servers acting as a messaging bridgehead server and operating as the messaging connector to other sites. These messaging bridgehead servers can run a variety of connectors including site connectors, X.400 connectors, dynamic RAS (DRAS) connectors, and Internet Mail Service (IMS) connectors. When these servers are upgraded to Exchange 2000, the connectors also must be upgraded. The following sections outline the processes you would deal with as a North American Air administrator performing the connector upgrades.

Upgrading a Site Connector

The most common method of connecting sites in Exchange 4.0/5.x is a site connector. A site connector is an RPC-based connector that can be used only to connect Exchange sites. A site connector has several advantages over other connectors. It is the fastest type of connector, it can be configured with multiple bridgehead servers on either side, and it is the easiest connector to set up and configure. Using multiple bridgehead servers ensures enhanced redundancy and the capability of load-balancing across multiple servers.

When you upgrade a messaging bridgehead server that is running the site connector, the upgrade process checks if any of the remote bridgehead servers are already running Exchange 2000. If this is the first bridgehead server to be upgraded, it upgrades the connector to an Exchange 2000 RPC-based X.400 connector. This connector is used only to connect Exchange 2000 servers to Exchange 5.5 in a different site when the Exchange 5.5 server is a messaging bridgehead server for a site connector. The process upgrades all the settings for the connector except the target server costs. Exchange 2000 does not have any target server cost configuration options.

If the Exchange server being upgraded detects that one or more of the messaging bridgehead servers in the remote site are running Exchange 2000, the upgrade process attempts to set up an SMTP routing group connector between the upgraded server and the destination server(s). If the account being used to upgrade the server does not have administrative permissions in the remote site, it upgrades the site connector to the Exchange 2000 X.400 RPC-based connector.

An Exchange 4.0/5.x site connector can be configured so that all the servers in a site act as the bridgehead servers for the connector, or so that one server acts as the bridgehead server. After you have upgraded the site connector to the Exchange 2000 SMTP connector, you might wish to change this setting, because the Exchange 2000 connector allows any number of servers to operate as messaging bridgehead servers, not just one or all.

Upgrading an X.400 Connector

The second method of connecting sites is the X.400 connector. The primary advantage of the X.400 connector is that since it is not RPC-based, it can be used on a slower network connection. The X.400 connector also can connect the Exchange system to a non-Exchange X.400-based messaging system. However, unlike a site connector, the X.400 connector can be configured with only a single messaging bridgehead server at each end of the connector.

When you upgrade a server that operates as a bridgehead server for an X.400 connector to Exchange 2000, the process upgrades the connector as well. If the bridgehead server in the remote site runs Exchange 2000, the upgrade process upgrades the connector to the Exchange 2000 SMTP connector. However, if the server is the first bridgehead server to be upgraded for the connector, and the remote server still runs Exchange 4.0/5.x, the process upgrades the connector to the Windows 2000 X.400 connector.

The only X.400 connector component that does not upgrade to Exchange 2000 is the TP4 transport stack for the connector. The TP4 transport stack is one of three possible transport stacks you can configure in Exchange 4.0/5.x for a connector. The others are X.25

and TCP/IP. Because Windows 2000 does not support the TP4 protocol, any X.400 connectors using TP4 are not upgraded. If you are using the TP4 protocol, you have to implement a different protocol before installing Exchange 2000 on the server.

Upgrading an Internet Mail Service Connector

The third method of connecting sites in Exchange 4.0/5.x is the Internet Mail Service (IMS) connector. The IMS connector uses SMTP mail to route messages between the sites, either through an actual Internet connection or through private WAN connections.

When you upgrade a server operating as a bridgehead server for an IMS connector to Exchange 2000, the process upgrades the connector to the Exchange 2000 SMTP connector. The default SMTP server on the server is configured as the bridgehead server for the connector by default. However, one of the advantages of Exchange 2000 is that you can configure additional SMTP virtual servers on a single server, so after the upgrade, you can create an additional SMTP virtual server and specify which virtual server will operate as the bridgehead server. You also can configure additional servers in the routing group to operate as bridgehead servers for the connector.

Almost all the configuration settings for the IMS connector are upgraded when you upgrade the server. One significant exception is the list of hosts that are allowed to connect to the Exchange server. In Exchange 4.0/5.x, you can configure the IMS connector to accept connections from only a specified list of computers. Exchange 2000 relocates this setting to the virtual server properties. The upgrade process does not transfer the previous settings to virtual server properties, however, so you must reconfigure the option manually on the virtual server properties after the upgrade. The option that prevents a server from relaying messages also has been relocated to the virtual server properties and also is not upgraded.

NOTE: The two settings that are not migrated to the SMTP connector can result in a potentially serious security breach. The default configuration for the SMTP virtual server prevents the server from relaying any messages, so in most cases you can just accept this default. If you are using the list of connecting hosts as a security mea-sure, you should configure the virtual server immediately after the upgrade.

Other settings from the connector are upgraded to Exchange 2000 but not configured on the connector anymore. In Exchange 4.0/5.x, for example, you can configure filtering based on e-mail domains on the IMS connector. In Exchange 2000, you'll find this configuration in the Global Settings/Message Delivery settings.

> **NOTE:** *I cover the configuration of the virtual servers and the global settings, as well the configuration of the SMTP connector in more detail, in the next chapter.*

Replacing a Dynamic RAS Connector

Exchange 2000 does not support the Dynamic Remote Access Service (DRAS) connector. In Exchange 4.0/5.x, you can use the DRAS connector to connect two sites that use a dial-up connection as the only connection between them, or that use a dial-up connection as a backup connection. For example, a corporation might have a small remote office that runs an Exchange 4.0/5.x server as part of the corporate Exchange organization. The corporation might use a DRAS connector to connect to the corporate office via a modem or an ISDN connector several times a day to transfer mail and directory information. When the server is upgraded to Exchange 2000, the DRAS connector must be replaced.

You can replace the DRAS functionality with one of the other connectors in Exchange 2000 and then use the demand-dial options in Windows 2000 to initiate the connection as needed. If the current DRAS connector uses a dial-up connection, replace it with the X.400 connector. If it uses an ISDN connector, replace it with either the routing group connector or the SMTP connector.

To set up the demand-dial option, you must configure Routing and Remote Access Service (RRAS) in Windows 2000. You can create a demand-dial interface using RRAS such that when any traffic des-tined for a remote network arrives at the server, the server automati-cally initiates a demand-dial connection to the remote network. In most cases, you can then create static routes within RRAS so that the server dials the correct interface when the packet intended for the remote network arrives.

After you configure RRAS, the next step is to configure the Exchange connector with the name of bridgehead server in the remote site. When the Exchange connector needs to connect to the remote server, it queries DNS for the IP address of the destination server. Since the IP address for the remote server is included in the network address in the routing table, the Exchange server initiates a demand-dial connection and delivers the messages. You also can configure the routing group connectors with selected schedules, so that it initiates the remote connection only during certain times of the day.

Another way to use the demand-dial option when connecting Exchange servers is to use the Internet as a backbone. This has become a viable alternative for many smaller organizations because of the availability of fast, inexpensive Internet connections, such as DSL or cable modems. In this case, you would configure the demand-dial interface to initiate a VPN connection to the remote network (again based on a static routing table). You can then use the VPN connection to route all types of traffic between the sites, including the Exchange traffic.

NOTE: *When messages are not being delivered between servers in Exchange 4.0/5.x, it is often useful to examine the queues on either the MTA or the connector that should be delivering the message. In Exchange 2000, however, the intersite connectors do not have queues. The queue objects appear instead under the virtual server objects on each server. The intrasite and intersite connector queues for connections to Exchange 4.0/5.x servers appear under the X.400 virtual server in Exchange System Manager. (See Figure 10-1.) I cover queue management on the Exchange 2000 connectors in more detail in Chapter 11.*

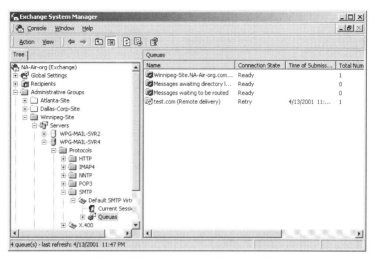

Figure 10-1: Viewing the Queue Objects in Exchange System Manager.

Migrating from Other Messaging Systems

In many organizations, the migration to Exchange 2000 includes not only migrating the Exchange 4.0/5.*x* servers to Exchange 2000, but also migrating other messaging systems. North American Air is a typical company in this respect in that it supports more than one messaging system. Sometimes, as in North American Air's case, one company has taken over another that used a different messaging system and has not switched over the acquired locations to the corporate standard. In other companies, a corporate standard might not exist at all, or might not be enforced.

Different messaging systems can coexist for a period of time until the organization is ready to migrate to a single system, but is not an ideal situation. Supporting multiple messaging systems increases network administration complexity because administrators must learn and support two different messaging systems, and because there are often interoperability issues between the systems. Exchange 2000 provides tools for both coexistence and migration from non-Exchange messaging systems to Exchange 2000.

NOTE: In the following section, I discuss migration from two popular non-Exchange messaging systems: Microsoft Mail for PC Networks (MS Mail) and a Domino Server/Lotus Notes. These are not the only platforms that Exchange 2000 supports, but the processes of migrating from other systems (such as Novell Groupwise or Lotus cc:Mail) are similar to the processes covered in this chapter.

Migrating from MS Mail

To coexist with MS Mail, Exchange 4.0/5.*x* includes the Microsoft Mail Connector, which provides messaging connectivity between the two messaging systems. In addition, Exchange 4.0/5.*x* also can exchange directory information with an MS Mail system so that the recipients from each messaging system appear in the GAL for each system's clients. MS Mail uses a directory synchronization process in which every server operates as either a directory synchronization server (only one per MS Mail organization) or a directory synchronization requestor. During the MS Mail directory synchronization cycle, the requestors all update the directory synchronization server with their directory changes and also accept updates from the server. Exchange 4.0/5.*x* can function as either a directory synchronization server or requestor. Exchange 4.0/5.*x* servers and MS Mail servers also can exchange free and busy information for user calendars and scheduling.

The Microsoft Mail Connector runs as a service on Exchange 4.0/5.*x* servers. When you upgrade an Exchange 4.0/5.*x* server that is running the Microsoft Mail Connector, the connector is upgraded to the Exchange 2000 version of the same connector. Messaging connectivity is maintained between the servers. Almost all the configuration options for the directory synchronization also are upgraded. Like Exchange 4.0/5.*x*, Exchange 2000 servers also can operate as either directory synchronization servers or requestors. The Free/Busy Connector also is upgraded.

One option that is *not* migrated when you upgrade the server is the destination container for the objects that the container creates. In Exchange 4.0/5.*x*, you can configure the objects to be created in the Recipients container or in a different container in Exchange. When you upgrade the connector to Exchange 2000, you can specify the Active Directory OU in which the objects the connector creates will reside. You also must configure the address space, message size restrictions, and the schedule specifying when the connector is active. The Exchange 4.0/5.*x* connector also uses trust levels to specify which directory objects are synchronized with the other organization. Trust-level configuration is not available in Exchange 2000, and these settings are not migrated. To control what recipient information is replicated to the MS Mail servers, you can either select the source domain or an OU in Active Directory.

The Microsoft Mail Connector enables the two messaging organizations to coexist, but many companies prefer to use the Exchange Server Migration wizard in Exchange 4.0/5.*x* to migrate the mailboxes from the MS Mail to Exchange 4.0/5.*x*. Exchange 2000 provides essentially the same Exchange Server Migration wizard for direct migration from Microsoft Mail to Exchange 2000. For an organization such as North American Air, the Exchange Server Migration wizard provides an easy-to-use tool for migrating both the directory information and the mailboxes from MS Mail to Exchange 2000.

Migrating users and mailboxes from MS Mail to Exchange 2000 using the Exchange Server Migration wizard is quite straightforward. To begin, you install an Exchange 2000 server in the location where the MS Mail server(s) are located. You then use the wizard to create Active Directory accounts for all the users from the MS Mail post offices and then migrate the contents of the mailboxes to Exchange 2000. Like other procedures, however, this one requires careful planning and testing. North American Air's project team must test this migration process thoroughly in the lab and put the backup and restore procedures in place, before starting the migration.

To migrate users from MS Mail to Exchange 2000 using the Exchange Server Migration wizard, perform the following steps:

1. Start the Exchange Server Migration wizard from the Microsoft Exchange folder on the Start menu.

   The wizard prompts you to choose the type of messaging system you are migrating to Exchange. See Figure 10-2.

2. Select Migrate from MS Mail for PC Networks and click Next.

A message dialog box informs you that you are migrating from MS Mail for PC Networks and that you can configure connectivity between the systems using a connector or gateway.

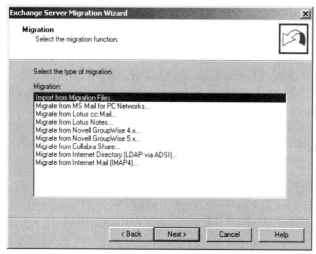

Figure 10-2: Choose the Message System Being Migrated.

3. Choose either a one-step migration or a two-step migration. See Figure 10-3.

   If you choose one-step migration, the wizard connects to the MS Mail server, extracts the user information from the MS Mail directory, and creates user objects in Active Directory for each mailbox. Then the wizard moves the contents of each mailbox from the MS Mail server into the mailbox created for each recipient.

   If you choose two-step migration, the wizard extracts the directory information from the MS Mail server and then creates a comma separated values (.csv) file listing all the directory entries. You can edit the .csv file using a text editor or a spreadsheet application. When you run the wizard again, you can create the Active Directory objects based on the .csv file and then migrate the contents of the mailboxes. You might use the two-step migration if you needed to change some of the directory information for each user. For example, you might be using a different naming scheme in Exchange than was used on the MS Mail server; you could modify the names in the .csv file before importing the objects into Exchange.

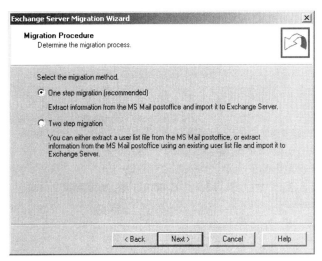

Figure 10-3: Configuring a One-Step or Two-Step Migration.

The format of the .csv file is similar to the files used for directory import and export in Exchange 4.0/5.*x*. As the following listing shows, the .csv file consists of a header that defines the attributes for each object to be migrated and then a line that details the migration information for each user.

```
Version,SFS-POID,SFS-POSN

1,"SANDIEGOPO",1111113

SFS_UserName,SFS_FullName,MigrateUser,Obj-
    Class,Mode,Common-Name,Display-Name,Given-
    Name,Surname,Home-Server,Comment,Secondary-Proxy-
    Addresses,Mail-Nickname,Obj-User

"TomP","Tom Perry",Y,Mailbox,Create,"Tom Perry","Tom
    Perry","Tom","Perry",~SERVER,"",MS:SANDIEGONET/
    SANDIEGOPO/TomP,"TomP","TomP"
```

If you do a two-step migration, the next step is to choose which step you are performing. (See Figure 10-4). If you are performing the first step, select the Extract a user list file option. The wizard extracts the directory information and exports it to a .csv file. If you are performing the second step, the server uses the edited .csv file and completes the migration.

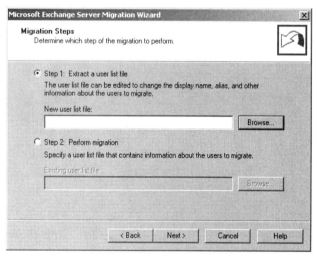

Figure 10-4: Choosing the Two-Step Migration.

4. Chose the destination Exchange server. (See Figure 10-5).

    You can migrate the information either to an Exchange 2000 server or to a .pst file. If you choose a .pst file, the wizard creates a separate .pst for each of the mailboxes on the MS Mail server. You can then manually import the mailboxes using a messaging client such as Outlook.

    You also can migrate the mailboxes to a .pst file as a backup measure for the actual migration. You can run the Exchange Server Migration wizard once and migrate all the mailboxes to a .pst. Migrating the information copies the information to the .pst file, but maintains the mailboxes on the MS Mail server. Then you can run the Exchange Server Migration wizard again, this time performing a one-step migration. If the migration fails, you can use the .pst files to import each user's information into their Exchange mailbox.

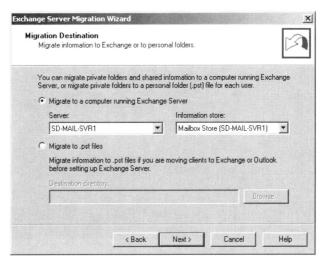

Figure 10-5: Configuring the Destination for the Migrated Mailbox Contents.

5. Enter the information required to connect to the MS Mail server.

    To connect to the server you need the server name and share name for the MS Mail post office. You also must enter the name of an account that has administrative access to the mailboxes on the server.

6. Choose what types of information to migrate to Exchange 2000. (See Figure 10-6.)

    You must choose to import the user information into Active Directory. You also can choose to import the e-mail messages (either all messages or from a selected time period), shared folders, personal address books, and schedule information from Schedule+.

7. Choose which user accounts and mailboxes to migrate to Exchange 2000.

The wizard presents a list of all the users with mailboxes on the selected MS Mail server. You can select individual mailboxes or all the mailboxes to import.

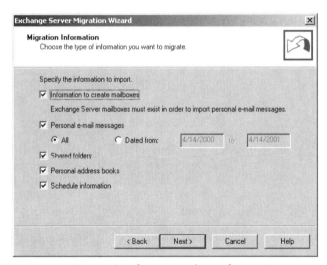

Figure 10-6: Configuring the Information to Migrate to Exchange 2000.

8. Choose the destination container for the MS Mail users.

You can choose any Active Directory container. When the Exchange Server Migration wizard creates the Active Directory information at the beginning of the migration, it tries to match the user accounts from the mailboxes to existing accounts in Active Directory. If it can match the mailbox name to an account, it displays that information, as shown in Figure 10-7. If the wizard cannot match the mailbox account to an Active Directory account, it creates a new account. You also can select Find Existing Account to browse for the account that you want to match to the mailbox name.

This option of linking the mailbox to an existing account is important for an organization like North American Air. Before administrators install the Exchange 2000 server into the San Diego location (where the MS Mail server is located), they will upgrade the domain to Windows 2000 Active Directory. This means that all the mailboxes on the MS Mail server should already be linked to an Active Directory account. When the wizard runs, it maps the existing Active Directory accounts to the migrated mailboxes.

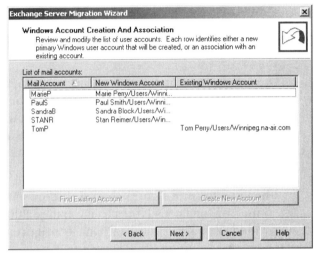

Figure 10-7: Choosing the Accounts and Name Mapping in the Exchange Server Migration Wizard.

9. Configure the level of permissions the default user has to any shared folders that are migrated to Exchange 2000 as public folders.

10. Enter the user name that you want to assign as the owner of the migrated public folders.

The wizard runs and creates the accounts, and then migrates the mailboxes.

The actual procedure for migrating from MS Mail to Exchange 2000 is fairly straightforward. In most cases, the mailboxes are migrated to Exchange 2000 and connected to the Active Directory users. As always, however, you need to test your actual migration in your test lab and prepare for any possible problems during the migration by ensuring that you have complete backups of your Exchange and MS Mail servers before the migration.

Migrating from Lotus Notes

Exchange 4.0/5.*x* and Exchange 2000 provide connectors for Lotus Notes organizations, both for messaging and for the replication of directory information. The connectors also can connect schedule information between the organizations to so that meetings can be booked between users in the two organizations.

The Connector for Lotus Notes is useful in an environment in which you must continue using Lotus Notes for some time after implementing Exchange 2000. North American Air needs this connector because they plan to upgrade the Exchange servers at the Corporate location to Exchange 2000 before they upgrade the Domino/Lotus Notes server.

When you upgrade an Exchange 4.0/5.*x* server that is running the Connector for Lotus Notes to Exchange 2000, the connector also is upgraded. You also can install and configure the Lotus Notes connector on an Exchange 2000 server.

You also can use the Exchange Server Migration wizard to migrate the directory information and mailboxes from the Domino Server/Lotus Notes organization into the Exchange organization. The process for migrating the information is similar to the process described earlier for migrating from MS Mail, with the following differences:

▲ You must install the Lotus Notes client software on the computer that is running the Exchange Server Migration wizard. The Lotus Notes client must be version 4.5.2 or later.

▲ You must configure the Exchange Server Migration wizard with a Lotus Notes account for the migration. The user ID file and the notes.ini file that the Lotus Notes Client installs must be available on the computer running the wizard.

▲ If you are doing a two-step migration, you must choose the two-step migration option when you run the wizard the first time. The wizard creates the .csv file. After editing the file, choose the Import from Migration Files option when you run the wizard again.

▲ The list of object types that migrate from Lotus Notes are slightly different than for MS Mail. (See Figure 10-8.) You must still choose to migrate the information to create the mailboxes, and you still can migrate the personal e-mail messages and schedule information. However, you also can configure how the Exchange Server Migration wizard converts Notes DocLinks. DocLinks are document links inside one Notes document pointing to a different document. One option is to convert the DocLinks to a URLs, which means that the linked document remains on the Lotus Notes server. The Lotus Notes server must then be running a Web server component for you to access the document. When the link is selected in the document, the linked document is displayed in the user's browser. If you convert the DocLinks to OLE, the linked document migrates to the Exchange mailbox and displays as an attachment on the mail message. The attachment retains its file extension, so that when the user opens the file, the correct application opens. The third option is to convert all the DocLinks to RTF format, which converts all linked documents to rich text format documents and stores them as attachments to the mail messages. When an attached document is opened, it opens as an RTF document.

After choosing which objects to migrate, you can choose which mailboxes to migrate, which container to migrate the user information to, and how to migrate the user accounts to Active Directory. When you have finished making your selections in the wizard, it creates the Active Directory accounts and migrates the selected information.

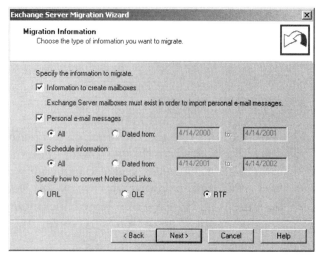

Figure 10-8: Configuring the Migration Options for the Domino
Server/Lotus Notes Migration.

Completing the Migration at North American Air

The first site at North American Air to be migrated to Exchange
2000 was the Winnipeg site. Now that it is complete, the project team
is ready to begin implementing the rest of the migration process.

Migrating the Atlanta and Chicago Locations

The next locations to be upgraded at North American Air are the
Atlanta and Chicago sites. Atlanta runs a single Exchange 5.5 server
that hosts 800 mailboxes, as well as an Internet Mail Service connector and a site connector to the Dallas corporate site. When the corporate applications are deployed, this server also will host the public
folders for the applications, which could mean a significantly
increased load on the server. The only decision to make in this case is
whether to perform an in-place upgrade of the existing server or to
install a new Exchange 2000 server into the site and move the mailboxes and connectors to the new server. Because of the extra load
placed on the server with the additional public folders, the project

team has decided to install a new, more powerful server and move all the mailboxes, public folders, and connectors to the new server.

The Windows 2000 domain migration plan called for the Chicago and Atlanta domains to merge into a single domain. The project team contemplated merging the two Exchange 5.5 sites into a single site before the upgrade to Exchange 2000, and as part of that consideration, they used the Move Server wizard to move all the servers from the Chicago site into the Atlanta site in a test environment. However, the project team ultimately decided to maintain two separate sites and upgrade each of them to Exchange 2000. This means there will be two administrative groups, with a separate routing group in each location. The project team decided to use this approach for two primary reasons. First, the bandwidth between Chicago and Atlanta is limited, such that it would have been difficult to combine the two Exchange 5.5 sites. Second, the Exchange 2000 configuration is fairly easy to change after the migration.

The project team plans to maintain a separate routing group for each location, but if the need to change the administrative configuration ever arises (for example, if most of the users are moved to Atlanta and the need for full-time Exchange administrators in Chicago decreases) the project team has two options. One option is to install a new Exchange 2000 server in Chicago but make it a part of the Atlanta administrative group, and then move all the users to the new server. After the organization has been switched to native mode, administrators can move mailboxes between servers in different administrative groups. The second option is to wait until Microsoft or a third party develops an application that can move servers between administrative groups. Microsoft did provide this functionality in early beta releases of Exchange 2000, so they are likely to make it available again.

The Chicago location has two Exchange servers. One is used primarily as a mailbox server, while the other has some mailboxes and the connectors on it. The project team decided to consolidate both servers onto a single new server. Even though the load on the server could potentially increase with the increased use of public folders, a single powerful server should be able to handle such a load.

Migrating the Texas Locations

Once the team has migrated the Winnipeg, Chicago, and Atlanta locations, it is ready to migrate the Texas locations. Before migration, the Texas Exchange configuration is as listed in Table 10-1.

Table 10-1: Exchange Server Configurations for the Texas Locations of North American Air

Site	Exchange Server	Information Store	Bridgehead Server and Connectors
Dallas_Corp_Site	Dal-C-Mail-Svr1	2,000 mailboxes 10 public folders	Not Applicable
Dallas_Corp_Site	Dal-C-Mail-Svr2	2,000 mailboxes	Not Applicable
Dallas_Corp_Site	Dal-C-Mail-Svr3	2,000 mailboxes	Not Applicable
Dallas_Corp_Site	Dal-C-Mail-Svr4	2,000 mailboxes	Not Applicable
Dallas_Corp_Site	Dal-C-Mail-Svr5	0 mailboxes	Connector to all other Exchange 5.5 Sites Microsoft Mail Connector (for San Diego) Internet Mail Service for Internet mail
Dallas_Corp_Site	Dal-C-Mail-Svr6	0 mailboxes	Connector to all other Exchange 5.5 Sites Connector for Lotus Notes (for Portland) Internet Mail Service for Internet mail
Dallas_Manu_Site	Dal-M-Mail-Svr1	2,000 mailboxes 10 public folders	Not Applicable
Dallas_Manu_Site	Dal-M-Mail-Svr2	2,000 mailboxes	Not Applicable
Dallas_Manu_Site	Dal-M-Mail-Svr3	2,000 mailboxes	Not Applicable

Table 10-1: Exchange Server Configurations for the Texas Locations of
North American Air (Continued)

Site	Exchange Server	Information Store	Bridgehead Server and Connectors
Dallas_Manu_Site	Dal-M-Mail-Svr4	2,000 mailboxes	Not Applicable
Dallas_Manu_Site	Dal-M-Mail-Svr5	1,000 mailboxes	Connector to Dallas_Corp_Site
Dallas_Manu_Site	Dal-M-Mail-Svr6	1,000 mailboxes	Connector to Dallas_Corp_Site
Houston_Manu_Site	Hou-Mail-Svr1	2,000 mailboxes 10 public folders	Not Applicable
Houston_Manu_Site	Hou-Mail-Svr2	2,000 mailboxes	Not Applicable
Houston_Manu_Site	Hou-Mail-Svr3	1,500 mailboxes	Connector to Dallas_Corp_Site
Houston_Manu_Site	Hou-Mail-Svr4	1,500 mailboxes	Connector to Dallas_Corp_Site

The project team plans to combine all three locations into a
single routing group, thus eliminating the need for several connector
servers. However, the additional public folder servers, real-time collaboration servers, and OWA servers require additional servers. Table
10-2 outlines how the server configuration will be after the migration.

Table 10-2: The Exchange Servers in the Texas
Locations after the Migration

Server Name	Administrative Group	Routing Group	Functionality
Dal-C-Mail-Svr1	Dallas_Corp_AG	Texas_RG	Mailbox server (3,000 mailboxes)
Dal-C-Mail-Svr2	Dallas_Corp_AG	Texas_RG	Mailbox server (2,500 mailboxes)
Dal-C-Mail-Svr3	Dallas_Corp_AG	Texas_RG	Mailbox server (2,500 mailboxes)
Dal-C-PF-Svr1	Dallas_Corp_AG	Texas_RG	Public folder server

Table 10-2: The Exchange Servers in the Texas
Locations after the Migration (Continued)

Server Name	Administrative Group	Routing Group	Functionality
Dal-C-Con-Svr1	Dallas_Corp_AG	Texas_RG	Connector server
Dal-C-Con-Svr2	Dallas_Corp_AG	Texas_RG	Connector server
Dal-C-OWA-Svr1	Dallas_Corp_AG	Texas_RG	OWA front-end server
Dal-C-Col-Svr1	Dallas_Corp_AG	Texas_RG	Instant Messaging Test server Conferencing Test server
Dal-M-Mail-Svr1	Dallas_Manu_AG	Texas_RG	Mailbox server (2,500 mailboxes)
Dal-M-Mail-Svr2	Dallas_Manu_AG	Texas_RG	Mailbox server (2,500 mailboxes)
Dal-M-Mail-Svr3	Dallas_Manu_AG	Texas_RG	Mailbox server (2,500 mailboxes)
Dal-M-Mail-Svr4	Dallas_Manu_AG	Texas_RG	Mailbox server (2,500 mailboxes)
Dal-M-PF-Svr1	Dallas_Manu_AG	Texas_RG	Public Folder server
Hou-Mail-Svr1	Houston_Manu_AG	Texas_RG	Mailbox server (3,000 mailboxes)
Hou-Mail-Svr2	Houston_Manu_AG	Texas_RG	Mailbox server (3,000 mailboxes)
Hou-Mail-Svr3	Houston_Manu_AG	Texas_RG	Mailbox server (1,000 mailboxes) and Public Folder server

NOTE: *When you install an Exchange 2000 server in an Exchange 4.0/5.x site, or upgrade an Exchange 4.0/5.x server to Exchange 2000, the administrative group and the routing group both receive the same name as the site. You can rename the administrative and routing groups in Exchange System Manager.*

The project team also decided to implement additional administrative groups for specific roles throughout the organization, as specified in Table 10-3. These additional administrative groups help centralize administration of the specific service in one location with a single group of administrators. This means that one group of administrators can manage all the routing group connectors in the organization, while another group can be responsible for the public-folder administration.

Table 10-3: Administrative Group Configuration at the Texas Location in North American Air

Administrative Group	Containers	Manages
Dallas-Corp-AG	Servers	All Exchange servers in corporate location.
Dallas-AG-Manu-AG	Servers	All Exchange servers in the Dallas manufacturing location.
Houston-Manu-AG	Servers	All Exchange servers in the Houston manufacturing location.
Texas-Routing-AG	Routing Groups	Routing groups and routing group connectors for the entire organization.
Texas-PubFolder-AG	Folders	All public folders in the entire organization.

The biggest changes that the migration brings in the Texas locations is to the message-routing configuration. Administrators upgrade and maintain each site as a distinct administrative group for now, but they group all the Texas servers into one routing group. This approach enables messages to be delivered between servers in the routing groups more quickly and with fewer connector servers required.

The project team decided to upgrade the connector servers in the Dallas_Corp_Site first, because these servers operate as the connector servers to the Winnipeg, Atlanta, and Chicago locations. As a result, they can use SMTP and the link state table in Exchange 2000. Therefore, the first servers to be upgraded are Dal-C-Mailsvr5 and Dal-C-Mailsvr6.

Because the servers in the Dallas_Manu_Site and the Houston_Manu_Site cannot be moved into a single routing group until they switch the organization to native mode, administrators next upgrade the connector servers in these locations. After upgrading the connector servers, the team will upgrade the mailbox servers to Exchange 2000. In most cases, they will deploy new servers and move the mailboxes to the new servers, in some cases consolidating the number of servers by increasing the maximum number of mailboxes per server from 2,000 to 3,000. Some of the connector servers or mailbox servers removed from the network can be redeployed as public folders servers or as collaboration or OWA servers.

Migrating the Vancouver Location

With only 300 mailboxes in the Vancouver site, a single server can easily host all the mailboxes as well as host the public folders and connectors. The only factor that makes the Vancouver migration different is that the connector to the Dallas location is an X.400 connector. When administrators upgrade the connector server in the Dallas site to Exchange 2000, the Exchange 4.0/5.x X.400 connector automatically upgrades to the Exchange 2000 version. When administrators upgrade the server in Vancouver, an SMTP connector replaces the X.400 connector.

Migrating the San Diego MS Mail Server

San Diego uses two MS Mail servers that host a total of 500 mailboxes. The connection to the North American Air Exchange organization is through an MS Mail connector hosted on one of the connector servers in the Dallas corporate sites. To upgrade the location to Exchange 2000, administrators install a single Exchange 2000 server at the location and migrate all the mailboxes to the Exchange 2000 server using the procedure outlined previously. They configure the Exchange 2000 server with a routing group connector to the Dallas routing group. An SMTP connector on the Exchange server in San Diego provides Internet e-mail access.

Migrating the Portland Domino/Lotus Notes Server

The Portland location runs a single Domino/Lotus Notes server. This server is connected to the North American Air Exchange organization through a Connector for Lotus Notes running on one of the connector servers at the corporate headquarters. Administrators migrate the Domino/Lotus Notes server at Portland to Exchange 2000 using the Exchange Server Migration wizard. They install an Exchange 2000 server in the Portland location and configure it with a routing group connector to the Dallas Corporate routing group as well as an SMTP connector for Internet Mail. Then they use the Exchange Server Migration wizard to migrate the mailbox information from the Domino servers to Exchange 2000.

Switching to Native Mode

When you install an Exchange 2000 server into an existing Exchange 4.0/5.x organization, or install an Exchange 2000 server to create a new organization, the Exchange organization always starts out running in mixed mode. In mixed mode, the organization can support both Exchange 2000 and Exchange 4.0/5.x servers. When the migration is complete, and all the Exchange 4.0/5.x servers have been upgraded to Exchange 2000 or removed, you can switch the organization to native mode.

Running the organization in mixed mode imposes some restrictions on the organization:

▲ You must map all Exchange 4.0/5.x sites directly to Exchange 2000 administrative groups.

▲ All the servers in the same administrative group must belong to a routing group in the administrative group.

▲ You cannot move servers into a routing group outside the administrative group.

▲ You cannot move mailboxes between servers in different administrative groups.

For these reasons, an organization like North American Air should switch to native mode soon after the last Exchange 4.0/5.x server has been removed from the network. North American Air can benefit in particular from having the option to change the administrative structure and routing group configuration. After the organization switches to native mode, administrators can create a new administrative group in the Dallas corporate location and move all the routing groups for the entire organization into this administrative group. They can then give one group of administrators the rights to administer routing throughout the organization. In addition, once they have switched the organization to native mode, they can combine all the servers in the three Texas locations into one routing group.

 NOTE: *Switching an organization to native mode is a one-way process; once you have switched to native mode, you can never switch back. For this reason, you should make sure that there are no plans to include Exchange 4.0/5.x servers in your organization before you make the switch.*

To switch to native mode, open Exchange System Manager, right-click the organization name, choose Properties, and then click Change Mode.

Conclusion

This chapter discussed the completion of the Exchange 2000 migration process at North American Air. The primary issues that North American Air had to deal with were the migration of the site connectors to Exchange 2000 and the migration of the non-Exchange messaging systems.

North American Air is now running an Exchange 2000 organization. The next chapters describe the management of the Exchange 2000 organization and the implementation of some of the new Exchange 2000 features that North American Air needs to utilize to achieve their migration goals. The next chapter looks at the basics of managing the Exchange 2000 organization through the Exchange System Manager.

Part 5

Managing and Maintaining the Exchange 2000 Server Organization

Chapter 11

Managing the Exchange 2000 Organization

AFTER MONTHS OF WORK, the migration to Exchange 2000 is finally finished at North American Air. All Exchange servers are running Exchange 2000, and the Exchange organization has been switched to native mode. That means the Exchange administrators now manage an Exchange 2000 organization.

The remaining chapters in this book focus on Exchange 2000 organization management. This chapter covers messaging-connectivity management between servers and routing groups in Exchange 2000, with particular emphasis on virtual server and routing-group connector configuration. Chapter 12 looks in detail at some of the enhancements to Exchange 2000, such as OWA, Instant Messaging, and Conferencing server, and describes how an organization like North American Air might implement these technologies to enhance communication flow. The final chapter looks at monitoring and disaster-recovery procedures for Exchange 2000.

The configuration of message routing is significantly different in Exchange 2000 compared to Exchange 4.0/5.*x*. With Exchange 2000, you can configure several global settings, including default messaging options for Internet mail. In addition, Exchange 2000 uses SMTP virtual servers to configure how messages are sent and received. To configure messaging between different company locations, Exchange 2000 uses routing group connectors. I discuss each of these topics in this chapter.

Configuring Global Settings

The global settings in Exchange 2000 include the defaults for how messages are delivered to and from the Internet. You can set defaults for all users in the organization that define values, such as message size and automatic replies to the Internet. In most cases, you can override these default values by configuring a different value on a specific object, such as a connector, virtual server, or mailbox. The Internet message formats specify messaging formats as well as whether automatic replies are enabled for Internet connections. The message delivery options specify default message sizes and configure filters to block the acceptance of messages from specified e-mail addresses on the Internet.

Configuring the Internet Message Formats and Automatic Responses

You can use the Internet message format settings to configure global options that define how Internet messages are handled. When you install Exchange 2000, a default policy is configured that applies to all messages sent to any SMTP address outside of the organization. By adding additional domain-specific policies, you can modify how messages are sent to specific domains. For example, one of the configuration options in the Internet message formats is whether out-of-office messages are forwarded to the Internet. The default is No, because in most organizations people do not want to inform others outside the office when they are not in. However, if your company is working closely with a partner organization, you might want to allow the out-of-office messages to be forwarded to the partner organization. To do this, you would leave the default format as-is and configure a new format for the partner organization's domain.

To modify the global settings or add a new domain format, open the Exchange System Manager and expand the Global Settings container and the Internet Message Formats container.

To configure a new message format based on a particular domain, right-click Internet Message Formats, point to New, and click Domain. Type a name for this message format configuration and the domain name to which this configuration will apply. See Figure 11-1.

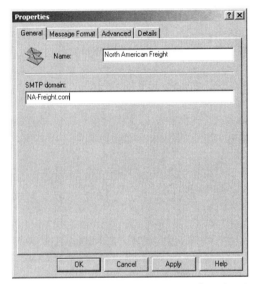

Figure 11-1: Entering the Name for the New Message Format Configuration.

To configure the message format for this policy, select the Message Format tab, shown in Figure 11-2. Select the format with which to encode messages sent to the domain. The default setting of MIME encoding is almost always appropriate, as most mail systems support MIME. To configure how Exchange handles automatic responses for messages from the specified domain, choose the Advanced tab, shown in Figure 11-3. The default message settings block all automatic replies, forwarding, and out-of-office replies from going to the Internet, and allow delivery and nondelivery reports. You can enable or disable any of the options. The Preserve sender's display name on message option forwards the display name for a user to Internet recipients; if you clear this check box, only the sender's e-mail address is forwarded to the Internet.

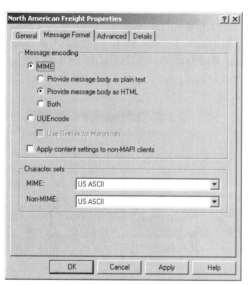

Figure 11-2: Selecting a Message Format.

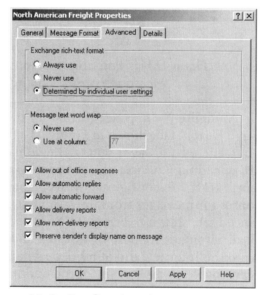

Figure 11-3: Configuring Automatic Responses.

Configuring Message Delivery Options

You also can configure the message delivery options for the entire organization. To configure this set of options, start from the Global Settings container and open the Message Delivery properties (by right-clicking Message Delivery and choosing Properties).

The Defaults tab of the Message Delivery Properties box enables you to set a limit for the maximum size message that recipients in your organization can send or receive. (See Figure 11-4.)

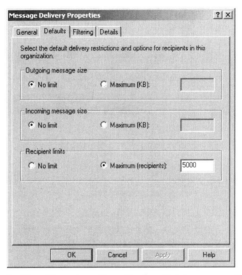

Figure 11-4: Configuring the Default Message Size for the Organization.

By default there is no limit on the size of messages sent and received, and a 5,000 limit to the maximum number of recipients per message. You might limit the message size if you had several slow network links in your organization, or if the Exchange servers were being overloaded with large messages. Remember, these settings apply to all messages sent within the organization, including messages between users within your organization and messages to and from the Internet.

NOTE: *If you want to allow messages of any size within the organization but limit the size of messages sent to the Internet, you can override the global setting on either the SMTP virtual server or the SMTP connector used to send and receive mail from the Internet. You also can configure maximum messages sizes on each individual mailbox.*

The Filtering tab enables you to configure the domains from which you do not want to accept e-mail. This option is useful to prevent unwanted e-mails (or spam) from entering your organization. (See Figure 11-5.)

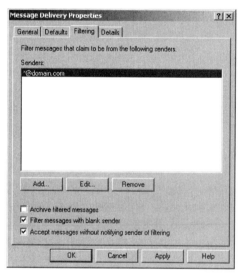

Figure 11-5: Configuring Message Filtering for the Organization.

To configure a filter, click Add and type the address of the domain or user that you want to exclude. You can use wildcards to filter all messages coming from an entire domain (*@*domain*.com, for example). In most cases, you also should select the Accept messages without notifying the sender of filtering option. When you select this option, the message is filtered but a nondelivery report (NDR) is not sent to the sender of the message. If you are filtering out a large amount of unwanted e-mail every day, this option decreases the load on your server because it eliminates the need for an NDR for each filtered message. You must apply the filter to a SMTP virtual server for it to take effect. (The procedure for applying filters to virtual servers is covered in the next section.)

Administering Exchange 2000 Virtual Servers

In Exchange 2000, all Internet protocol support has been moved into IIS. This means that rather than directly configuring a protocol object, you configure an IIS virtual server for each of the protocols. Exchange 2000 delivers almost all messages through the SMTP virtual server, including messages within routing groups or between routing groups.

Because the SMTP virtual server handles almost all messages, I describe the SMTP virtual server configuration in the following section. The virtual servers for other protocols have similar configuration options, plus their own protocol-specific options.

NOTE: *I cover the HTTP virtual server configuration in more detail in the next chapter, when I discuss OWA implementation.*

To configure the SMTP virtual server, locate the administrative group that contains the server with which you are working and expand the Servers container. Locate the server, expand the server container, and expand the Protocols container. Expand the SMTP container, right-click the SMTP virtual server, and select Properties. Figure 11-6 shows the Default SMTP Virtual Server Properties box.

Setting General Options

On the General tab, you can configure the IP address that this virtual server uses. If you have more than one IP address for the server, you can configure multiple virtual servers, with each virtual server using one of the IP addresses.

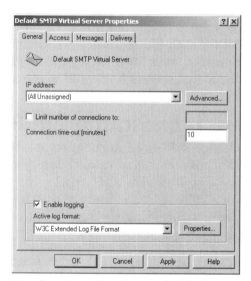

Figure 11-6: Configuring the General Tab for an SMTP Virtual Server.

If you have only one IP address, you can still configure multiple servers, but you must create a unique identity for each virtual server. To do this, click Advanced, and then add a new identity. (See Figure 11-7.) The new identity must use a different port number if you have only a single IP address. You also can enable filtering for each virtual server from this screen. When you enable filtering, you apply the filter list configured at the organizational level to this virtual server.

You also can limit the number of connections to this virtual server on the General tab and set a connection timeout. The connection timeout defines how long the server waits before disconnecting an idle client. You also can configure logging for the virtual server here. To log all connections to this virtual server, select Enable logging and then choose the logging format to use.

Setting Access Options

To configure the options for accessing the virtual server, select the Access tab, shown in Figure 11-8.

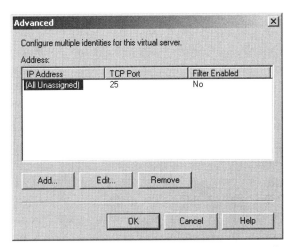

Figure 11-7: Configuring the Advanced Properties for a Virtual Server.

The settings available from the Access tab include:

▲ **Authentication.** The Authentication option specifies whether this virtual server accepts anonymous connections or whether all users must authenticate to connect to the server. You also can choose between basic authentication and integrated Windows authentication. If this virtual server is your SMTP server for receiving Internet mail, you must accept anonymous connections so that the SMTP servers from other organizations can connect to your server. However, if the virtual server were only for internal clients using an Internet protocol client, you might configure the virtual server to require authentication.

▲ **Certificates.** Clicking the Certificate button starts the Web Server Certificate wizard. This wizard creates a certificate request that can be forwarded to a commercial certificate authority such as VeriSign. If you are configuring this virtual server only for internal clients, you also can install a certificate server in Windows 2000 and use it to grant a certificate for the virtual server.

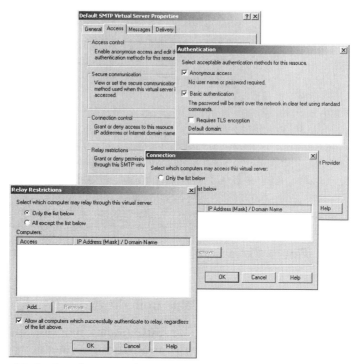

Figure 11-8: Configuring the Access Tab for a SMTP Virtual Server.

NOTE: *Transport Layer Security (TLS) enables you to encrypt all communication between the server and clients, including the logon process, even when using basic authentication. If you want users to use TLS to connect this virtual server, however, you must install an X.509 certificate on the server. Use the Web Server Certificate wizard to do so.*

▲ **Connection**. Use Connection to configure which computers can access this virtual server. You can specify that all computers can connect and then configure a list of exceptions, or you can specify that only the computers you identify can connect. You can define the list of exceptions based on a single IP address, an IP subnet, or a domain name. If this server is receiving SMTP mail from all SMTP servers on the Internet, you cannot set any restrictions.

▲ **Relay Restrictions.** Use Relay Restrictions to define which servers can relay e-mail messages through this server. If this virtual server is your Internet SMTP server, you should choose to allow only the listed computers to relay and then leave the list empty. If you then select the Allow all computers which successfully authenticate to relay...option, clients using SMTP will be able to relay mail through the server if the client is configured to authenticate to the SMTP server.

Setting Message Options

You can set the following options on the Messages tab, shown in Figure 11-9.

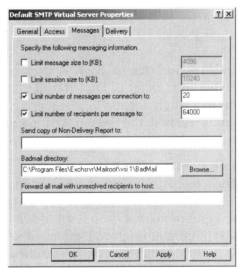

Figure 11-9: Configuring the Messages Tab for an SMTP Virtual Server.

▲ **Limit message size to (KB).** This setting defines the maximum message size that this connector accepts from other servers. If you have limited bandwidth for your Internet mail, or if your corporate policy sets limits on the size of incoming mail messages, you might want to set a limit here.

When an Internet e-mail server with a message that is larger than the limit connects to this server, one of two things can happen. If the sending server supports Extended SMTP (ESMTP), the receiving server informs the Exchange 2000 server of the size limitation during the initial connection. When the sending server receives the message limit and determines that the message being delivered is too large, an NDR is generated for the sender. If the sending server does not support ESMTP, it begins to send the message. When the message reaches the limit, the receiving server stops accepting the message. Because the message cannot be delivered, the sending computer sends an NDR to the sender.

NOTE: If you want to set message size limits for outgoing messages, you also can configure these settings at a global level or at a mailbox level. Message size limits at these levels apply to both incoming and outgoing messages.

▲ **Limit session size to (KB).** You can use this option to limit the maximum number of kilobytes of e-mail messages that can be sent in a single session between two SMTP servers. When the limit is reached, the session terminates and a new session must be established to deliver the rest of the messages.

▲ **Limit number of messages per connection to.** You can use this option to optimize server performance. If the server is sending a large number of messages to another server, and the number of messages per connection is set low (for example, to 20) the server must open multiple connections to deliver all the messages. Having multiple simultaneous connections between servers can increase message delivery speed.

▲ **Limit number of recipients per message to.** This option defines how many recipients for a single message can be sent on one connection. When the limit is reached, the SMTP server opens a new connection to send the rest of the messages.

Other settings on the Messages tab configure how the server responds to undeliverable messages. If a message cannot be delivered, the server automatically sends an NDR to the message sender.

You also can specify that a copy of the message be sent to an alternate SMTP address, or that a copy be saved in the Badmail folder.

You also can specify that any nondeliverable messages be forwarded to a specific host. You might find this useful if you have two SMTP servers in different organizations that are both configured as mail servers for the same domain name. For example, the Exchange server might be configured to handle all mail for the NA-Air.com domain, but another SMTP server also might be configured as a mail server for the same domain. Suppose that the two servers are configured so that they do not share any directory information with each other, and therefore each is unaware of the mailboxes on the other. When one Exchange server receives a message intended for a user on the other, this option can be used to forward the message to the other server.

Setting Delivery Options

The Delivery tab, shown in Figure 11-10, controls the delivery options for the server. The options on this tab define how the server deals with message retries and messages that cannot be delivered.

There are two main sections on this tab: Outbound and Local. Under Outbound, the first four settings define the time between retries on remote messages — that is, messages being delivered to another server. You can set a different time for First, Second, Third, and Subsequent retries.

The Delay notification setting defines the time at which the server sends a notice to the sender that the message is being delayed during delivery. The default setting is 12 hours. If the message cannot be delivered within the specified amount of time, the user receives a message indicating that the original message has not yet been delivered. The Expiration timeout setting defines the time at which the server stops trying to send the message and sends a NDR to the sender.

The Local settings define at which point the server sends the delay report and the NDR for local messages.

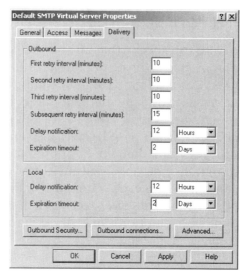

Figure 11-10: Configuring the Delivery Tab for a SMTP Virtual Server.

Outbound Connections

The Outbound Connections button on the Delivery tab opens the Outbound Connections dialog box, shown in Figure 11-11. You can use these controls to configure the number of connections the server can have open at one time, both the total number of connections and the total number of connections per domain.

Outbound Security

The Outbound Security button opens the Outbound Security dialog box, shown in Figure 11-12. It specifies authentication settings for outgoing connections. By default, the virtual server uses anonymous access when connecting to other servers, but you can configure different levels of authentication, as well as the accounts used for authentication. When the Exchange server is connecting to other Exchange servers in the organization, it uses the Local System account for authentication. You should configure the outbound security only if you need authentication to connect to servers in other organizations.

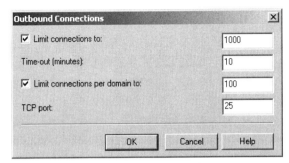

Figure 11-11: Configuring the Outbound Connections for a SMTP
Virtual Server.

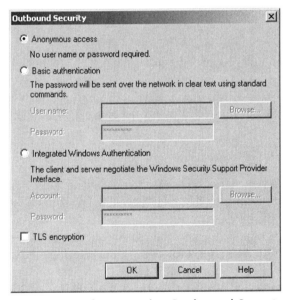

Figure 11-12: Configuring the Outbound Security for a
SMTP Virtual Server.

Advanced

The Advanced button opens the Advanced Delivery dialog box, shown in Figure 11-13. You can use it to configure the maximum hop count for the message, which defines the number of SMTP servers the message can be sent through on the way to the final destination.

407

When a message exceeds the maximum hop count, the message is dropped, and the message sender receives an NDR.

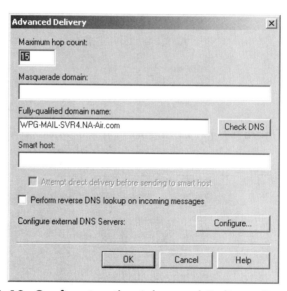

Figure 11-13: Configuring the Advanced Delivery Options for a SMTP Virtual Server.

You can use the Masquerade domain option to specify a different domain name to be used during the SMTP negotiation at the beginning of a message delivery. The Masquerade domain does not affect what the destination client sees as the message sender when the message is opened, because that information is included in the body of the message. However, the Masquerade domain does affect the destination for NDRs. The only reason to use a different masquerade domain would be to send the NDRs to a different domain than the originating domain.

You can use the Fully-qualified domain name option to specify a name for this virtual server. In most cases it should be the same as the host name assigned to the computer, but you can configure a different name.

You also can configure a smart host for this virtual server. A *smart host* is a server that this virtual server uses for forwarding all messages, rather than delivering the messages using DNS.

When Perform reverse DNS lookup on incoming messages is enabled, the server tries to resolve a message sender's IP address to the host name or domain name sent during the initial SMTP negotiation. Because this option requires a DNS lookup for every message received, it can significantly degrade the performance of the server.

If you configure the virtual server to use DNS to determine the destination servers for Internet messages, you can click the Configure button to configure external DNS servers that are specific to this virtual server.

SMTP Extensions in Exchange 2000

Exchange 2000 has implemented several extensions to the SMTP protocol to optimize the use of the protocol for messaging. Two of the most significant are the use of pipelining and chunking.

Pipelining speeds up the initial SMTP negotiation when a message is sent between two servers. When one server connects to another server to send a message, the first server sends an EHLO or HELO message. The receiving server responds with a list of the SMTP extensions it supports. The sending server then sends packets that include the message sender, the intended recipient, and the message body. If the message has multiple recipients, it sends a RCPT TO: command for each recipient. Without pipelining, the sending server sends a single command to the receiving server and then waits for a response. For example, the sending server might send a MAIL FROM: command and then wait for an OK response. When both servers support pipelining, however, the first command after the initial EHLO is the PIPELINING command. The sending server then sends multiple commands to the receiving server without pausing after each command to wait for a response.

The sending server might send an entire list of intended recipients to the receiving server before waiting for the receiving server to acknowledge.

Chunking speeds up the delivery of large messages between servers. Normally, SMTP signals the end of the DATA part of a message with a return character, a period, and another return. The receiving server must scan the entire message to locate this marker. Chunking speeds up the delivery process by informing the destination computer of the size of the message before it transmits the packet. To do so, it includes a BDAT command followed by the size of the message in bytes. The receiving computer can use this size value to determine the end of the message rather than looking for the end of DATA marker. For more information on ESMTP, see RFC 1869.

Managing the Virtual Server Queues

In Exchange 4.0/5.*x*, the Configuration dialog box for each connector, including the MTA on each server, has a Queue tab from which you can view the queued messages. You can use this feature for troubleshooting to determine where messages routed through the organization are being blocked. In Exchange 2000, you still can view these queues, but the queue objects have been relocated to the virtual servers. To access the queue for a virtual server, double-click the virtual server object in the Protocols container for the server. Then expand the Queues object.

The Queues object contains two types of queues: system queues and link queues. Exchange 2000 uses *system queues* for internal routing. For example, as Figure 11-14 shows, the SMTP virtual server includes system queues for messages waiting for directory lookup, messages waiting to be routed, and the local domain queue. System queues are always visible in the queue container regardless of whether there are any messages in the queues.

A *link queue* is created only when a message intended for a particular domain is submitted to the virtual server. For example, Figure 11-14 shows link queues for the test.com domain, the domain.com domain, and the RGC to Dallas routing group connector. The existence of these queues indicates either that a message is waiting in the queue or that a message has just been forwarded through the queue.

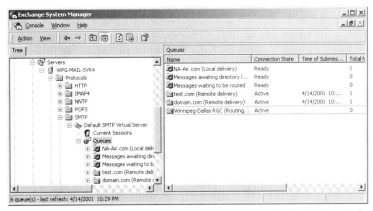

Figure 11-14: System and Link Queues on an SMTP Virtual Server.

A queue can be in one of six states:

▲ **Active.** A connection is open with a remote server.

▲ **Retry.** A connection to a remote server has failed and the server is waiting for the retry interval to elapse.

▲ **Ready.** A connection is not currently open, but the queue is ready to accept a connection.

▲ **Scheduled.** The server is waiting for a scheduled connection.

▲ **Remote.** The connection is open and waiting for a remote dequeue command such as TURN or ETRN.

▲ **Frozen.** The administrator has frozen the queue. The queue accepts new messages, but no messages can leave the queue.

Exchange 2000 provides several tools for managing the queues. To manage the queue, right-click the queue and select the command you want to use. The available commands include the following:

▲ **Enumerate 100 messages.** This command lists the first 100 messages in the queue in the Details pane.

▲ **Force Connection.** If a queue is in a Ready or Retry state, forcing a connection forces an immediate attempt to deliver the message.

▲ **Freeze All Messages.** This command prevents the virtual server from creating any connections to deliver messages, but it continues to accept new messages into the queue. To unfreeze the messages, choose Unfreeze All Messages.

▲ **Delete All Messages (no NDR)** or **Delete All Messages (send NDR).** This command deletes the messages in the queue and can send an NDR to the message sender (if the Send NDR option is selected).

▲ **Custom Filter.** This option sorts the messages in the queue based on selected criteria. For example, you may want to sort by size to find the messages in the queue that are over a specified size, or to sort by sender to see messages being sent from a particular mailbox.

▲ **Properties.** This tab lists the number of messages in the queue, the total size for the messages in the queue, the time of submission for the oldest message in the queue, the time for the next retry, and the reason why the last connection failed.

SMTP Messaging and IP Security

A significant drawback to SMTP is the lack of security for SMTP-based messages. By default, SMTP sends all traffic in clear text across the network, including the message sender and recipient addresses and the message body. This can create security issues, particularly when the messages are crossing a public network, such as the Internet.

The only way to protect SMTP mail is to encrypt the messages using IP Security (IPSec). IPSec encrypts the packets at the IP layer. This means that the applications using IPSec do not need to be IPSec-aware. When you configure an SMTP virtual server, you need not be concerned that the SMTP traffic will be encrypted using IPSec. At the physical network layer, the packets appear as ordinary IP packets, so there are no special requirements at the physical layer for supporting IPSec.

When you configure two servers to use IPSec, you can encrypt all or some of the traffic between them. When one server initiates a connection to another server, it checks to see if an IPSec policy applies to the connection. For example, the IPSec policy might be configured such that all SMTP traffic between two particular servers must be encrypted but SMTP traffic to any other server need not be. If a policy applies, the servers negotiate a security association and agree on encryption settings such as encryption algorithms, and key lengths. The security negotiation can use Kerberos, certificates, or a pre-shared key for authentication. Once the security negotiation is complete, all traffic specified in the policy is encrypted between the two servers.

You can enable IPSec at the individual Windows 2000 server level, or you can use group policies to configure and enforce the IPSec policies through Active Directory. The best way to configure the use of IPSec is to create an OU in Active Directory that includes all the Exchange servers. Then you create a group policy for the OU that specifies the types of traffic to encrypt between the servers. If you want to encrypt only SMTP traffic, then you create a policy to encrypt all IP traffic using port 25. When you apply the group policy, all the Exchange servers use IPSec based on the same policy.

Because IPSec's encryption and decryption use a significant number of CPU cycles, server performance degrades if you use IPSec for all traffic. If you want to encrypt only the SMTP traffic, configure the policy to encrypt only that traffic. If you want all traffic to and from a particular server to be encrypted, be prepared to optimize the processor on that server.

Configuring Exchange 2000 Routing Group Connectors

One of an administrator's primary responsibilities in any large Exchange 2000 organization is to manage the routing group connectors within the organization. As the routing group connectors replace the site connectors from Exchange 4.0/5.*x*, you must manage and configure these connectors.

Configuring the Routing Group Connector

The routing group connector replaces the site connector as the preferred connector between remote locations. Like the site connector, the routing group connector can support multiple bridgehead servers at each end. You can configure a cost for the routing group connector, but it does not support different target costs for each server. Also like the site connector, the routing group connector can be used only to connect two Exchange routing groups and not to connect to any other messaging system. When you configure a routing group connector in one location, you can choose to configure the routing group connector in the remote location as well.

The routing group connector uses SMTP to deliver messages between routing groups. Just like any other SMTP server, a server using the routing group connector must resolve the IP address for the destination server before it can deliver the messages.

The SMTP server can use any of three methods to resolve the IP address. The first method is to query a DNS server for the MX records for the destination domain. For this to work, you must have some way of distinguishing the locations within the organization on the basis of the domain name.

For example, North American Air might decide to configure the domain names for each location based on the Active Directory domain names. Each user in the Atlanta location would then have an e-mail address configured as *alias*@Atlanta.NA-Air.com. Administrators could then configure the DNS servers with MX records for the Atlanta.NA-Air.com domain. If there were multiple Exchange servers in the Atlanta location, they could use the MX records as a way of load balancing. If they give the MX records equal priority numbers, the load would be balanced between the servers using DNS round robin.

To use one server as the bridgehead server for a location and a second server for redundancy, you can configure the primary server with a lower priority number. When a sending SMTP server queries the DNS server for the MX record, it always tries the record with the lower priority first. Exchange 2000 servers do not automatically register MX records with the DNS servers, so you must enter these MX records manually.

The second method of name resolution is to use a DNS query based on the destination server's host name. If you use a version of DNS that supports dynamic updates for the host records, each of the Exchange 2000 servers is registered in DNS, so the names can quickly be resolved. (Windows 2000 DNS servers and BIND 8.1.2 and later support dynamic updates.)

The third method is NetBIOS name resolution. If you are using a WINS server or LMHOSTS files, the Exchange server uses the NetBIOS information to resolve the host names.

To create and configure the routing group connector, from Exchange System Manager, expand the administrative group that contains the routing group where you want to add the connector. Then expand the routing group container and right-click the Connectors container and choose New/Routing Group Connector.

I describe the configuration options in the following sections.

General
Your first stop should be the General tab, shown in Figure 11-15. On the General tab, you can perform the following:

▲ If you are creating the connector, enter/change the name for the connector. Use a descriptive name so that you can easily identify which connector is used between different routing groups.

▲ Select the routing group to which this connector connects.

▲ Assign a cost to this connector. The cost is similar to the cost assigned to different site connectors in Exchange 4.0/5.*x* — it helps determine the best (that is, lowest cost) route through the organization.

▲ Select the servers in the local routing group that operate as the bridgehead servers. In many cases, accepting the default Any local server can send mail over this connector option is advantageous because of the fault tolerance that this option provides. However, if you are dedicating one or more servers as connector

servers, select the These servers can send mail over this connector option and then click Add to select the connector servers.

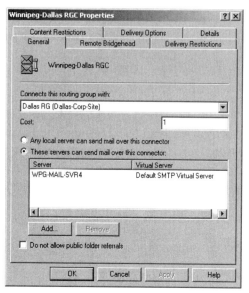

*Figure 11-15: Configuring the Routing Group
Connector General Tab.*

▲ Choose whether to allow public folder referrals. The Do not
allow public folder referrals feature is equivalent to the public
folder affinity feature in Exchange 4.0/5.x. By default, this option
is unselected, which means that clients from this routing group
can connect to any Exchange server in the remote routing group
to locate the contents of a pubic folder. You can use the cost of
the connector to specify which site the client tries first. For example, North American Air might configure a routing group connector from Chicago to Atlanta and from Chicago to Dallas. If
the default option to allow public folder referrals is not modified,
the clients from Chicago could connect to either Dallas or Atlanta
to access a public folder. If the cost of the Atlanta connector is
higher than the cost of the Dallas connector, the client always
tries to connect to the public folder in Dallas first.

NOTE: *The public folder referrals also are transitive. That means that if the connector from Chicago to Dallas is configured to allow public folder referrals, and the connector between Dallas and Winnipeg is configured the same way, then clients from Chicago could access a copy of a public folder in Winnipeg.*

Remote Bridgehead

To configure the remote bridgehead servers, select the Remote Bridgehead tab. (See Figure 11-16.) On this tab you can configure the servers in the remote site that operate as bridgehead servers for the connector.

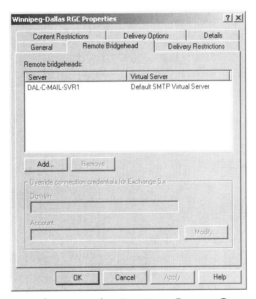

Figure 11-16: Configuring the Routing Group Connector Remote Bridgehead Tab.

To select the servers to use, click Add. When you add a server, you can choose which of the virtual SMTP servers in the remote location are used. Multiple servers provide redundancy. When a server from the local site tries to connect to the remote site, it tries all of the remote bridgehead servers before deciding that the connector is not available and beginning the process of updating the link state tables throughout the organization.

You also can choose to override connection credentials for Exchange 5.*x*. You need this option if you use the connector to connect to an Exchange 5.*x* server in a remote site. If you are using one site service account for the entire organization, you don't need to add any information here, because the server uses the service account configured in the administrative group properties. However, if you have different service accounts for different sites in Exchange 5.*x* and you need to connect to a site that is using a different service account than the one configured for the administrative group, you must configure the override account.

Delivery Restrictions

To specify who is allowed to send mail using this connector, select the Delivery Restrictions tab, shown in Figure 11-17.

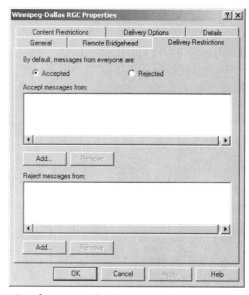

Figure 11-17: Configuring the Routing Group Connector Delivery Restrictions Tab.

The configuration options here are similar to the delivery restrictions in Exchange 4.0/5.*x* except that when you configure the users or groups that are allowed or not allowed to use the connector, you create Active Directory user and group accounts rather than just mailboxes. You can configure a default rule for this connector that specifies that messages from everyone are either Accepted or Rejected and then define exceptions to the rule.

Content Restrictions

The Content Restrictions tab (Figure 11-18) enables you to define a minimum priority for messages to cross this connector.

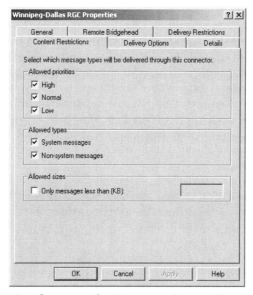

Figure 11-18: Configuring the Routing Group Connector Content Restrictions Tab.

By default, messages of any priority can cross the connector. However, situations might arise in which you want to change that default. For example, if the connector joins two routing groups via a WAN connection with limited bandwidth, you might want only messages with a high priority to be able to cross this connection during the regular working hours to alleviate some of the bandwidth congestion. To do this, configure this connector on the Delivery Options tab to Always run, and then clear the check boxes for the Normal and Low priority messages on the Content Restrictions tab. Then configure an additional connector to accept messages of all priorities, but send the messages only at specified times of the day.

> **NOTE:** *If you configure the connector to accept only high priority messages, you also must configure restrictions on who can use the connector. This prevents large numbers of users from bypassing the restriction by setting the priority of their messages to High.*

You also can configure the connector to accept system or non-system messages. System messages are messages sent by the Exchange server or Windows 2000 server itself rather than by a specific user. Examples of system messages include public folder replication messages, monitoring messages, and delivery or nondelivery reports. Nonsystem messages include messages from users.

You also can configure the maximum size for any message that are sent using this connector. Again, you may want to use this option to control the traffic across a slow WAN link.

Delivery Options

To configure when the link sends messages, use the settings on the Delivery Options tab. These options can help prevent bandwidth problems on the connection between the two routing groups. (See Figure 11-19.)

The Connection time setting specifies when the connector is active. In addition to the default Always run setting, you can choose to run the connector only once per day, or every one or two hours, or never to run. You also can choose Customize to specify precisely at what times of day the connector should deliver messages.

You also can choose a different schedule based on message sizes. If you choose the Use different delivery times for oversize messages option, you can specify a size limit. You also can configure a customized schedule for oversize message delivery.

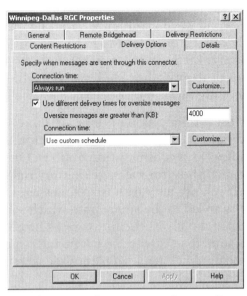

Figure 11-19: Configuring the Routing Group Connector Delivery Options Tab.

Details

The Details tab provides information about the connector's creation and last modification date and time, as well as an option to include an administrative note. An administrative note can be useful as a change-control mechanism when working with the connector. When you make a change to the connector configuration, you can use the note to document the change.

When you finish configuring the routing group connector and click OK, Exchange asks whether you want to configure a routing group connector in the remote routing group. If you choose Yes, Exchange creates the routing group connector in the other routing group with exactly the same configuration as connector that you just configured, including the same name. You can rename the connector using System Manager if desired or modify any of the settings for the new connector.

Configuring the SMTP Connector

The second way to configure a routing group connector is to use the SMTP connector. The SMTP connector is similar to the IMS in Exchange 4.0/5.*x* in that you can use it to connect to other routing groups or to any other SMTP server, either on the Internet or in another organization.

Most configuration options are quite similar for the SMTP connector and the routing group connector, but the SMTP connector has a few extra configuration options. One of these is the option to use a smart host for message delivery rather than DNS name resolution. If you use a smart host, all messages from the Exchange server are forwarded to the smart host, which then performs the DNS lookup and delivers the messages. The SMTP connector also can be configured to use dequeue commands, such as ATRN and ETRN, to download SMTP mail from another server using an intermittent connection.

Configuring the SMTP server is similar to configuring the routing group connector when you use the connector between Exchange routing groups. To configure the SMTP connector, start in Exchange System Manager. Expand the administrative group that contains the routing group where you want to add the connector, and then expand the routing group container. Right-click the Connectors container and choose New/SMTP Connector, opening a Properties box for the connector. Figure 11-20 shows the interface.

General

On the General tab, you can choose to use DNS to resolve the domain names for any messages sent from this server, or you can choose to use a particular smart host for delivery.

If you are using this SMTP connector as a routing group connector, you must enter the name of a smart host. You can use either the IP address of the smart host server or the DNS host name. If you are using the IP address, enclose the IP address in brackets ([and]). The server always tries to do a DNS lookup for the name provided for the smart host; enclosing the IP address in brackets informs the server that it is connecting to an IP address rather than to a host name.

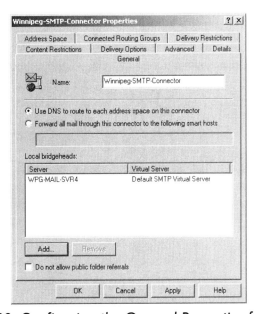

Figure 11-20: Configuring the General Properties for the SMTP Connector.

You also can configure the local bridgehead servers on the General tab. You can choose from any of the SMTP virtual servers in the routing group. In addition, you can specify whether the routing group connector is used for public folder referrals.

NOTE: *The Content Restrictions and the Delivery Restrictions are identical for the SMTP connector as they are for the routing group connector.*

Delivery Options

The Delivery Options tab, shown in Figure 11-21, enables you to configure when and how messages are sent using this connector. The first part of the tab is the same as the delivery options for a routing group connector. You can configure when messages are sent using this connector, and you can configure a different schedule for larger messages.

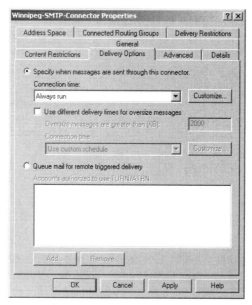

Figure 11-21: Configuring the Delivery Options for the SMTP Connector.

Advanced

The Queue mail for remote triggered delivery option specifies the accounts that have permission to initiate a TURN or Authenticated TURN (ATRN). To configure additional settings for TURN and ETRN, as well as for outbound security, you use the Advanced tab, shown in Figure 11-22.

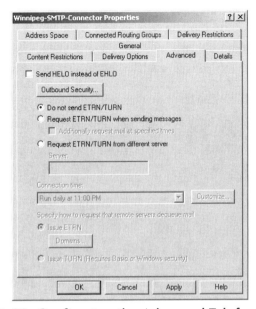

Figure 11-22: Configuring the Advanced Tab for the SMTP Connector.

TURN, ATRN, and ETRN

SMTP is based on the principle that all SMTP servers are always connected to the network and are always available for message delivery. However, there are several situations in which the destination host of an e-mail message might not be accessible. For example, you might have a dial-up client that connects only occasionally to the mail server to download the messages from a particular mailbox. Because SMTP cannot be used in this case, message retrieval protocols, such as POP3 and IMAP, serve to access a mailbox on a mail server and retrieve the messages from the mailbox. This is not only an issue with mail servers and e-mail clients. In some cases, the SMTP server that is the e-mail server for a particular domain might not be accessible from the Internet. If the server is temporarily down, the sending server retries message delivery until the message can be delivered. In other cases, the SMTP server for a domain might be using a dial-up connection to an ISP for access to the Internet.

This means that the SMTP server is accessible from the Internet only while the dial-up connection is active.

To deal with this type of situation, dequeuing protocols, such as TURN, ATRN, and ETRN, were developed. These protocols are all similar in concept. The first component is an SMTP server (usually an ISP's SMTP server) that is always accessible on the Internet. This server is configured as an SMTP server for the domain with an MX record pointing to the SMTP server. When a message arrives at the server, the message is not delivered to a mailbox, but instead placed in a queue for the destination domain. When the offline SMTP server connects to the ISP's SMTP server via dial-up, it uses one of the dequeue commands to download the messages that are queued for its domain. For example, if North American Air used this solution and was using the ETRN command, the SMTP server would connect to the ISP's SMTP server, authenticate, and then issue an etrn na-air.comcommand. The SMTP server at the ISP would then send all messages queued for that domain to the requesting server.

TURN, ATRN, and ETRN are all types of dequeuing commands. TURN is the most basic of these. It does not require a static IP address on the requesting server and does not support any authentication beyond the authentication on the dial-up connection. ATRN is similar to TURN, except that it can be configured to require another level of authentication by using the ESMTP Auth command. ETRN supports authentication but requires a static IP address for the requesting computer.

Exchange 2000 can operate as either the queuing server for the dequeue commands or as the client server that issues the dequeue commands. Both of these options are configured on the SMTP connector.

The option to use HELO rather than EHLO depends on the type of mail server that you are connecting to. If the destination mail server supports Extended SMTP (ESMTP), it responds to the EHLO command with the list of extended SMTP commands the server supports. If the destination server does not support ESMTP, the HELO command initiates the SMTP connection. In most cases, you can accept the default of using the EHLO command, which tells the

Exchange server to use the EHLO command first. If the destination server does not support this command, it replies with a code 500 error message indicating that it does not support ESMTP, and the Exchange server then tries to initiate the connection with the HELO command.

The other options on this tab specify how the dequeuing commands are implemented on the server. In most cases, the default Do not send ETRN/TURN option is the correct setting. However, in cases where you are connecting to a SMTP server that is queuing messages for your domain, you must use one of the dequeuing commands. You can configure the connector to issue the commands when sending mail, as well as at other times. You also can use the Domains option to configure the domains for which the dequeuing commands are issued.

If you configure ETRN or TURN, you must configure a setting for outbound security by identifying the user account and password for the account that is used during the authentication.

Address Space

Select the Address Space tab to configure the address space settings for the SMTP connector. (See Figure 11-23.) The address space defines the domains to which this SMTP connector can deliver mail.

When you choose Add, the default address space that gets added is the SMTP address space with an asterisk (*) as the address. This means that this connector can deliver messages to any SMTP connector. You can specify that this connector can deliver mail only to a particular domain.

The Connector scope setting specifies the visibility of this address space within the organization. The default value, Entire organization, makes the address space accessible to all clients in all routing groups in the organization. Everyone can use this connector to send messages to the Internet. If you choose instead to limit the scope to just the routing group, then the address space is visible only to clients in the routing group in which the connector is defined.

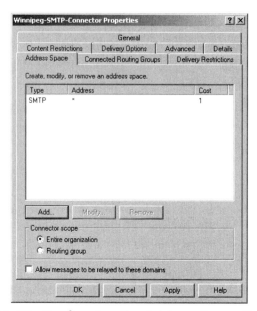

Figure 11-23: Configuring the Address Space Tab for the SMTP Connector.

Changing the default connector scope setting is useful if you have two locations (with a routing group in each location) and each location has an SMTP connector for Internet mail. If you want to ensure that messages intended for the Internet do not cross the WAN link between the two locations, you can configure the SMTP connection in both locations to limit the connector scope to the routing group. This means that the clients in each routing group can send Internet mail only through the connector at their own location, and even if the connector is down, the messages are not sent to the other routing group.

NOTE: *In Exchange 5.x, you also could limit the visibility of the address space based on the server's location setting within the site. This option is not available in Exchange 2000.*

Connected Routing Groups

Because you can use the SMTP connector to connect to any SMTP server, not just other SMTP servers in another routing group in the organization, you must configure the connector if it is to operate as a routing group connector. You do this by adding the routing group information on the Connected Routing Groups tab, shown in Figure 11-24.

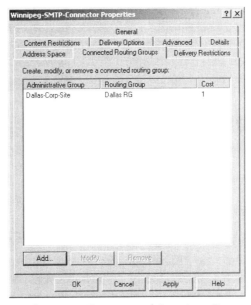

Figure 11-24: Configuring Connected Routing Groups on the SMTP Connector.

Configuring the X.400 Connector

The third method of configuring routing group connectors is to use the X.400 connector. The X.400 connector is the only connector in Exchange 2000 that uses the MTA rather than the SMTP for message delivery. In Exchange 4.0/5.*x*, administrators use the X.400 connector in situations where there is limited bandwidth between Exchange sites. Because the other connectors in Exchange 2000 are based on SMTP rather than RPCs, the SMTP connector can replace most of the X.400 connectors that are used as site connectors in earlier Exchange versions. The primary use for the X.400 connector in Exchange 2000 is to connect the Exchange 2000 server to a different messaging platform that is based on X.400.

> **NOTE:** *The configuration options for the X.400 connector in Exchange 2000 are virtually identical to the options for the X.400 connectors in Exchange 4.0/5.x. Because of this, and because the requirement for the X.400 connector is greatly decreased in Exchange 2000, I do not describe the configuration options for this connector. If you are configuring an X.400 connector and you have not configured this connector in Exchange 4.0/5.x, consult online help.*

Conclusion

This chapter examined the process of configuring messaging connectivity between servers and routing groups in Exchange 2000. For the most part, you use routing group connectors or SMTP connectors for message routing between routing groups and SMTP connectors for sending Internet e-mail. Virtually the only time you use the X.400 connector is to connect to another X.400 messaging system.

The next chapter continues describing the activities involved in managing an Exchange 2000 network. In particular, the next chapter examines some of the new options in Exchange 2000 that are of interest to North American Air, including Outlook Web Access (OWA), instant messaging, and Conferencing Server.

Chapter 12

Implementing Additional Exchange 2000 Services

EXCHANGE 2000 IS MUCH MORE THAN an e-mail server. Some of the most significant enhancements in Exchange 2000 are the new options for information sharing and collaboration between people within an organization, or between organizations. When an organization like North American Air considers migrating to Exchange 2000, these new features are an important part of that decision.

This chapter examines the Exchange 2000 enhancements to Outlook Web Access and public folder administration. Both of these technologies were available in Exchange 5.*x*, but Exchange 2000 provides some interesting new options that make these technologies more scalable and reliable. The chapter then discusses two completely new technologies in Exchange 2000: Instant Messaging and Conferencing Services.

Implementing Outlook Web Access

Exchange 5.0 marked the first appearance of Outlook Web Access (OWA) for Exchange, and it quickly became a popular option in many organizations. OWA is a great technology for remote users because the only client software that the users need to access their e-mail is a Web browser.

With each service pack in Exchange 5.0 and 5.5, OWA has become more scalable and stable, but significant limitations remain in all 5.*x* versions. One of the limitations, from a user perspective, is that public folders containing calendar or contact information cannot be accessed through OWA. OWA under Exchange 5.*x* also provides no options for offline access to the user's mailbox, and the user interface is limited compared to a MAPI client such as Outlook. OWA does provide more functionality than POP or IMAP clients such as Outlook Express, but the biggest limitation with OWA before Exchange 2000 is scalability. OWA in Exchange 5.*x* is implemented using Active Server Page (ASP) scripts on an IIS server running OWA. When a client connects to the OWA server, the ASP script initiates a MAPI session with the Exchange information store, either on the same server or on a back-end server. The number of MAPI sessions that can be opened in an ASP session is limited, so a limited number of clients can connect to the OWA server simultaneously without seriously affecting the OWA server's performance.

Despite these limitations, OWA has been implemented in many organizations. The reason for this is that OWA provides excellent functionality in a number of scenarios:

▲ **Non-Windows clients.** If you support non-Windows clients, such as Apple Macintosh or Unix clients, the users can access their e-mail with no additional software except for a Web browser.

▲ **Remote users.** OWA is an ideal solution for remote users who might have access to an Internet connection, but not to any other messaging client. All they need to access OWA is a Web browser.

▲ **Migration scenarios.** If you are migrating a number of users from a messaging system to Exchange 2000, and you do not yet have the Outlook clients installed, the users can access their e-mail through OWA as an interim solution.

▲ **Multiple use workstations.** OWA makes accessing private e-mail easy in an environment where many users share a single computer. OWA makes use of URL addressing to the individual mailbox, so users do not need to log on with their user account. They can connect to their mailboxes using the URL and then authenticate when connecting to the mailboxes.

OWA in Exchange 2000

OWA has been significantly improved in Exchange 2000, especially in the area of client access. For example, all public folders, including public folders containing contact and calendar information, are now accessible through OWA. You also can now add multimedia attachments to messages sent through OWA. When using Internet Explorer 5 or later, you also can perform many MAPI client functions, such as using drag-and-drop to move messages between folders and creating new folders on the Exchange server.

> **NOTE:** *While the interface for OWA has been greatly enhanced, it is not as full-featured as a real MAPI client. In particular, it lacks support for any kind of offline use (where you can continue to use the messaging interface without being connected to the server). It also does not provide an easy way to view the entire GAL, so users must perform a search to access the address book.*

Microsoft has completely redesigned the architecture for OWA in Exchange 2000 and has moved it into IIS along with all the other Internet protocols. The OWA server now appears in the Exchange System Manager as the Exchange Virtual Server object in the HTTP Protocol container. The Exchange Virtual Server object points to the default Web site on the IIS server. Inside the Exchange Virtual Server container are the Exadmin, Exchange, and public objects, which are the virtual directories created in IIS. Virtual directories are additional directories in IIS that you access by adding the virtual directory alias to the URL for the server. For example, when you type http://OWA.NA-Air.com/Exchange, you connect to the Exchange virtual directory. You also can view the same objects using the Internet Services Manager. Figure 12-1 shows the relationship between the two administrative interfaces.

As you can see in Figure 12-1, the virtual directories under the default Web site all point to the Exchange components on the server. The Exchange virtual directory points to the mailbox store through the M: drive, the public virtual directory points to the public folders store (also through the M: drive), and the Exadmin virtual directory points to the M: drive itself. The other Exchange-related virtual directory is the Exchweb directory, which contains the graphics and scripts used by OWA.

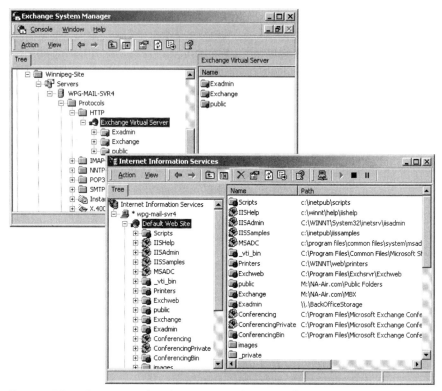

Figure 12-1: Viewing the OWA Virtual Server from Exchange System Manager and Internet Services Manager.

NOTE: *OWA does not use the Exadmin virtual directory. The Exchange System Manager uses Exadmin to manage public folders.*

OWA is automatically enabled on all Exchange 2000 servers and requires no configuration to enable it. Almost all OWA server configuration takes place in the Internet Services Manager in Exchange 2000, rather than through the Exchange administration tools. The only configuration options for OWA objects in the Exchange System Manager are found on the Access tab on Exchange and public objects, where you can view and modify the permissions and authentication methods for the virtual directory.

Rather than using MAPI, the Exchange 2000 version of OWA accesses the information store through HTTP and Web-DAV. Web-DAV, which is described in RFC 2518, is an extension of HTTP that Web browsers use to communicate with Web servers. The client uses Web-DAV when manipulating files on a Web server. It supports options, such as file locking (so only one person can change the file at one time), the display of property information about a document such as owner, creation date, and so on, and collections and namespace operations (used to view and manipulate directory structures on the server). The only Web browser that currently supports Web-DAV is IE 5.0 or later. Office 2000 and Web Folders (installed on a Windows 9.x or Windows NT client) also are Web-DAV clients and you can use them to directly access the Web Store on the Exchange server through Web-DAV.

Because OWA's architecture is different in Exchange 2000, the process of connecting to a server and opening an e-mail message also has changed significantly. The following ten steps describe what happens when a client connects to an OWA server and opens a message. Figure 12-2 outlines the process.

> **NOTE:** *This example illustrates an environment in which none of the servers involved have been configured as front-end servers. I explain the differences between this approach and the process when using distributed servers (using a front-end/back-end server configuration) later in the chapter.*

1. You access the Exchange server by typing the URL for the Exchange server. For example, you might type http://Dallas-OWA-S1.na-air.com/Exchange/*alias*/inbox.

2. If you are logged in to your computer with a user name and password that has access to the mailbox, Exchange automatically authenticates you. If the logged-in account does not have access to the mailbox, OWA prompts you to enter a user name and password.

3. The IIS server checks with Active Directory to determine your home server.

4. If your mailbox is on a different server, the Web request is redirected to your home server and the authentication process begins again.

OWA displays the default page for the mailbox on the client PC.

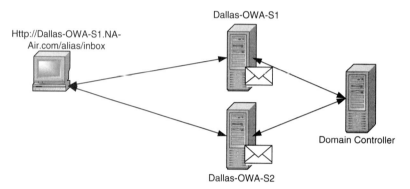

Http://Dallas-OWA-S1.NA-Air.com/alias/inbox

Dallas-OWA-S1

Domain Controller

Dallas-OWA-S2

Figure 12-2: Accessing Exchange 2000 through OWA.

5. When you double-click a message to open it, the client software sends a Get request to the server. The Get request identifies the URL for the message that you requested.

6. The Get request is sent to the Exchange Internet Services Application Programming Interface (ISAPI) application, DavEx.dll. An ISAPI application on an IIS server redirects client requests by calling an application to manage the request. The Exchange ISAPI application takes the client request and forwards the request to the Exchange information store. The request includes information, such as the browser type and operating system for the client computer, as well as the information identifying the object being requested.

7. The store process checks the permissions on the item to ensure that you have permission to access the item and then returns the item information, such as the type of item, to the ISAPI application.

8. The ISAPI application uses the properties of the item to determine the object type (that is, whether it is a contact item, calendar item, mail message, and so on). The ISAPI application then selects the correct type of form definition for the object type. The form definition specifies how the item displays on the client PC.

9. The ISAPI application extracts the information from the store to fill in the form.

10. The form and the data are rendered into HTTP and XML (if the client supports XML), and the information is sent to the client.

Most popular Web browsers, including Netscape Navigator 4.08 or higher and Microsoft Internet Explorer 4.01 (Service Pack 1) or higher, can access OWA. However, because only Internet Explorer 5.01 or higher supports Web-DAV, it is the only browser that supports the following features:

▲ **Drag and drop.** Messages can easily be moved from one folder to another.

▲ **Preview pane.** You can configure the client to display a preview pane of each message.

▲ **Rich text formatting.** You can change the font size, style, and color of the content of a message.

▲ **Right-click functionality.** Right-clicking opens a context menu in the folder view. One of the options on this menu enables you to create a new folder for any item type, not just mail items.

Every Exchange 2000 server also is by default an OWA server because of the integration of IIS with Exchange 2000. If you want to disable access to OWA on a server, you can remove the virtual directories created under the Default Web Site in Internet Services Manager. If you remove the Exadmin folder, you cannot administer public folders on the server. Because the Exadmin folder is not accessible through the Web interface, you can leave this virtual directory on the server. You also can prevent users from accessing OWA on a server by setting the permissions on the Exchange virtual directories so that no one can access the directories.

Configuring Distributed Servers

One of the reasons why OWA is so much more scalable in Exchange 2000 is because you can use distributed servers with it. By configuring one or more front-end servers and one or more back-end servers, you can scale the OWA configuration in Exchange 2000 to support almost any number of users.

> **NOTE:** *The distributed server configuration also is available for POP3 and IMAP4. When you configure a server to be a front-end server, it is a front-end server for all three protocols.*

Using distributed servers provides a number of benefits. These include the following:

▲ **Secure Sockets Layer (SSL) encryption and decryption offloading.** The process of encrypting and decrypting messages through a secure Web site is processor-intensive. By configuring a front-end server to handle this process, you can decrease the load on a back-end server.

▲ **Single name space.** Users need not remember multiple server names for accessing their mailboxes. They can use a single URL to connect to the front-end server and gain access to their mailboxes on any back-end server.

▲ **Enhanced security.** You can set up the front-end server as the only point of contact from the Internet, and it can redirect the client request to the back-end servers.

The processes of authentication and mailbox access change very little when you use distributed servers. The main change is that when the client authenticates to the front-end server, the server does not refer the client connection to the user's home server. Rather, the front-end server proxies the client request to the back-end server and uses HTTP and Web-DAV to communicate with IIS on the back-end server.

To configure a server as a front-end server, access the server properties through the Exchange System Manager. Figure 12-3 shows the interface.

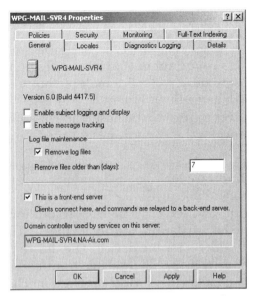

Figure 12-3: Configuring a Front-End Server.

Select the This is a front-end server option and then stop and restart the HTTP, POP, and IMAP services using the Services Administration tool. Once the server has been configured as a front-end server, the information store on that server is no longer accessible to OWA, POP or IMAP clients. Instead, all requests to the server using these protocols are redirected to a back-end server. Even though the information store on the front-end server is still accessible with a MAPI client, you should not put any mailboxes on the front-end server. After ensuring that there are no mailboxes or public folders on the front-end server, you can dismount the mailbox store and the public-folder store on the front-end server.

By using distributed servers for OWA, you can provide service for almost any number of users. As the number of OWA clients increases, you can provide additional capacity by adding servers, either front-end, back-end, or both. You can enable load balancing for the back-end servers by distributing the mailboxes for the clients using OWA equally across the back-end servers.

Configuring load balancing for the front-end servers is a little more complicated. With multiple front-end servers you have three options for load balancing:

▲ **DNS round robin.** You can configure the DNS records for the front-end servers with multiple host records all using the same host name but different IP addresses. As clients query the DNS server to resolve the host name to an IP address, the DNS server provides the IP addresses for the front-end servers on a rotating basis.

▲ **Hardware load-balancing devices.** You can place a hardware load-balancing device between the OWA clients and the OWA front-end servers. The DNS record for the OWA server points to the load-balancing device so that all clients connect to the single IP address for the device. The device then distributes the client requests across all available front-end servers. Using hardware load-balancing devices provides much more flexibility than DNS round robin. The devices can monitor each server to determine server capacity and load and refer the client request to the server that can provide the fastest response time to the client.

▲ **Network Load Balancing.** Windows 2000 Advanced Server provides load-balancing functionality for IIS-based services through Network Load Balancing. (Network Load Balancing also is available in Windows NT 4.0 Enterprise Edition, where it is called Windows Load Balancing Service.) All servers in a Network Load Balancing cluster share one IP address (as well as maintain a unique IP address). The DNS server has a host record that points to the shared IP address. When a client connects to that IP address, Network Load Balancing determines which computer in the cluster can provide the fastest response time to the client and directs the client request to that server.

Configuring Secure OWA

Security is an important concern when using OWA, especially when the OWA server is accessible from the Internet. The two most significant security issues are password security and data security. To create a secure OWA environment, you should ensure that both the passwords and the data being transferred to and from the OWA server are encrypted. That way, even if someone captures the network packets using a packet sniffer, the contents of the packets are unreadable. You can secure an OWA environment by configuring authentication options and setting up OWA to use SSL.

> **NOTE:** *Whenever you make any server accessible from the Internet, including an OWA server, you create an entrance point to your network. To protect your network, you need to have a firewall between the Internet and the OWA server in addition to the OWA-specific options described in the following sections.*

Configuring Authentication Options

The first step in securing OWA is to configure the authentication options correctly. OWA supports the authentication methods described in Table 12-1.

Table 12-1: Authentication Options for OWA

Authentication Method	Description
Anonymous	Users need not authenticate when connecting to the server. Users have access to all content to which the Anonymous user account has access. This method should be used only for providing anonymous access to selected public folders.
Basic	Users must enter a user name and password. The password is sent across the network with minimal encryption. This method can be used in a distributed server configuration. It should be used in combination with SSL to provide encryption for the authentication information.

Table 12-1: Authentication Options for OWA (Continued)

Authentication Method	Description
Digest	Users must enter a user name and password. A mathematical function (hash) is applied to the password before transmission. This method requires that the passwords for all users using digest authentication be stored in reversible encryption on the domain controller. This decreases the security of the passwords on the domain controller. You cannot use this method in a distributed server configuration, but you can use it to authenticate across proxies and firewalls. Only HTTP 1.1-compliant browsers support this method.
Certificate-based	The server and client use certificates, public keys, and private keys to authenticate and encrypt all traffic. This method provides a high level of security when combined with basic authentication. Almost all Web browsers support it. This method requires a public-key infrastructure to create and distribute the certificates. It can be used in a distributed server configuration.
Integrated Windows	The user must enter a user name and password. The password is encrypted before it is sent over the network. Pre-Windows 2000 clients use NTLM as the authentication protocol. Windows 2000 clients use Kerberos. You cannot use this method in a distributed server configuration.

Any of the authentication methods from Table 12-1 except Anonymous can provide secure access to OWA. However, almost all of these authentication protocols have serious limitations. If you use Basic authentication, passwords are not secure because they are sent across the network in an easily decrypted format. Digest authentication provides password security on the network, but the passwords are stored on the domain controller in a less-secure format. Integrated Windows authentication provides for secure authentication but you can't use it in a distributed environment, so all your back-end servers must be accessible from the Internet.

The most secure and flexible option to provide secure access to OWA is to use Basic authentication with Secure Sockets Layer (SSL) to provide authentication and encryption. The primary problem with this option is that it requires a great deal of planning and effort to create and distribute the certificates needed to use SSL.

Using SSL with OWA

The default OWA installation has some inherit security risks. First, it sends all the traffic between the server and client using HTTP, in clear text. Second, with basic authentication, the user's password crosses the network with minimal encryption. Anyone capturing the OWA traffic on the network not only can extract the user passwords but also can read all messages read or sent through OWA.

Virtually the only way to provide the necessary security is to use SSL to encrypt both the authentication process and the transmitted data between the host and client. However, to implement SSL, you must provide certificates to all the OWA servers to enable the secure communication. The most difficult part of implementing SSL is acquiring and configuring these certificates.

Public Key Infrastructure Concepts   You can use a public key infrastructure (PKI) to create and acquire the certificates you need to implement SSL. A PKI consists of four components:

▲ **Certificate Authority (CA).** The CA is a server component that issues the digital certificates for the OWA servers.

▲ **Digital certificates.** These certificates authenticate the identity of either the server or the client during an SSL session. The issuing CA digitally signs the certificates and provides a public key and a private key.

▲ **Public key.** The public key for a certificate confirms the identity of the certificate holder and creates a secure channel between the client and server. A client requests and receives the public key from the certificate holder. You can also store a public key in a directory service, such as Active Directory, and clients can retrieve it from there.

▲ **Private key.** The private key is known only to the certificate holder. You can store a private key on the local computer's hard drive, as part of a roaming profile, or on an external device such as a smart card. The certificate holder uses the private key to digitally sign certificates and messages and to decrypt messages sent using the public key. The public key and private key are mathematically related, but there is no way to derive the private key from the public key.

PKI-based security is quite different from the regular network security in Windows 2000 or Windows NT. Both Kerberos and NTLM are "shared secret" security protocols. The shared secret in these protocols is the user's password. When a user logs on by entering his password, the server compares its copy of the password with the password that the user entered. If the passwords match, it assumes that the user is authentic, and the user receives network access.

A PKI-based system, in contrast, does not use a shared secret for authentication, but rather certificates and public and private keys. Every user or computer involved in the information exchange has a certificate that includes two keys: a private key and a public key. Instead of checking for a shared secret during the authentication process, the server and the client check the certificate validity. When a client connects to a server, the client checks the server's certificate to confirm that the certificate is valid and that it trusts the CA that issued the certificate. If both of these conditions are met, the client assumes that the server is authentic, and the connection can continue.

PKI-based security is also a trust-based authentication process. The trustworthiness of any certificate depends entirely on the trustworthiness of the CA that issued the certificate. With Windows 2000, you can set up a CA by installing the Certificate Service on a Windows 2000 server, but most clients do not accept the certificate issued by your CA as trustworthy. If you want clients from outside your organization to accept your certificates, you must acquire a certificate from a third-party CA. The responsibility then rests with the third-party CA to ensure that your organization is trustworthy before issuing a certificate to you.

For the SSL Web site to be completely secure, three components are required:

▲ **Server authentication.** Server authentication verifies that the server's certificate is valid and that the server is the holder of the private key associated with the certificate. Server authentication is required for every SSL Web site.

▲ **Client authentication.** Client authentication verifies that the client's certificate is valid and that the client is the holder of the private key associated with the certificate. Client authentication is not required on most SSL Web sites, because it would require that every client obtain a certificate from a CA.

▲ **Data encryption.** The authentication process generates a session key that is used to encrypt the data flowing between the computers. Encrypting with the session key is much less processor-intensive than encrypting using the certificate's public and private keys, so the certificate-based encryption is used only for authentication; the session key then takes over the job.

When a client connects to an OWA server using SSL, the following processes take place:

1. The client sends a request to the server for access to its resources. The client request includes its SSL capabilities and some randomly generated data.

2. The server responds to the client request by sending the client a copy of the server's certificate, which includes a copy of the server's public key and a digital signature based on the server's private key. If the server is configured to request or require client authentication, the server also requests the client's certificate.

3. The client checks the server's certificate, ensuring that the date on the certificate is valid and that the certificate was issued by a CA that the client is configured to trust. It then uses the server's public key to check the digital signature on the certificate. If the

server requested a client certificate, the client sends the certificate to the server at this point. The server goes through the same process of authenticating the client certificate.

4. The server and client then negotiate a session key. The process of negotiating the key makes use of the randomly generated data that has been exchanged between the computers, as well as the server's public key and private keys. At the end of the negotiation, the server and the client have agreed on a shared session key that they will use to encrypt all the data during the remainder of the session.

5. Once a secure channel exists, the server sends the OWA authentication request to the client. Because all traffic between the server and client is encrypted, the client's password is encrypted at this point even when using basic authentication. In addition, all data between the server and client is now encrypted.

The primary planning issue involved in configuring OWA to use SSL is to determine what to use as the CA. You have two CA options when setting up SSL; you can create your own CA by using the Certificate Server included with Windows 2000 Server, or you can use a third-party commercial CA such as VeriSign.

The choice depends on the types of clients that access your Web site. If only internal corporate clients access your Web site (usually the case if you are using SSL for OWA), you can configure your own CA using the Certificate Service in Windows 2000. If you install an Enterprise CA, the Certificate Service is integrated with Active Directory. You can then configure group policies in Active Directory to automate the process of managing certificates. Active Directory also stores the certificates, and you can create certificate mappings in Active Directory that link a certificate to a specific user account.

NOTE: The planning and implementation of Certificate Services in Windows 2000 is beyond the scope of this book. The Windows 2000 Server Resource Kit includes detailed information on these topics.

Configuring OWA for SSL The first step in creating the secure Web site is to obtain a server certificate for the OWA server. To do this, perform the following twelve steps:

1. On the OWA server, open the Internet Services Manager from the Administrative Tools folder.

2. Right-click the Default Web Site and choose Properties.

3. Select the Directory Security tab. (See Figure 12-4.)

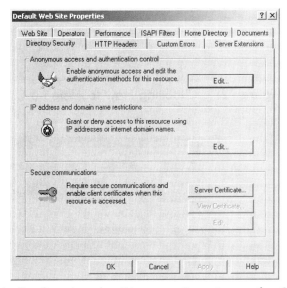

Figure 12-4: Configuring the Directory Security on the OWA Server.

4. Select Server Certificate. The Web Server Certificate wizard begins.

5. Choose how you are going to assign the certificate for the Web site. (See Figure 12-5.)

   If this is the first certificate you are assigning to the server, choose the Create a new certificate option.

6. Choose to create a request to send either to an offline CA or to an online authority. (See Figure 12-6.)

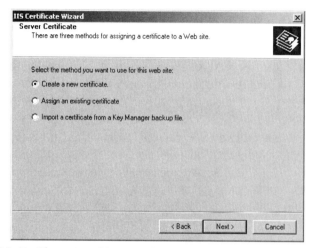

Figure 12-5: Choosing How to Assign a Certificate to a Web Site.

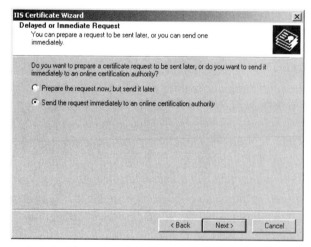

Figure 12-6: Choosing How to Apply for the Certificate.

If you are using a Windows 2000 Certificate Service to manage your own certificate requests, choose the Send the request immediately to an online certificate authority option.

You can use the Prepare the request now, but send it later option to create a request for a certificate to be sent to a commercial CA. If you chose this option, the wizard asks you for additional information, such as the name of the Web site that uses the certificate, the key length, and the organization details. The wizard then generates a random key that you must include in your request to the commercial CA.

NOTE: The rest of this procedure assumes that you have an online CA and send a request directly to it. If you want to prepare the request now and send it to an offline CA, the wizard asks for the same information but generates a text file containing the key at the end of the procedure.

7. Enter the name that you want to use for the certificate, and choose an encryption key length. The longer the key, the more secure the encryption is, but longer keys require more server resources to encrypt and decrypt.

8. Type the organization name and organizational unit information. This information is for the certificate only and does not need to correspond to your Active Directory or Exchange organization names.

9. Type the name of the Web site for which this certificate is to be used. This name must match the DNS name that clients use to access the Web site. For example, if the Web site is called OWA.NA-Air.com, that name should appear on the certificate. If the names are not identical, the clients receive a warning message every time they connect to the site indicating that the certificate name does not match the Web site name.

10. Type the geographic information required for the certificate request. The information must include the country, state or province, and city.

11. Chose the CA to which the certificate request is to be sent.

12. Review the certificate request information and then submit the request to the CA. If you have an online CA and it is configured to grant certificate requests automatically, the CA immediately issues the certificate and installs it on the Web site.

You can now configure the Web server to use SSL. To do so, open the Properties page for the Web site for which you just created the certificate and choose the Directory Security tab. Under Secure communications, select Edit to open a Secure Communications dialog box. (See Figure 12-7.)

Figure 12-7: Configuring the Web Site to Use SSL.

To force all clients connecting to this Web site to use SSL, select the Require secure channel option. You can enforce a higher level of encryption by selecting the Require 128-bit encryption option.

You also can configure whether the clients need certificates when connecting to the server. If you select the Ignore client connection option, the server never requests a client certificate. The Accept client certificate option configures the server to request a certificate from the client but to accept connections if the client does not have a certificate. The last option, Require client certificates, configures the server not to accept connections from any client that does not have a certificate from a trusted CA.

The other two options in the dialog box are for more advanced certificate configuration. You can use the client certificate mapping option to map a certificate to a user account so that when the user connects using the certificate, the user has the same permissions as the mapped user account. You can use the certificate trust lists to configure trusted CAs for this Web site.

The procedure I just outlined describes how to configure the default Web site for SSL. In some cases, however, you might not want to use SSL for the default Web site, but only for OWA. You can configure this by creating an additional HTTP virtual server through the Exchange System Manager and then using Internet Services Manager to obtain a certificate for that virtual server.

Implementing Public Folder Enhancements

Also of interest to North American Air are the new Exchange 2000 options available for administering public folders. While public folders have been available in Exchange since Exchange 4.0, their support had not changed a great deal until Exchange 2000. Since North American Air uses public folders extensively in Exchange 2000, several of these new options, such as the capability to create additional public folder trees and configure full-text indexing, will prove useful for the company.

Configuring Multiple Public Folder Trees

Exchange 2000 enables you to have more than one public folder tree. This means that you can create multiple public folder hierarchies within an organization.

Exchange 4.0/5.x supports only a single public folder hierarchy, which it automatically replicates to all Exchange servers that contain a public folder store. When you create a new public folder in this hierarchy, the information about the new folder is replicated to all Exchange servers, potentially including an Exchange server from which no one will ever need to access it. For example, administrators might create a public folder at North American Air's Atlanta location that contains information that applies only to the avionics component in the corporation, and so would be of interest to only the Chicago, Atlanta, and Corporate locations. With the Exchange 4.0/5.x implementation of public folders, there is no way to limit the replication of the public folder hierarchy to only these three locations. If someone sends a new message to any public folder in the organization, the header information for the message replicates throughout the organization, again resulting in needless replication traffic.

Another limitation of the single public folder hierarchy is that you must create all public folders within that hierarchy. In organizations that use many public folders, it can take some time to browse to the correct public folder through the client interface.

Exchange 2000 addresses these issues by enabling the use of multiple public folder trees. When you create a new public folder tree on a server, Exchange does not replicate the information about the new public folder tree to any other server unless you configure the tree on another server. This means that if North American Air wanted the avionics public folder information to be replicated only in the Chicago, Atlanta, and Corporate locations, they could configure the tree on a server in each of those locations. Any public folders that related to this topic could then be created in that public folder tree, and the information about the folders would be replicated only to those servers.

Configuring additional public folder trees does introduce some complications, however. The default public folder tree is accessible from any client that can access public folder information on an Exchange server, including MAPI, IMAP, NNTP, and HTTP clients. When you configure a new public folder tree, the information is accessible only through NNTP and HTTP clients, and then only if you configure an additional virtual server for these protocols that points to this new public folder tree. A second complication is that each new public folder tree must be stored in its own public store, so that each server that gets a new public folder tree must have a public store dedicated to that tree. Each additional public store on a server requires hard disk space as well as at least 10 MB of additional RAM.

To configure additional public folder trees, perform the following steps:

1. In Exchange System Manager, locate the Folders container in which you want to create the additional public folder tree.

    Any administrative group in the organization can contain a Folders container, and you can create the public folder tree in any Folders container in the organization. However, normally you would create the new public folder tree in an administrative group that contains the server on which the public store is to be created. If you have centralized all public folder administration in one administrative group, create the new public folder tree in the Folders container in that group.

2. Right-click the Folders container and choose New/Public Folder Tree. A Properties box appears for the new tree, as shown in Figure 12-8.

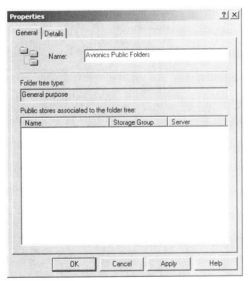

Figure 12-8: Creating a New Public Folder Tree.

Type a name for the tree in the Name box. The Folder tree type is General purpose, and cannot be changed. Close the Properties box when you're finished.

3. As you can see in Figure 12-8, there are no public folder stores associated with this public folder tree yet. The next step is to create the public folder store and associate it with the public folder tree.

4. Locate the server where you want to create the public folder store that is associated with the new public folder tree.

   This server can be anywhere in the organization, including in any administrative group for which you have Exchange Administrator rights.

5. Expand the server container, right-click the storage group in which you want to create the new store, and choose New/Public Store. A Properties box appears, as shown in Figure 12-9.

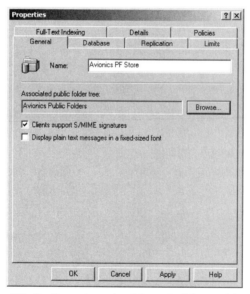

Figure 12-9: Creating the New Public Folder Tree.

Type a descriptive name for the new public store in the Name box, and click Browse to select the new public folder tree that you just created.

Configure the rest of the properties for the public folder store, and close the Properties box.

NOTE: If you create the new public folder tree in one location and then immediately try to create the public folder store on a server in a remote location, the new public folder tree might not have replicated to the remote location. When you try to create a new public store on a server, it checks the Active Directory configuration container on the closest domain controller for the available public folder trees. If the information has not yet replicated, you get an error message indicating that all public folder trees already have an associated public store on the server and that you need to create a new public folder tree before creating the new public store. This is the same error message that you get if you try to create a new public store before creating a new public folder tree.

After you create the public folder tree and public store, the next step is to create a new HTTP or NNTP virtual server to provide client access to the new public folder store. The following steps show the procedure for creating the HTTP virtual server.

1. Expand the Protocols container for the server on which you want to create the additional virtual server. Right-click the HTTP container and choose New/HTTP Virtual Server. Figure 12-10 shows the interface.

2. Type a Descriptive name for the server.

3. Choose a unique IP address, port number, or host name to identify the virtual server.

   As with any other virtual server, you must provide some unique way of identifying this virtual server, either by using a unique IP address, port number, or host name. The host name option is available only for HTTP virtual servers and enables the option of identifying a unique name for the server. For example, in this case you could use host name of Avionics.Na-Air.com for the host name and use the same settings for the IP address and port number as the default Web site. (See Figure 12-11.) When clients connect to this virtual server, they use the host name identified for the virtual server rather than the host name associated with the default Web site. For clients to be able to connect to this new host name, a DNS entry must exist.

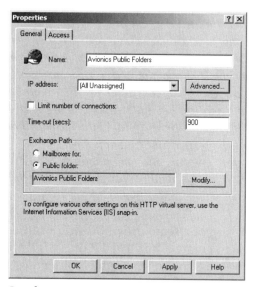

Figure 12-10: Configuring an HTTP Virtual Server for a New Public Folder Tree.

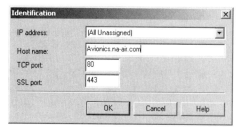

Figure 12-11: Configuring the Advanced Identification of an HTTP Virtual Server for a New Public Folder Tree.

NOTE: When you create the new virtual server, it appears in Internet Services Manager. The host name in the Exchange System Manager is called the host header name in Internet Services Manager.

4. Under Exchange Path, choose Public Folder and then choose Modify. Select the public folder tree that this HTTP virtual server will connect to.

The home directory for the virtual server that you create in this procedure is the new public folder tree. When clients connect to this Web site using a Web browser, they connect directly to the public folder tree, and they need not include any virtual directories such as /public in the URL they type. They can, however, specify public folders in the tree, or specify messages in a public folder, by appending them to the URL. For example, a URL of http://Avionics.na-air.com/Updates/Price List.eml would open a message that has Price List as its subject in the Updates public folder in the Avionics public folder tree.

NOTE: The procedure I outline here describes how to configure the public folder tree on one server. If you want the public folder tree to be replicated to any other servers, you must create the public folder store on that server and then configure the virtual servers to provide client access. You also must configure public folder replication for the actual contents of the public folders to replicate between the servers.

Administering Full-Text Indexing

North American Air might also find full-text indexing useful. Full-text indexing can improve search performance for systems on which users frequently search a large folder for specific information. For example, North American Air might use public folders to store technical manuals and troubleshooting procedures. This public folder could become very large and could include hundreds or thousands of documents. Searching through this list of documents for a particular term would be slow for the client and would utilize significant resources on the server.

With full-text indexing, however, Exchange indexes the entire public folder tree before the user needs to search it. Then, when the user searches the folder for a specific term, Exchange searches the index rather than the actual public folder. The search is much quicker and consumes fewer server resources.

You can enable full-text indexing on either a public folder store or a mailbox store. When you enable full-text indexing on a public folder store, all of the public folders on the store are indexed. When you enable full-text indexing on a mailbox store, all mailboxes on the store are indexed. Exchange indexes all messages in the store, including the message subject, the message body, and most attachments.

> **NOTE:** *Exchange can index attachments of these types: Word (.doc), Excel (.xls), PowerPoint (.ppt), HTML (.html, .htm, .asp), text (.txt), and embedded MIME messages (.eml).*

Full-text indexing also has two important limitations:

▲ Only complete words are indexed. A search for the term *admin* would return only messages that included the word *admin* and would not return messages that had the word *administrator*.

▲ Only the message subject, body, and attachments are indexed. If you want to search for other attributes, such as message recipient or message date, you must use a regular search of the database. You can combine an indexed search with a regular search. For example, if you searched a public folder for all messages that included a particular word that was sent to a particular recipient during a selected week, Exchange would first do a search of the full-text index for the selected word and then would search only the returned messages for the other criteria.

Implementing Full-Text Indexing

You enable full-text indexing at an individual store level. To enable and configure full-text indexing, follow these six steps:

1. Locate the information store for which you want to enable full-text indexing.

2. Right-click the information store and choose Create Full-Text Index.

3. Select the location where the catalog is to reside.

4. To initiate the first full-text indexing, right-click the information store again and choose Start Full Population.

   By default the Microsoft Search service does not initiate the full-text indexing until you manually start the process, or until the next scheduled indexing period occurs. This means that you can configure the full-text indexing during the day and then have it actually do the indexing during nonwork hours.

5. To view the details of the full-text index, expand the store for which you configured full-text indexing and then expand Full-Text Indexing. (See Figure 12-12.)

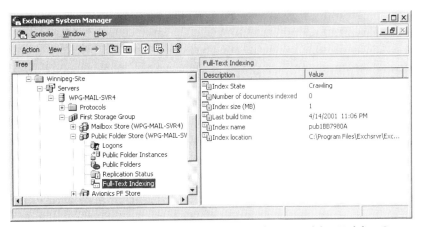

Figure 12-12: Full-Text Indexing Details for a Public Folder Store.

6. To configure how frequently Microsoft Search re-indexes the store, access the store Properties, and choose the Full-Text Indexing tab. (See Figure 12-13.)

   The Update interval specifies when Microsoft Search will perform an incremental index of the selected store. You can choose to index the store once a day, to index it several times a day, or create a custom schedule. You also can configure the indexing process to Always run, which means that Microsoft Search service is always running and messages are indexed throughout the day. The correct setting depends on how important it is in your organization to have an up-to-date index at all times of the day. If you must have an up-to-date index, select Always run. However, for a large store that receives many messages during a day, this option has a significant impact on the server performance. In most cases, running the index once a day during nonpeak times is a better choice.

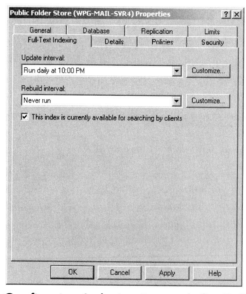

Figure 12-13: Configuring Indexing Intervals for Full-Text Indexing.

You also can configure the Rebuild interval, which defines how frequently Microsoft Search performs a complete rebuild of the index. In most cases it is best to leave this setting at the default of Never run and use the Update option to keep the Index current.

You should also select the This index is currently available for searching by clients option. You can leave this feature turned off while the index is being created, but then you must turn it on to make the index available to clients.

When you first initiate full-text indexing, Microsoft Search processes the entire store. During the initial indexing, it heavily utilizes the server's CPU. The initial indexing of a large information store can take several hours, so you should configure the initial indexing to occur during nonworking hours. An index for a store is approximately 20 percent of the size of the store being indexed.

Once you have enabled full-text indexing, MAPI and IMAP4 clients can take advantage of full-text indexing when searching for messages in a folder.

Try it out yourself using a MAPI client such as Outlook 2000. In Outlook, choose Tools/Advanced Find. Type the criteria on which you want to search and click Find Now. (See Figure 12-14.)

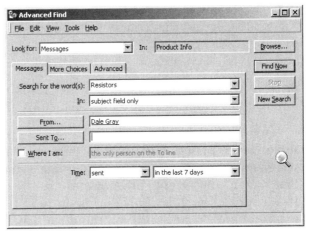

Figure 12-14: Using Full-Text Indexing from Outlook 2000.

The search shown in Figure 12-14 uses both the full-text index search and the regular message search. The search first uses the full-text index to return a list of all messages in the Product Info public folder that have the word Resistors in the subject or body of the message (including attachments). Then it searches that subset of messages to extract only the ones sent in the last 7 days by Dale Gray.

To configure other search criteria in Outlook 2000, such as searching only unread messages, or only messages with attachments, click the More Choices tab in the Advanced Search dialog box. You can use the Advanced tab to search for any of the standard properties for any of the Outlook objects. For example, if you were searching a public folder containing contacts, you could use the Advanced tab to configure a search based on a specific ZIP code or postal code.

Optimizing Full-Text Indexing

You must plan full-text indexing carefully. Indexing a large store can take a long time and consume significant server resources. If the information in the store changes constantly and the index must always be up to date, server resources are constantly used to maintain the index. Because of this, you might not want to implement full-text indexing on every mailbox store. Full-text indexing is ideal when you have a public folder store in which the information does not change frequently, but which users frequently search. For North American Air, a public folder that contains technical documentation is an ideal example.

To optimize the full-text indexing process, configure the index to be rebuilt during times when the server resources are not being used for any other process. In most organizations, this is at night.

Full-text indexing is processor- and memory-intensive on the server. If you plan to index a large store, or multiple stores on the server, and you must maintain a completely current index, make sure that you have sufficient CPU power to handle the constant indexing. If you update the index only during off-peak times, the CPU usage is not as critical. In addition, you should add an extra 256 MB of RAM to a server you use heavily for indexing. Hard disk space is an issue as well. The Microsoft Search service requires at least 15 percent free hard disk space to run, in addition to the space that the index itself uses. Ideally, you should locate the index files on a hardware RAID disk system.

NOTE: *An organization might use a full-text index for some public folder stores, but not for others. You can implement this option by creating multiple folder trees and linking each tree to a different store, and then indexing only the required stores.*

Implementing Instant Messaging

One of the new collaboration technologies available in Exchange 2000 is Instant Messaging. Instant Messaging makes it possible for users to have short real-time conversations across the network using an Instant Messaging client. In many ways, Instant Messaging is like a phone call, except that messages are typed rather than spoken.

Instant Messaging enables you to create a list of users that you need to contact frequently, and it maintains presence information for your contacts, so you can see at a glance who is available for messaging and who is not. Then when you want to Instant Message one of the people on your list, you can check to see if she is online, and then connect directly to the Instant Messaging client on her computer. You can have a brief typed conversation and then close the application. You can choose to save a transcript of the conversation, but by default none is saved.

Instant Messaging Overview

Instant Messaging in Exchange 2000 requires a number of components:

▲ **Instant Messaging home servers.** These servers host the user accounts for Instant Messaging and maintain the presence information for the each user. The Instant Messaging home server can be the same Exchange 2000 server that hosts a user's mailbox, but need not be because the two processes do not share information.

▲ **Instant Messaging routers.** These servers act much like front-end servers in a distributed-server environment. Routers are not required for Instant Messaging; however, any organization that requires more than one home server should implement Instant Messaging routers. Users connect to the Instant Messaging router, and the router redirects or relays the client requests to the home servers. Instant Messaging routers maintain a single Instant Messaging namespace when user accounts are spread across multiple home servers.

▲ **RVP protocol.** Instant Messaging uses this protocol. It is an extension of the HTTP 1.1 protocol, using elements of Web-DAV and XML.

▲ **Firewall topology configuration.** You can configure Instant Messaging for intranet use only, or it can support users on the Internet as well. If you make Instant Messaging accessible from outside your intranet, the firewall topology configuration defines which clients are inside the firewall and which clients are outside it. The Instant Messaging router handles clients inside and outside the firewall differently.

▲ **Exchange 2000.** You can install Instant Messaging as an optional component when you install Exchange 2000. Exchange 2000 provides the node database that stores presence information for each user. If you are implementing Instant Messaging in a large scale (more than a couple of thousand users), you must dedicate servers to operate as Instant Messaging servers.

▲ **Active Directory.** You must enable user accounts for Instant Messaging in Active Directory Users and Computers. When the user tries to connect to the Instant Messaging servers, the user must authenticate to Active Directory.

▲ **DNS.** For client computers to connect to an Instant Messaging server, DNS must contain a host record for the server. In addition, you can configure DNS with SRV records that point to the Instant Messaging domain name. This simplifies the user logon process by allowing users to use their email addresses when logging on, rather than using the Instant Messaging domain name.

When you enable a user account for Instant Messaging, the user account receives three Instant Messaging-specific attributes:

▲ **Instant Messaging user address**. The user can log on to Instant Messaging by using this name. The format is *alias@InstantMessagingDomainName*.

▲ **Instant Messaging URL address.** This is the name of the domain for Instant Messaging and points to the Instant Messaging router. The format is http://*InstantMessagingDomainName*/inst-msg/aliases/*alias*.

▲ **Instant Messaging home server URL address.** This address points to the user's home server for Instant Messaging. The format is http://*HomeServer*/instmsg/local/*InstantMessagingDomain-Name* aliases/*alias*.

To understand how these components work together, suppose that North American Air decides to implement Instant Messaging in the Texas locations. They might come up with an Instant Messaging network topology like the one shown in Figure 12-15.

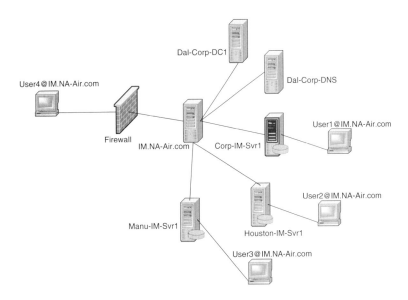

Figure 12-15: The Instant Messaging Topology at the Texas Locations in North American Air.

They plan to deploy an Instant Messaging home server at each of the three Texas locations. An Instant Messaging home server can host up to 10,000 user accounts. They configure a single Instant Messaging router at the corporate location. An Instant Messaging router can manage up to 50,000 user accounts, so both servers are within the limitation. They configure the Instant Messaging domain as IM.Na-Air.com, which also is the host name for the Instant Messaging router at the corporate location. They configure the clients with Instant Messaging user addresses of *alias*@im.na-air.com.

When a user from the corporate location logs on to Instant Messaging using his Instant Messaging user address, the client sends this address to the Instant Messaging router. The router queries Active Directory to determine the user's home server. The router then redirects the client software to point to the user's home server URL. The client connects to the home server, sending the user name and password, and the home server authenticates the user.

The clients connect to the HTTP server on the Instant Messaging server using port 80. When Instant Messaging is installed with Exchange 2000, it creates a new virtual directory called InstMsg under the default Web site.

Once the users are enabled for Instant Messaging, they can add other users in the organization as contacts from within the Instant Messaging client. A contact in this context is someone whose presence information the user wants to monitor. The user can add additional contacts based on user e-mail addresses, or by searching Active Directory for Instant Messaging-enabled users.

NOTE: The Instant Messaging client is the same client as the MSN Messenger client used on the Internet. Earlier versions of the client restricted you to using either MSN Messenger or Exchange Instant Messaging. Starting with the client version 2.2, however, you can maintain contacts both in Exchange and through MSN and log on to both at the same time.

Each home server includes a node database that stores the presence information about each user. Each user's home server then keeps all the user's contacts informed about the user's information. At North American Air, the home server at the corporate location maintains User1's presence information. Because other users have User1 listed as a contact, Corp-IM-Svr1 keeps them informed about User1's presence information. When User1's information changes, Corp-IM-Svr1 connects to the Instant Messaging URL for each user to update the information.

When one of the internal Instant Messaging users wants to contact one of the other Instant Messaging users, the client software sends a request to the Instant Messaging router. For example, if User1 tries to contact User2, the router examines the source IP address of the connection and determines from the firewall topology configuration that both clients are inside the firewall. The router queries Active Directory to determine the home server for User2. The router then redirects User1's client to connect directly to the home server for User2. User1's client sends a message to User2's home server URL. User1's client then caches the information on how to connect to User2's home server, so it need not go back to the router for the rest of the conversation.

When an outside client, such as User4, connects to the Instant Messaging router, the router again examines the source IP address. In this case, the router determines that the client is outside the corporate network. Rather than redirecting User4's client to connect to the home server for the internal user, the router relays the request. When User4 sends a message to User3, the message is sent to the Instant Messaging router, which forwards the message to User3' s home server. The Instant Messaging router is the only computer that is directly accessible from the Internet.

DNS plays an essential role in the Instant Messaging process by providing regular hostname resolution. When the client needs to connect to the Instant Messaging router, it queries DNS for the router IP address. For example, if the router name is IM.Na-Air.com, this record must exist in DNS. When the router needs to connect to an Active Directory server to determine a user's home server, it uses DNS just like any other client to locate the closest domain controller. All of the home servers must have records in DNS for the router and clients to locate them.

You can also use DNS to simplify the configuration of Instant Messaging by using an SRV record. Without any special DNS configuration, each of the clients in the North American Air scenario uses the login name of *alias*@im.na-air.com to log on to Instant Messaging. If the e-mail address and the Universal Principal Name (UPN) for all users is *alias*@na-air.com, having a second similar login name may lead to confusion. By using SRV records in DNS, you can modify the logon name for Instant Messaging to match the regular e-mail addresses or UPNs. To do this, you must configure an SRV record that creates the link between the domain name for the user's e-mail addresses and the Instant Messaging domain name. The SRV record might look like this:

```
_rvp._tcp.NA-Air.com 600 IN SRV 0 100 80 IM.NA-Air.com
```

This record indicates that the RVP server for the NA-Air.com domain is IM.NA-Air.com. When a user logs on to Instant Messaging using the regular e-mail address (*alias*@na-air.com), the Instant Messaging router checks with DNS and determines the RVP server for the NA-Air.com domain and substitutes IM.NA-Air.com for the domain name.

Planning for Instant Messaging

You can deploy Instant Messaging in an organization of almost any size. In a small organization that needs only one Instant Messaging server, the planning issues are not complicated. In larger corporations with multiple locations and the need for multiple Instant Messaging servers, however, the planning issues become more complex.

If you have a small company with fewer than 500 users, you can implement Instant Messaging on the same server as the other Exchange services. Because all clients use a single Instant Messaging server, the name that you provide when you configure the RVP virtual server is the domain name for all users as well as for the home server.

If you have a medium-sized company (500 to 10,000 users) and you plan to provide Instant Messaging only for internal use, you can implement Instant Messaging on a single dedicated server. Again, because you are using only a single server, the domain name and home server name are the same for all users. The single server in this case operates as the home server and the router.

If you are working for a larger corporation, or a corporation that wants to provide Instant Messaging to users outside the internal network, you should use an Instant Messaging router. Corporations with more than 10,000 users must have more than one home server, and all users cannot share a single Instant Messaging domain name unless you implement an Instant Messaging router between the servers. With an Instant Messaging router, the domain name for all users can be based on the DNS name for the router.

If your corporation anticipates having more than 50,000 Instant Messaging users logged on at one time, you must set up multiple Instant Messaging routers. You can configure all routers with the same Instant Messaging domain setting and then use Network Load Balancing or DNS round robin to balance the load across the routers.

If your company plans to make Instant Messaging available on the Internet, you also should use an Instant Messaging router. Make the router the only Instant Messaging server accessible from the Internet; it can relay all client traffic to the home servers. You can set up multiple routers to provide load balancing if many clients connect from the Internet at the same time.

Implementing Instant Messaging

The first step in implementing Instant Messaging is to configure a new Instant Messaging virtual server. To do this, perform the following steps:

1. Open the Exchange System Manager and locate the server that you want to configure as an Instant Messaging home server in the administrative group/Servers container. Expand the server container and the Protocols container.

2. Right-click Instant Messaging (RVP) and choose New/Instant Messaging Virtual Server. The New Instant Messaging Virtual Server wizard starts.

3. Type a display name for the virtual server.

4. Select the Web site to use for Instant Messaging. Unless you have configured an additional HTTP virtual server for Instant Messaging, accept the default selection of the Default Web Site.

5. Type the DNS domain name for the server. (See Figure 12-16.)

    If the server is a home server, the DNS name should be the host name for the computer. All user accounts configured on this server then use this name as part of the home server URL.

If the server is an Instant Messaging router, the DNS name should be the Instant Messaging domain name to which the users connect. If this is not the actual host name for the server, you must configure a host header for the default Web site that points to this host name.

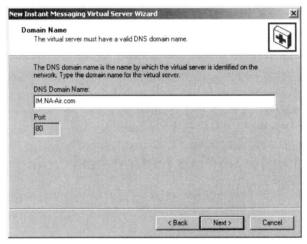

Figure 12-16: Configuring the DNS Domain Name for the Instant Messaging Server.

6. Select the Allow this server to host user accounts option. (See Figure 12-17.)

    By selecting the option to host user accounts on this server, you make this server an Instant Messaging home server. Don't select this option if the server is to be an Instant Messaging router.

    The New Instant Messaging Virtual Server wizard finishes and the new virtual server is created.

    If you are providing Instant Messaging functionality outside your corporate network, you also must configure the firewall settings. To do this, expand the Global Settings container in Exchange System Manager and locate the Instant Messaging Settings object. Right-click this object and choose Properties. Select the Firewall Topology tab. (See Figure 12-18.)

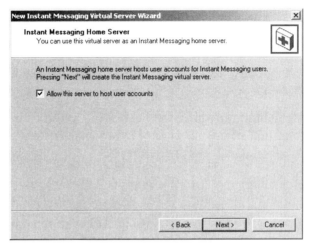

Figure 12-17: Configuring the Instant Messaging Server to Host User Accounts.

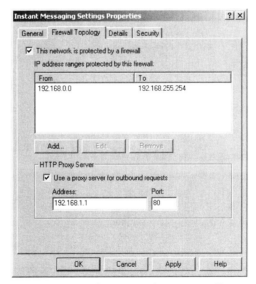

Figure 12-18: Configuring the Firewall Topology for Instant Messaging.

The range of IP addresses defines the internal network. When an Instant Messaging router receives a message from any client from the list of defined addresses, it redirects the client request to the user's home server. When the Instant Messaging router receives any client requests from an IP address outside the defined range, the router acts as a relay between the client and the home server.

You also can define a proxy server to use for all outgoing Instant Messaging traffic.

After you configure the servers and the firewall configuration, the next step is to enable users to use Instant Messaging. To do this, perform the following steps:

1. Open Active Directory Users and Computers and locate the user account that you want to enable for Instant Messaging.

2. Right-click the account and choose Exchange Tasks.

3. Select Enable Instant Messaging.

4. Select the Instant Messaging home server and the Instant Messaging Domain Name. (See Figure 12-19.)

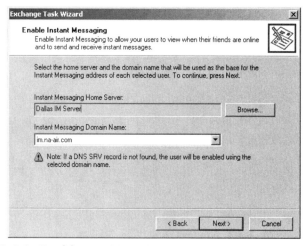

Figure 12-19: Enabling a User Account to Use Instant Messaging.

When you enable a user account for Instant Messaging, the user account receives three Instant Messaging addresses. Figure 12-20 shows the information for a user in the NA-Air.com domain. The domain name for Instant Messaging at North American Air is configured as im.na-air.com, an Instant Messaging Router has been configured with that domain name, and the user's home server is Atlanta-Mail-s1.na-air.com.

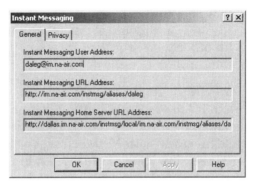

Figure 12-20: Multiple Instant Messaging Related Address Are Assigned to Instant Messaging Enabled Accounts.

Once you have enabled the users for Instant Messaging, you can then distribute and install the Instant Messaging client. Microsoft updates the client frequently, so you should download the latest client from the Microsoft Web site (www.microsoft.com/exchange). After installing the client, you can configure the contact information and begin using Instant Messaging.

Implementing Conferencing Services

Another new technology in Exchange 2000 is Conferencing Services. Instant Messaging is useful for one-to-one conversations containing only text, while Conferencing Services provide a more full-featured conferencing environment. Multiple users can connect to a conference hosted on the Exchange Conferencing Server. The conference can include audio and video information, as well as application sharing, a whiteboard application, a chat program, and a file-transfer program.

> **NOTE:** *Conferencing Server is the only Exchange component that is not included with Exchange Server. Conferencing Server comes on a separate CD-ROM that must be purchased separately and requires a separate installation and administration.*

In some ways, using Exchange 2000 Conferencing Services is similar to running a conference using a client such as Microsoft Net-Meeting. When using NetMeeting, a user can create a meeting and then invite other users to join the meeting. While in the meeting, users can share a whiteboard, share applications, transfer files, and chat with other users. For those users with audio and video equipment, the conference also can include audio and video conferencing.

However, the functionality of meetings hosted with NetMeeting is limited. If the computer hosting the meeting shuts down, or leaves the meeting, the meeting is over. In addition, there is no way to schedule meetings with NetMeeting; you can only join conferences that are in session. One of the biggest limitations with hosting conferences using NetMeeting is network bandwidth. The computer hosting the NetMeeting establishes a unicast session with each of the other computers in the meeting. This means that if six computers join the meeting, the host computer sends the same information to six different IP addresses, each using a unicast session.

Hosting meetings on Conferencing Services addresses all these issues. When the Conferencing Server hosts the meetings, the Conferencing Server uses multicast rather than unicast sessions. This means a significant saving in bandwidth, especially when the meeting includes video conferencing. The Exchange server also becomes the host server for the meeting, so people can leave and enter the meeting without affecting the meeting status. In addition, users can schedule meetings on the Conferencing Server using Outlook clients.

Conferencing Services consists of a number of services and components:

▲ **Conference Management Service.** This server component manages the reservation and scheduling of Conferencing Server online conferences. The Conference Management Service uses two components:

- **Conferencing Resource.** This is a mailbox-enabled account used to reserve and schedule meetings. When a user sets up an online meeting, a conferencing resource also is invited to the meeting, serving as a virtual meeting room for the conference.

- **Conference Calendar Mailbox.** This is a mailbox-enabled account that the Conference Management Service uses as a storage location for information about online conferences format and structure. All scheduled online conference information also is stored in this mailbox.

▲ **Conference Technology Provider.** The Conference Technology Provider server component provides the service that clients use when attending online conferences. Exchange 2000 provides two types of conference technology providers:

- **Data Conferencing service.** This service uses the T-120 standard to deliver online data conferences to clients. The T-120 standard provides the facilities to share applications and whiteboard sessions, chat, and file transfer during the data conference.

- **Video Conferencing service.** This service provides the video conferencing services. By default, video conferencing is configured to use IP multicasting, but Conferencing Server also provides an H.323 Bridge Server for clients that do not support IP multicasting.

▲ **T-120 Multipoint Control Unit (MCU).** Clients attach to this component when they connect to an online meeting. You can install the T-120 MCU component on any Windows 2000 Server with IIS 5.0 installed, even on servers that are not running any other Exchange components.

▲ **H.323 Bridge Server.** The H.323 Bridge Server provides video conferencing for clients that do not support multicasting. If you have clients, such as Windows 9x or Windows NT, that do not support multicasting, they connect to the conferencing bridge, which unicasts the video conference to each client.

▲ **Conference Access Web pages.** These Web pages display when a client connects to the online conference.

▲ **Client applications.** The user must be running a compatible client to connect to Conferencing Server. To connect to a data conference, the user must be running a T.120 client such as NetMeeting. To connect to a video conference, the client must support multicasting (or connect to the H.323 Bridge Server) and then download and install an ActiveX control from the conference server when the client connects for the first time.

You install Exchange 2000 Conferencing Server as a separate installation from Exchange 2000. The computer where you are installing Conferencing Server must run Windows 2000 Server with IIS 5.0. The server can run Exchange 2000 Server, but this is not a requirement. However, you should install the Exchange System Manager if you want to manage the Conferencing Server from this computer. All clients that will join online meetings hosted on the server must be able to connect to the Web server.

When you install Conferencing Server, you can choose the administrative group in which to install it. The first time you install Conferencing Server, you can chose any administrative group in the Windows 2000 site. If a Conferencing Server is already installed in an administrative group in the site, all subsequent installations of Conferencing Servers are placed in the same administrative group.

During the installation of the Conferencing Server, you can choose to do a complete or custom installation. If you choose a custom installation, you can choose which components to install. (See Figure 12-21.)

If this is the first Conferencing Server in the site, you should install all components. Subsequent installations of Conferencing Server in the same site might not require all the components. For example, you might want to install an additional T.120 MCU on a server without installing all the management tools.

Once the Conferencing Server is installed, you can use the Exchange Conferencing Manager or the Exchange System Manager to configure the Conferencing Services.

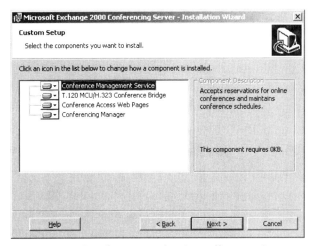

Figure 12-21: Configuring the Installation Options for Conferencing Server.

NOTE: *To configure the Conferencing Services, you must have Exchange Full Administrator rights in the administrative group where the server is installed.*

You must enable Exchange Conferencing before clients can begin using Conferencing Server. To enable Exchange Conferencing, perform the following steps:

1. Open the Exchange Conferencing Manager, right-click Exchange Conferencing, and choose Manage.

   A dialog box appears listing all the Windows 2000 sites where you have administrative permissions.

2. Select the site where you are configuring the conference management.

A warning message appears indicating that there is no Conference Calendar Mailbox designated for the site and asking whether you want to specify the account now.

3. If you have not created a Conference Calendar Mailbox, use this interface to create one.

A Conference Calendar Mailbox dialog box appears. (See Figure 12-22.)

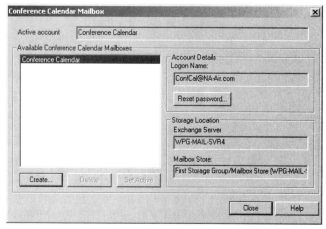

Figure 12-22: Configuring the Conference Calendar Mailbox.

The Conference Calendar Mailbox is required for the Conferencing Server to store the configuration and conference booking information.

4. To create a new Conferencing Calendar Mailbox, click Create and fill in the details for the new mailbox. (See Figure 12-23.)

You can configure the Conference Calendar Mailbox on any Exchange server in the organization. However, you should configure the mailbox on the same server as the Conferencing Server so that the Conferencing Services does not need to connect to the other Exchange server to access the mailbox. When you create the mailbox, a user object is created in Active Directory in the Exchange System Objects/Conferencing container. The object is visible as a mailbox-enabled user in the GAL.

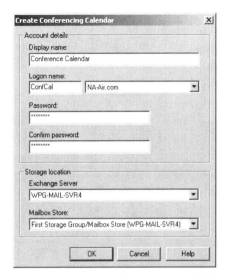

Figure 12-23: Creating a New Conference Calendar Mailbox.

Before any clients can connect to the Conferencing Server, you must configure the site settings. To do this, perform the following steps:

1. To configure the Conferencing settings for the site, right-click the conferencing site and select Properties.

   The General tab displays the Conferencing Host Server and the site conference calendar mailbox. By default the first server installed as a Conferencing Server is the active Conferencing Host Server. This means that it is the only server that is running the Conference Management Service in the site. You can have only one Conferencing Management Service per site. You can change the server, but when you do this the Conference Management Service on the current server becomes inactive.

   You also can change the site Conference Calendar Mailbox, but you lose all information about meetings that have already been booked.

2. Select the Conference Settings tab to configure the default settings for the online conferences. (See Figure 12-24.)

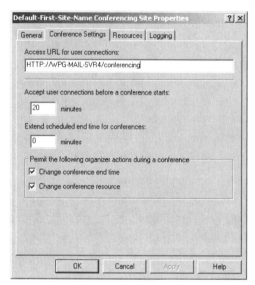

Figure 12-24: Configuring the Conference Settings.

You can configure a different IIS server to host the user connections. By default the access URL is the conferencing virtual directory on the Conferencing Server. If you want to change this to another server, you must create an IIS virtual server for the directory on the other server and then change the URL to point to that server.

You also can configure some conferencing settings on this tab. You can specify when the server begins to accept user connections, whether a conference time is extended beyond the scheduled end of the conference, and whether the conference organizer can extend the conference and change the conference resource during a conference.

3. To configure the conference resources, select the Resources tab. To add additional resources, click Add. (See Figure 12-25.)

The conference resources are virtual rooms that are invited as a resource to each online conference. After you create the conference resource, you specify the type of Conference Technology

Provider for the resource. You can choose Data Conference Provider, or Video Conference Provider, or both.

When you choose one of the providers, you can configure the settings for the data or video conferences. The settings include the number of users that are allowed to connect to the conference (for both data and video conferences) and other video conference-specific settings.

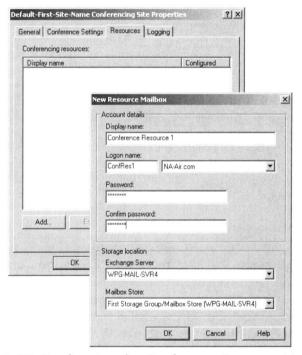

Figure 12-25: Configuring the Conference Resource Mailboxes.

4. Select the Logging tab to configure the level of logging you want to enable for the conferencing service.

Once the server has been configured, the next step is to configure the clients. For clients to book online meetings on the Exchange Conferencing Server, they must be running Outlook 2000 or later. To configure the client, add the following key to the Registry on each client PC. Do not assign any value to the key.

```
HKEY_CURRENT_USER\Software\Microsoft\Office\9.0\Outlo
ok\ExchangeConferencing
```

After making these changes to the Registry, the user can book an online meeting through Outlook 2000 with the regular calendar interface. (See Figure 12-26.)

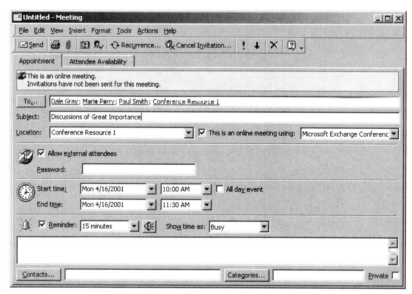

Figure 12-26: Creating an Exchange Conferencing Meeting.

Unlike with a regular meeting request, the This is an online meeting using: Microsoft Exchange Conferencing option is selected and a conferencing resource also is invited to the meeting. The conferencing resource appears as the conference location.

To connect to this meeting, the clients can accept the meeting in Outlook 2000, and then right-click the calendar entry and choose Join Conference. The clients also can connect to the HTTP server identified on the site Conference Settings tab and select the meeting to join. If NetMeeting has not been used before on the client PC, a NetMeeting Configuration wizard appears. After completing the wizard, the user connects to the conferencing site. (See Figure 12-27.)

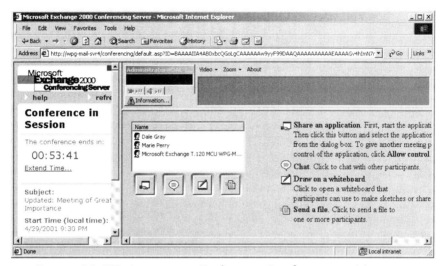

Figure 12-27: Joining an Exchange Conferencing Meeting.

Conclusion

For many organizations, Exchange 2000 will become a center for information exchange that goes well beyond e-mail service. Enhanced features in OWA and improved public-folder administration mean that these services can be used to make more information available to more users. In addition, totally new technologies, such as Instant Messaging and Conferencing Services, provide exciting new ways for users to communicate and collaborate. This chapter provided an overview of these technologies in Exchange 2000.

The next chapter examines another topic that is essential to managing an Exchange 2000 organization: monitoring and maintenance. In this last chapter of the book, I cover the monitoring tools available in Exchange 2000 and look at backup and disaster recovery options.

Chapter 13

Monitoring and Maintaining Exchange 2000

THE LAST ESSENTIAL TASK IN UPGRADING to Exchange 2000 is to develop a workable monitoring and maintenance plan for the servers and connectors. Exchange 2000 provides several utilities to make this task easier. You can use them to monitor the Exchange services on each server in the organization, as well as to monitor the messaging queues on the servers. You also can configure the Exchange server to notify you when things go wrong on the server.

You also must be constantly prepared for failure of some component on a server. A consistent backup regimen is the only protection against a complete failure of a server, so the first step in disaster-recovery planning must be to develop a backup plan.

This chapter details the essential monitoring and maintenance activities for managing an Exchange 2000 organization. The first part of the chapter covers the monitoring tools available, and the second part discusses backup and recovery procedures.

Monitoring the Exchange Organization

To ensure that the Exchange organization is performing optimally, you must monitor the Exchange servers and connectors on an ongoing basis. Monitoring can often detect potential problems before they become critical. For example, if you are monitoring the growth of the SMTP queue and notice that it is growing steadily for 10 minutes, you can determine the cause of the growth of the queue before there are thousands of messages in the queue and users start complaining that messages are not being delivered.

An ongoing monitoring program also can detect performance bottlenecks and performance issues. Data gathered when monitoring the Exchange organization often can be useful for troubleshooting problems. For example, if you set diagnostic logging at a moderate level, the logs created can provide valuable information about what has failed when messages are not delivered.

Effective monitoring of the Exchange organization maintains a balance between having too much information and having too little. If you monitor and log every possible object in the Exchange organization, you won't have enough time to review the data that you collect. If you monitor or log too little data, you might not collect the crucial piece of data that you later need to detect a bottleneck or solve a problem. The best way to deal with this issue is to begin with a fairly high level of monitoring and logging. As you gain experience with your Exchange organization, you can determine what data is important for your organization and focus your monitoring on that data.

Monitoring Server Performance

In Exchange 4.0/5.*x* you can use server monitors to monitor the Exchange services on any Exchange server in the organization. When you set up a server monitor in Exchange 4.0/5.*x*, you can configure which servers you want to monitor and then configure which services to monitor on each server. You also can set up the server monitor to notify an administrator when a service stops on one of the monitored servers. The notification can be delivered as an e-mail message or an alert, or you can define a customized event to be triggered.

> **NOTE:** *One of the configuration options on the Exchange 4.0/5.x server monitor is to restarts services automatically when it detects a service stop. In Exchange 2000, this functionality has been moved into Windows 2000. Using the Services administration tool, you can set any Windows 2000 service to automatically restart, reboot the server, or execute a program when the service stops.*

Exchange 2000 provides a similar tool to the Exchange 4.0/5.x server monitor It's located in the Monitoring and Status container, which is in the Tools container in Exchange System Manager. The Monitoring and Status container contains two subcontainers: Notifications and Status. Figure 13-1 shows the interface.

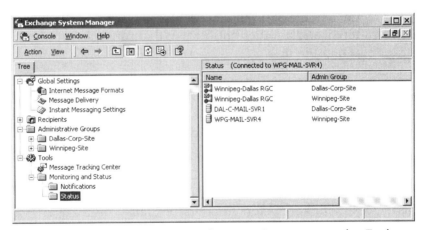

Figure 13-1: The Monitoring and Status Container in the Exchange System Manager.

The monitoring of the Exchange organization is configured in both the Notifications and the Status containers. In the Status container, you can configure a variety of objects to be monitored in the Exchange organization. By default, the Exchange services on all of the servers in the organization are monitored, as well as the connectors. You can configure the monitoring to include additional objects, such as monitoring the growth of the SMTP queues or monitoring the remaining hard disk space. For each of the monitored objects, you can set a warning level and a critical level. These are threshold levels.

When one of the monitored objects reaches the level that you configure as the warning level, the computer registers a warning state and then performs a defined action. For example, you can monitor the amount of available hard disk space on the Exchange server. You can configure the service to register a warning when the disk space drops below a specified number and then e-mail you with the warning message. When the space decreases further, to the critical level you specify, the service can register a critical state and then run a script.

The objects in the Status container define what objects you want to monitor. In the Notifications container, you can define what happens when a warning or critical state is reached. You can configure a notification that sends e-mail when a warning state is registered, and another notification that runs a script when a critical state is registered.

By default, the Status container lists all servers and connectors in the entire organization. To limit the servers or connectors that appear in the list, right-click the Status container and choose Custom Filter. Select only those servers and connectors that you want to monitor. For example, in a large organization, your only monitoring responsibility might be to monitor the connectors. By configuring the filter, you can display only the connectors, and not all the servers.

The connectors listed in the Status container are monitored automatically and appear as either Available or Unavailable. No additional information is provided about the connectors.

All the servers also appear in the Status Container. To manage what components are monitored on a server, right-click the server name and choose Properties. Some of the Microsoft Exchange services and the World Wide Web Publishing Service are monitored by default on every server. (See Figure 13-2.)

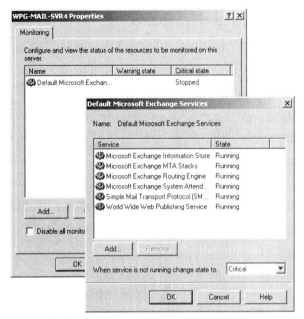

Figure 13-2: The Default Monitoring Configuration for Exchange 2000 Servers.

You might want to use Disable all monitoring of this server when you are troubleshooting a server problem and you know that you will be stopping and restarting the services. To avoid triggering the notifications that would normally be triggered when a service stops, you can disable monitoring temporarily. While monitoring is disabled, the server status appears as In maintenance mode in the Status container.

When a service stops, the state for the service changes to Critical by default. You can modify this setting so that when the service stops, the state changes to Warning. You cannot set individual services differently; changing the setting for one service makes the same change for all.

You also can monitor additional services by clicking Add and choosing from a list of all Windows 2000 Services running on the server. You should add any other critical services that are running on the server. For example, if this server functions as POP3 or IMAP4 server, add these Exchange services to the monitored list. If the monitored server is also a DNS server, monitor the DNS Server service as well.

You also can add new resources to the monitored list on the Monitoring tab. To monitor additional resources, select Add from Monitoring tab, and then select a resource from the Add Resource box, shown in Figure 13-3.

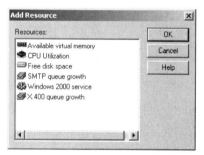

Figure 13-3: Adding New Resources to Monitor.

In Exchange environments, you should monitor several additional resources. For example, because of the increased importance of SMTP in Exchange 2000, monitoring the SMTP queue growth on your servers is also essential. If an SMTP queue grows continuously for several minutes, one of the SMTP connectors might not be functioning. To add the SMTP queue growth resource to the monitored list, select the object and then click OK. Then configure the thresholds that you want to monitor, as shown in Figure 13-4.

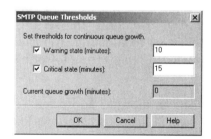

Figure 13-4: Configuring the SMTP Queue Thresholds.

You can configure the thresholds for the monitor to register a warning state and a critical state. The actual numbers that you choose depend on the server that you are monitoring and the topology of your Exchange organization.

If the monitored server is a member of a routing group and does not function as a bridgehead server for any routing group or SMTP connector, the queue should not grow for more than five to ten minutes or so. On this server, configure the queue growth numbers at a low level, such as a warning state after 10 minutes and a critical state after 15 minutes.

If this server operates as a bridgehead server for a routing group or SMTP connector, set the numbers at a higher level. If the connector activates according to a schedule, make sure that you take the schedule into account when configuring the queue growth thresholds. To determine the best threshold numbers for your organizations, choose a number that you think is accurate and then monitor the notifications. If you start receiving many notifications when there are no problems with the connectors, increase the number. If you set the number too high, you might have hundreds of messages in the queue before find out that a problem exists.

The other resources that you can add to the monitoring list are outlined in Table 13-1.

Table 13-1: Configuring Additional Resources to Monitor

Resource	Threshold Settings
Available virtual memory	The length of time that the available virtual memory can fall below the defined thresholds before entering a warning or critical state (minutes). The minimum virtual memory that must be available before entering a warning or critical state (percent).
CPU utilization	The length of time that the CPU utilization must exceed the defined thresholds before entering a warning or critical state (minutes). The maximum CPU utilization before entering a warning or critical state (percent).

Table 13-1: Configuring Additional Resources to Monitor (Continued)

Resource	Threshold Settings
Free disk space	The drive(s) to be monitored (based on the logical drives on the server). The minimum drive space that must be available before entering a warning or critical state (MB).
Windows 2000 service	The additional Windows 2000 services to be monitored on the Exchange servers. You can monitor any services on the Windows 2000 server either using this option or by adding the service to the default list of monitored services. Use this option if you want to configure a different response when a service stops. For example, you might want to register a critical state when the Exchange services stop, but only a warning state if the DNS service stops. The only way to configure this is to add the DNS service as an additional resource and configure it to enter a warning state when it stops.
X.400 queue growth	The length of time the queue can continue to grow before entering a warning or critical state.

NOTE: *Exchange 4.0/5.x provides a link monitor that monitors the connections between servers within the organization and between the organization and the external mail servers. Exchange 2000 does not provide an equivalent service. The only way to monitor connectivity with other servers and organizations is to monitor the growth of the queues and then troubleshoot the connectors when they reach the queue growth threshold.*

Configuring Notifications

After you configure the services and objects to monitor, the next step is to configure the notifications. Exchange 2000 supports two types of notifications: e-mail or script. To configure the notifications, perform the following steps:

1. Right-click the Notifications container, choose New, and select either E-mail notification or Script notification.

If you select E-mail notification, the dialog box shown in Figure 13-5 appears.

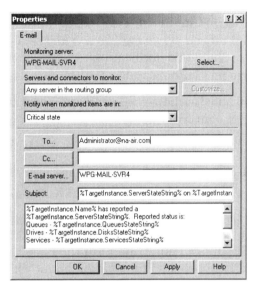

Figure 13-5: Configuring an E-mail Notification.

2. Chose a monitoring server.

   The monitoring server is the server that monitors whether the server(s) or connector(s) are in a warning or critical state. If you have more than one server in a location, configure the servers to monitor each other. That's because if a server's Exchange services stop, it cannot send mail to the designated mailbox. You also can install Exchange System Manager on a separate computer that is not running Exchange and use this computer to monitor the Exchange servers.

3. Choose the servers or connectors you want to monitor.

   You can choose to monitor all servers, the server that you are configuring, all servers in the routing group, or a selected list of servers. You also can choose to monitor all connectors, all connectors in a routing group, or a selected list of connectors. You cannot configure one notification to monitor both servers and connectors. To monitor both servers and connectors, configure multiple notifications.

4. Specify whether this notification notifies the recipient when the monitored servers are in a critical state or warning state. If you are using this notification to monitor connectors, the notification triggers automatically when a connector enters a Down state.

5. Specify to whom the notification is to be sent. You can choose any recipient from the GAL.

6. Configure which e-mail server sends the notifications.

   If you select one of the Exchange servers in the organization, you can browse the list of all servers by clicking E-mail server. You also can type the fully qualified domain name of any SMTP available server.

   The subject and content of the message are configured automatically to provide information about which server has entered the warning or critical state and what resource triggered the event. You can change the message if you want.

The second type of notification you can choose is to run a script. To do this, follow this procedure.

1. Right-click the Notifications container, choose New, and select Script notification The dialog box shown in Figure 13-6 appears.

2. Configure the monitoring server, which server(s) or connectors to monitor, and what event triggers the notification. These options are all the same as for e-mail notification.

3. Enter the path to executable and the command-line options.

   The path to executable points to the script that runs when this notification is triggered, and the command-line options list any command-line switches to use when the script runs.

You can use the monitoring and notification tools in Exchange 2000 for monitoring Exchange servers as well as message queues. These tools free you from monitoring the servers individually because you can quickly receive a message when one of the services fails or one of the queues on the server grows continually.

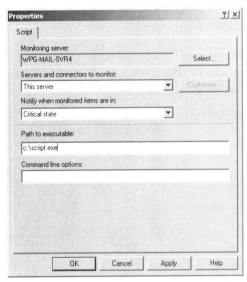

Figure 13-6: Configuring a Script Notification.

NOTE: *In addition to the monitoring and notification tools provided with Exchange 2000, you can also use third-party tools to alert you when the Exchange services fail. A popular option is to install a pager gateway that can call a pager when a critical state occurs on the servers.*

Configuring Diagnostic Logging

You also can configure Exchange 2000 to perform detailed diagnostic logging on many of the server processes and protocol events. The notifications and status information discussed in the previous section can alert you that a problem exists, but they do not provide much help in determining the exact cause of the problem. For example, the SMTP queue growth may display a critical state, indicating that the queue has been growing for several minutes, but it does not tell you *why* the queue is growing. Diagnostic logging can help you determine why the service has entered the warning or critical state.

You also can use diagnostic logging to collect advance information about potential problems on the Exchange server. By monitoring the Exchange services for warning messages, you can sometimes get advance notice of a problem that may be developing before it becomes a major problem.

To configure diagnostic logging on a server, access the server properties in the Exchange System Manager and select the Diagnostics Logging tab. (See Figure 13-7.)

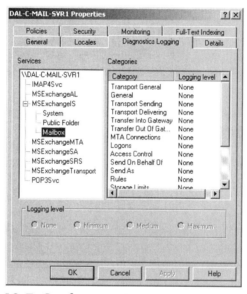

Figure 13-7: Configuring Diagnostic Logging on the Exchange Server.

To configure the diagnostic logging, select the service that you want to log within the Services box, and then select the category in the Categories box. After selecting the category, select the logging level for the category.

NOTE: *In addition to the services shown in Figure 13-7, other options, such as monitoring Lotus Notes Connector, MS Mail Connector, Directory Synchronization, and so on, also are available on the server if the server is running these services.*

You can choose one of four logging levels:

▲ **None.** Only error messages are logged.

▲ **Minimum.** Error and warning messages are logged.

▲ **Medium.** Error, warning, and informational messages are logged.

▲ **Maximum.** Error, warning, informational, and troubleshooting messages are logged.

If you choose a high level (Medium or Maximum), the event logs fill up rapidly and you might not have time to examine all the information. Minimum is an appropriate level for most of the counters because the resulting event log is smaller and easier to work with. Setting the logging at Maximum is useful when troubleshooting a difficult problem, but you should lower the logging level after solving the problem.

The SMTP, HTTP, and NNTP services do not appear in the list for diagnostic logging. To configure logging for these services, you must enable logging on the virtual servers for these protocols (in Exchange System Manager for SMTP and NNTP, and in Internet Services Manager for HTTP). (See Figure 13-8.)

To configure the logging of these protocols, right-click the virtual server and choose Properties. The option to enable logging is on the General tab. You also can select the type of logging to use:

▲ **NCSA Common Log File Format.** Logs a fixed set of values for the virtual server. This format logs the least amount of information.

▲ **Microsoft IIS Log File Format.** Logs a fixed set of values for the virtual server. This format provides more information than the NCSA Common Log File Format.

▲ **ODBC Logging.** Logs a fixed set of values and writes the information to any ODBC data source. The Online Help in Internet Services Manager provides the details of the table that you have to create on the ODBC data source.

▲ **W3C Extended Log File Format.** Logs the greatest amount of information. This is the only log file format in which you can configure what information to log.

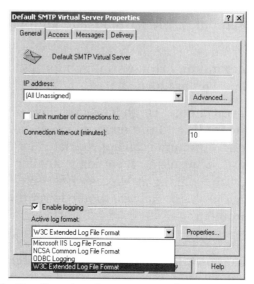

Figure 13-8: Configuring Logging on the SMTP Virtual Server.

To configure more advanced settings for the logs (when W3C Extended Log File Format is selected), click the Properties button and make your selections in the Extended Logging Properties box shown in Figure 13-9.

You can specify how frequently a new log is created and choose the storage location for the log files. If you are using W3C Extended Log File Format, you also can configure precisely what extended properties you want to log on this server.

On a busy server, logging all information on the SMTP server results in very large log files. Again, configure detailed logging only for troubleshooting purposes.

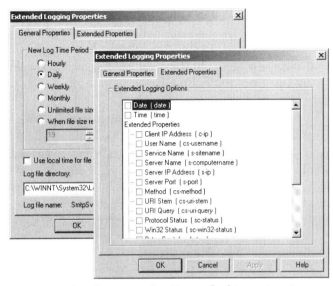

Figure 13-9: Configuring the Extended Logging Properties.

Monitoring Message Flow

Another useful troubleshooting and monitoring tool in Exchange 2000 is the Message Tracking Center. This tool is similar to messaging tracking in Exchange 4.0/5.x. The Message Tracking Center enables you to trace the path of a message through the Exchange organization, often determining exactly where the delivery failed. When you know where the message delivery failed, you know where to begin troubleshooting.

Message tracking is also useful when dealing with user complaints about nondelivered or delayed messages. By tracking the message, you can determine exactly when the message was sent (or *if* it was sent) and identify the reason why the message was not delivered.

Before you can track messages through the organization, you must enable message tracking on all the Exchange servers. In Exchange 4.0/5.x, you have several locations in which you must configure message tracking, including the MTA and connectors. In

Exchange 2000, you can enable all message tracking on the server object in Exchange System Manager.

To enable message tracking in Exchange 2000, access the server property pages. On the General tab, select the Enable message tracking option. (See Figure 13-10.)

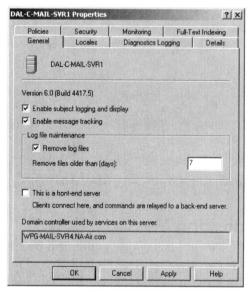

Figure 13-10: Configuring Messaging Tracking on an Exchange Server.

When you enable message tracking, the server logs all messages that are sent through it. Selecting Enable subject logging and display turns on message subject logging as well, which helps when you want to track messages through the organization.

You also can configure how long the server retains message tracking logs. The default setting of seven days is appropriate in most cases. If you are low on hard disk space, you might choose a lower number. If you find that you need to track messages more than a week old, you might increase this number.

Because message tracking is such a useful tool, you should enable it on all your servers. The easiest way is to create a server system policy that enables message tracking and sets the log retention limits, and then apply this system policy to all servers in the organization. Enabling message tracking on all servers in the organization can result in a slight decrease in performance on busy servers because of the additional logging. In most cases, however, the value of message tracking outweighs the small performance decrease.

Once you have enabled the message tracking on the servers, you can use the Message Tracking Center to track messages throughout the organization. To track a message, perform the following steps:

1. Expand the Tools container in the Exchange System Manager, right-click Message Tracking Center, and choose Track Message. The Message Tracking Center screen appears. (See Figure 13-11.)

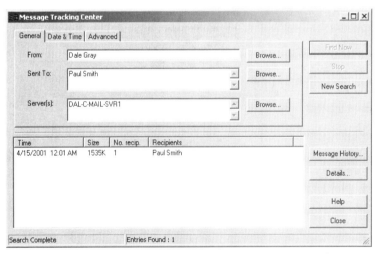

Figure 13-11: Tracking a Message in the Message Tracking Center.

2. Select the criteria you want to use when tracking the message.

    You can select a number of criteria, including the sender and the recipient. When you select a sender, the sender's home server name is automatically inserted in the Server(s) box.

3. Select the Date & Time tab or the Advanced tab to configure other tracking criteria.

On the Date & Time tab you can specify a date, or range of dates, for which you want to search. You can use the Advanced tab to track a message using the message ID, if you know it. To locate the ID of a particular message, examine the properties of the message using a mail client.

4. After selecting the criteria for the search, click Find Now.

The program searches the message tracking logs for all selected servers, and all the messages meeting the criteria listed in the bottom window. To view the message tracking, select a message and then click Message History. The message details appear as well as the entire path that the message took through the organization. From the message history, you can determine exactly where the message went and where it could not be delivered. See Figure 13-12.

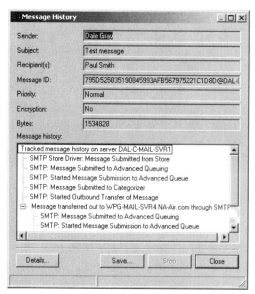

Figure 13-12: Viewing the Message History for a Tracked Message.

Message tracking can be a useful tool for troubleshooting and monitoring your Exchange organization. This is especially true if you have a large organization with multiple routing groups and multiple connectors. By tracking messages being sent between routing groups, you can monitor what routes messages are taking. You also can track undelivered messages.

> **NOTE:** *In addition to the Exchange 2000 tools for monitoring the Exchange server, Windows 2000 also includes several tools that you can use to monitor the Exchange server. Two of the most useful are the Event Viewer and System Monitor. The Event Viewer displays the event logs. The warning and error messages that Exchange 2000 generates appear in the Application log. The System Monitor provides a graphical view of the server performance and can also be configured to log server performance. Almost all Exchange services add performance counters to the counters available in System Monitor.*

Monitoring the North American Air Exchange Organization

The project team at North American Air implemented all of the monitoring options as part of the Exchange 2000 migration. The monitoring of the servers and connectors in the organization is configured as follows.

For monitoring and notification:

▲ The team has enabled monitoring on all Exchange servers. They have maintained the default monitoring settings of the crucial Exchange services on all servers and also added monitoring for virtual memory, CPU utilization, and free disk space. The actual settings for the servers vary depending on the server role. For example, on a mailbox server at the corporate location, the transaction logs grow quickly. Therefore, they have set the warning levels for the hard disks containing the transaction logs to 25 percent free space to provide early warning as the disks fill up.

▲ The team has enabled monitoring for the growth of the SMTP queue on all servers. For servers that do not operate as routing group connector bridgehead servers, they have set the warning level for the growth of the SMTP queue at 10 minutes, with the critical level at 15 minutes. For servers that are operating as bridgehead servers, they have set the warning level at 20 minutes and the critical level at 30 minutes.

▲ They have specified that when any warning state is reached on the server, the local Exchange administrators group receives an e-mail message indicating the problem. When a bridgehead server's SMTP queue reaches a warning state, both the local administrative group and the corporate routing group administrators receive e-mail notification. Two servers are set up for monitoring so that if one server fails, the other server can alert the administrators.

For diagnostic logging:

▲ The team members have set diagnostic logging on all Exchange servers at a warning level, so that only errors and warnings are logged. They will increase the level of diagnostic logging for troubleshooting purposes on an as-needed basis.

▲ The local administrators at each location are responsible for monitoring the log files that diagnostic logging creates. The local administrators also are responsible for resolving the problems identified by error and warning message logs.

For message tracking:

▲ The team has enabled message tracking on every server in the entire organization by using a server system policy and applying the policy to all servers. The message tracking logs are set to be retained for seven days on all servers.

▲ Administrators use message tracking primarily as a troubleshooting tool. Exchange administrators initiate message tracking when a user contacts them with a complaint about a nondelivered message.

▲ The local administrators at each location are responsible for tracking any messages sent between recipients in their location.

▲ The group of Exchange administrators responsible for managing the routing groups and routing group connectors are responsible for tracking messages between company locations. These administrators also use message tracking as a monitoring tool by regularly sending and then tracking messages between company locations.

Maintaining the Exchange Organization

One of the most important components of Exchange Server management is to implement a consistent and comprehensive backup and restore plan. It is almost inevitable that at some point a hard disk on your server will fail, and the only copy of your Exchange databases might be on a backup tape. If you have been adhering to a well-designed backup regimen, you can recover the databases fairly quickly.

Understanding Exchange Database Design

To understand how the backup and restore operations work in Exchange 2000, you must first understand how the Exchange databases are designed.

For the most part, the Exchange 2000 database design is similar to that of Exchange 5.*x* databases. While the underlying technology has not changed a great deal, there are some significant changes when dealing with backup and restore issues. In Exchange 2000, you can have multiple storage groups and stores on a single server. This means that you have more flexibility in your backup and restore procedures. In addition, the Exchange database in Exchange 2000 consists of two files: a Microsoft Exchange format (.edb) file and a streaming (.stm) file. Because these two files make up the database, you almost always work with both files at the same time for backup and restore. Another change is that Exchange 2000 uses Active Directory as its directory service, so you no longer have to back up the Exchange directory database. However, backing up Active Directory must be part of your backup strategy.

Exchange Databases
Each Exchange database is made up of two files. The first is an .edb file, which stores rich-text messages received from MAPI and X.400 connections. The second is an .stm file, which stores messages

received from Internet protocol connections. The messages, which could include text or multimedia content, are stored as streams of MIME data in the .stm file, rather than converting the data to the Exchange database format when the message is received. Each file consists of 4KB pages, and each database can contain up to 2^{32} pages, for a total storage space of 16 terabytes.

Each page in the database includes a header that takes up the first 82 bytes of the page. The header contains information about the page, including the type of page, the kind of data on the page, a page number, and a checksum. The checksum is used to ensure the integrity of the data on the page. When Exchange writes a page to the database, it calculates the checksum and writes it to the page header. When Exchange reads the page from the database, it recalculates the checksum and compares it to the checksum in the header. If the checksums do not match, the page has been damaged. When Exchange detects damage, it unmounts the database and writes an error to the event log. In some cases, the database utilities described later can fix the error; in other cases, you must restore the database from backup.

Each database receives a GUID at its creation. The GUID for the database is the same for both the .edb file and the .stm file, and is stored as part of the database as well as in Active Directory. The GUID for the database must match the GUID for the database in Active Directory, or the database does not mount. Each mailbox on the server also is assigned a GUID. When a user in Active Directory is linked to a mailbox on the Exchange server, one of the attributes on the Active Directory object identifies the GUID for the mailbox.

Other Exchange Data Files
In addition to the Exchange databases, the Exchange server uses a number of other files to provide performance and recoverability for the databases.

Transaction Log Files Whenever an Exchange database changes (for example, when a new message is received or deleted), the change is first written to a transaction log file and then to the database. Transaction logs improve the performance of the server and provide improved recoverability in the event of an unexpected server shutdown or hard disk failure.

Exchange 2000 uses a transaction-based database system in which every change to the database is considered a transaction. A single transaction can consist of several steps. For example, when a message arrives on the Exchange server from an SMTP connection, the message is written to the .stm file. The message header also is written to the .edb file, so that when a user connects to the Exchange server using a MAPI client, the message header appears in the client. For the transaction to be complete, both steps must finish. If one step fails, the transaction is rolled back so that neither step completes. When all steps in a transaction have completed, the transaction is written to the transaction log and then committed to the database.

When a message arrives at an Exchange server, the message is written first to the transaction log. Because a transaction log is essentially a flat file in which the changes to the database are written sequentially, writing to a transaction log is fast. Writing data to the database is much slower. When the data is written to the database, the server must first search for a page in the database on which the information is to be written, and then must read the database page into memory, make the changes to the page, and then write the page back to the database.

The transaction log provides recoverability if the server shuts down unexpectedly while some of the transactions have not yet been written to the database. When the Exchange server restarts, the Extensible Storage Engine (ESE) examines the state of the database and the transaction logs and detects any changes listed in the transaction logs that have not yet been written to the database. It then writes these changes to the database. The transaction logs also provide recoverability if the hard disk storing the database fails. After restoring the database from the most recent backup and restarting the information store, the ESE again examines the database and reapplies all the transaction logs.

To provide this recoverability, you must ensure that the server is *not* using circular logging for the transaction logs, so that all the transactions since the last backup are stored in the transaction logs.

When circular logging is disabled, the transaction logs accumulate on the server until they are removed by performing a backup. In contrast, when the server is configured to use circular logging, a limited number of transaction logs are created and reused repeatedly. While this saves on hard disk space, it makes it impossible to recover the database beyond the last backup because most of the transaction logs have been overwritten.

> *NOTE: In Exchange 5.x, circular logging was enabled for all Exchange databases. In Exchange 2000, circular logging is disabled by default. The only time to ever enable circular logging is if you have limited hard disk space, or you are not concerned about recoverability. For example, if you are using the Exchange NNTP server to accept news feeds from USENET newsgroup servers, and you can recover the messages from the USENET servers, you can turn on circular logging for the storage group that contains the news feeds. Because circular logging is configured at the storage group level, you must make sure that no stores that require recoverability are located in the storage group.*

To make use of the recoverability provided by the transaction logs in the event of a hard disk failure, you must store the transaction logs on a hard disk that is separate from the database files. If both the transaction logs and databases are on the same hard disk and that hard disk fails, you can recover the database only up to the point of the last good backup.

All databases in a storage group share one set of transaction logs. Each transaction log file is always exactly 5,242,880 bytes (5MB) in size. If the transaction log file is any other size, it is corrupt. The transaction log files that the Exchange server uses are incrementally numbered. The current transaction log for the first storage group is E00.log. Current transaction logs for additional storage groups are incremented by one (E01.log, E02.log, and so on). As the current log file fills up, it is renamed to E*yyxxxxx*.log (where E is a constant, *yy* is the log file name and xxxxx is a hexadecimal number.) As additional transaction logs are filled up, the hexadecimal number for the used transaction logs increments by one for each new file.

Checkpoint File   The Exchange server uses a checkpoint file to keep track of which transactions in the transaction logs have been written to the database. The checkpoint file operates as a pointer. As the transactions in the transaction logs are written to the database, the checkpoint file indicates which transactions have been committed to the database. The checkpoint file is named E00.chk, (the number increments for each storage group) and resides in the same folder as the log files.

When the server shuts down unexpectedly and restarts, the ESE uses the checkpoint file to determine which transactions in the transaction logs have been written to the database. If the checkpoint file is missing or corrupted, the ESE reads all the transaction logs and determines which transactions have not been written to the database. If the checkpoint file is available, this process is much quicker.

Reserved Files   The ESE for each storage group creates two reserved log files, res1.log and res2.log, when the storage group is created. It uses these files only when the hard disk containing the transaction logs runs out of space. When the ESE fills up one transaction log, it renames it and then creates a new E00.log. If the hard disk does not have enough space to create the new transaction log, all uncommitted transactions stored in the server's memory are written to the reserved logs, and the Exchange services are shut down to prevent the server from receiving any more transactions until more space is available on the hard disk.

Patch Files   Patch files are created only during an online backup of the Exchange databases. Because users can access the database while the backup is running, changes to the database can occur during the backup. When the backup starts, it creates a patch file for each store. If a user makes a change to a part of the database that has already been backed up, the backup process does not back up the change. Instead, it writes the change to the transaction logs and the patch file. At the end of the backup, it writes the patch file to the backup tape.

When you restore a database from an online backup, the restore process uses the patch file to restore any changes made to the database during the online backup.

Using the Database Utilities

Exchange 2000 supports many of the same database tools as Exchange 5.*x*. Some of the tools have been modified, however, because of the different database options available in Exchange 2000.

Online Defragmentation

Like Exchange 4.0/5.*x*, Exchange 2000 supports both online and offline defragmentation. Online defragmentation runs while the Exchange databases are mounted, while you must dismount the databases to perform an offline defragmentation. Online defragmentation is enabled by default on all Exchange 2000 databases. During online defragmentation, the utility scans entire database and removes any objects that are no longer in use, such as deleted messages and mailboxes. The utility also reorders the information on the database pages for more efficient storage. For example, if a user has deleted several messages from his mailbox, the utility makes the space taken up by these messages available and moves other messages into the space. The online defragmentation process moves data between database pages, but does not decrease the overall database size. Online defragmentation might create a number of empty pages in the database if many messages have been deleted, but the space used for the database is not released. As new messages arrive in the information store, the blank pages can be reused.

Online defragmentation runs every night at midnight by default. You can access the store properties to specify when online defragmentation occurs.

Offline Defragmentation

With offline defragmentation, you can reduce the size of the database. You should use offline defragmentation only when you have decreased the database size for some reason. For example, you might have moved some mailboxes from one Exchange server to another, or you may have decreased the storage limits on the Exchange server and forced everyone to delete a large number of messages. Offline defragmentation should not be a regular part of database maintenance in Exchange 2000 because the online defragmentation is efficient in reclaiming the database space under normal circumstances.

The Extensible Storage Engine Utility (ESEUTIL) performs offline defragmentation. To use the ESEUTIL, you must first dismount the database to be defragmented. When you run the offline defragmentation, ESEUTIL creates a new copy of the database and then copies all of the data from the original database to the new one. It discards any blank pages during this process, decreasing the database size if possible. After copying the entire database to the temporary database, ESEUTIL renames the temporary database to the original database's name and deletes the original database. (You can change this default behavior and retain the original database, as well as use a temporary database on a different drive, with command line switches. I cover these in detail in the following section.)

Performing an offline defragmentation assigns a new signature to the database. Because this signature identifies the transaction logs that belong with each database, you can't use the existing transaction logs with the new database. When the information store restarts after the offline defragmentation, a new set of transaction logs is created for the storage group. Before performing an offline defragmentation, back up the database and transaction logs so that you can recover the data if the offline defragmentation fails.

ESEUTIL

ESEUTIL is a command line database utility that can perform a variety of diagnostic and repair tasks on the Exchange database. ESEUTIL is a powerful tool, but also a potentially dangerous tool, especially when using the recovery operation in which some pages of the database may be deleted from the database. You should use ESEUTIL only under exceptional circumstance, such as when the database has been corrupted, not for any kind of routine maintenance.

ESEUTIL operates at a database page level, not at an individual mailbox or message level. This means that ESEUTIL can repair connections between pages or tables but not individual damaged messages. Table 13-2 lists the switches available with ESEUTIL.

NOTE: *Both ESEUTIL and ISINTEG are located in the C:\Program Files\Exchsrvr\Bin directory.*

Table 13-2: ESEUTIL Operations in Exchange 2000

Operation	Switch	Explanation

Defragmentation	/d	Performs an offline defragmentation of the Exchange databases. Before running the offline defragmentation, you must dismount the store in Exchange System Manager. You must provide the name of the database that you are defragmenting. For example, to defragment the Priv1.edb file, use the command
		
		`Eseutil /d path\priv1.edb`
		
		Since offline defragmentation makes a temporary copy of the database, there must be at least as much free space on the drive as the size of the database. If the drive containing the database does not have enough space, you can specify an alternative location for the temporary database using the following command.
		
		`Eseutil /d path\priv1.edb /t`
		`    path\temporaryfilename.edb`
		
		When you defragment the .edb file, the .stm file is automatically defragmented as well.

Recovery	/r	Repairs links between database tables. If the recovery process can detect and repair errors it does so, but it does not delete any pages or tables.
Integrity	/g	Verifies the database integrity. The integrity checker does not make any changes to the database; it only checks the database consistency. If it finds any inconsistency, it reports the error but does not fix it.

Table 13-2: ESEUTIL Operations in Exchange 2000 (Continued)

Operation	Switch	Explanation
File dump	/m	Prints the header or file contents for a database, checkpoint, or log file.
Repair	/p	Attempts to repair the errors in database pages. If the recovery process cannot repair a page completely, it deletes the page from the database. This means that you run the risk of losing data when running ESEUTIL in repair mode. You should use this mode only as a last resort.
Restore	/c	Manually applies the temporary transaction logs created when you restore one of the stores from a backup tape.

NOTE: *Each of the operations listed in Table 13-2 includes a number of options and switches. To see the full list of options and switches, open a command prompt, go to the Program Files\Exchsrvr\Bin folder, and type* Eseutil /?. *Then choose which of the operations on which you would like more information.*

ESEUTIL in Exchange 2000 works much the same way as in Exchange 5.*x*, with a couple of exceptions. One is that in Exchange 5.*x* you can use the switches /ispriv (private information store), /ispub (public information store), and /ds (directory database) when running some of the operations. When you use these switches, ESEUTIL determines the location of these stores and runs the operation. Because Exchange 2000 supports multiple information stores, however, you must specify the actual name of the database that you are working with in the Exchange 2000 version of ESEUTIL. If the database is in a different folder than the ESEUTIL files, you must specify the entire path to the database.

Information Store Integrity Checker (ISINTEG)

A second database utility provided with Exchange 2000 is ISINTEG, which tests the database for inconsistencies. In contrast to ESEUTIL, ISINTEG operates on message and folder level in the information store rather than the database pages and tables. To run the ISINTEG command, you must first dismount the store that you want to check. Table 13-3 lists the command line switches for ISINTEG.

Table 13-3: Command Line Switches for ISINTEG

Command Line Switch	Meaning
-s	Defines the server name where you want to run the command. The syntax for this command is: `Isinteg -s servername -fix -test testname(s)`
-fix	Configures ISINTEG to fix any errors it identifies in the database. The default mode is to check the database, but not repair any errors.
-verbose	Provides detailed information of the checking process.
-l filename	Indicates the log file for the utility output. The default file names are Isinteg.pri or Isinteg.pub, which are created in the same folder as the database.
- t tempdbname	Indicates the location of the temporary database that ISINTEG creates during the checking process. The default location is the same folder as the current database.
-test testname	Specifies which database tests the utility runs. There are 32 tests available. If you want to run all the tests at once, you can use Alltests as the test name. Running all of the tests on a large database can take several hours.

NOTE: *In Exchange 5.x, one of the main uses for ISINTEG is to repair a database after a restore from an offline backup. The syntax for this usage is ISINTEG –patch. This switch is no longer available in Exchange 2000. Instead the information store process automatically repairs the database when it detects an offline database restore during a service restart.*

Backing Up Exchange Servers

The databases on the Exchange servers in your organization probably contain some of the most valuable data in your company. If you ever irretrievably lost that data, the entire company might be at risk.

Therefore a thoughtfully planned and conscientiously followed backup regimen is an absolute must.

NOTE: In most cases, you have more time to do a backup than you have to do a restore. For most companies, a backup that runs for 4 or 5 hours every night is acceptable. However, taking 4 or 5 hours to restore a server in the middle of the working day is probably not acceptable. When designing a backup strategy, make sure that you devise an optimal restore strategy and disaster recovery strategy.

Backup Planning

The first and most important element in being able to recover the data in case of a server failure is a well-designed and well-implemented backup program. Most of the basic concepts in backing up Exchange 2000 have not changed a great deal from Exchange 5.*x*. However, there are two significant changes.

First, just backing up the Exchange configuration and databases is no longer sufficient in Exchange 2000. Because of the tight integration of Exchange with Active Directory and IIS, both of these components also must be backed up. To back up these components, you must back up the system state data in Windows 2000. The system state data includes all configuration information for the computer. In addition, for any server running IIS, the system state data includes the IIS metabase, which is the IIS configuration information. When you back up the system state data on a domain controller, the backup also includes the Active Directory database as well as the complete configuration of the computer.

This means that the regular backup procedures in Exchange 2000 must include complete backups of all domain controllers and system state data on the Exchange servers. The system state data must be backed up and restored as a single unit in Windows 2000. When you restore the system state data on a computer, it overwrites all the system state data on the computer.

NOTE: Most medium to large organizations use an enterprise backup solution that can back up multiple servers across a network using a single backup server. As you implement Windows 2000 and

Exchange 2000, you must upgrade the backup application to be able to back up the system state data on all the servers. In addition, some backup applications restore the system state data only if the backup server is running Windows 2000.

A second difference when planning for backup in Exchange 2000 is that you can now back up and restore individual stores on the server. In most cases, this does not affect the backup procedures because you back up the Exchange server by backing up entire storage groups at a time. If you do decide to back up individual stores, each backup must include all the transaction logs, and the transaction logs are not flushed until the last store is backed up. You can back up multiple storage groups either sequentially or in parallel. If you have a tape library system with which you can write to multiple tapes at once with multiple backup jobs, you can back up all the storage groups on the server at once.

When backing up the Exchange 2000 server, you have the same options that you have when doing any other backup. Table 13-4 summarizes the options.

Table 13-4: Backup Option with Exchange 2000

Backup Type	Explanation
Full backup	Backs up all Exchange databases and transaction logs that contain committed transactions. Deletes the transaction logs after backup. Only one tape is needed to do a complete restore, so this is the best backup option if you have the time and tape capacity.
Copy backup	Backs up all the Exchange databases and transaction logs that contain committed transactions. Does not delete the transaction logs after backup. Only one tape is needed for a complete restore, but because this option does not clean up the transaction logs, this backup type is usually used only for archival purposes or for an extra backup just before performing a system change or running a database utility.

Table 13-4: Backup Option with Exchange 2000 (Continued)

Backup Type	Explanation
Incremental backup	Backs up only the transaction logs on the server and then deletes them. This is the fastest backup option, but the slowest restore option. When performing a restore, you must first restore the last full or copy backup, and then restore from each backup tape in sequential order. Circular logging must be disabled.
Differential backup	Backs up only the transaction logs on the server, but does not delete them after the backup. The backup tape size increases with each backup until a full backup is used to clean out the transaction logs. When performing a restore, you must first restore the last full or copy backup, and then restore just the last differential backup tape. Circular logging must be disabled.

The methods listed in Table 13-4 are all online backups. In other words, the backup is running while the store is mounted. In almost every situation, performing an online backup is best because it is easier to restore an online backup and because users can access their mailboxes during an online backup. You can perform an offline backup by dismounting the Exchange stores and then backing up the database and transaction log files. The only time that an offline backup is advantageous is if you cannot mount the store and you want to back up the store before using the database utilities to try to repair the store.

You can use the backup program included with Windows 2000 to back up the Exchange server. This backup program is a significant improvement over the backup program available in Windows NT, especially if you are backing up a single server. However, the Windows 2000 backup program is not designed to be an enterprise backup solution.

Restoring Exchange Servers

Restoring the data in your database might mean recovering a single, very important message, a single database, or an entire server. There are many different Exchange server recovery scenarios, each of which I discuss in the following sections.

Recovering a Single Message

In software versions prior to Exchange 5.5 and Outlook 98, recovering a single message that had been deleted from the information store was a long and painful experience. The only way to restore the message was to rebuild completely the Exchange server on a new computer, restore the Exchange databases to the server, and then use a messaging client to get access to the mailbox and message. With Outlook 98 and Exchange 5.5, you can configure the server to retain deleted messages in the information store for a period of time after they are deleted from the Deleted Items folder and then use the messaging client to recover the message.

Exchange 2000 provides the same options as Exchange 5.5 for recovering individual messages. You can configure the Exchange server to retain deleted messages so that they can easily be recovered. To configure this option in Exchange 2000, access the store properties and select the Limits tab. Figure 13-13 shows the interface to do this.

Use the Keep deleted items for (days) option to define how long deleted items should be retained. The appropriate number of days depends on how much space you have for your store and how long you want to provide the option to recover messages. Any message deleted from the Deleted Items folder is retained in the store for the specified number of days. This means that the store size includes all deleted items until the time limit expires.

After you have configured this option on the server, users can restore their own messages using Outlook 98 or higher. To do this, they need to select the Deleted Items folder and then select Tools/ Recover Deleted Items. A list appears of messages that have been deleted but are available to restore.

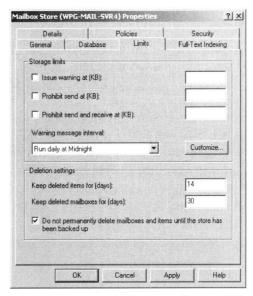

Figure 13-13: Configuring the Deleted Item Retention Time.

NOTE: *If you do not configure the deleted item retention time or if the message you are trying to recover is older than the deleted item retention time, you have to use the same procedure to recover the message as you would use in Exchange 4.0/5.x. You have to build an offline Exchange server and then restore the mailbox that contains the message to the server. Then connect to the server with a messaging client and retrieve the message.*

Recovering a Single Mailbox

Almost every Exchange administrator who has worked with messaging for a while has been faced with a situation in which a single mailbox needs to be recovered. Usually this happens when an employee leaves the company and his mailbox is deleted, only to have someone find out some time later that they need a mail message from that mailbox. In Exchange 5.*x*, the only option for recovering a single mailbox is to rebuild the server and restore the entire database using a backup tape from before the mailbox deletion. Because of the difficulty in restoring a mailbox in Exchange 5.*x*, many companies have a policy of not deleting a mailbox from the Exchange server until months after an employee leaves the company.

Exchange 2000 provides an easy way to recover a deleted mailbox. On the Limits tab for each mailbox store (shown in Figure 13-13) you can configure the Keep deleted mailboxes for (days) option. Enabling this option retains a mailbox in the store even after it has been deleted. A deleted mailbox does not appear in the GAL, but the actual mailbox still exists for the specified length of time. To access the messages in the mailbox, you can reconnect the mailbox to another user account. To reconnect the mailbox, expand the mailbox store in Exchange System Manager and then expand the Mailboxes container. Figure 13-14 shows the interface.

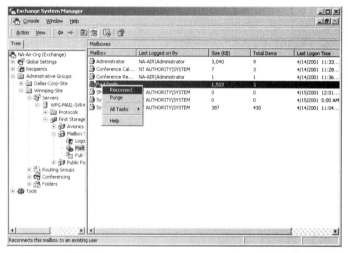

Figure 13-14: Reconnecting a Deleted Mailbox.

Deleted mailboxes are marked with a red X. Right-click the mailbox and choose Reconnect, and then select the user account to which you want to connect the mailbox. That user can then connect to the mailbox.

Restoring a Single Store

One of the biggest enhancements in Exchange 2000 is the capability of having more than one information store on a server. This is particularly advantageous when you want to restore individual stores. If one of your information stores has become corrupted, or if you are restoring an entire server, you can mount all the other information stores and restore one mailbox store at a time.

To restore an individual store, you must dismount it. Start the backup program and load the tapes or other media that contain the store backup. Catalog the tape if necessary, and then select the store that you want to restore. Figure 13-15 shows the interface if you are using the Windows 2000 Backup program to restore the database.

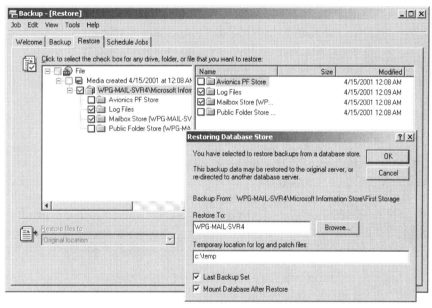

Figure 13-15: Restoring a Single Information Store.

You can configure a number of options when performing a restore. You can restore the information store to the same server from which it was backed up, or you can restore the store to a different Exchange server. You should restore it to a different server only if you need to recover an individual item (message or mailbox) that exists only on the backup tape. When you restore the store onto a different server, the directory information is not restored — only the store itself.

NOTE: *If you are restoring the store to a different server, the server must be in a different forest than your production forest. In addition, the display name for the storage group and the store must be the same as the original names, and the organization and the administrative group name must be the same. After restoring the store, you must then reconnect the mailboxes in the store to user accounts in the new forest.*

You must configure a Temporary location for log and patch files. Because other stores in the storage group might still be mounted, you cannot overwrite the log files for the storage group. Instead you must configure an alternative location to restore the transaction log and patch files. After you have restored the information store, the transaction logs from the temporary location are replayed to commit any changes that have not been committed to the database. After the changes from the restored transaction logs have been committed, the log files are deleted. The restore process then examines the active transaction logs for the storage group for any changes to the store and applies the changes.

The Last Backup Set option defines whether this backup set is the last of the restore set. If you are restoring the store from multiple tapes from an incremental or differential backup, you must select this option only when you are restoring the last backup tape. If you are restoring the database from a full backup, this option must be selected. When you select the Last Backup Set option, you also can select the Mount Database After Restore option.

When you are restoring an individual store, the restore process creates a temporary storage group on the Exchange server and restores the store into that temporary group. After the restore program commits the temporary transaction logs to the database, it mounts the restored store into its original storage group on the server.

Restoring an Exchange Server

The worst-case scenario in terms of disaster recovery is that the Exchange server fails and you need to rebuild the entire server. This might happen when a hard disk crashes on the server and there is no way to restart the server.

The procedure that you use to recover a failed Exchange 2000 server depends on whether the server is also an Active Directory domain controller. Because Exchange 2000 depends on Active Directory for its directory service, including the organization and server configuration information, Active Directory must be available before you can restore the Exchange server.

To rebuild an Exchange server after a complete server failure, perform the following steps:

1. Install Windows 2000 as a stand-alone server. When installing, follow these rules:

   ▲ Install the same version of server (Server, Advanced Server, or Datacenter Server) as the original server.

   ▲ Do not join the computer to the domain. If you do, you must delete the original server from the domain and the new server receives a different SID.

   ▲ Install Windows on the same hard disk and in the same folder where the original server was installed.

   ▲ Use the same computer name.

   ▲ Install the same components as on the original server.

   ▲ Install the same service packs and hot fixes as were on the original server.

2. Restore the system state data on the server. If this server is also an Active Directory domain controller, restoring the system state data restores the Active Directory database. If the server is not a domain controller, restoring the system state data restores the server configuration and connects the server back to the domain with the same SID as it had before the failure.

3. Install Exchange 2000 on the server using the Setup/DisasterRecovery option. When you run Setup using this option, Setup queries Active Directory for the configuration information for the server. This option displays the Component Selection screen shown in Figure 13-16, with Disaster Recovery in the Action column for each installation option.

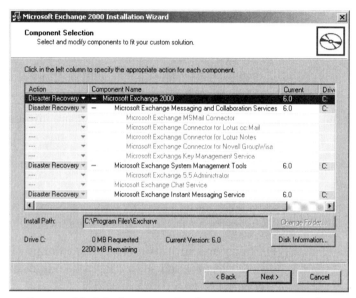

Figure 13-16: Running Exchange Setup with the Disaster Recovery Option.

4. After Setup is finished, the Exchange databases on the server are not mounted and a warning message to restore the databases from backup appears. Restore the databases from the backup tape and then restart the server.

The Disaster Recovery option makes it significantly easier to restore an Exchange 2000 server than to restore one in Exchange 5.*x*. The Exchange Setup program reads the server-configuration information from Active Directory and sets up the new server with a configuration identical to original server.

Maintaining the North American Air Organization

The project team at North American Air has implemented a thorough backup and recovery program for the organization. It features the following:

▲ Administrators back up every Exchange server every day during nonbusiness hours. In the smaller locations, they perform a full backup of the entire server, including the system state information and all the Exchange information. In larger locations, where a full backup might not be possible every night due to time restrictions, they perform a full backup every weekend and a differential backup of the transaction logs during each night of the week.

▲ All information stores retain messages for 14 days. Deleted mailboxes are retained for 30 days.

▲ The administrators at each location are responsible for managing the backup plan. In addition, they are responsible for managing the recovery of mailboxes.

▲ As part of the backup and restore plan, the administrators perform a test backup from the backup tapes on a monthly basis. The administrators at each location also perform a regular disaster recovery simulation every six months.

▲ The three locations in Texas and the Winnipeg location maintain a test lab for testing patches and new releases of software. Each lab includes at least one high-end server that can be used as a restore server to restore mailboxes and messages for situations when these objects exist only on backup tape.

Conclusion

To ensure that the servers and connectors are functioning at peak efficiency, you must establish a consistent monitoring program. By using the Exchange 2000 tools, such as status monitoring and notifications, you can receive alerts when some component in your Exchange organization fails. In addition to monitoring your Exchange servers, you also need to implement a backup and disaster recovery plan, so that if one of your servers ever fails, you can recover your data as quickly as possible.

Epilogue

NORTH AMERICAN AIR IS ONE OF MANY companies migrating from Windows NT and Exchange 5.*x* to Windows 2000 and Exchange 2000. As described in this book, this migration is a lengthy and complicated task. Due to the reliance of Exchange 2000 on Active Directory, the organization must first migrate the Windows NT domain structure to Active Directory. Then the Exchange 5.*x* directory must be integrated with Active Directory using the Active Directory Connector. Only then is the corporation ready to start installing Exchange 2000 servers.

One of the primary goals for North American Air in migrating to Active Directory and Exchange 2000 is to ease the process of adding new companies to the organization as the corporation expands. After migrating to Exchange 2000, the network administrators are familiar with the tools, such as the Active Directory Migration Tool and the Active Directory Connector, that can be used to merge organizations. In addition, Exchange 2000 provides the connectors and migration tools to interoperate with most messaging systems as well as migrate the users when necessary. North American Air is using Exchange as the platform for many of its business applications, so as new companies join the corporation, they need only to give the new employees access to Exchange to enable them to access the applications.

As the organization looks further down the road, a number of options become available. As new operating systems, such as Windows 2002 are released, the organization needs to look at enhancements offered by the new OS. Windows 2002 promises several enhancements for Active Directory, including:

▲ **More control of the Active Directory replication.** Windows 2002 enables administrators to manage some parts of the Active Directory replication so that some of the information in Active Directory is replicated to a limited set of domain controllers, rather than all domain controllers.

▲ **More options for storing dynamic data in Active Directory.** You can configure some applications to store frequently changing data in Active Directory. Windows 2002 enables this option while still providing control of how that information is replicated to other domain controllers.

▲ **Improved universal group membership replication.** The entire membership list need not be replicated between global catalog servers when a single change is made to the membership list.

▲ **Less reliance on global catalog servers to log.** You can configure domain controllers to cache universal group information so that a user can log on to the domain without having a global catalog server accessible to determine universal group membership.

While these enhancements (and others) are significant changes, the basic structure of Active Directory does not change in Windows 2002. This means that the migration to the next version of Windows does not have major implications for the Exchange 2000 organization.

Microsoft also is working on improving the tools available for managing connections between multiple Exchange 2000 organizations. Microsoft Metadirectory Services (MMS) is a powerful tool for synchronizing a variety of directories, including Active Directory data from multiple forests. However, MMS is a complex application that requires extensive training to implement successfully. To make tasks, such as managing the replication between forests easier, Microsoft is working on a version of MMS called the Interforest Toolkit, which is a wizard-based utility that can synchronize directory information between multiple forests. For Exchange 2000 administrators managing multiple forests, the Interforest Toolkit looks like a relatively easy solution. The Interforest Toolkit also provides the tools to migrate user information from one forest to another, in much the same way that the Active Directory Connector enabled you to migrate user information from Exchange 5.*x* to Active Directory.

Migrating to Exchange 2000 is a large, complicated task that many organizations will undertake. However, the end result of having a reliable and flexible messaging system is worth the effort.

Index